Why Do You Need This New Edition?

- Updates every chapter with the latest research and ethical and theoretical writing from all of the major helping professions.

- Incorporates school counseling internships to a much greater degree than prior editions, including the ASCA ethics code and multiple articles from school counseling literature.

- Includes expanded discussion of competency-based education and evaluation in the context of supervision.

- Incorporates substantial updates and revision of multicultural discussion; includes expanded discussion of working with veterans and survivors of traumatic events caused by human actions or natural occurrences.

- Has updated and expanded coverage of technology in all aspects of clinical work and training, with special attention to social media, ethics, and personal safety.

D0148765

THE INTERNSHIP, PRACTICUM, AND FIELD PLACEMENT HANDBOOK

A GUIDE FOR THE HELPING PROFESSIONS

Seventh Edition

BRIAN N. BAIRD

Boston   Columbus   Indianapolis   New York   San Francisco   Upper Saddle River
Amsterdam   Cape Town   Dubai   London   Madrid   Milan   Munich   Paris   Montréal   Toronto
Delhi   Mexico City   São Paulo   Sydney   Hong Kong   Seoul   Singapore   Taipei   Tokyo

Executive Editor: Susan Hartman
Editorial Assistant: Nicole Suddeth
Executive Marketing Manager: May Kelly
Production Manager: Tom Benfatti
Manufacturing Buyer: Tom Benfatti
Editorial Production and Composition Service: Integra Software Services, Pvt, Ltd.
Cover Designer: Brice Kenselaar
Creative Director: Jayne Conte
Editorial Project Manager: Reena Dalal

Library of Congress Cataloging-in-Publication Data
Baird, Brian N.
  The internship, practicum, and field placement handbook : a guide for the helping professions/
Brian N. Baird.—Seventh edition.
    pages cm
  ISBN-13: 978-0-205-95965-5 (alk. paper)
  ISBN-10: 0-205-95965-2 (alk. paper)
  1. Counseling—Study and teaching. 2. Social work education. 3. Counselors—Training of. 4. Human services personnel—Training of. 5. Internship programs. I. Title.
  BF636.6B35 2014
  158.3071'55—dc23
                                                          2013011806

10 9 8 7 6 5 4 3   EBM   14

ISBN-10: 0-205-95965-2
ISBN-13: 978-0-205-95965-5

Brief Contents

Contents

Preface

Professionals and students in the helping professions consider internships, practicums, and field placements among the most influential experiences of their careers. At the same time, however, students also report that their normal course work typically provides only indirect and, in many cases, insufficient preparation for their first "real-world" exposure. This book is designed to bridge the gap between academic course work and the knowledge, skills, and emotional challenges that are found beyond the classroom.

As a strong proponent of evidence-based practice and competency-based education, throughout this book I have drawn on the best *and most current* information available from psychology, social work, counseling, school counseling, psychiatry, and other helping professions. On the basis of this research and having worked with hundreds of students and trainees in beginning and advanced placements, my goal with every edition has been to write a book that will be valuable at many levels. Students in their first or second field experience will likely get the greatest benefit from this text, but even advanced graduate students and their instructors consistently tell me that they find the book covers key areas and material that might otherwise not be addressed in their training.

For this seventh edition, every chapter has been updated to reflect a thorough and comprehensive review of the latest research and clinical literature across all of the major helping professions. This edition also addresses the most recent ethical codes of the leading professions along with the latest legal and regulatory developments at federal and state levels. I have also continued to consult with numerous faculty and supervisors in each discipline and in various types of academic institutions and internship settings. Equally important, I have sought and received feedback from interns themselves about how to make the text the most meaningful and helpful to the most important people of all, those who are actually using it.

Based on feedback from students and faculty who use the text, several changes have been made since the sixth edition. Overall, the text is more streamlined to make chapters easier and quicker for students to read while still addressing the most important information. For prior users, the most immediately notable outcome of this is that material from Chapter 2 of the sixth edition has now been divided into two chapters, with the topic of classes and peer groups now occupying a new Chapter 3 in the seventh

edition. As the result of this change, all subsequent numbers have increased by one, but the overall length of the text has actually been somewhat shortened. Prior users may also note that a number of references that had become somewhat dated have been removed and replaced by more current sources. This is not to say that all older references have been supplanted. In a number of cases, the original sources simply said what needed to be said in the best way possible and in ways that remain just as valid today.

Other changes in this edition include expanded discussion of the role of social media as a clinical, ethical, and personal safety issue for interns. So too, the topic of online service delivery and supervision also receives added attention as do issues such as treatment of veterans and disaster victims.

MAKING THE MOST OF THIS BOOK

OVERVIEW OF THE CONTENTS

A glance at the table of contents reveals that this text is organized along both chronologic and thematic lines. The chapters have been organized sequentially to anticipate the stages interns pass through and the understanding or skills that will be required in those stages. Initial chapters deal with selecting placements and supervisors, meeting staff and clients, peer groups and classes, and key ethical and legal issues. Middle chapters deal with supervision, working with individuals of diverse cultural and ethnic backgrounds, clinical writing, self-care, and personal safety. Discussions of termination, finishing the internship, and lessons learned conclude the book. Finally, appendices provide examples of forms useful for establishing learning plans, supervision agreements, ethical guidelines, evaluations, and other procedures.

Although the book is organized chronologically, an important difference between this text and others is that the material in this book is heavily "frontloaded." Compared to courses in which you may read a chapter each week or so during a quarter or semester, with this book you may want to read much or all of the content during the first few weeks of your placement, then refer to specific chapters again as you proceed through the internship. For example, many students find it helpful to review the chapters dealing with clinical writing and case notes at the very start of their internships. It is also a good idea to give some consideration to the chapters on personal safety issues and self-care at the outset of your experience rather than waiting until after some issue arises. Of course, some chapters, such as that on termination and ending the internship, can wait till later, but even these topics are good to consider at the beginning because understanding how to close cases and conclude a placement successfully can help you better prepare for these events ahead of time.

RESOURCES AND REFERENCES

A second difference between this book and other texts is its emphasis on practical skills and knowledge. In writing this book, I have tried to present information that will be immediately relevant to your internship and will be of practical use to you in the field. I recognize, however, that entire books have been written about the topics of each of the chapters. If you are interested in more detail about a topic, references are provided throughout the text, and I hope you will refer to these as you read and as you work at your internship. The practice of going beyond a textbook to pursue additional resources is an essential part of how professionals pursue topics of interest. Throughout your internship and your future study and training, make it a practice to not simply accept a single source of information but to seek different sources and learn from different perspectives both within your own discipline and across professions.

DOING THE EXERCISES

Part of the reason I enjoy working with interns is that I believe strongly in the value of experiential and discovery-based learning. Because internship training and clinical work involve a constant process of self-exploration and change, the textual material of each chapter is accompanied by self-exploration and experiential learning exercises. The more one works in this field, the more acutely one realizes the importance of self-examination and understanding. I encourage you to use these exercises and be open to the experiences.

If your goal is simply to get through the book or if you are pressed for time, you may be tempted to skim over an exercise or suggested activity. I hope you will resist that temptation and devote some time to the exercises. A given exercise may seem unnecessary to you, but you will not really know unless you test your knowledge. It is one thing to tell yourself that you already know something, but it is another matter to really explore and reflect on an issue in a structured, systematic way. In my experience as an instructor and supervisor, and in my own work as a practicing clinician, I am constantly surprised by how often I think I know something but then discover a completely new insight or understanding.

KEEP THIS BOOK

Some students indiscriminately sell their textbooks the minute a class is over. In this case, that would be a mistake. If you plan to go on to work or further study in the field, this book as well as your other basic textbooks should begin to make up the core of your professional library; you should have them handy as references for future classes and as you work in the field. The marginal return you might gain from a resale is far outweighed by the value of having your own resources to draw on and refer back to in the future. Developing a personal library is part of the process of becoming a professional, and you might as well begin that process with this book. If you do go on to work in the field or to future internships, you will have many occasions to refer back to the chapters on ethics, writing, supervision, diversity, stress, and other topics. Keep this book when the course is over and read it again in the future.

ACKNOWLEDGMENTS

This book reflects the influence and contributions of many people, and it would not be possible to list everyone to whom I owe a debt of thanks. My many colleagues, friends, and students in recent years, as well as my instructors, supervisors, and mentors during undergraduate, graduate, and postgraduate training have all shaped this book and its author. I am grateful for all the positive, and even some of what at the time seemed to be negative, experiences they have given me.

Among the individuals I want to thank directly, I begin with Andy Carey, who was instrumental in helping formulate the initial plan for this book and provided insightful comments and information throughout its development. Andy's understanding of how students learn and the challenges they face as beginning counselors has been extremely valuable. I have great respect for his skills as a counselor and educator and am fortunate to consider him both a friend and colleague.

I am grateful for the support of Pacific Lutheran University (PLU), which granted me the sabbatical leave during which much of the writing of the book was completed. The input and support of my colleagues in the PLU Department of Psychology, especially that of Dana Anderson, Mike Brown, Jerry LeJeune, and Christine Moon, have been and are much appreciated.

In addition to the individuals acknowledged in prior editions, this seventh edition benefited significantly from the insightful reviews and many helpful suggestions provided by Robert Weis, Denison University; Joseph Bertinetti, University of Nebraska at Omaha; Susan Holbrook, Sothwestern Illinois College; Sheryl Reminger, University of Illinois Springfield; Pamela Brouillard, Texas A&M-Corpus Christi; Lisa Coyne; Ronnie Priest; Laura Roberts, Lehman College; and David Carter, University of Nebraska Omaha. I wish to thank the editorial staff of Pearson: Susan Hartman, executive editor; Reena Dalal, Editorial Project Manager and Mogana from Integra. I want to thank each of them for their time, professionalism, and abilities to be direct with criticism and constructive in their suggestions.

Thanks also to some of the many professors and mentors who helped me get into the field and learn some things along the way: Thomas Schenkenberg, Raymond Kesner, Don Strassberg, Dick Hemrick, Randy Linnel, B. J. Fitzgerald, Wilson Walthall, Richard Pasewark, Judith Olson, Max Rardin, Karen Nicholas, Helen Crawford, Leo Sprinkle, Steve Bieber, Geoff Bartol,

Lance Harris, Marvin Brown, Mark Seeley, Jarret Kaplan, Vic Ganzer, Katherine Mateer, and Tedd Judd; to peers, who shared the challenges and fun: Mike Hawkins, Rita Valentine, Rick Jensen, Walthall's Warriors, Doreen Daly, Dick Shepherd, Mike Whitley, Warner Karshner, Deborah Frank, and Kirk Strosahl; for friendship and support during dissertation work: Dave Droge and Ray Preiss.

And most important of all, I want to thank my wife, Rachel Nugent, for her support, advice, friendship, and love through this project and so much more. I also thank our two young sons, William and Walter, for periodically running into the room and lighting up my spirit with their smiles and laughter.

Brian N. Baird

CHAPTER 1
PREPARATION

I've learned more in this experience than I have in any of my classes. Every student should have the opportunity to do a practicum.

Every day there was something new that I realized I didn't know. If for no other reason than that, I'm glad I did an internship.

Comments from student evaluations of their practicum and internship experiences

THEORY INTO PRACTICE

A friend of mine who was working overseas in the Peace Corps decided it would be fun to teach the children of his village how to play baseball. The children were enthusiastic and eager to learn, so he rounded up some equipment; drew pictures of the playing field; explained the rules of the game; and had everyone practice throwing, catching, and hitting the ball. He even gave them a test that included questions about the number of balls and strikes allowed, how many outs per inning, the distance between bases, and famous players of the past. With the basics mastered, the class improvised a field in a nearby pasture, divided up into two teams, and prepared to play ball.

As the villagers looked on, the excited children took their places on the field. My friend, the teacher, asked the children if they were ready, and all assured him that they understood what to do. The leadoff batter, a wiry young boy of 13, looked nervous but determined. My friend surveyed the field and aligned his players. Then, taking an exaggerated windup, he delivered the first baseball pitch the village had ever witnessed.

To everyone's astonishment, the batter smacked the ball into deep left field. The batter was so shocked by this that he just stood watching as the teacher shouted for him to "Run, Run, Run!" Turning to see how his team fared as fielders, my friend found that all of his players had left their positions and were running as fast as they could around the bases, tagging each one, screaming, laughing, and heading for home plate. The ball, meanwhile, rolled to a stop far out in the field with no one making any effort to chase it.

When the commotion subsided, my friend was the only player left on the field. All of his team, even the batter, had raced from the field to home, thrilled with how many runs they believed they had just scored. "Somewhere," my friend declared to himself, "we've got a gap between theory and practice." With that, he ran for first base and raced around the diamond just as his players had. When he crossed home plate, he made baseball history by scoring the tenth run from a single hit. His students loved it, and the village still talks about the game today.

Students beginning their first practicum or field placement can identify with my friend's players. Enthusiasm, nervousness, determination, and uncertainty will be familiar feelings (Gelman, 2004; Gelman & Lloyd, 2008; Hill, Sullivan, Knox, & Schlosser, 2007). Regardless of all the coursework and study, there is no substitute for real experience. Only by getting out there and trying things can we discover what we do or do not know.

This is why field placements are so valuable. They give you the chance to experience firsthand what you have been learning in your readings and classes. You will quickly discover that reading in a textbook about schizophrenia, alcoholism, child abuse, or other issues is not the same as meeting and interacting with real people who experience the situations or conditions you have studied. Similarly, reading about, or role-playing, therapy and counseling techniques in a classroom differs greatly from participating in actual therapy sessions.

You will also discover that many things you need to know in the "real world," such as ethical and legal issues, how to write case notes, how to deal with supervision, and a host of other topics, may not have been addressed sufficiently in your academic classes. Even when subjects have been studied in class, as my friend learned from his base-running fielders, instructors too often assume that students will be able to transfer what they learn in the classroom directly to the field. Students recognize the error of this assumption the moment they enter their internship and ask themselves, "Now what do I do?" My goal in writing this book is to help you answer that question.

TERMINOLOGY

FIELD PLACEMENTS, PRACTICUMS, OR INTERNSHIPS?

Because this text deals with issues that are common across multiple disciplines and for students at various levels of study and training, a brief word about terminology is in order. Different disciplines use different terminologies to describe field learning experiences, and the terms depend on the level of the student's training. For example, social work programs often refer to learning opportunities beyond the classroom as "field placements" or "field experiences" (Council on Social Work Education [CSWE], 2001; Gelman, 2004). Psychology and counseling use "practicum" to describe field experiences early in one's career and "internship" for more advanced field training (American Psychological Association Committee on Accreditation, 2005; American School Counselor Association [ASCA], 2009; Council for Accreditation of Counseling and Related Educational Programs [CACREP], 2009; Hatcher, Grus, & Wise, 2011; Hatcher & Lassiter, 2007). While recognizing and respecting the terminology differences across disciplines and levels of training, for simplicity, we will use the word *internship* in this text, primarily because it happens to carry the convenient noun *intern,* which describes the individual receiving training. Thus, throughout the text, except where direct quotations are cited, all field experiences, regardless of discipline or level of training, will be called internships, and all those receiving training will be referred to as interns.

SUPERVISORS AND INSTRUCTORS

With the exception of the final internship training for advanced graduate students, in most internship experiences students will be under the guidance of persons in two different roles. *Instructors* are faculty from the student's educational institution who monitor the student's progress and interface with those employed by the field placement site. Those who directly monitor and direct the student's work at the placement site are referred to as *supervisors.*

All field placements are part of students' overall academic training (Wayne, 2004), and they should work closely with both their academic instructor and their field supervisor. Although the amount of direct contact students have with instructors or supervisors will vary from program to program and across placements, throughout this text I will emphasize repeatedly that both instructors and supervisors should be kept closely informed of the intern's activities and should be notified of any questions, concerns, or problems that develop.

MEETING WITH YOUR INSTRUCTOR

Your first task as an intern is to meet with the academic instructor who will work with you during your internship. Some academic programs offer structured classes along with internships. Other programs leave internship support or supervision to be arranged individually between students and instructors (Hatcher et al., 2011). In either case, initial contact with an instructor is vital for a number of reasons.

The most important reason is to ensure that you receive the best possible educational experience from your internship.

Instructors can help you select placements or supervisors best suited to your needs, and they may assist in making contact with placement sites or individual supervisors. If your department has established procedures governing internships, meeting with your instructor right at the outset will ensure that you follow those procedures. You may need to complete some paperwork before you begin an internship and fulfill certain requirements to receive credit or a grade for your internship.

An additional concern that many interns do not consider is the liability risks that instructors and supervisors face when their students work in the field (National Association of Social Work Insurance Trust, 2004; Pollack & Marsh, 2004; Zakutansky & Sirles, 1993). Given this shared liability, the faculty in your department must be involved in all aspects of your internship, from the very beginning until the conclusion.

Students should also be aware that it can take a great deal of effort on the part of instructors and supervisors to establish a relationship with various internship sites (Cornish, Smith-Acuña, & Nadkarni, 2005). Many programs have a fixed set of placement sites and long-established relationships with the supervisors of their students. Such arrangements ensure that the academic program will have placements for students and, simultaneously, that the treatment agencies can rely on interns to help them carry their workload. Students who might wish for greater autonomy or flexibility in placement settings sometimes find this frustrating, but it should be remembered that having well-established placement sites with experienced supervisors is certainly preferable to situations in which adequate placement sites or supervisors cannot be arranged at all.

Research and reports from the field of social work (Bogo, 2005; Wayne, Bogo, & Raskin, 2006) have shown that changes in health care and academia are making it harder to find field placement sites willing to accept interns. Within academia, as a result of increasing pressures on faculty to produce research and cutbacks in the number of faculty, the role of field liaison is being relegated to part-time faculty. Thus, the decision to accept an intern or establish an intern program within an agency is not one that is taken lightly by the agency or the supervisors and staff. Although this background work may not be transparent to you, it is worth keeping in mind how much time and effort goes into creating and maintaining placement opportunities for students.

FINDING AND SELECTING A PLACEMENT

As a result of the various approaches to selecting or assigning internships, some of the material that follows may not be equally relevant to all readers. If your academic program makes all the internship arrangements for students, you may skim or skip this section and move on to the discussion of establishing formal institutional and individual agreements. On the other hand, if your program provides little structure or support for its interns, the material that follows should help you find and choose the best placement for your interests and abilities.

INSTRUCTORS, PEERS, AND CAMPUS RESOURCES FOR LOCATING INTERNSHIPS

Your academic instructors will generally be your primary source for internship recommendations. As discussed earlier, your first step in finding an internship should be to meet with the designated instructor responsible for internship courses. Your instructor will likely have a number of preapproved sites from which you can choose. She or he may also be able to give you specific recommendations based on your personal interests or training needs. Your instructor can also tell you if a particular site meets the requirements of your department and major. This is especially important because it would be unfortunate to select an internship or practicum, spend months working there, and then discover that the experience did not count for credit or would not be recognized by your professional association or department.

In addition to the resources of your instructor, many campuses have offices dedicated to coordinating field learning experiences. These often go by such names as "Cooperative Education" or "Community Learning" programs. Agencies with available internship positions typically send position announcements to these offices, which then post them for students. Even though you may not have heard of a program of this sort on your campus, check around to see if one is available.

One other campus resource to check is the career services or job placement center. You may be less likely to find internship openings there, but you should nevertheless become familiar with the services available through these offices. Internships provide an excellent opportunity to begin developing your job application file and honing the interview skills that you will need when you eventually apply for employment. Career service offices can help you develop those skills. They can also help you write a curriculum vitae or resume, and many offices will help you establish a complete job application file, including letters of reference and other material commonly requested by employers. These offices also receive regular announcements of position openings, so stop by periodically to see if they have received word of any openings in your subject area.

Peers or prior graduates are yet another source of information and may be able to offer insights not available from instructors or campus referral offices. Along with identifying placements to pursue, your peers may suggest places to avoid. Such information can be valuable, but keep in mind that another student's experiences will not necessarily match yours. Still, if a student advises that a certain internship amounted to little more than typing data into a computer or watching television on the midnight shift, you can predict that the placement may present limited learning opportunities.

COMMUNITY RESOURCES

Interns who look to faculty or campus resources sometimes overlook the many community resources available. Many communities have volunteer coordinating programs to help match programs with volunteers. United Way sometimes supports such programs and has been involved in efforts to establish 2-1-1 call centers that connect people in need with resources and people seeking to volunteer with community opportunities. More information about 2-1-1 resources in general and those in your local area can be obtained at http://www.211.org/. Another resource that may be available locally is a telephone crisis line. These lines make referrals to programs of all kinds, and many have books listing different agencies. If there is a community mental health center in your area, call there, explain that you are a student seeking an internship, and ask whether they have openings or could provide lists of local agencies that you might contact.

Three other sources that can be helpful are Internet listings, newspapers, and phone books. On the Web, sites such as Craigslist have special listings for nonprofit jobs that often include positions in mental health and social services. In the newspaper, classified advertisements sometimes list position openings in agencies that also offer internships. Try looking in the Employment Offerings section under the headings "Counselor," "Mental Health," or "Therapist" or under your specific discipline's title. These may be listed alphabetically in the general section or in special sections for "Health Care" positions. The added benefit of finding positions this way is the possibility of locating a paid position for an internship. The disadvantage is that such positions may require more job experience than beginning interns have. Also, in some paid positions, it may be more difficult to find suitable supervision. That should not discourage you from calling to discuss a position. Interns often start a position as a student in an unpaid status but are later hired in a paid capacity as openings become available. If you inquire about a position that requires more experience than you have at present, do not be afraid to suggest working as an unpaid intern to gain the requisite experience.

National, state, and local professional associations also can be useful resources. Most organizations have membership directories that you can use to locate individuals working in settings or areas that interest you. Many professions maintain national catalogs listing available field training opportunities. These catalogs tend to be directed toward graduate training, but there are often opportunities for undergraduates as well.

INTERNATIONAL PLACEMENTS

As you are considering where you might like to seek an internship, do not be afraid to think outside your national borders. Students who have had the opportunity to work or study abroad often rate the experience as the most significant of all their educational activities. Most campuses have special study abroad offices that offer their expertise in locating international opportunities and assistance in navigating issues such as visas, insurance, and vaccinations.

If you do pursue an international placement, be sure to consider cultural and linguistic differences that may substantially alter how and why people seek and deliver certain mental health services in other countries. Do not assume that the helping and communication models you are familiar with at home will apply well or at all in another country and culture. You may also want to review some of the ethical and clinical issues associated with online supervision. These are discussed in Chapters 4 and 5 of this book.

CHOOSING A PLACEMENT

Finding potential placements is the first step. The next step is to select an internship from among the possibilities. I encourage interns to approach this process thoughtfully because it is important that your first clinical experience be positive.

One way to determine what features to look for in an internship is to consider what other interns have found important in their selection process. The features that will be most important to you will depend on your program and your level of training, but surveys of interns have shown several key variables that influence decisions: the match of interests between the training site and the intern, the reputation of the training site, special training opportunities, the breadth of clinical populations available, location, quality of supervision, and the intern's gut feeling about the site. In addition to the variables just mentioned, you should also consider unique personal circumstances. For example, many graduate students are somewhat older, have families, and may be taking their coursework or internship on a part-time basis or in addition to other employment. For this group of students, scheduling flexibility may be especially important.

EXERCISE

To help you select an internship that best matches your needs, skills, and interests, take a moment to list key factors that will be important to you. Then rate each possible internship on each of these key factors. For example, you might list such factors as type of setting, clients served, treatment approaches, and supervisor qualities. You might also list pragmatic considerations, such as location, compensation (if any), hours, and flexibility. Once you have done this for yourself, I suggest that you share your assessment with a peer and with your instructor to get their feedback about what you have included or what you might want to add.

After you have given some thought to the features that are most important to your own interests, the next step involves matching those interests with the internships available. Appendices A and B in this text provide forms I have developed to help gather information about placement sites. On one form, interns list their interests, experience, available times, and other information relevant to internship selection. The parallel form presents agency information, such as location, types of clients, treatment approaches, supervision, and available days and times.

Comparing information from the intern and agency allows instructors, students, and the agency to make informed decisions about the suitability of a given placement for a specific intern. Such information may also reduce the likelihood of placements not working.

To supplement the information provided in Appendices A and B, Appendix K provides a form that interns can use to evaluate their placements at the end of their experience. Some programs make these evaluations available to other students (typically with individual identifying information removed or edited) so that students seeking placements can read what their predecessors have reported about their opportunities and experiences at a particular site. If such reports are available, you might want to read those from various internships before making a selection for yourself.

SUPERVISION

Although many interns select placements based on clients served, location, treatment approach, or other considerations, perhaps the most important factor to consider involves the professionals who will work with you and provide supervision. Particularly in more advanced internships, the quality of the internship experience is closely related to the quality of the supervision received.

Interns who are selecting placements need to ask this basic question about a supervisor: "Is this someone I think I can work with and who will be interested in helping me learn?" In answering this question, consider the supervisor's personality, professional qualifications, and areas of interest, as well as the likelihood that this person will give you sufficient supervision time and instruction.

In selecting a supervisor, also consider compatibility of clinical philosophy or approach. Many interns broaden their views and become more confident when working with supervisors whose theoretical orientations differ from their own, but others have experienced significant conflicts. Although placement with a supervisor with a different orientation can be stimulating, if either the supervisor or the intern is dogmatic and intolerant of differing views, it can leave both feeling frustrated and discouraged.

The best way to get to know potential supervisors is to schedule a meeting or phone interview with them. Remember that in this meeting, both of you will be evaluating how well an internship together would work. Supervisors will want to know about your academic training and practical experiences. They will also be interested in your personality, character, and skills. Can they rely on you? Are you diligent in your work? Will you take suggestions or instructions well? And will it be in some way worth the supervisor's time to work with you?

On your part, it is a good idea to do a bit of background work, perhaps by consulting the agency website or doing an Internet search for information about the placement setting and your potential supervisor. Once you both meet, you will be asking some of the same questions the supervisor asks about you. You will be interested in this person's professional experience and in any specific training or experience as a supervisor. You will also want to know if the supervisor will be a good teacher, someone who lets you take some risks and make mistakes in the process of learning but who also is there with guidance and support when you need them. I recommend that students ask specific questions about a potential supervisor's education, training, and experience in supervision. Questions about the supervisor's philosophy and approach to the role can also be helpful.

Finally, ask how much time the supervisor has to spend with you. One of the most common frustrations interns describe about their experience is lack of availability or time with their supervisor. To avoid this, before you reach the stage of formalizing your arrangement, be certain the supervisor can devote sufficient time to working with you.

LEARNING OPPORTUNITIES

Along with identifying a supervisor with whom you would like to do an internship, also consider the kinds of learning opportunities that will be available to you and clarify your role before starting an internship. The lack of sufficiently interesting or challenging learning opportunities is one of the most common causes of complaints and frustration among interns. It is not unusual for interns to select what appear to be ideal placements only to discover that all they are allowed to do is code data for research, help with reorganizing files, or "babysit" students while teachers or counselors are out of the room. Knowing from the outset what opportunities you desire and what the internship can and will make available will avoid such disappointments.

In your first internship, most of the focus will be on learning by observing. This means you should have the opportunity to observe many different elements of the activities at your placement. Ideally, interns should have some opportunity to observe everything that goes on, from staff meetings and paperwork to direct treatment and other service delivery. This gives interns the broadest exposure to all elements of the placement. It is important for interns to know both the rewarding and the mundane aspects of the profession. If it is your first field experience, you should remember that for your benefit and that of clients, you will likely be given only very limited responsibilities to begin with.

As your abilities and training allow, you will gradually go beyond observational learning and begin to accept responsibility in clinical activities. This must be closely coordinated with the supervisor, but your goal should be to take new challenges in stages, pushing yourself slightly each time but never extending beyond your level of competence. Again, if you hope to have a certain kind of experience on your internship, check with potential placements and supervisors to determine whether that experience will be available to you.

TREATMENT APPROACHES

Internships provide your best opportunity to experience firsthand what a therapy or technique that appeals to you in theory is like in actual practice. If you have a particular interest in a treatment approach, you may want to seek a placement where you can receive supervision and experience in that approach.

If you already have experience in one intervention approach, consider seeking training in a completely different one. This does not mean you must become a convert to the other approach. It merely suggests that you should be open to different methods and give them a try to see what there is to learn from another perspective. When interns actually experience a different approach in practice, those who may have once been quite critical come to recognize that each method has something useful to offer.

CLIENTS

The next factor to consider in selecting a placement is the client base served by the program. Just as it is advisable for interns to be exposed to a variety of treatment approaches, experience with diverse client groups is also desirable. In your first internship, the exact makeup of the client population is less important than that you are out in the real world working with people. Still, there is nothing wrong with seeking a placement based on the type of client served. If you want to eventually work with a specific client group, it might be ideal to find a placement with a program for that group.

In my own training, I sought opportunities to work with clients of virtually all ages and diagnostic groups. By selecting a series of internship and practicum placements, I was eventually able to work with clients ranging from very young children to elderly adults and with diagnostic groups ranging from college students in a counseling center to patients in a unit for mentally ill criminal offenders. In each placement, I learned something new and expanded both my awareness and my skills. This diversity of experience also helped me gain a clearer sense of the kinds of therapy and clients I was most interested in and for which my skills were best suited.

PROGRAMS AND SETTINGS

Theoretical approaches and client types are frequently foremost on interns' minds when they select internships, but you should also consider the different kinds of internship settings available. For example, although the ages of the clients may be similar, an internship in a school setting is likely to differ in many ways from an internship in a home for runaway adolescents. Similarly, although many of the clients served and treatment techniques found in mental health clinics may be similar to those in inpatient facilities, some important characteristics will be specific to each setting. Thus, apart from the clients served and the treatment approaches used, if you have experience in only one kind of setting, a placement in a completely different setting could be very educational.

RESEARCH OPPORTUNITIES

Because so much of the focus of practicums and internships is on clinical experience, it is easy to overlook the opportunities field training can provide for hands-on research experience. Especially for students in master's- or doctoral-level programs who must complete theses or dissertations, and for pre-graduate-level students seeking to continue their studies, it is a good idea to explore how supportive of research activities a placement may be and what opportunities it offers to be involved in research.

CAREER PLANS

Most interns should avoid premature specialization, but this does not mean you should completely ignore your career plans when you choose an internship. This is particularly important if you hope to seek employment or further education in the field soon after you complete your internship. Interns who are about to enter the job market or go on to further studies often desire placement sites that make them more marketable to potential employers or graduate schools.

If your career or academic plans are not yet clear, you may want to discuss any career or educational questions with your instructor before you choose an internship. You could also review any current publications about careers in your chosen field. These are often published by and available through your professional organization. By getting a sense of your interests and the feasible options, you can better select an internship that gives you the experience to make decisions about future career directions.

PRACTICAL ISSUES: LOCATION AND TIMES

The issues addressed thus far have primarily been concerned with the nature and quality of the clinical experience and training you will receive. More mundane, but not to be overlooked, are such practical considerations as where the placement is located and how your available days and times match those of the placement site. Particularly for students who are trying to juggle obligations of parenting, work, and academic classes with an internship, it will be important to match the internship placement expectations with other scheduling needs.

If you can, try to pick readily accessible placement sites. This will allow you to spend more time at the placement site and less time in transit. In some areas, you should also consider safety factors associated with getting to and from a placement. Wherever you find an internship, it is a good idea to ask your supervisor and other staff members about any safety issues associated with the location. Some areas assumed to be "terribly dangerous" are really not so if you take a few precautions. Do not be embarrassed to express any concerns or to ask your coworkers for their suggestions.

It is important for interns to be on their placement site at regularly scheduled times—ideally, a minimum of two to three hours a day for at least three days per week. Interns who are on site at irregular or infrequent times do not fully integrate into the routine of the placement. Unless interns are present on a regular basis, staff and clients are unlikely to be sufficiently comfortable or confident with them to involve them in activities. Keep in mind, too, that insofar as the internship serves as preparation for employment, dependable attendance is a key way to demonstrate employment readiness.

As you consider your schedule and make arrangements with an internship placement, be as realistic as possible about the times you will be available. Many interns do not heed this advice and overextend themselves because they have a great desire to learn and will try to do whatever their placement agencies ask. The motivation to learn is admirable, but if you extend yourself too far, you may end up disappointing yourself and the agency.

If academic and other time demands severely limit the time available for the internship or if your schedule is so variable that you cannot set aside consistent times for the internship, consider doing the internship at some other time or perhaps changing the other elements of your schedule to better accommodate the internship. It is better to postpone an internship than to try to force one into an overcrowded schedule and have a bad experience.

COMPETENCE AND SAFETY

The final consideration here is by no means the least important. When you select an internship, carefully consider your level of ability and training in relation to the tasks you will be expected to perform. An internship should stretch your knowledge and skills, but you must not extend your responsibilities to a point that would be dangerous to yourself or your clients. If you are concerned about personal safety at an internship, you may want to read Chapter 9 now and discuss any safety concerns with your instructor and supervisor. So too, if the kinds of clients served or the technical demands of treatment, assessment, or other services are beyond your current abilities, you need to recognize this and discuss any limitations fully with your instructor and supervisor before you begin a placement.

PREPARING YOUR INTERNSHIP APPLICATION

As you consider which internship sites best match your interests, keep in mind that the people at those sites are also looking for specific qualities in applicants. Suggestions and tips about selecting and applying to internship sites are offered later in this chapter and can also be found in Madson, Aten, and Leach (2007).

You can take several steps to prepare in advance and improve your chances of being accepted wherever you decide to apply. Two key elements are preparation of letters of application and recommendation and practice for the interview. Given the importance assigned to clinical writing and the frequency with which supervisors express concerns about deficiencies in their interns' writing skills, you may also want to review Chapter 7, which addresses clinical writing and case notes. Another good source of suggestions for writing applications and interview preparation is the workbook produced by the American Psychological Association of Graduate Students (Williams-Nickelson, Prinstein, & Keilin, 2008). Although written for graduate-level psychology students, the suggestions about letters, interviews, and other application procedures apply well across disciplines.

LETTERS OF APPLICATION AND RECOMMENDATION

Your application letter and supportive letters of recommendation are two key areas in which you can strengthen your application.

In your own letter of application, it is important to tell something about yourself that is not simply a reiteration of your curriculum vitae but will help you stand out in some way to the reader. This might be a noteworthy personal experience or achievement of some kind. Based on my own experience reviewing applications, I find that such personal elements often serve as important mnemonics that help selection committees recall and distinguish individuals. For example, a member of a committee discussing applicants might say something like, "Isn't that the person who played in the band?" or "I liked the one who had volunteered in Guatemala." As you write your own application, think about what might help you stand out in addition to your academic achievements, research, and clinical and other experiences.

In describing yourself, it is also a good idea to be honest about not only what you consider to be your strengths but also about areas you hope to develop further. A mix of accurate self-confidence with sincere humility and a desire to learn are desirable qualities in letters and in interns themselves. Letters that are too self-aggrandizing or self-deprecating tend to raise red flags.

Along with describing you, your letter should address your specific reasons for seeking the particular internship and mention specific goals you hope to achieve while there. Showing that a particular site matters to you in some specific way demonstrates that you have done your homework about where you are applying and that you have a personal interest and commitment to that location. This goes a long way to help a site select between students who are looking for just any placement versus those who are seeking that particular placement.

Just as you give attention to writing your own letters, I suggest you also give some time to helping others write letters of recommendation on your behalf. When asking someone to serve as a reference, be sure to give plenty of advance notice and make his or her task as easy and convenient as possible. Always ask permission in person before giving a name as a reference. When you provide written material, such as recommendation forms, it is a courtesy to complete as much of the form as you can, leaving only the evaluative sections for the reference source to complete. Also provide preaddressed, stamped envelopes along with notes indicating how and when the letter should be sent (e.g., some programs request that the outside of the envelope be signed over the seal). Follow-up inquiries a week before the due date are usually welcomed and are considered a courtesy. After someone has written a letter on your behalf, be sure to send a note of thanks and let the person know the result of your application process.

INTERVIEWS

Most people do not realize it, but the key to an effective interview is what you do *before* the interview, not simply what happens *during* the interview. Careful preparation beforehand will substantially increase the likelihood of the interview going well; if you are well prepared, the actual interview will usually take care of itself.

As you prepare for an interview, begin by studying information about the prospective internship site. Know about the history of the site, something about the clients served and about the staff, especially the person with whom you will have the interview. Also make an effort to speak with other interns or staff to learn about the day-to-day operations of the site, what is expected of interns, and what opportunities are available. In addition to learning about the site, review your own qualifications so that you can confidently describe your experiences and what you have to contribute to the internship.

It is also extremely helpful to practice responding to questions the interviewer may ask you. This practice should not just be mental; have another person fill the role of the interviewer and ask you questions directly. You might even want to video the process so that afterward you can review the practice session and get feedback about both the content and the style of your responses. As you practice for an interview, be sure to have your portfolio ready and use it to illustrate your experiences and work products.

Some of the questions you are likely to be asked during an interview include the following: "Why are you applying to this particular internship site?" "What are your primary learning and training goals?" "What supervisory experiences are you seeking?" "What specific skills or abilities do you bring that make you well suited to the internship?" "What areas or skills do you believe you need to improve?" "What are your long-term career goals?"

In addition to answering specific questions, you may also need to respond to hypothetical case situations. A good strategy in such situations is to approach the task systematically. Begin by reviewing out loud the information you have just been given. Then, proceed through a step-by-step process of identifying what you would consider and why. In most cases, the goal in responding to such questions should not be to quickly arrive at the "right answer." Rather, it is to demonstrate that you are capable of careful, systematic, and informed reasoning. In this process, do not be afraid to ask for further details. The questions you choose to ask and how you ask them may be just as informative as the answers you give. The key is not so much to demonstrate what you would do, but to demonstrate how and why you reached that decision. Remember that it is perfectly acceptable to indicate an awareness of the need for consultation or assistance if a case is beyond your experience or knowledge.

A final element of interviews that applicants frequently overlook is sending a thank-you note a day or so after the interview. Interviewers will notice and appreciate this simple courtesy, and it is too often neglected.

Get together with a fellow student and prepare for an internship interview by asking each other the questions identified earlier. Each of you should role-play both the interviewer and the applicant. Try to video record the interactions so you can watch them later. If feasible, have a third person watch both of you to give constructive feedback. You may also want to meet with someone from your university's career service center and ask for help in preparing for a job interview. As with any skill, repeated practice will lead to further improvements, so practice the interview several times and with different people who ask slightly different questions each time.

Once you have located and selected an internship setting and found a supervisor willing to work with you, a formal agreement should be established to clarify the nature and details of your learning arrangement.

INTERNSHIP AGREEMENTS

Two types of agreements should be formalized before you begin an internship. The first is a written agreement between your academic institution and the internship site. Next, together with your instructor and supervisor, you need to formulate an agreement that describes the specific features and learning goals of your individual internship experience (Hatcher et al., 2011). Establishing such agreements in writing at the outset will help avoid later misunderstandings or confusion about what the internship site and supervisor expect of you and what you expect of them.

INSTITUTIONAL AGREEMENTS

As society in general and health care in particular have become increasingly litigious, the need for formal and detailed internship agreements has grown. Wayne emphasized that for certain legal purposes, particularly for performance evaluations or disciplinary actions, field placements are treated by the courts like academic courses, thereby making it essential that programs have "clearly defined learning objectives and evaluation criteria that are known to the student, the field instructor and the faculty liaison at the start of the course" (Wayne, 2004, p. 409).

At the beginning of your internship, it is certainly reasonable to ask both your instructor and your field supervisor if a formal written arrangement exists and for you to have a chance to review it. Of course, you should not be responsible for drafting the agreement, but asking the questions may help spur action if explicit accords are lacking. If there are extant agreements, knowing with clarity from the outset what the expectations are between institutions can help prevent problems or misunderstandings down the road.

Because no two internship sites or academic programs are identical, there is no single model for such agreements. As a general rule, however, most institutions prefer agreements that begin by recognizing the importance, mutual benefits, and shared responsibilities of field learning opportunities for the academic institutions, students, and field placement sites. This initial recognition is then typically followed by a description of the agreed-upon expectations for each of the parties involved. The expectations for the field setting include allowing the student to observe or participate in specified activities, providing certain kinds of learning opportunities, providing supervision by persons with specific qualifications and at specified intervals, and maintaining contact with the academic institution and instructor. Identifying the degree and other qualifications of the supervisor and specifying with clarity the number of hours spent on site and in supervision can be of particular importance as these may be required for formal credit or approval to be granted by professional associations and licensing boards (e.g., see CACREP, Standards, 2009).

For its part, the academic institution affirms in such agreements that the student is in good standing and has sufficient preparation to participate in the specified internship activities. The academic institution also agrees to provide a liaison instructor to work with the field setting. The agreement may also clarify the role of the instructor and address the evaluation process to be used. The student's responsibilities as described in such agreements include adhering to the professional code of ethics, attending the internship as scheduled, carrying out any agreed-on responsibilities, and informing the supervisor and instructor of any problems or concerns. Guidelines for dress and conduct and, again, a description of evaluation procedures are sometimes included in the description of the student's responsibilities.

Two of the most common areas of legal concerns covered in agreements are (1) the possibility that the intern might be involved in activities that injure or otherwise harm a client or other person at the internship site and (2) the possibility that the intern might be injured or otherwise harmed while at the internship site. Portions of the agreement that deal with these issues specify how responsibilities will be shared in the event of such incidents. This includes clarification of liability insurance.

The value of liability insurance for interns was demonstrated by Gelman, Pollack, and Auerbach (1996), who found that 2.3% of programs reported that one of their students, and in five of six cases the supervising faculty member as well, had been named in liability cases. In light of this finding, it is certainly advisable for more institutions to provide insurance for students and supervisors alike. Many field agencies do in fact provide both liability and injury coverage for interns under their existing insurance for volunteers or employees. If so, it is essential for the intern and the school to complete any necessary paperwork officially designating the intern as a member of the class of individuals covered by the policy. The fact and extent of such coverage should also be specified in the field learning agreement.

Even if you believe you are covered by the institutions, and whether or not individual coverage is formally required by your placement site, it is good advice to obtain a policy for yourself so you can be sure you are covered personally. Fortunately, most professional associations offer discounted policies for student members. For example, the American Psychological Association Insurance Trust (http://www.apait .org/apait/products/studentliability/) offers policies to student members for very reasonable rates. The National Association of Social Workers Assurance Services (http://www.naswassurance .org/student_liability.php?page_id=12) offers comparable policies for social work student members, and the American Counseling Association (http://www.counseling.org/students/) and the American School Counselor Association (http://www .schoolcounselor.org/content.asp?contentid=185) actually include liability insurance as part of their student member benefits. Other professional associations offer similar benefits. More will be said about liability risks and insurance in Chapter 4, but considering the reasonableness of the rates, the potential risks, and as a start to your professional development, I strongly encourage you to join your professional association and to sign up for insurance as soon as possible if you have not already done so.

INDIVIDUAL INTERNSHIP AGREEMENTS

Beyond the more general institutional-level agreement is one specifically focused on what you will learn and do on the internship; what sorts of supervision experiences will be provided; what specific competencies will be developed and through what means; how your performance will be evaluated; and other such matters. Somewhat surprisingly, Hatcher et al. (2011) found that only 37% of the psychology practicum programs they surveyed reported the use of an individualized training plan that included specific goals, competencies, and learning sequences.

To help you develop a plan along with your instructor and supervisor, a sample individual internship agreement form is provided in Appendix C. As illustrated by that form, internship agreements should record the days and hours you will be expected to work, what your responsibilities will be, and the nature and extent of supervision to be provided. The internship agreement should also provide space to identify your goals and how you hope to achieve them during the internship.

EVALUATION

Because each internship offers different experiences and sets different expectations, and because interns differ in their personal goals, it is a good idea to be involved in the evaluation process from the beginning. To ensure the most effective and constructive learning experiences and to avoid future misunderstandings, interns, instructors, and supervisors should agree on the evaluation and grading criteria and process before the internship begins (Wayne, 2004). Everyone can then work together to ensure that the evaluation process is predictable and productive and contributes to the overall learning experience of the intern (Bogo, Regehr, Hughes, Power, & Globerman, 2002; Regehr, Regehr, Leeson, & Fusco, 2002).

As you think about the evaluation process, it is important to understand that you are not doing yourself a service if you seek, expect, or accept only positive feedback from an evaluation. I say this for several reasons. First, it is unrealistic to believe that you will excel in everything you do from the very outset. Therefore, you should expect that in some areas your performance may be exemplary and in others it may need some improvement. That is what learning is all about. Second, if you receive only positive feedback, you will not be able to identify or improve in those areas in which you are not strong or as skilled. Kadushin and Harkness (2002) emphasized that in many instances, student evaluations of supervisors reflect a desire for more, not less, critical feedback and for more specific constructive comments rather than general impressions.

Hoffman, Hill, Homes, and Feitas (2005) made a similar observation and report that supervisee attitudes toward feedback can influence the willingness of supervisors to address challenging issues. Furthermore, Hoffman et al. (2005) found that supervisors who avoid giving difficult or critical feedback often wished later that they had offered the feedback or critical evaluation for the sake of the student, their clients, and ultimately the profession. Smith and Agate (2004) described a method of addressing overconfidence among counselor trainees as a way of encouraging interns to reflect more critically on their own inferential and assessment processes. In my own experience as a supervisor and instructor, the students who eventually go on to be most successful are not only open to constructive criticism, they actually seek it out so they can learn more about themselves and their work.

Along the same lines, students should also keep in mind that one of the most difficult but important roles faculty and supervisors fill is that of "gatekeeper" for the profession (Busseri, Tyler, & King, 2005; Gibbs & Blakely, 2000; Hatcher & Lassiter, 2007; Johnson & Campbell, 2004; Morrow, 2000; Vacha-Haase, Davenport, & Kerewsky, 2004; Wayne, 2004; Wilkerson, 2006). Not everyone who seeks to work in the helping professions is up to the task, and, like it or not, your faculty and supervisors have the difficult but essential responsibility of identifying those who do not make the grade and should not continue with their studies or training.

Given the concerns just mentioned, there is no single evaluation approach that works best. Hatcher and Lassiter (2007) described the "Practicum Competencies Outline," which grew out of a lengthy process involving the Directors of Psychology Training Clinics and the Council of Chairs of Training Councils (http://www .psychtrainingcouncils.org/Practicum%20Competencies%20 FINAL%203-07.pdf). The Practice Competencies Outline builds on a developmental approach to practicum training and then sets defined levels of competencies that should be achieved in various skill and knowledge areas by the end of the practicum. Also included are certain personality characteristics and skills that are deemed essential prerequisites to successful clinical performance. Hatcher and Lassiter recommended that this instrument may provide a useful basis for evaluating practicum performance. They also suggested that further research be conducted to validate this use and that the outline itself be updated as additional research informs the practice of practicum training.

Regehr et al. (2002) described comparable skill and knowledge areas for social work. These authors reviewed a variety of approaches to evaluation in field placements and emphasized the importance of obtaining a baseline of student competence at the beginning of an internship. Such an assessment helps identify the learning needs and opportunities to be addressed during the internship and serves as a foundation for subsequent evaluation. Regehr and colleagues then recommended identifying specific learning goals that meet the needs of the student and the agency and the expectations of the school and the supervisor.

Evaluation has also received increasing attention within training of school counselors. Murphy and Kaffenberger (2007) built on the American School Counselor Association's National Model® and emphasized the importance of coordinating field learning, supervisory activities, and evaluation with the elements of the model. This coordination of training and evaluation is part of the accountability component of the National Model®. Murphy and Kaffenberger noted that accountability involves using data for three purposes—monitoring student progress, assessing counseling programs, and demonstrating counselor effectiveness.

I find this three-purpose approach to accountability particularly valuable, as it helps everyone involved keep in mind that evaluation is not simply a method for assessing the intern or trainee performance. Ideally, evaluation should give valuable information about the training and the academic programs as well. In turn, this should help specific institutions and professional disciplines as a whole demonstrate the adequacy and efficacy of their training and of the professionals who hold the relevant degrees.

If your instructor or supervisor has an established format for evaluation, review it carefully to be sure you understand it. If your instructor or supervisor does not have a fixed format, you may want to consider the sample evaluation forms provided in Appendices D and E. More will be said about the evaluation aspect of supervision in Chapter 5.

REFERENCES

American Psychological Association Committee on Accreditation. (2005). Guidelines and principles for accreditation of programs in professional psychology. Retrieved from http://www.apa.org/ed/gp2000.html

American School Counselor Association. (2009). State certification requirements. Retrieved from http://www.schoolcounselor.org/content.asp?contentid=242

Bogo, M. (2005). Field instruction in social work: A review of the research literature. *The Clinical Supervisor, 24,* 163–193.

Bogo, M., Regehr, C., Hughes, J., Power, R., & Globerman, J. (2002). Evaluating a measure of student field performance in direct service: Testing reliability and validity of explicit criteria. *Journal of Social Work Education, 38,* 385–399.

Busseri, M. A., Tyler, J. D., & King, A. R. (2005). An exploratory examination of student dismissals and prompted resignations from clinical psychology PhD training programs. *Professional Psychology: Research and Practice, 36,* 441–445.

Council for Accreditation of Counseling and Related Educational Programs. 2009 Standards. Retrieved from http://www.cacrep.org/doc/2009%20Standards%20with%20cover.pdf

Council on Social Work Education. (2004). Educational policy and accreditation standards. Retrieved from http://www.cswe.org/About/governance/CommissionsCouncils/CommissiononAccreditation.aspx/

Cornish, J. A. E., Smith-Acuña, S., & Nadkarni, L. (2005). Developing an exclusively affiliated psychology internship consortium: A novel approach to internship training. *Professional Psychology: Research and Practice, 36,* 9–15.

Gelman, C. R. (2004). Anxiety experienced by foundation-year MSW students entering field placement: Implications for admissions, curriculum, and field education. *Journal of Social Work Education, 40,* 39–54.

Gelman, C. R., & Lloyd, C. M. (2008). Pre-placement anxiety among foundation-year MSW students: A follow-up study. *Journal of Social Work Education, 44,* 173–184.

Gelman, S. R., Pollack, D., & Auerbach, C. (1996). Liability issues in social work education. *Journal of Social Work Education, 32,* 351–361.

Gibbs, P., & Blakely, E. H. (Eds.). (2000). *Gatekeeping in BSW programs.* New York: Columbia University Press.

Hatcher, R. L., Grus, C. L., & Wise, E. H. (2011). Administering practicum training: A survey of graduate programs' policies and procedures. *Training and Education in Professional Psychology, 5*(4), 244–252.

Hatcher, R. L., & Lassiter, K. D. (2007). Initial training in professional psychology: The practicum competencies outline. *Training and Education in Professional Psychology, 1,* 49–63.

Hill, C. E., Sullivan, C., Knox, S., & Schlosser, L. Z. (2007). Becoming psychotherapists: Experience of novice trainees in a beginning graduate class. *Psychotherapy: Theory, Research, Practice Training, 44,* 434–449.

Hoffman, M. A., Hill, C. E., Holmes, S. E., & Freitas, G. F. (2005). Supervisor perspective on the process and outcome of giving easy, difficult, or no feedback to supervisees. *Journal of Counseling Psychology, 52,* 3–13.

Johnson, W. B., & Campbell, C. D. (2004). Character and fitness requirements for professional psychologists: Training directors' perspectives. *Professional Psychology: Research and Practice, 35,* 405–411.

Kadushin, A., & Harkness, D. (2002). *Supervision in social work.* New York: Columbia University Press.

Madson, M. B., Aten, J. D., & Leach, M. M. (2007). Applying for the predoctoral internship: Training program strategies to help students prepare. *Training and Education in Professional Psychology, 1,* 116–124.

Mangione, L., VandeCreek, L., Emmons, L., McIlvried, J., Carpenter, D. W., & Nadkarni, L. (2006). Unique internship structures that expand training opportunities. *Professional Psychology: Research and Practice, 37,* 416–422.

Morrow, D. F. (2000). Gatekeeping for small baccalaureate social work programs. *Journal of Baccalaureate Social Work, 5*(2), 67–80.

Murphy, S., & Kaffenberger, C. (2007). The ASCA national model®: The foundation for supervision of practicum and internship students. *Professional School Counseling, 10*(3) 289–296.

National Association of Social Work Insurance Trust. (2004). Supervisor beware: Reducing your exposure to vicarious liability. Retrieved from http://www.naswinsurancetrust.org/understanding_risk_management/pointers/PP%20Vicarious%20Liability.pdf

Pollack, D., & Marsh, J. (2004). Social work misconduct may lead to liability. *Social Work, 49*(4), 609–612.

Regehr, C., Regehr, G., Leeson, J., & Fusco, L. (2002). Setting priorities for learning in the field practicum: A comparative study of students and field instruction. *Journal of Social Work Education, 38,* 55–65.

Smith, J. D., & Agate, J. (2004). Solutions for overconfidence: Evaluation of an instructional module for counselor trainees. *Counselor Education and Supervision, 44*(1), 31–43.

Vacha-Haase, T., Davenport, D. S., & Kerewsky, S. D. (2004). Problematic students: Gatekeeping practices of academic professional psychology programs. *Professional Psychology: Research and Practice, 35,* 115–122.

Wayne, J., Bogo, M., & Raskin, M. S. (2006). The need for radical change in field education. *Journal of Social Work Education, 42,* 161–170.

Wayne, R. H. (2004). Legal guidelines for dismissing students because of poor performance in the field. *Journal of Social Work Education, 40,* 403–414.

Wilkerson, K. (2006). Impaired students: Applying the therapeutic process model to graduate training programs. *Counselor Education and Supervision, 45,* 207–217.

Williams-Nickelson, C., Prinstein, M. J., & Keilin, W. G. (2008). *Internships in psychology: The APAGS workbook for writing successful applications and finding the right fit.* Washington, DC: American Psychological Association.

Zakutansky, T. J., & Sirles, E. A. (1993). Ethical and legal issues in field education: Shared responsibility and risk. *Journal of Social Work Education, 29,* 338–347.

CHAPTER 2
GETTING STARTED

ANXIETY AND EXCITEMENT

Now that you've made arrangements for your internship and are set to go, let's start by acknowledging again that when we undertake any new venture, it is normal to feel a combination of anxiety and excitement. Anxiety comes because we are not sure what lies ahead and may not be certain we can meet all the challenges. At the same time, we are excited because this, after all, is what we have trained for, and we're now getting a chance to try out in the real world what we learned from coursework. The key to dealing with these emotions is, first, to recognize that you are not alone and, second, to understand that with experience, time, and support, you will get more comfortable more quickly than you might imagine.

In a study of MSW students entering their foundation-year practicum, Gelman and Lloyd (2008) found that 72% of their respondents rated themselves moderately anxious or more as they looked toward their internship. Prior experience, age, and specific coursework all contributed to lower anxiety scores than those reported by younger, less experienced students with less prior coursework. When asked to identify specific concerns, respondents identified lack of skill or knowledge, logistical details such as commuting, safety issues, questions about the workload and expectations, and concerns about the kind of relationship and support that would be provided by the supervisor. Several concerns relating to work with clients were cited. These included clients reacting to the intern's inexperience; concerns about linguistic, ethnic, or socioeconomic differences; and questions about becoming overinvolved with clients. Trainees in a study by Hill, Sullivan, Knox, and Schlosser (2007) identified comparable concerns.

On the positive side, the concerns expressed by respondents in the Gelman and Lloyd study were counterbalanced by a sense of excitement, with the average positive score on a 10-point scale being 7.3. To help students explore the strengths they would bring to their practica, Gelman and Lloyd asked the trainees to list the knowledge and skills they believed they already possessed. The most commonly identified strengths in this group included prior experience, knowledge, and basic listening and empathy skills. Students also identified strategies for managing anxiety, including relaxation, positive thinking, social support, and personal therapy. A number of students suggested that schools and practicum settings could do more to help students adjust at the beginning of their placements. What follows in this chapter is designed to do just that, to help make your entry into the internship a positive and successful experience.

This chapter addresses common questions and concerns that arise in the first few days of an internship. It also discusses the role of the intern, some of the opportunities you can expect, and the limitations inherent in internships. Typical areas of concern include working with other staff, meeting clients, fees for service, managing paperwork, and coping with other tasks that are part of professional life but will probably be new to most interns. Finally, although there is much you can and should learn on internship sites, there may also be lessons that are best left unlearned. Recognizing these can be just as important as discovering the positive things you want to retain from your experience.

FIRST IMPRESSIONS

One of the great things about aphorisms is that for every famous saying there is an equal and opposite saying. Two mutually contradictory sayings relate particularly well to internships. The first is "You never get a second chance to make a first impression." The counterpoint advice is "Don't judge a book by its cover." As you begin your internship, keep in mind the importance of the first impressions you make on others. Remember also not to judge an internship setting or the people there solely on the basis of your first impressions.

When you begin an internship, first impressions will go both ways. On the one hand, as you are introduced to the staff, clients, and internship facility, you will begin to form your impressions of them. At the same time, the staff and clients will begin to form their impressions of you. Because first impressions can leave lasting effects, you should think about what kind of first impression you want to give others.

It would be foolish to tell interns exactly what they should wear or precisely how they should act on their first days on the job. Fortunately, expensive suits and the latest styles are not an expected part of the helping professional's wardrobe. Nevertheless, interns would be well advised to consider the nature of their internship setting, the kinds of activities they will be involved in, and the institutional norms for attire and conduct.

Most people have had the awkward experience of arriving at an event for which they were dressed either more formally or more informally than everyone else. One simple way to avoid this experience at internships is to ask your supervisor beforehand what the norms for clothing are and what activities will be happening on the first day.

The value of this advice was demonstrated by the experience of an intern who, keen on making the best first impression he could, arrived at his internship on his first day dressed in a suit and tie. The intern could not have looked finer, but it happened that his first day was "games" day at the internship site. Everyone else on staff was wearing shorts or jeans because, among other things, the games day activities included softball, egg tossing, and a tug-of-war through a mud pit. Dressed as he was, the intern did not participate in any of the events. What could have been a wonderful way to get to know people resulted in a rather uncomfortable experience of feeling out of place.

Experiences in the opposite direction have also befallen interns. Some students, accustomed to dressing, talking, and acting any way they want on the college campus, may insist on their right to "be themselves" at the internship. I know this argument rather well, not only because I have heard it from students on occasion but also, more personally, because I made it myself when I arrived at a rural internship placement with my very long hair and beard and dressed casually in Levi's ® and a flannel shirt. My supervisor was not at all happy with how I presented myself on the first day of work, so he summarily sent me home with advice to return looking more professional. Very reluctantly, and with a degree of righteous indignation, I trimmed my beard and hair, traded my jeans for khakis, and put on the only sport jacket I owned. In turn, the supervisor, also reluctantly, allowed me to continue the placement and, though this rough introduction took some time to work through, I ended up learning a great deal and somehow managed to demonstrate that even long-haired, bearded guys can have something to offer. I also came to realize that lost in the defense of an intern's own individuality is the more important principle that in clinical work our focus needs to be on caring for clients in the most effective way possible, not simply "being ourselves." Just as therapists or counselors must understand the needs of clients and adapt their interventions accordingly, interns should be sensitive to the institutional needs of their placement site. If that includes dressing, acting, or talking in a way that is different from the way one would outside the internship, so be it. In a very real sense, you are a guest at the internship site and should dress and conduct yourself in a way that respects the internship customs and needs.

Interns should carefully consider the first impressions they will make on others, even though many people at the internship will not be as concerned about the first impressions they make on the interns. This is to be expected because the experience and perspectives of staff are substantially different from those of interns.

Recently, one of our promising young interns returned from the first day at her internship site terribly distraught and convinced that the next three months were sure to be awful. When she went to visit her supervisor, he was at first too busy to meet with her. When they finally met later in the day, he asked a lot of questions about her approach to treatment, her experience, and

what she was doing there. During the conversation, he corrected some of the things she said, used "rough" language, and never asked her about who she was as a person. Almost in tears, she said to her instructor, "I'm sure there's no way we'll ever get along. I'm sure he hates me already, and I just can't work with someone like that."

As it turned out, the instructor knew the supervisor and was aware that his style was often perceived to be gruff. The instructor also knew that the supervisor was extremely dedicated to his clients and to the interns he trained. The gruffness was his natural style, in part because he was overworked and in part it was his way of getting past the surface talk to see how interns performed in response to stress. The supervisor had worked with many interns and had come to believe that given the type of clients encountered and the nature of the work at that internship site, interns had to be able to cope with confrontation.

In response to a request from the intern, the instructor called the supervisor, who reported that contrary to the intern's first impressions, he was quite impressed by her and thought she would work out just fine. The next day he apologized for any misunderstandings, complimented the intern on how she had responded, then set to work providing her with the best training and supervision received by any student that semester. Not all supervisory relationships work out as well as this one did, but it demonstrated the importance of not making decisions solely on the basis of first impressions.

ENTHUSIASM MEETS EXPERIENCE

Supervisors and staff who work with interns consistently say that the greatest assets interns bring to placements are their enthusiasm and optimism. Fresh from their studies and eager to try out their knowledge and skills, some interns practically radiate energy. Other interns, perhaps less sure of themselves, may radiate insecurity. What all interns have in common is that they bring something new to the institution. This is one of the reasons institutions and supervisors agree to accept interns. For the most part, they appreciate the interns' new perspectives, and they value the opportunity to be part of training future professionals (Globerman & Bogo, 2003).

Interns should be aware, however, that their own perspectives and experiences differ markedly from those of the staff and clients who are already at a placement site. Caught up as they are in their own feelings and in all there is to do and learn, interns often do not pause to think about this difference. For the intern, each placement is a new and potentially exciting experience, but each placement is also transitory. Throughout their time in the placement, interns will be on the steep upward slope of the learning curve, and every day can bring new discoveries and opportunities. By comparison, many of the staff at placement sites will have worked there for years and have different perspectives. They already know the people, the system, and the clients. They may also have seen many interns come and go. As a result, although each intern's experience is unique, having interns at the site may be a frequent occurrence for the staff members, and they may not share in the intern's sense of novelty or enthusiasm.

This does not mean the staff members are any less invested than the interns in the treatment of clients. It simply means that their perspective will differ from that of the interns. One long-time staff member explained it to an intern by comparing the experience to "falling in love versus marriage. The initial sense of wonder is fantastic, but it can't last forever. That doesn't mean the love is gone; it's just taken a different form that might not be so easy to see from the outside."

The same staff member went on to point out another factor that differs for staff and interns. For interns, the experience is limited in time. At the completion of the internship, the intern will go back to school, move on to another internship, or do something else, but seldom will the intern stay on at the site. Staff, on the other hand, were there before the intern came and will be there after the intern leaves. This is partly why interns may feel that some staff members do not reach out to form the close contacts the interns might desire. The staff may have become accustomed to interns coming and going; it is not realistic to expect them to form repeated close relationships that will almost certainly be temporary. Many interns do form valuable and lasting relationships with supervisors and others at internships, but it is helpful for interns to understand the situation so that they will not be disappointed if such relationships do not develop.

EXERCISE

Take a moment to think about the role of an intern as viewed from several perspectives. For example, how does each of the following view interns: supervisors, other professional staff, staff with less formal education, administrators, clients, the interns themselves? As you think about these perspectives, ask what positive and negative ideas each group might hold about interns. Giving some thought to this beforehand will better prepare you for the different relationships and reactions you will encounter during your internship.

THE ROLE OF THE INTERN

The role of an intern occupies a gray area somewhere between student and professional. As an intern, you will still have many things to learn, but you may also be counted on to possess certain knowledge and skills. Depending on your experience and training, you may be given gradually increasing responsibilities, but your position will probably not be equal to that of a full staff member. This ambiguity is compounded because others at the internship, including staff and clients, may also be unclear about what interns are and what the purpose of the internship is.

Precedents set by previous interns may further complicate your role as an intern. Many placement sites have had many interns over the years, and your predecessors have created certain expectations, positive or negative, with which you are likely to be compared. If a terrific intern preceded you, staff members at the placement are likely to welcome you but may hold you to high standards. If the former intern did not do well, a negative attitude toward interns may carry over to you. Although you cannot do anything about what happened before you arrived, being aware of

these possibilities can help you understand that the ways in which people relate to you are often influenced by experiences that have nothing to do with you as an individual.

Two principles can help interns deal with role ambiguity and any precedents that other interns may have set: (1) Be honest with yourself and with others and (2) do your best. Although these rules may sound simplistic, many interns have reported that remembering these basic principles helped them keep it together when things became confusing at their placements.

Being honest with yourself means you accept that your role is ambiguous, not only for yourself but for others as well. It also means that you are open about your relative strengths and limitations. If you have no experience doing something, let people know and be open to learning. If you have some experience or knowledge, do not be afraid to share it. If situations arise in which you need clarification about your role or the expectations others have, do not try to read people's minds. Ask for clarification, and be willing to share your own thoughts and feelings about the matter. Your goal at an internship is not to impress everyone with how smart or skilled you are. If you want to impress someone, show how eager and open to learning you are, not how much you already know.

Friedman and Kaslow (1986) described how supervisees in the early stage of training are "frequently plagued by the self-doubts and ambivalent feelings which reflect both the inchoate nature of their professional identities and the minimal degree of skill they as yet have amassed with which to perform their work" (p. 36). Kaslow and Rice (1987) and Stoltenberg (2005) made similar observations in their discussions of the developmental phases interns experience during their placements. Deal and Clements (2006) reported that when supervisors received training in understanding such developmental issues, students reported more positive experiences as compared with supervisors who did not have developmental training.

Precisely because interns are not expected to know everything, they can ask questions others might be afraid to raise. Similarly, interns who are new to settings may see things in ways that people working in that setting for years have never noticed. By acknowledging what you do not yet know, you not only enhance your potential to learn, you also gain a unique kind of permission and influence not always accorded to professionals. You should appreciate this opportunity while you still have it. When you obtain your degree and are in the role of professional, it may not be so easy to admit that you do not know everything.

WORK NEAR YOUR "LEARNING EDGE"

If acknowledging what you do not know is a first step toward learning, being willing to take some risks and extending yourself are key elements of the second step. Internships allow you to try new skills that you may have only read about before. To develop these skills, you have to test them and learn from both your successes and your mistakes. A concept that is useful to interns, and will later be useful in practice, is the idea of a *learning edge*. This term refers to the point just beyond one's present level of knowledge or skill. It is not so far ahead that we are in danger of making mistakes that could be calamitous for ourselves or others, but it is beyond our habitual level of functioning and comfort.

In your internship, you will often be right at your learning edge. This is comparable to Vygotsky's concept of the "zone of proximal development," namely, functioning in the skill area between your actual development and your potential development (Van Geert, 1998). If you find yourself feeling too comfortable, you should probably talk with your supervisor about extending your activities in some way. If you recognize that there is an area of knowledge or skill that you need to develop, you can expect that it will be a bit uncomfortable, but you must also realize that you need to accept this discomfort and push yourself in order to advance. Apart from specific skills you might develop or information you might acquire, becoming familiar and comfortable with your own learning edge is one of the most important lessons you can learn from internships.

Doing your best means that as someone in training, you do not already have to be the world's greatest therapist, social worker, psychologist, or counselor; it is not your sole responsibility to save all of the clients or do everything anyone asks of you. As an intern, you should set the highest possible standards for yourself, but do not set or try to meet unrealistic expectations. If people around you seem much more experienced than you are, do not be intimidated. They probably do have more experience, and that gives you the opportunity to learn. Enjoy the opportunity and make the most of it.

There may be times when you feel pressured by time or other constraints to do less than your best work. People tend to remember the quality of your work, not the circumstances under which it was done. For this and other reasons, it is generally advisable to concentrate on providing a high quality of service rather than emphasizing quantity. If you think that time or other demands are causing you to compromise quality, discuss this with your instructor and supervisor so that adaptations can be made.

THE ROLE OF THE PROFESSIONAL

Because interns are exploring and beginning to establish their professional identity, it is important to consider how the role of professional differs from that of student (Elman, Illfelder-Kaye, & Robiner, 2005). The easiest way to understand this difference is to think in terms of standards. I use this word often because, for me, being a professional means setting the highest possible standards for what I do in my professional life. As an intern, I hope you will aspire to this as well. Because our work as professionals impacts the lives of others, we must always conduct ourselves ethically and must do our utmost to stay current with research literature, clinical practices, organizational standards, legal issues, and other matters that may affect our practice, the people we serve, or our profession.

Students tend to have an implicit assumption that learning about a subject has a start and an end point at the conclusion of class. For students, the goal is often to get the best possible grade or, perhaps, simply to do the minimum needed to pass a course. For a professional, however, learning is ongoing, it never stops, and the standard cannot be the minimum needed to pass a course. If there is something you need to know to better serve a client or perform some other function, then you must do what it takes to

fully and solidly acquire the necessary skill or knowledge. There is no room for "just good enough to pass," and there is no room for kidding ourselves into thinking we know or can do something when, in fact, this is not so. The demand for meeting high standards will be ongoing throughout your professional work; it can be very challenging but also rewarding and is part of what you sign up for when you enter a profession.

To appreciate why this is so, ask yourself what you expect from other treatment professionals when you put your life in their hands in some way. Do you expect anything less than their full commitment to adhere to the highest standards of ethics and quality care? Do you expect them to pay full attention to your concerns and do whatever it takes to study and learn about your condition and treatment? Of course you do, which is why you must set the same high standards for yourself.

Another important difference between students and professionals is that students are viewed as individuals and their conduct can vary accordingly. Professionals, on the other hand, are expected to meet certain standards of conduct because they are members of and represent a larger, identified group. Earlier I described my own unpleasant experience of being sent home from an internship because I was not dressed suitably. In addition to dress, there are standards for the kind of language that is acceptable, the way one relates to others on the job, and the quality of work one produces. Professional and student standards are also different in the more mundane but nevertheless extremely important details, such as coming to work on time and keeping appointments. Students typically have a great deal of freedom in each of these areas, but the professional must be prompt, reliable, and act in ways that maintain an image of respectability.

For most students, this will not be a problem; but if you find it difficult to balance your personal habits or identity with your professional role, you might want to reexamine your own conduct or select another internship that more closely matches your style. I also encourage you to understand that meeting standards does not mean abandoning your individuality. If all professionals were clones, they would not be able to meet the needs of diverse clients. There is room and need for individuality among therapists, but it is also your responsibility to find ways to remain an individual while still serving your internship and clients (Pipes, Holstein, & Aguirre, 2005).

JOINING YOUR PROFESSIONAL ASSOCIATION

This was mentioned in the prior chapter, but it bears repeating here. If you have not already done so, I strongly encourage you to join your professional association. The easiest way to sign up for membership is to access the website for your profession. As you will discover, membership provides a host of benefits and helps advance your entry into the role of a professional. Among the benefits are the chance to get to know, work with, and learn from others in your profession from your own area and from across the nation and the globe. Membership also brings discounted access to journals, newsletters, and other communications that help you stay current with your field. In addition, as discussed before, membership may include coverage by or discounts for select insurance programs—including professional liability insurance. Associations also offer continuing education programs that are valuable today and will be essential to continuing licensure when the time comes. Knowledge of and participation in policy and advocacy efforts on behalf of your profession and the people you serve is also part of your association's work and allows you to help advance the profession itself both for your own interest and the interests of the next generation of professionals. For many associations, membership may also include somewhat more mundane but nevertheless useful benefits such as rental car discounts or special rates on magazine subscriptions.

Although most students and interns do not fully appreciate it, you are able to study and practice today because people who came before you worked hard and made sacrifices to build the profession you are entering and created the educational and training opportunities you now enjoy. By joining your professional association yourself, you can take up the torch and make your own contributions before passing it on to the next generation.

MAKING THE MOST OF YOUR INTERNSHIP

ACADEMIA MEETS THE "REAL WORLD"

One thing all interns discover is that internships require a different set of skills and knowledge than those required by academic classes. Formal academic classes emphasize knowledge of facts. The focus of most academic exams is on what you know, and the "what" that you must know has been explicitly taught in the class. By the time they are in college, most students know this system pretty well. If you pay attention in class, study hard, and memorize the material, you are likely to pass the exam. Contrast this situation with the internship world.

In an internship, the focus is not on what you *know*, but what you *do*. Being able to identify the founders of every major therapy technique or to describe in detail five theories of personality is fine if you are in a class; however, such abilities may be of limited use at your internship, where usefulness of information depends on what you do with what you know and how you relate your knowledge to the situations you encounter. If you experience this gulf when you begin your internship, you are not alone. Indeed, the issue of translating academic knowledge to practical applications was at the core of the first internships in psychology (Routh, 2000; Thorp, O'Donohue, & Gregg, 2005). Lewis, Hatcher, and Pate (2005) described this difference from the perspective of academic training directors compared with that of practicum site coordinators, noting that the willingness of the latter to accept interns into their facilities depends on weighing the benefits of the service provided by the trainee against the costs of providing training and supervision.

The other difference between internships and classroom study is that it is never clear beforehand just what you will have to know. One of the truest statements I know about life applies well to internships: "Life gives the test first, then the lesson." At an internship, at any given moment you may be called on to use any knowledge or skills you have and possibly some you do not have. Therefore, your study approach must prepare you with the skills of understanding people and interactions in general. It must

also teach you to be flexible, think on your feet, expect the unexpected, and understand that the measure of success is much different from what you may be accustomed to.

TAKE RESPONSIBILITY FOR LEARNING

In all aspects of learning, students need to take personal ownership for what and how they learn. Merely accepting passively what an instructor tells you to read or do is not a recipe for success as a student, and it is certainly not a recipe for success as a professional. Taking responsibility for learning is particularly important in the context of internships, because the nature of the learning setting and opportunity is so different from that of a typical classroom. Internships do not usually provide structured syllabi, reading assignments, exams, or any of the other methods that tend to direct students. At the same time, it is possible that your supervisor will be busy and not able to give the time you might need or want unless you assert yourself in some way.

An especially useful resource for all students is *On Course* by Skip Downing (2010). This text was recommended to me by one of the reviewers of this edition, and I want to pass the recommendation on to you. Now in its sixth edition, Downing's book and its accompanying website (http://www.oncourseworkshop .com/) helps students take control of their own learning by first assessing how they learn and then offering a host of tips and exercises to develop key principles of success, including accepting self-responsibility, discovering self-motivation, and mastering self-management. Students report that they find Downing's text and the exercises tremendously helpful, and institutions that have adopted the program report substantial gains in student performance.

Whether you use this program or some other strategy, the key point is to take charge and be proactive in your education and training. Ultimately, your education is your responsibility, and it is in your own best interests to be as assertive and focused as you can be.

REMEMBER THAT YOU DO KNOW SOME THINGS

Along with the opportunity to develop and try out your skills, the internship should also give you a chance to bring together information learned during your academic program. Courses in human development, culture, gender issues, community systems, theories of personality, assessment, abnormal psychology, and other subjects are all relevant to your internship.

Students who have studied a subject in class often seem to forget what they have learned when they begin their internships. Try to avoid that mistake. If you have had a course in human development, consider what you learned as you work with people of different ages. If you have taken a class on the theories of personality, ask yourself how different theorists might view the people in your clinical setting. If you are working in a community agency, give some thought to ways in which knowledge from a community systems course helps you understand the agency and its clients. Such opportunities will strengthen your understanding and give you the chance to compare theory with reality. Again, the emphasis is not just on what you know. It is on what you can do with that knowledge in the context of your internship.

EXERCISE

To boost both your confidence and your humility, take a few moments to list the courses or learning experiences you have had that you think will help you on your internship site. For each course, try to identify specific concepts, theories, findings, or applications that you can put into practice to understand the setting and the people you will work with as clients. For example, a course in human development might help you understand the challenges adolescent clients are facing. Similarly, a course in systems theory might give you insights into the family dynamics of your clients. When you have listed what you know that will help you, give some thought to identifying the areas in which you do not know something and wish you had further training. This list can alert you to areas you should be cautious about approaching and may help you plan your studies to fill in any noticeable deficits.

GET HELP WHEN YOU NEED IT

This final suggestion for making the most of an internship will be offered repeatedly in this text: If you have any problems or questions, be sure to get assistance. It is essential that you recognize when situations or assignments are beyond your ability and you need help to deal with them. You may need help with anything from questions about ethics to how to write a certain kind of case note. You may be working with a particularly challenging client, or perhaps you are not getting along well with a staff member or supervisor. Whatever the difficulty, when problems develop, get help, and do so early.

Resources include your faculty instructor, placement supervisor, peers, and other faculty or staff. If none of these persons is available, other professionals outside the setting or university may also be helpful. The main point is that you are not alone and are not expected to be able to do everything yourself. This is not a precept you must practice only in your internship—it is a fundamental principle of responsible professional conduct. You will be off to a good start if you follow it in your first placement.

Because it is absolutely essential that interns be willing to seek help and know where to get it, especially in an emergency, it is a good idea to complete the Emergency Contact and Procedures Information form provided in Appendix F. The form lists the names, phone numbers, and other information needed to contact site supervisors, faculty instructors, or other individuals as backup if the immediate supervisors or instructors are not available. The form also lists step-by-step procedures and specific people to contact for dealing with crises and situations involving possible hospital commitment.

Completing this crisis contact form may not seem necessary at present, but if a crisis occurs in the middle of the night and you cannot locate your primary supervisor or instructor for help, you will be very glad to have the numbers of other contacts readily available. Needing just such support when I was an intern, and having provided it to students in my roles as supervisor and instructor, I cannot emphasize this too strongly. Complete the form when you start your internship, keep a copy at work and at home, and use it whenever you need help. Any supervisors or faculty members worth their salt would much rather be called unnecessarily than find out later that they were not consulted about a serious problem.

MEETING CLIENTS

When they first begin placements, interns are most commonly concerned about how they will be received by clients.

EXERCISE

Before reading further, write down some of your hopes and concerns about meeting clients. Talk about these with your peers and, if possible, with students who have recently completed internship experiences. Also schedule some time to discuss your concerns with your supervisor and instructor. They will undoubtedly be familiar with these problems, but it can be useful for you to express any concerns openly.

In most cases, the anxieties of interns about meeting clients are often quite different from the realities. In spite of the common fears of interns, most clients readily accept interns and relate to them as they do to other staff members. Clients generally understand the need to train future professionals. Some are even solicitous, wanting to help ensure that the interns have a good experience. Other clients may be overly accepting of interns, and some may be extremely trusting of the intern's skills. Friedman and Kaslow (1986) contrasted the supervisee's anxieties with the client's trust by noting that client reactions "attest to the fact that at least one member of the trainee–patient dyad believes that the former is actually a therapist" (p. 34).

This does not mean that all clients will welcome all interns. There will be clients who reject working with interns and want to work with a "real therapist." Clients who resist working with the intern can be intimidating and remarkably capable of making interns feel unwelcome or incompetent.

As you prepare for your first interactions with clients, remember that whether clients are extremely trusting or instantly hostile or react in some other way, your task is to understand these reactions in the clinical context. This means you should not necessarily be overly flattered by clients who are immediately trusting, nor should you be deeply hurt or intimidated by clients who are initially distant or hostile. Instead, your primary task is to understand the client's reaction from the client's perspective and be aware that each interaction is part of the overall clinical process. It also helps to beware of first impressions, both positive and negative, because first impressions can often be misleading.

Along with concerns about how clients will respond to them, interns also ask questions about how they should introduce themselves to clients. As recommended earlier, the best practice is to be honest. When asked, interns should say they are interns, what their field of study is, and, if it is relevant, explain a bit about why they are at the internship. For example, "Hi, I'm Alyson Jones. I'm an intern in counseling, and I'll be working here for the next three months." That is usually sufficient. If more information is requested, such as what experience you have, be honest about that as well. If you have experience working with a certain treatment approach or setting, it is fine to say so. If you have no such experience, you might say, "I haven't had any experience working in a setting of this kind. That's why I'm here. I'll be working closely with my supervisor and hope to learn some things."

Zakutansky and Sirles (1993) asserted that whenever interns work directly with clients, the intern's field supervisor should make it a point to meet directly with those clients at the start of treatment. In addition to ensuring that clients are aware that the intern is being supervised, meeting with the supervisor allows clients to know that there is someone they can speak with if they have concerns about their treatment. These issues are discussed further in Chapter 4 in the context of the ethical obligation to provide informed consent. Before working directly with clients, all interns should read that chapter carefully and be well versed in their ethical obligations.

AGE AND EXPERIENCE ISSUES WITH CLIENTS AND SUPERVISORS

The age and experience of interns are issues that sometimes arise when interns meet with clients or supervisors. These issues are particularly likely with undergraduate students, many of whom will be in their early 20s or perhaps even in their late teens. For school counselors, especially those working in high school settings, this can be especially difficult as some of the youths who will be receiving services may be just a few years younger than the counseling intern. On the other hand, it can also happen, especially with returning adult students, that the intern will be older than not only clients but also the field supervisor and perhaps the instructor (Fox, 2004; Hopkins, Bloom, & Deal, 2005).

Considering first the situation of interns who are younger than their clients or near their clients in age, two types of problems are most likely to arise. If you are young and working with clients near your age, clients may expect you to relate to them as a friend rather than as an intern. They may also test your limits and your role and authority, or they may ask you to let them do things that other staff would not. If this happens, you will need to be clear with yourself and with the clients that you are, indeed, part of the staff and have the same responsibilities and authority as the staff.

A different sort of problem can arise if you are working with older clients, who may ask, "So how can somebody your age have anything to tell me?" In response, interns should first try to understand what the question might mean to the client. Does it mean, for example, that the client is sincerely interested in the treatment program and wants to know whether he or she can rely on the intern for help? Or does it mean that the client is interested in taking a position of power over the intern because that is how the client relates to most people? What else might a question of this type mean to clients?

How one understands the meaning of the client's question should help in forming a response. As a general guideline, interns need not be defensive about age, experience, or for that matter any other issues on which clients might challenge them. Instead, the intern might wish to acknowledge the importance of the question. Then, without being defensive, the intern may explore any specific concerns or issues with the client. This displays genuine concern for the client's needs and shows that the intern is honest. The following example shows one way this might occur in practice.

A male client has been court ordered to seek counseling because he has been abusing his wife and children. The following dialogue takes place when the client meets a new intern who will be working with his primary therapist. The intern will also be observing interactions between the client and his family members:

Client (rather gruffly): So you're an intern from the college, huh? How old are you?

Intern: I'm 21. And you?

Client: Forty-two. Old enough to be your father. (Pauses for a moment looking over the intern. Then, with some hostility, asks) What the hell are you supposed to tell me that I don't already know?

Intern (calmly, but assertively and without being confrontational): I'm not here to "tell" you anything. I'm here to observe and learn.

Client: Well, I don't need any know-it-all kid telling me how to raise my family. I've got enough of those already.

Intern (still calmly): I don't think it's my job to tell you how to raise your family. But I might be able to listen to how things are going and maybe help you folks get things back together.

Client: Yeah. We'll see.

In this example, the client appears to want to diminish the intern's credibility or provoke a conflict. This reaction may be based on legitimate concerns about the intern's qualifications, or it may be an attempt to shift the focus from the client's reason for being in treatment to why the intern is there. The intern's response is thoroughly professional. She does not attempt to elicit the client's approval on the spot, nor does she become defensive, counterattack, or apologize. Instead, she stays right with the client and with the interaction process. She acknowledges the presence and legitimacy of the client's concerns and offers to do what she can to be of help. That is all that can reasonably be expected.

An interaction such as this would probably not be very pleasant for the intern or the client, but not all clinical work is pleasant. It may also happen that, despite the intern's best efforts, a client will continue to be hostile and challenging. This can make the situation even more unpleasant, but it provides important clinical information that can help the intern understand the client. The intern should keep in mind that it is perfectly legitimate for clients to have questions about the intern's age and experience. At the same time, however, the real issue of importance is the one the client brings, not the intern's age. By remaining professional and receiving what the client is saying without becoming defensive, the intern can help keep the focus where it needs to be.

In contrast to scenarios that arise when interns are much younger than clients, a host of different, but not entirely unrelated, issues arises when an intern is older than supervisors or instructors. This situation is becoming more common as increasing numbers of adults return to college or take on new careers later in life. Two rather paradoxical challenges can be present in these situations.

Many older students describe feeling some anxiety as they interact with much younger peers and feel self-conscious or worry that they cannot keep up with the seemingly hypersonic speed of the younger students. On the other hand, older students may also become frustrated with younger classmates they perceive as naive or overly confident. So too, it can sometimes be difficult for interns who are older than their instructors or clinical supervisors to really trust and respect the guidance of someone who is younger and, presumably, has less life experience.

A couple of practical suggestions may be helpful in these circumstances. First, in internship settings, one is not in competition with other students, or for that matter with supervisors, regardless of age differences. Rather, the task at hand is to develop one's own skills to the greatest extent possible. To achieve that goal, openness to learning will be a much more beneficial perspective than a sense of competition or anxiety. An attitude of openness can also help make it easier for older students to take instruction or guidance from younger faculty or supervisors. The mere fact that one person has logged more time on the planet than another does not mean he or she knows more about everything than does the other person. Before concluding that younger faculty or supervisors do not have all that much to offer, older students may wish to give some thought to how much time and experience their instructors and supervisors have had, not simply on the planet, but doing whatever it is they are trying to learn to do. For their part, instructors can also benefit by recognizing that older or nontraditional students bring valuable experiences and knowledge that can be assets to the class as a whole and from which the instructor can help build new learning opportunities.

TIME LIMITS

Although some clients may not want to work with interns, others often form close connections with them, perhaps because many clients are in great need and interns are usually approachable, interested, and eager to work with them. Whereas relationships between interns and clients can be highly beneficial to both, they also raise unique clinical issues that must be carefully considered in selecting clients to work with interns and in developing treatment approaches.

One of the real strengths of interns is that their enthusiasm and openness often make it possible to form contacts with difficult clients. Indeed, some experienced supervisors make a habit of assigning the most hopeless cases to interns because they have learned that where others may have failed, the enthusiasm and effort of an intern can sometimes break through.

Interns know from the first day, however, that their placement is time limited and that termination may be inevitable within just a few months. Under such circumstances, is it therapeutic, or even fair, to encourage interns and clients to build strong relationships that must end in a short time?

This question has no easy answer, but it must be addressed. First, interns must be clear about the time limits of their placements when dealing with staff; clients; and, most important, themselves. This means that when they begin working with individual clients, in groups, on projects, or whatever else they may participate in, interns must inform those involved of the time constraints. This is part of the informed-consent process.

Interns must also remember their own time constraints; they should not create unrealistic fantasies about what they can accomplish or should attempt within the time available. It is dishonest, for example, to tell clients that you will always be there for them if you know that in another two months you will be gone. Similarly, taking on a project that will require a year to complete is unwise if the internship lasts only six months. It may be difficult to limit a relationship with a client or to decline involvement in an interesting project, but it is better to be realistic than to create false hopes that will inevitably lead to disappointment.

When interns hear this advice, they sometimes wonder if they should avoid working with any clients or projects at all. That would be going too far. Rather than avoiding all involvement or contact, the wise response is to be selective about one's involvement. This is the second element of working within limited time. Not all cases or projects will require extended periods. Many clients can be helped within a few weeks or months, and many projects can also be completed in a short time. One of the intern's responsibilities is to select cases and activities wisely. Supervisors should play a role in these choices and should be aware of time constraints when they assign interns to clients or duties. An intern who is assigned a case or project for which time limitations will pose a problem should discuss this with the supervisor.

A third element to working within time constraints is to consider the approaches used. It is not necessary to limit involvement to short-term cases or activities, as long as the treatment selected takes the time factor into account and includes provisions for continuing the treatment or other work after the intern leaves. An intern can also deal with time constraints by working with clients in the presence of another professional who will continue the case after the intern leaves. Arrangements of this type often involve interns seeing clients jointly with their supervisor. The supervisor can then maintain the case after the internship concludes. A comparable situation also holds when the intern is involved in treatment groups. Because the group provides the continuity for clients, there is a less dramatic change when an intern leaves.

However limits are addressed, interns need to consider termination issues even before they accept a case. By thinking about termination as part of selecting cases and choosing intervention techniques, interns can prevent many potential difficulties of termination from the outset. More is said about concluding treatment in Chapter 10, but for the reasons described here, interns should keep time limits in mind at all stages of their internship and work with clients.

FEES FOR SERVICE

Most interns who are just starting out do not have to deal with charging for their individual services, but the agencies where they work will very likely have at least some fees. Whether or not this is part of your internship, the idea of charging for helping people is an awkward issue for many interns so it is useful to discuss this matter briefly here. It is also important to be aware that important ethical and legal issues are associated with fees.

Fees can pose a challenge for many reasons, but one of the more prominent is the apparent conflict many interns experience with the altruistic motives that initially brought them to the helping professions. If a person goes into a profession out of a desire to help people but then charges those people money, the conflict between the motives of altruism and profit is likely to create dissonance (Wolfson, 1999). Resolving this dissonance is not easy because of the risk of compromising the altruism or simply rationalizing away one's sense of guilt.

To address this question, it may help to recognize that what we as human service professionals are really billing for is our time and presumed knowledge and expertise. We are not necessarily promising to cure clients or solve their problems. We are, however, agreeing to spend time with clients and do the best we can to help them in some way. Psychologists, counselors, and social workers are not the only professionals who bill for services in this way. Attorneys, physicians, and many others bill in similar ways. The common element is that billing is based on the professional's time. Attorneys do not always win their cases, doctors do not always cure their clients, and even plumbers cannot always fix sinks.

One question this raises is, Are interns sufficiently skilled to justify charging for services? By their nature, internships involve a trainee working in a clinical setting under the guidance and instruction of a supervisor. Thus, when clients are billed for services provided by interns, they are not being charged solely for the intern's time. The bill must also include the time of the supervisors and the resources of the internship sites. What is more, although interns may not yet be ready for independent practice, this does not mean that their time is without value. Many interns, particularly those completing graduate degrees, are, in fact, quite skilled, and in conjunction with the aid of their supervisors and the support and resources of their internship sites, it is thoroughly appropriate that they and the agency be compensated for their services. For a more extensive discussion of when trainees are ready to practice independently, see Rodolfa, Ko, and Petersen (2004).

Speaking personally again and returning to the matter of altruism versus fees, I did not enter this field because I wanted to get rich. If that was my goal, I could have pursued any number of other occupations. My primary motive was the desire to help people and society in the best way I could. In selecting a profession, I set out to find a way to combine altruistic motives with the legitimate need to earn an income. For me, it was not altruism *versus* income; it was altruism *and* income. The helping professions seemed to fit that aim well. I have found that my students and interns share many of the same motives that led me to this field. Berger (1995) described similar motives, noting that few of the senior therapists he interviewed even mentioned financial rewards as a factor sustaining their commitment and enthusiasm for the profession. More important than monetary compensation, such factors as personal experience, mental attitude, and interpretation of the work that we do may be bigger determinants of the happiness or satisfaction we gain in our careers (Csikszentmihalyi, 1999).

CLINICAL AND ETHICAL ISSUES PERTAINING TO FEES

Although this discussion has pointed out the similarities between fees in the helping professions and other fields, an important difference must be understood. In psychotherapy, how clients and therapists deal with fees is not just a business arrangement; it is also part of the material and process of therapy. For example, Rabkin (1994) described how clients with such diagnoses as dependent personality or obsessive-compulsive personality may react in unique ways to fees, and this reaction can become part of the therapeutically useful material therapists address in treatment.

Some research evidence suggests that charging fees may enhance the effectiveness of therapy (Conolley & Bonner, 1991; Wong, 1994). A matter of pride is involved for many clients who sincerely need help but do not want to accept "charity." For these clients, it is important to respect both their need and their pride and allow them to pay for services to the best of their ability. For a review of other research on this topic, see Wolfson (1999).

Along with clinical considerations, interns need to be aware of certain ethical issues pertaining to fees. As an intern, you are unlikely to deal with the matter directly, but you should realize that having fees collected when clients fail to pay could raise delicate and ambiguous ethical issues (Goodman, 1994). For example, in some agencies, unpaid client bills are given to a collection agency, which raises questions about confidentiality. Some experts on legal issues have advised against the practice, arguing that the fees that might be obtained through such means are probably not sufficient to justify the risks (E. Harris, personal communication, February 3, 1995).

Again, all of these issues will be more relevant to you when you have completed your training, but even in your role as intern, you need to know your agency's policy concerning fees, and you need to know clearly how to address this matter with clients. If you are interested in more information about this topic, see the National Association of Social Workers (NASW) handbook, *2008 Third-Party Reimbursement in Clinical Social Work Services,* 13th ed. (NASW, 2008). This concise resource, which is relevant to all related professions, reviews and provides contact information pertaining to a host of reimbursement sources, including managed-care and government insurance providers. In addition, ethical and legal issues are discussed along with the Health Insurance Portability and Accountability Act (HIPAA) 1996 rules as they pertain to reimbursement. For insights into setting fees in the current professional climate, see Sears (2005), and for results of a study of gender differences in fee structures, see Newlin, Adolph, and Kreber (2004).

IS TREATMENT EFFECTIVE?

Along with the other issues just addressed in regard to fees, interns may also ask more fundamental questions that should be addressed early on in training; "Does what we do really work?" "Does it make a difference?" "Is it really worth anything?"

For the mental health or human service professional, this is a core existential matter. Because the services we provide and the outcomes we seek are largely intangible, what those services are or how much they are worth is not always clear. Personally, I believe it is actually desirable for interns to question the effectiveness of treatment.

An example of this happened just as I was writing this chapter. During a recent internship class, I noticed that one of the students seemed to be considerably more relaxed and comfortable than he had previously appeared. It turned out that the student, who was involved in a research internship involving biofeedback, had decided to experience biofeedback himself as part of his training. When I commented on the apparent change in his level of comfort, the student said with genuine surprise and pleasure, "You're right. I've been doing biofeedback myself, and it's working great. Really great. I can't believe it. I thought it was all a bunch of baloney, but some of this stuff really works!"

Such personal experience of therapy effectiveness is tremendously valuable. It can help students understand the client's experience in treatment, and it can help build confidence in the potential for treatment to be helpful (Norcross, 2005).

Apart from personal experience, concerns about treatment effectiveness can also be addressed by reviewing the research literature. Paul (1967) pointed out that we should not simply ask whether therapy in general is effective. Instead, we should ask, "What treatment, by whom, is most effective for this individual with that specific problem, and under which set of circumstances?" (p. 111).

Although a number of methodological issues complicate research in this area, numerous reviews over the past several decades (APA, 2012; Boisvert & Faust, 2003; Bovasso, Eaton, & Armenian, 1999; Chorpita et al., 2011; Hunsley, 2007; Roth & Fonagy, 1996; Seligman, 1995) have concluded that for most clients, including adults, children, couples, and families, psychotherapy has positive effects and produces results superior to what would be expected if the client had not been in therapy or had received placebo treatment (for more detailed information, see the Resolution on Recognition of Psychotherapy Effectiveness by the APA (2012) and the review of research with children and adolescents by Chorpita et al. (2011)).

Although studies of treatment effectiveness are encouraging, it should also be acknowledged that some clients may get worse rather than better in therapy (Barlow, 2010; Castonguay, Boswell, Constantino, Goldfried, & Hill, 2010; Lilienfeld, 2007; Orlinsky & Howard, 1980; Shapiro & Shapiro, 1982). Strupp (1989) identified some of the factors, notably "communications that are experienced by patients as pejorative" (p. 717), that may contribute to negative outcomes. More recently, Lilienfeld (2007) established a list of "potentially harmful treatments"

(PHTs), and Castonguay et al. (2010) stressed the importance of teaching the potentially harmful effects of treatment as part of professional training.

EVIDENCE-BASED PRACTICE AND EMPIRICALLY SUPPORTED TREATMENTS

In theory, one might assume that health care practice and social service have always been driven by research. In practice, however, there are numerous examples in which this has not been the case. On the one hand, too often treatments, diagnostic procedures, or social services are applied without sufficient empirical or clinical evidence to support their use and, in some instances, in spite of evidence that would contraindicate their use. On the other hand, treatments, diagnostic approaches, and services that have demonstrated efficacy and positive cost/benefit returns are often left unused or underused either because of lack of awareness in practitioners, the inertia of existing practices and biases, or social or economic forces.

In response to growing pressures to constrain health care costs and improve outcomes, the question of treatment effectiveness has gained attention well beyond the professional community of practitioners and researchers. Growing and legitimate calls insist that only empirically studied, evidence-based diagnoses and treatments should be paid for by insurance. This increased scrutiny is coming from private insurers as well as from government entities that administer Medicare, Medicaid, and other programs (McHugh & Barlow, 2010; Edmond, Megivern, Williams, Rochman, & Howard, 2006; Goodheart, Kazdin, & Sternberg, 2006; Hunsley, 2007; Kazdin, 2008; Steinfeld, Coffman, & Keyes, 2009).

Two terms are commonly used to describe the movement to counter these problems. In the field of medicine, the term *evidence-based practice* (EBP) is predominant, whereas in the social sciences, one also finds reference to *empirically supported treatments* (EST) (Baker, 2012; Hunsley, 2007; McNeill, 2006; Norcross, Beutler, & Levant, 2006). For an informative review of efforts to disseminate evidence-based treatments, see McHugh and Barlow (2010).

As an intern and throughout your practice, you need to be aware of EBP and EST for a number of reasons. First, to ensure that your own treatment or assessment activities are well founded and effective, you will need to appreciate and be able to put into practice the underlying principles, terminology, research methods, and findings (Hershenberg, Drabick, & Vivian, 2012). Second, it is very likely that the internship setting in which you work will be coming under increasing pressure to implement and demonstrate that its interventions are evidence based and cost effective. Third, for legal reasons, you are well advised to know and practice the most empirically sound methods because if challenged in court, your ability to demonstrate both knowledge of and adherence to such methods affords a strong defense against liability claims. Fourth, professional associations are weighing in heavily on this matter and establishing official policies and guidelines. Useful guidelines for integrating EBP in training have been offered by Hershenberg et al. (2012), who described the importance of trainees developing the skills to evaluate best available research and then applying that knowledge to understanding client characteristics and developing clinical expertise.

Limitations of EBP have also been identified. Edmond et al. (2006), McNeill (2006), Yunong and Fengzhi (2009), and Gilgun (2005) describe four "cornerstones" of EBP: (1) knowledge from research and theory; (2) "practice wisdom," including knowledge gained from clients and experience; (3) the personal experience of the provider; and (4) the knowledge, information, and experience clients bring to the situation. Gilgun (2005) emphasized that in addition to considering research findings, it is important in the human service professions to incorporate unique client values and provider qualities, elements not so easily incorporated into empirical research. McNeill (2006), in particular, also stressed the role of clinical judgment, whereas Nelson and Steele (2006) emphasized the importance of looking at factors other than just treatment outcome, including economic considerations as well as client and provider preferences.

The most important point for you to understand as an intern is that across all disciplines in mental health and social services, there is growing attention to basing practice on research and paying close attention to issues of costs and benefits in everything we do. In your training now and later in your professional work, I strongly encourage you to at all times have certain questions in your mind: "What is the clinical and research evidence behind doing what we are doing in the way we are doing it with this particular client in this particular situation?" "What other options are we not using, and have we considered them carefully?" "How can we evaluate, either through formal empirical studies or careful, critical clinical examination, the efficacy of what we are doing?" "What are the total costs of this treatment relative to the likely benefits, and how do the costs and benefits compare with other options?" Finally, as will be discussed in the next section, it is always worth asking, "What are the risks and possible harm of doing what we are doing with this particular client in this situation?" "Have we carefully and critically evaluated the possibility that we may be doing more harm than good?"

All of these questions are not simply ones you should ask yourself; they are also legitimate topics for discussion with your internship supervisor and instructor. If you ask these questions, be aware that in many instances, there may not be fully satisfactory answers. In part, this is inherent in the nature of the work we do, and in part it is simply a reflection of the limitations of human knowledge in all fields. It may also happen that you will ask these kinds of questions of individuals or in settings where an empirical, evidence-based approach to practice is not a core value. Sometimes the answer you will be given may simply be, "Because that's how we've always done it." Other times there may be references to personal clinical experience, a particular theoretical orientation, or "expert knowledge" without other substantiation or empirical evidence.

Should this happen, it does not mean that the questions are not legitimate or that you cannot learn from the setting or individuals. It may, however, mean that you will want to explore answers yourself beyond the responses you are given by others. Do not be disappointed or discouraged by this. In fact, it is the reality of how one learns as a professional. There often is no one right answer,

but by asking questions, gathering information and ideas from multiple sources, carefully reviewing the literature, and keeping a critical and questioning attitude not only about what others do and say but also about what you do and say yourself, you will gradually grow in your understanding and skill and will be less likely to make errors of either commission or omission.

INOCULATION: WHAT NOT TO LEARN AT AN INTERNSHIP

Throughout this text, you will be encouraged to be open to learning, but that does not mean you must uncritically model everything you observe or accept everything you are told as truth. Although EBP may represent the kinds of knowledge and skills you hope to acquire during your internship, you may also be exposed to some things you should not emulate. At all times, it behooves you to be aware and thoughtful about the behaviors you observe or the information you receive.

For example, in some placement sites, staff members constantly express negative attitudes toward clients through a hostile tone of voice, derogatory statements, mean-spirited jokes, or in other overt or subtle ways. Interns who observe this attitude may not feel comfortable with it at first; but if the atmosphere of a setting and the behavior of the staff set an example of negativity, it is easy for the intern to adopt similar attitudes and behaviors, often without even realizing what is happening. I have observed interns who began with positive, idealistic feelings start to shift toward negativity and hostility within just a few weeks at a placement. When I point this out, the interns are often surprised and somewhat ashamed of themselves, but most are glad to have the feedback and to understand what they have modeled and why.

Similar issues were voiced by Gross (2005), who solicited student perceptions of their practicum experiences and, in addition to many positive reports, also discovered a number of concerns. These included the presence of negative attitudes of staff toward clients, poor treatment quality, unmotivated staff, cultural insensitivity, inefficient procedures, dysfunctional organizational culture, and violations of ethical strictures on confidentiality and boundaries. Unfortunately, Gross reported, many of the students who had these concerns did not share them with their placement site staff, their supervisor, or their academic instructor because there was no established mechanism to do so or because they did not feel safe in doing so. Gross believes these issues must be better addressed and recommends that field training sites and academic institutions review their own mechanisms that allow or discourage critical and constructive feedback from interns. It is easy for faculty or supervisors to become accustomed to certain conditions or overlook legitimate concerns, but interns can bring fresh eyes to a setting, and the feedback they can offer needs to be received.

In addition to actions or conditions that might be easily recognized as negative or ineffective, interns may also be exposed to, and tempted to model, more subtle but nevertheless counterproductive behaviors. In most institutions, for example, it is common for staff to use jargon—"stock" words or phrases—when speaking to or about clients. A commonly seen example of this is the word *inappropriate*. This is probably the most overused word in all the helping professions: In response to a client's statement or action, a staff member might say, "Tim, that is inappropriate," or a therapist might write a note that says, "Tim acted very inappropriately in group today." Interns observe this usage and quickly incorporate it into their own vocabulary. Unfortunately, more often than not this blocks rather than enhances intern and client understanding and growth.

When I introduce this example into discussions, many interns and practicing professionals insist that they and the rest of the staff use the word *inappropriate* all the time, and they do not perceive anything wrong with it. Others argue that it is just a word, and I am making too much out of it.

In response, I offer two observations. First, the fact that interns so quickly accept and adopt this jargon is evidence of just what I have been saying about how people model others unconsciously. Second, it is instructive to ask interns or others what they mean when they say "inappropriate." When asked this question, most interns initially have great difficulty defining their meaning without resorting to the tautology of using the term to define itself. When they begin to work toward a definition, it becomes apparent that the meaning depends on the situation and alternative words might be more informative.

The underlying point here is not simply about one word. Rather, it is about thinking carefully about what we do and say and what we model in our training.

In place of the word *inappropriate*, I suggest to interns that they try addressing more specifically the real issues in a given situation. For example, suppose a client told a staff member that he thought the staff member was ugly. Instead of saying, "Tim, that is inappropriate," the staff member might respond by saying, "It hurts my feelings when you say that" or "You sound angry today. Shall we talk about what is going on?" The first response, "That's inappropriate," does not tell the client what is inappropriate, why it is inappropriate, or what *inappropriate* means in a given situation. By comparison, the alternatives give specific information about the effects of the statement or about possible motives behind it. Formulating an alternative response requires more effort and insight from the staff, but compared with a meaningless reflex response, it is much more likely to be therapeutic.

Other terms or phrases that are used excessively and imprecisely include *manipulative, denial, acting out, resistant, doing it to get attention,* and certain diagnostic categories that come in or out of vogue. If you are attentive, you will no doubt encounter many others along the way.

Communication is the primary tool of our treatment and assessment efforts. Beginning with your internship and throughout your career, you will do well to think about everything you do, say, and observe. Try to not simply accept or model behaviors, words, or attitudes without asking questions and seeking explanations. In the end, the ability to think critically and act wisely is the most important skill you can gain from any internship experience.

REFERENCES

American Psychological Association Presidential Task Force. (2006). Evidence-based practice in psychology. *American Psychologist, 61,* 271–285.

American Psychological Association (APA). (2012). Resolution on recognition of the effectiveness of psychotherapy. Retrieved from http://www.apa.org/news/press/releases/2012/08/resolution-psychotherapy.aspx

Baker, S. B. (2012). A new view of evidence-based practice. *Counseling Today.* Retrieved from http://ct.counseling.org/2012/12/a-new-view-of-evidence-based-practice/

Barlow, D. H. (2010). Negative effects from psychological treatments: A perspective. *American Psychologist, 65,* 13–20.

Berger, M. (1995). Sustaining the professional self: Conversations with senior psychotherapists. In M. B. Sussman (Ed.), *A perilous calling: The hazards of psychotherapy practice* (pp. 302–321). New York: Wiley.

Boisvert, C. B., & Faust, D. (2003). Leading researchers' consensus on psychotherapy research findings: Implications for the teaching and conduct of psychotherapy. *Professional Psychology, Research and Practice, 34*(5), 508–513.

Bovasso, G., Eaton, W., & Armenian, H. (1999). The long-term outcomes of mental health treatment in a population-based study. *Journal of Consulting and Clinical Psychology, 67*(4), 529–538.

Castonguay, L. G., Boswell, J. F., Constantino, M. J., Goldfried, M. R., & Hill, C. E. (2010). Training implications of harmful effects of psychological treatments. *American Psychologist, 65,* 34–49.

Chorpita, B. F., Daleiden, E. L., Ebesutani, C., Young, J. Becker, K. D., Nakamura, B. J. Phillips, L., Hershberger, A., Stumpf, R., Trent, L., Smith, R. L., Okamura, K., & Starace, N. (2011). Evidence-based treatments for children and adolescents: An updated review of indicators of efficacy and effectiveness. *Clinical Psychology: Science and Practice*, 18, 153-171.

Conolley, J. C., & Bonner, M. (1991). The effects of counselor fee and title on perceptions of counselor behavior. *Journal of Counseling and Development, 69,* 356–358.

Csikszentmihalyi, M. (1999). If we are so rich, why aren't we happy? *American Psychologist, 54*(10), 821–827.

Deal, K. H., & Clements, J. A. (2006). Supervising students developmentally: Evaluating a seminar for new field instructors. *Journal of Social Work Education, 42*(2), 291–306.

Downing, S. (2006). *On course: Strategies for creating success in college and in life* (6th ed.). Boston: Houghton Mifflin.

Edmond, T., Megivern, D., Williams, C., Rochman, E., & Howard, M. (2006). Integrating evidence-based practice and social work field education. *Journal of Social Work Education, 42,* 377–396.

Elman, N. S., Illfelder-Kaye, J., & Robiner, W. N. (2005). Professional development: Training for professionalism as a foundation for competent practice in psychology. *Professional Psychology: Research and Practice, 36,* 367–375.

Fox, R. (2004). Field instruction and the mature student. *Journal of Teaching in Social Work, 24,* 113–129.

Friedman, D., & Kaslow, N. J. (1986). The development of professional identity in psychotherapists: Six stages in the supervision process. In F. W. Kaslow (Ed.), *Supervision and training: Models, dilemmas and challenges.* New York: Haworth Press.

Gelman, C. R., & Lloyd, C. M. (2008). Pre-placement anxiety among foundation-year MSW students: A follow-up study. *Journal of Social Work Education, 44,* 173–184.

Gilgun, J. F. (2005). The four cornerstones of evidence-based practice in social work. *Research on Social Work Practice, 15,* 52–61.

Globerman, J., & Bogo, M. (2003). Changing times: Understanding social workers' motivation to be field instructors. *Social Work, 48,* 65–73.

Goodheart, C. D., Kazdin, A. E., & Sternberg, R. J. (Eds.). (2006*). Evidence-based psychotherapy: Where theory and practice meet.* Washington, DC: American Psychological Association.

Goodman, K. J. (1994). When patients don't pay: Practical aspects of fee collection. *Independent Practitioner* (Bulletin of the Division of Independent Practice, Division 42 of the American Psychological Association), *14*(1), 24–25.

Gross, S. M. (2005). Student perspectives on clinical and counseling psychology practica. *Professional Psychology: Research and Practice, 36,* 299–306.

Hershenberg, R., Drabick, D. A. G., & Vivian, D. (2012). An opportunity to bridge the gap between clinical research and clinical practice: Implications for clinical training. *Psychotherapy, 49*(20), 123–134.

Hill, C. E., Sullivan, C., Knox, S., & Schlosser, L. Z. (2007). Becoming psychotherapists: Experiences of novice trainees in a beginning graduate class. *Psychotherapy: Theory, Research, Practice and Training, 44,* 434–449.

Hopkins, K. M., Bloom, J. D., & Deal, K. H. (2005). Moving away from tradition: Exploring the field experiences of part-time, older, and employment-based students. *Journal of Social Work Education, 41,* 573–585.

Hunsley, J. (2007). Addressing key challenges in evidence-based practice in psychotherapy. *Professional Psychology: Research and Practice, 38,* 113–121.

Kaslow, N. J., & Rice, D. G. (1987). Developmental stresses of psychology internship training: What training staff can do to help. In R. H. Dana & W. T. May (Eds.), *Internship training in professional psychology* (pp. 443–453). Washington, DC: Hemisphere.

Kazdin, A. E. (2008) Evidence-based treatment and practice. *American Psychologist, 63(3)* , 146–159.

Lewis, B. L., Hatcher, R. L., & Pate, W. E., II. (2005). The practicum experience: A survey of practicum site coordinators. *Professional Psychology: Research and Practice, 36,* 291–298.

Lilienfeld, S. O. (2007). Psychological treatments that cause harm. *Perspectives on Psychological Science, 2,* 53–70.

McHugh, R. K., & Barlow, D. H. (2010). Dissemination and implementation of evidence-based psychological interventions: A review of current efforts. *American Psychologist, 65*(2), 73–84.

McNeill, T. (2006). Evidence-based practice in an age of relativism: Toward a model for practice. *Social Work, 51,* 157–156.

National Association of Social Workers. (2006). *Third-party reimbursement for clinical social work services.* Washington, DC: Author.

Nelson, T. D., & Steele, R. G. (2006). Beyond efficacy and effectiveness: A multifaceted approach to treatment evaluation. *Professional Psychology: Research and Practice, 37*(4), 389.

Newlin, C. M., Adolph, J. L., & Kreber, L. A. (2004). Factors that influence fee setting by male and female psychologists. *Professional Psychology: Research and Practice, 35,* 548–552.

Norcross, J. C. (2005). The psychotherapist's own psychotherapy: Educating and developing psychologists. *American Psychologist, 60,* 840–850.

Norcross, J. C., Beutler, L. E., & Levant, R. F. (2006). *Evidence-based practices in mental health: Debate and dialogue on the fundamental questions.* Washington, DC: American Psychological Association.

Orlinsky, D. E., & Howard, K. I. (1980). Gender and psychotherapeutic outcome. In A. M. Brodsky & R. Hare-Mustin (Eds.), *Handbook of psychotherapy and behavior change* (pp. 3–34). New York: Guilford Press.

Paul, G. (1967). Strategy in outcome research in psychotherapy. *Journal of Counseling Psychology, 29,* 268–282.

Pipes, R. B., Holstein, J. E., & Aguirre, M. G. (2005). Examining the personal-professional distinction: Ethics codes and the difficulty of drawing a boundary. *American Psychologist, 60,* 325–334.

Rabkin, L. Y. (1994). On some character styles and fees in psychotherapy. *Independent Practitioner* (Bulletin of the Division of Independent Practice, Division 42 of the American Psychological Association), *14*(1), 26–28.

Rodolfa, E., Ko, S. F., & Petersen, L. (2004). Psychology training directors' views of trainees' readiness to practice independently. *Professional Psychology: Research and Practice, 35,* 397–404.

Roth, A., & Fonagy, P. (1996). *What works for whom? A critical review of psychotherapy research.* New York: Guilford Press.

Routh, D. K. (2000). Clinical psychology training: A history of ideas and practices prior to 1946. *American Psychologist, 55,* 236–241.

Sears, M. (2005). How to decide what fees to charge. *National Psychologist, 14(5),* 21.

Seligman, M. E. P. (1995). The effectiveness of psychotherapy: The *Consumer Reports* study. *American Psychologist, 50,* 965–974.

Shapiro, D. A., & Shapiro, D. (1982). Meta-analysis of comparative therapy outcome studies: A replication and refinement. *Psychological Bulletin, 92,* 581–604.

Sklare, G., Thomas, D. V., Williams, E. C., & Powers, K. A. (1996). Ethics and an experiential "Here and Now" group: A blend that works. *Journal for Specialists in Group Work, 21,* 263–273.

Steinfeld, B. I., Coffman, S. J., & Keyes, J. A. (2009). Implementation of an evidence-based practice in a clinical setting: What happens when you get there. *Professional Psychology: Research and Practice, 40,* 410–416.

Stoltenberg, C. D. (2005). Developing professional competence through developmental approaches to supervision. *American Psychologist, 60,* 855–864.

Strupp, H. H. (1989). Psychotherapy: Can the practitioner learn from the researcher? *American Psychologist, 44,* 717–724.

Thorp, S. R., O'Donohue, W. T., & Gregg, J. (2005). The predoctoral internship: Is current training anachronistic? *Professional Psychology: Research and Practice, 36,* 16–24.

Van Geert, P. (1998). A dynamic systems model of basic developmental mechanisms: Piaget, Vygotsky, and beyond. *Psychological Review, 105,* 634–677.

Wolfson, E. R. (1999). The fee in social work: Ethical dilemmas for practitioners. *Social Work, 44,* 269–273.

Wong, J. L. (1994). Lay theories of psychotherapy and perceptions of therapists: A replication and extension of Furnham and Wardley. *Journal of Clinical Psychology, 50,* 624–632.

Yunong, H., & Fengzhi, M. (2009). A reflection on reasons, preconditions, and effects of implementing evidence-based practice in social work. *Social Work, 54,* 177–182.

Zakutansky, T. J., & Sirles, E. A. (1993). Ethical and legal issues in field education: Shared responsibility and risk. *Journal of Social Work Education, 29,* 338–347.

CHAPTER 3

INTERNSHIP CLASSES AND PEER GROUPS

Internships can be tremendous learning opportunities, but they can also feel pretty lonely if you are not connected to others having similar experiences. In many programs, formal classes or peer groups are designed to help interns learn from and with one another and to provide valuable emotional support in the process. This chapter describes some of the ways classes or peer groups can be structured and some of the learning activities that typically take place.

OFFERING AND RECEIVING FEEDBACK WITH PEERS

As part of an internship class or study group, you will be involved in a give-and-take of ideas, observations, and suggestions. In a moment, we will discuss some of the structured activities that can facilitate discussion and development in classes or groups. It is useful to begin, however, by reviewing some core principles for giving and receiving feedback with peers.

Some of the most valuable guidelines I have found for peer-to-peer feedback actually came from advice offered to supervisors by Kadushin and Harkness (2002). In a discussion of how supervisors can most effectively give feedback to supervisees, these authors emphasized the importance of keeping feedback descriptive rather than judgmental, remembering the importance of positive feedback, focusing on behaviors rather than personal qualities of the person receiving the feedback, and offering comments in the form of tentative statements instead of authoritative conclusions or directions. Also highlighted were the value of giving specific rather than vague suggestions or examples; focusing on concrete, objective behaviors; and considering feedback as part of an idea-sharing, rather than advice-giving, process. Finally, the comments and observations offered must be selective and not overwhelm the recipient by their number or nature.

Whenever one offers feedback about a case, and particularly when students offer suggestions for peers, it is important to remember that the role of outside observer is much easier than the role of therapist. Statements that might seem obvious to an observer may be difficult to recognize or accept when one is directly involved in the complex role of treatment provider. Thus, peers should not let themselves become overly confident or feel superior to one another if it happens that one person recognizes something about a case that others did not.

Even though it may be easier to be in the role of observer than therapist, peers should also keep in mind that whatever impressions they might draw from a case description or tape, there will always be many things they do not know about the history of the case or the interaction between therapist and client. This suggests another reason to avoid becoming overly confident as an observer. It is entirely possible that overconfidence is based not on an accurate impression but on a misunderstanding the case.

Consistent with these principles, it is a good idea for interns to offer feedback to one another with a degree of "intentional tentativeness" rather than as conclusive statements. Instead of saying, "This client is clearly manipulating you!" or "At that point, you should have asked him to...," peers might try, "As I watched the video I got a feeling the client was trying to get your approval or permission. Did you have that feeling, too, or is something else happening?" or, "I wonder what might have happened if you had asked the client to..."

Phrasing feedback in this way respects the difference between observer and therapist and does not imply that the observer has all the answers. Not only is this practice useful in peer feedback, it is also a valuable technique in therapy. Just as observers of therapy can mistakenly think they have the answers for their peers, therapists sometimes think they have the answers for their clients. Tentative phrasing can help reduce resistance and encourage clients to explore possibilities.

THE IMPORTANCE OF EMPATHY

In many instances, the most helpful response interns can give one another is empathic understanding. On numerous occasions, I have observed interns being overwhelmed by suggestions from instructors and peers. Often, what the intern needed most was for a peer to acknowledge how tough the case was and how frustrated, sad, or angry the intern must have felt. This is so important that before offering suggestions or feedback about a case, interns are well advised to ask themselves if they really understand how their peer is feeling and what he or she needs most at the moment.

Empathy and support are important also because as you are going through the internship or other learning experiences, the rest of your life is going on as well. This means that you and your peers, in addition to the responsibilities of school and your internships, may also be dealing with everything from the illness or death of loved ones to sorting out romantic relationships. Depending on how they are dealt with, these personal life events can interact positively or negatively with your academic and internship training experiences. Furr and Carroll (2003) studied "critical incidents" in the development of student counselors and found that students often cited events occurring outside the training program as having the most impact on their personal growth. Furr and Carroll also noted an intriguing synergy in which insights and knowledge gained as part of internship training impacted the personal lives of interns, and events in personal lives, in turn, influenced the internship training. Again, if handled well, this synergy can be tremendously productive and helpful in both spheres of life.

When an intern needs empathy and support, the relief that comes when a peer provides it is almost palpable. It is sometimes as if a great weight has been removed from the intern, and he or she is at last able to breathe again. By comparison, until the empathic connection has been made in a group, all the well-intentioned technical suggestions, no matter how valid, are likely to be of little benefit. Interns are in a unique position to provide empathic understanding and support to one another because they are most closely in a position to feel what their peers are experiencing both within the internship training and in life outside. Instructors and supervisors easily get caught up in the theoretical or technical aspects of a case and may forget to attend to the intern's affective needs. By remembering to attend to empathy, peers can meet an essential need for one another and, in the process, can both practice and directly observe the effects of this key therapy skill. More will be said about dealing constructively with the stresses of training and life in Chapter 8.

RECEIVING FEEDBACK

Along with considering ways to give feedback, it is equally important to think about how one receives feedback. The first thing to understand is that receiving feedback is not easy. This awareness will help you better understand your own experience at receiving feedback from supervisors or peers. It can also help you appreciate some of what clients experience in therapy.

Whenever you expose yourself to feedback from others, you make yourself vulnerable. You run the risk of revealing weaknesses, errors, or personal qualities that you might wish others were unaware of or at least would not comment on. As an intern in the helping professions, the stakes are even higher because you have been charged with the responsibility for helping others. This makes it easy to believe that perceived mistakes, failures, or

shortcomings mean you have somehow let down or perhaps even harmed the clients who have come to you for help.

The matter is complicated still further because therapy involves using the therapist's self, or at least the presentation of self, as part of the healing process. As a result, even the most well-intentioned suggestions or feedback can easily be experienced as intimations or outright assertions that something is amiss with one's presentation of self. That is seldom easy to cope with, but it is part of the learning process. It is also part of what clients experience whenever they come to therapy and must explore who they are.

ACKNOWLEDGING IMPERFECTION

To help interns accept feedback from peers and supervisors, they need to give themselves permission to be something other than perfect and flawless. Although interns should do their best, that does not mean they can never make mistakes. Therapists and interns are only human, and part of learning is that there will be some things you do not know.

If you do not feel you have to be or appear perfect, it is easier to accept the possibility that others can offer suggestions or observations that will help you improve. I encourage interns to experiment with an attitude that says, "I hope others will recognize some things I do well, but I also hope they will recognize some things I am not doing as well as I could. If people identify my mistakes, that will help me learn, and I am grateful to them." If you approach learning with this attitude, you are much more likely to be open to suggestions from others. You are also more likely to receive helpful suggestions, because people will recognize that suggestions are welcome.

Most students have not been taught to hope that others will recognize their weaknesses. The alternative, however, is actually absurd, if you think about it. Being in school or internship training includes the assumption that one has not yet mastered a body of knowledge or skill. Therefore, the best way to learn is to identify areas of deficiency and seek to remediate them. If one seeks to hide those areas, how can growth and learning occur?

The best thing that can happen to you as an intern or student is to discover what you do not know or what you think you know or understand but, in fact, do not. If this sounds strange, ask yourself whether you would rather go on to practice without knowing that you lack certain information or misunderstand key concepts.

One way to put this attitude into practice is to develop the habit of thanking people whenever they offer suggestions, corrections, or constructive criticism. I know a person who travels around the world and speaks several languages with fluency that most people would envy. Despite his proficiency, he makes a point of asking native speakers to correct him whenever he makes a mistake. My friend explains his approach this way:

> I know it might seem impolite to correct me, and, of course, I appreciate compliments, but for me the sign of true friendship is when someone cares enough to correct my mistakes. That is the only way I can learn, and I'd rather be corrected than go around thinking I'm speaking properly when I'm really making some glaring mistake.

My friend is quite sincere about this, and he always makes a point of acknowledging his appreciation and thanking people when they offer corrections. That attitude is probably why he speaks so many languages so well. By acknowledging mistakes and being open to feedback, he lets everyone become a teacher, and he is able to learn much more rapidly than people who fear mistakes and do not accept suggestions.

STRUCTURED CLASS OR GROUP ACTIVITIES

As in all your courses, different instructors will incorporate different activities in an internship class, but it can be helpful for you to consider some of the possible structured activities both to enhance your own understanding of what is done in class and in the event that you decide to create or participate in a peer group apart from a formal class setting.

Whatever structure is used, to be most effective, classes or peer groups need many of the same elements that are essential to effective therapy or counseling. Trust, support, openness, honest feedback, safety, and willingness to explore and experiment are all ingredients of successful groups. Peer support is also vital and is often cited by our interns as the single most important element of internship classes.

One example of a structured approach to peer or in-class supervision was originally described by Border (1991). In this approach, which has since been used with success in countless classes, an intern seeking assistance begins by briefly describing a case, then specifies questions he or she would like addressed and the kind of feedback being sought. A recorded therapy session or a description of a case is then presented to the group.

As the class or peer group listens to the case, peers in the group are assigned by the instructor or group leader to take different roles or focus on specific aspects of the interaction. One person might focus on the nonverbal behavior of the therapist or client. Another might listen for the sequence of the content addressed. Group members might also be invited to view the session from different roles, such as the client, therapist, or significant people in the client's life. Another approach to the case would be for members to listen from different theoretical perspectives. Some members might approach the case from a behavioral perspective, others from a psychodynamic model, and still others from a cognitive framework.

Borders (1991) pointed out that the focus, roles, or theoretical perspectives assigned to or chosen for group members provide instructional experiences for the group as well as for the person receiving the supervision. Interns who need to develop greater nonverbal awareness can be assigned to focus on this element of the interaction, whereas those who are learning about a certain theoretical model can apply that model as they view the case. Borders also noted that because the role of observer relieves the stress experienced as a therapist, trainees are often able to notice things or display skills as observers that they have not yet manifested when they are in the therapy role themselves.

Many of the elements described by Borders are also found in a model developed by Wilbur, Roberts-Wilbur, Morris, Betz, and

Hart (1991). Their Structured Group Supervision (SGS) model includes six phases: (1) the Request-for-Assistance Statement, (2) the Questioning Period and Identification of Focus, (3) the Feedback Statements, (4) a Pause Period, (5) the Supervisee Response, and (6) an Optional Discussion Period. Wilbur and colleagues noted that during the request for assistance, the supervisee may seek assistance with technical skills, personal growth, or integrating aspects of the therapy process. During the questioning period, group members use a round-robin technique, taking turns, with each member asking one question of the supervisee. Depending on the nature and focus of the initial request for assistance, the group members ask questions that tend to focus on what Wilbur and coworkers described as "skill-development and task-process," "personal growth and psycho-process," or "socio-process." These different foci are also referred to as "extra-, intra-, or interpersonal," respectively.

Following the questioning, group members offer feedback relating to the initial request for assistance. The supervisee can take notes during this feedback but is asked to remain silent and not respond immediately to the feedback. Wilbur et al. pointed out that this reduces the common "Yes, but…" or "I have tried that already" types of responses that supervisees often give to feedback. Group members are encouraged to offer feedback in the form of statements such as "If this were my client…" or "If I were in your situation…"

Perhaps the most unique feature of the SGS model is the "pause period" that follows the feedback statements. Remember that during the feedback, the supervisee can take notes but is not allowed to respond verbally. Following the feedback, there is a period of 10 to 15 minutes during which the supervisee is invited to think about the feedback but is not allowed to discuss the case further with group members. Group members may take a brief break to have coffee or interact with one another, but the supervisee's task is to reflect on the feedback.

In my experience, the concept of structuring a time for reflection is particularly valuable. The overriding American and Canadian cultures, and academia in particular, place a premium on quick responses and give relatively little value to thoughtful reflection. Yet instantaneous responses make it difficult for recipients of feedback to fully explore what they have heard or how they are reacting to the feedback. Quick responses also tend to go hand in hand with defensiveness rather than open receiving of feedback. By structuring time for thought, supervisees are encouraged to give deeper attention and consideration to the feedback they have received. This is likely to lead to more effective learning, and it models the importance of careful thought and time in the therapy process.

Regardless of the structure used, classes and peer groups are enhanced when students and instructors remember to intentionally address and promote a positive, supportive atmosphere within the group. On way to ensure this is to regularly ask participants to share how they think the class is going and how they feel about working together. As part of this engagement, interns can be invited to express any desires or concerns they might have for the class. The following exercise is designed to assist in that process.

As a beginning toward developing a caring class or peer group, each intern should explore several questions:

1. Am I willing to take some risks myself, ask for help, and be open about my questions, areas of competence, and feelings of inadequacy?
2. Am I willing and able to empathize with and support my peers as they deal with difficulties in their internship and in the class?
3. Am I willing and able to empathize with and support my peers as they deal with success and accomplishments in their internship and in the class?
4. As I imagine it and as I demonstrate it in my behavior, what is my goal in this class? Am I seeking to learn and help others learn, or am I (a) just trying to get the grade or (b) trying to improve my status by showing what a good clinician I am? What is my real goal in this class?
5. Do I realize that it often seems easier to understand what is happening from the outside looking in? This means that we must be gentle with ourselves when someone else points out something we have overlooked. We must also be gentle with our peers if we recognize something in their work that they have been overlooking.
6. When I have something to ask or say to another student, do I act on it, or am I passive and quiet? If I do act, is it in a way that conveys respect and empathy? If I do not speak up, is it because of my own characteristics or because I have determined in this instance that my input or questions are not necessary at this time?

VIDEO OR AUDIO RECORDINGS OF SESSIONS

In the models described by Borders and by Wilbur and colleagues, group case discussions often center on audio or video recordings of therapy sessions. Because these media enable the supervisor and the class to observe the actual clients and treatment interactions, they can be extremely valuable tools for clinical training (Huhra, Yamokoski-Maynhart, & Prieto, 2008; Romans, Boswell, Carlozzi, & Ferguson, 1995; Sobell, Manor, Sobell, & Dum, 2008). If you can incorporate recorded sessions in your training, several suggestions may be helpful.

One of the more useful models I have encountered is using the technique of "motivational interviewing" to help students constructively self-critique their own taped therapy sessions. As described by Sobell et al. (2008), this approach involves interns first reviewing their therapy recordings on their own and, in the process, identifying "examples of the 'good' and 'less good' parts of their therapeutic interventions with clients" (p.153). Interns are then asked to provide reasons for those judgments.

The purpose of this approach is to help reduce resistance and enhance motivation to learn and change by promoting greater self-reflection and awareness (Miller & Rose, 2009). Although many beginning trainees may be afraid their supervisors or peers will identify some shortcomings or evaluate them harshly, this technique helps reduce that fear first by putting the interns themselves in the position of self-appraisal and, second, and importantly, by focusing in a positive way on what was done well and what could have been done better rather than on what was done poorly or what mistakes were made. Sobell et al.'s research showed that trainees found this process very helpful. In fact, when asked if they would utilize this method if they were providing supervision, all of the 62 trainees responded affirmatively.

A question that often arises when recordings are to be reviewed with peers or supervisors is which parts of the session should be reviewed. This poses an interesting paradox. Most interns want to present a positive impression of their clinical skills and work, so there is a temptation to choose only those points in a session where one feels particularly confident in the work. At the same time, beginning therapists may not fully share their work with supervisors or others because they fear looking silly or incompetent.

Although understandable, this is not necessarily the best way to learn. As an alternative, interns might choose to pick a few sections where they believe they were doing their best work (it is perfectly valid and important to want and receive some positive strokes) and a few other sections where they felt lost, confused, overwhelmed, on the spot, tense, or frightened. One intern took this suggestion to heart and had the courage to bring in a video in which the client actually fell asleep during a session. For several minutes, the video consisted only of the client's snoring. Sharing this with the internship class and supervisor took courage on the part of the intern, but it took even more to play another portion and reveal that for a few minutes there were two people, the client and the intern, snoring. (This really happened.) In your own work, you will probably not have an experience exactly like this, but you will feel sleepy at times, and you will undoubtedly say and do things that you will immediately wish you could take back or try again. Do not be ashamed to acknowledge such mistakes or to share them with your peers so that you and they can learn from the experience.

As you listen to recordings of your sessions or those of peers, you may find it interesting to attend in various ways. When most beginning interns observe or listen to therapy sessions, they focus primarily on the words people say to each other. This focus is consistent with how people interact during ordinary conversations, but one of the lessons of therapy is that the content (the words) of an interaction often carries far less information than the process (the way the words are said, the position of the speakers, the sequence of the overall interactions, and a host of other nonverbal elements).

I learned this exercise during a supervision workshop presented by Jesse Geller. The exercise involves listening several times to a brief recorded portion of a therapy session. The first time through, simply listen with no specific instructions. Then play the recording and listen again, but this time focus intently on the words the participants use as they interact. Next, listen a third time, but this time focus on receiving not the words but the affect—the emotional messages and experiences of the participants. What do you experience as you receive with your attention focused on different elements of the interaction? Most people report that they get something different out of the interaction each time through. Moreover, in the third listening, in which the focus is on affect rather than words, people usually believe they begin to understand the client in a way different from before.

The preceding exercise introduced you to the experience of receiving elements of an interaction other than words. In this case, the focus was on affect, but it would also have been possible to emphasize such aspects as rate of speech, length of pauses, and tone of voice.

ROLE-PLAYS

An alternative to working with recorded therapy sessions is to enact therapy sessions within the group. Role-plays involve class members taking the roles of clients, trainees, or other staff members and acting these roles as they portray a situation or interaction of interest. Role-plays can be particularly helpful in developing basic helping skills and in learning to deal with difficult clients or staff. Role-plays can also help interns become more aware of their therapeutic style and, in some instances, of significant issues in their own lives. Field instructors can also use role-plays to learn about issues and techniques of supervision.

Role-plays are most productive when participants are aware of several principles. First, the goal of the role-play is not necessarily to provide an exact replication of the real situation or people. Although realism may be useful, role-plays also exist as experiences in themselves and need not be perfectly accurate for learning to occur. Indeed, the deviation from reality sometimes provides important clinical insights about what is happening and how things might change. Thus, although several of the following suggestions deal with enhancing the realism of role-plays, keep in mind that realism is not the primary goal; experiencing, understanding, and learning are the goals that matter.

A second key to successful role-plays is for the people involved to not just imagine or act their role but temporarily to "become" the person they are portraying. Role-players should not just talk about what they are doing. They should try to get out of their own minds, feelings, and behavioral sets and into those of the persons they portray. When you portray someone, feel what that person feels, hold or move your body as that person might, use the tone and volume of voice that person might use. Experience what life has been like for that person. Experience what this moment and interaction mean for that person and how his or her body feels.

Becoming someone else not only facilitates role-plays, it is also an excellent way to develop or enhance empathy. By trying to get inside someone else's skin, we gain understanding at a much deeper level than if we merely discuss the person as some abstract object of clinical interest. This was brought home to me when I worked with a combat veteran in his late 30s who had lost both his arms below the elbow. To increase my awareness of what life was like for this man, my supervisor induced a light hypnotic trance, suggested that I too had lost my arms and hands, and then created images of otherwise mundane activities, such as opening doors, dressing, shaking hands, and going to the bathroom. The images progressed from these activities to the more profound awareness of wanting to hug a child, caress a lover, or wipe away a tear. The point of the exercise was not to evoke pity for the client. Rather, it was to help me get some sense of an important aspect of the client's life that I had never experienced myself.

In some form, this kind of learning experience applies to all our interactions with clients. We have never experienced exactly what another person has, yet we must try to get a sense of what it is like to be that person. In your role-plays, do your best to make this happen. As you do so, it is also important to be open to suggestions about how to adjust your actions to more closely approximate the person you are representing. If you are unsure of how to play a role, ask for suggestions. Similarly, if you are directing a role-play, you may need to give feedback to your players about how they need to act, move, and speak. For example, if two students who are good friends are trying to role-play a relationship between people who despise each other, it may help to suggest that the friends not think about each other as friends but instead try to imagine someone else whom they detest. I once observed an instructor deal with a similar situation by asking the students in the role-play to think of a time when they had been sick to their stomach and at the point of vomiting. When this image became very real and the students were almost sick themselves, the instructor said, "Okay, now imagine that you feel that way whenever you are around this other person."

Suggestions for images and deep involvement in characters can enhance the accuracy and benefits of role-plays, but there will probably be times when you find it almost impossible to portray certain clients or situations. During role-plays, some interns who normally do well in such exercises suddenly find they are blocked and cannot act like a particular type of person or cannot play a certain kind of behavior. This may be experienced as an inability to understand the character intellectually or as feeling a strong emotional reaction to the role.

Such experiences can lead to valuable insights for the participants. When a person who is otherwise skilled at role-plays is suddenly unable to portray a role or situation, this may be a clue that some unresolved issues are being touched. The exact issues may be unclear from the immediate experience, but it is a good sign that something important has been evoked and is worth exploring further. If you experience this kind of reaction, ask yourself if one of the characters, the situation, or the setting of the role-play is somehow reminiscent of an experience or person in your own life. Is it difficult for you now to portray anything about a person, or are there only certain qualities that you are blocking on or feeling troubled about?

Through awareness of your own experiences in role-plays, and by pursuing and trying to understand your reactions, you may learn more about yourself than about the specific situation or client that stimulated the role-play. This can be very beneficial. If something in your own life needed to be dealt with and was related to the client's issues, your own issues might block not only the role-play but also the work with the client. Experienced psychodramatists have observed that as people deal more effectively with underlying issues, their ability to portray the related roles also improves. Thus, just as the initial difficulty may be an index of underlying issues, changes in your role-playing can be an indication of progress in your self-awareness. As you become more aware of and able to deal with your own issues, your ability to interact therapeutically with clients is also likely to improve.

A final suggestion about role-plays is that, as a general rule, role-plays are more useful when not interrupted by frequent discussions or commentary. If you are involved in a role-play, it will probably work best if you get into the role, stay with it, and see what happens. Try not to stop and ask for guidance or talk about the role. If you find yourself frequently interrupting the role, that could be a sign, as was just discussed, of some issues in your own life. On the other hand, many interns interrupt role-plays because they are most accustomed to learning by talking "about" a subject, not by trying to experience something. After the role-play, it is useful to discuss what you experienced or observed, but during the role-play, be careful not to substitute intellectualization for experience.

INTRODUCTION TO JOURNAL WORK

To conclude this chapter, let me encourage you to begin using two tools that can be tremendously beneficial for personal and professional development. The first tool is a personal journal, and the second is a professional portfolio.

Consistent with the emphasis in this text on active learning and self-reflection, personal journal work can be an exceptionally valuable part of your internship experience. Effective journal use takes time, but journals that are done well provide a unique and valuable form of learning.

Many students and instructors who use journals do not make the most of the process because they are not clear about what should go into a journal or why. To get the most out of journal work, use a journal to (1) record experiences at your internship; (2) reflect on your experiences to better understand your emotional reactions, thoughts about clients, impressions of treatment, and so on; (3) make notes about questions, ideas, or discoveries that you wish to discuss or study further; and (4) complete exercises presented throughout this text.

A RECORD OF EXPERIENCES, REACTIONS, AND THOUGHTS

I recommend that you make a journal entry for every day at your internship (the root of the word *journal*, after all, means "daily"). Begin by listing the day, the date, and the hours you were at the internship. The entry should then list and briefly describe your major activities that day. A chronological format is convenient: Note the activities, clients, and staff you worked with and any other salient information for the day. Remember confidentiality issues as you write in your journal. As discussed in Chapter 4, it is

good practice to use generic terms or single-letter abbreviations, rather than names, to signify clients. Here is an example of a journal entry of this type:

Thursday, April 21, 2001, 10:00 A.M.–2:00 P.M.

10:00–10:30. Met with Rachel (Supervisor) and followed up on yesterday's group. Agreed that J. and R. had dominated group. B. was distracted by something, but we do not know what. We will discuss these observations in tomorrow's group. Also spoke with Rachel about plans to be at conference next Friday. She approved of my absence. In staff meeting the following Wednesday, I will report back to staff about the conference.

10:30–12:00. Participated in recreation activities with clients under supervision of Robert Jones, Rec Therapist. Played softball at Jefferson Park. Close game; clients seemed to enjoy it.

12:00–1:00. Lunch in dining room. Ate with two clients I had not met before, A. and N. Today was A.'s first day, and she was nervous but seemed to be coping. N. has been here three weeks. He is looking forward to visit from his family this weekend.

1:00–2:00. Administered and scored the Beck Depression Inventory for F. Discussed results with supervisor and with F. Wrote brief summary for patient records.

In addition to journal entries describing the events of the day, you should also establish a separate record in which you keep a running total of the number of hours spent in different activities, such as milieu observation, assessment, therapy, and case conferences. If you conduct intake interviews, write case reports, or perform psychological assessments, maintain a count of these, including specific information about which tests were given, interpreted, and/or scored by you.

Recording your experiences in the internship serves several purposes. This documentation of your activities can keep your supervisor or instructor apprised of what you are doing. Your journal record also will be useful later on when you seek employment and need to indicate your experience in various clinical activities. The record in which you document numbers of interviews, therapy sessions, assessments, and so on will be especially useful for this purpose. Such information is often requested for graduate-level internships, and in many states it is required as part of the professional licensing process.

Along with serving as a record of what you have done, the process of keeping regular journal entries helps establish a habit of record keeping. Accurate and current records are essential to responsible clinical practice, but record keeping is often neglected. By getting into the habit of keeping records each day, you are less likely to develop poor record-keeping practices later on. To serve this function and maintain accuracy, avoid the common intern strategy of neglecting the journal until the end of the term and then trying to fill it in by memory. Instead, as part of the time allotted for your internship, include a few minutes at the end of each working day for writing in your journal.

REFLECTION AND EXPLORATION

The record-keeping function of journals is important in itself, but their real value emerges when interns go beyond record keeping and use their journal as a place for deeper reflection on their experiences. By using their journals as opportunities to explore and process their experiences, interns can gain a deeper understanding of clients; the internship setting; the clinical process; and, most important, themselves. Journaling then becomes a form of self-supervision and can markedly enhance the benefits of the journal and the internship.

To illustrate this approach to journal work, suppose an intern noticed that a client who usually was quite talkative seemed extremely quiet. This observation might lead the intern to think and write about what might be associated with the change in the client's behavior. The intern might consider recent events at the internship or in the client's life. The general mood of the placement could also be taken into account, as could topics and stages of therapy, anticipated events on the unit, and a host of other pertinent factors. It is not necessary for the intern to arrive at the right explanation in the journal. What really matters is that the intern is observing events carefully and trying to understand them.

Of course, it is not possible to engage in detailed exploration of every event that happens every day at the internship. This means you will have to be selective about what you write about in your journal. One approach is to focus on two or three main ideas or concerns and write about them in detail. You might attend to the progress of a specific client, changes in the setting, supervision experiences, or other topics of interest.

Whatever external events your journal addresses, for maximum benefit, it is essential to include internal observations in your journal. Use your journal to reflect on your emotional reactions, thoughts, and behaviors. The goal of this reflection should not be to "evaluate" or reach conclusions about whether you did things well or poorly. Rather, the goal is to increase self-awareness and understanding by reflecting on what you experienced or did. A journal entry from one of my students illustrates this process:

> One of the students at the school really blew up at me today. T. has kind of been a favorite for me, and we usually get along great. Today he was causing all kinds of trouble, so I asked him what was up. He totally lost it. He called me all kinds of names and acted like he wanted to hit me. I was blown away. I didn't understand what caused him to act like that, and I was really hurt by what he said. I felt as though maybe it was my fault that he was so upset and that I should have been able to do something to help calm him down. It was especially hard because some of the other kids saw it all, and so did a couple of the staff. The staff members were nice afterward, but still I felt like I'd screwed up. I'm supposed to be here to help these kids, and sometimes it seems like there's nothing I can do to really reach them. Sometimes I wonder if I need everyone to like me too much.

This process of self-reflection can go a long way toward helping you work through, and learn from, your experiences as an intern. It also provides a useful basis for discussions with instructors or supervisors. The key to making the process worthwhile is to be as open and honest as you can about what you thought, felt, or did and what your impressions are after you have time to reflect.

NOTING QUESTIONS, IDEAS, AND DISCOVERIES

Because ideas that arise during an internship might be forgotten before you have a chance to discuss them, you can also use your journal to record any questions, exciting insights, or discoveries you want to remember. Questions about treatment approaches, agency procedures, or specific client diagnoses or behaviors would be examples of items an intern might want to note in a journal and later address with a supervisor. Discoveries could include themes that appear to be crucial for certain clients, newly acquired skills to emphasize in the future, or perhaps some ideas for possible research.

EXERCISES FROM THE TEXT

Journals are also an excellent place to write about and keep your responses to the exercises in this book. By keeping your work in the journal, you will be able to refer to it later in class discussions or supervision sessions. In the future, when you have been practicing for a few years, you can look back in your journal and remember where you started.

PORTFOLIOS

Whether or not your academic program or internship site explicitly incorporates portfolios into the curriculum or training, I strongly encourage you to begin and maintain a portfolio throughout your internship. I hope you will pass this suggestion on to your peers and beginning students. In essence, portfolios are collections of material from courses and other experiences during your academic coursework and field learning opportunities. A common practice is to organize a portfolio into sections based either on classes (with a different section for each class) or by type of material (e.g., course syllabi, books or other readings, exams, papers you have written, evaluations, honors or awards, extracurricular activities, letters of recommendation).

A somewhat different portfolio structure was offered by Alvarez and Moxley (2004), who suggested that portfolios serve several functions for students who are developing as professionals. These functions include the collection of tangible products that substantiate the intern's claims of competencies or achievements; the explanation of the relevance of these claims in regard to current practice; and a case for how the achievements, as manifested through the portfolio material, distinguish the individual as a practitioner. Consistent with these functions, Alvarez and Moxley recommended that each portfolio include a lengthy narrative describing and supplemented with material evidence of the individual's philosophical orientation, domain of practice, learning experiences, practice competencies, and professional development plan. This material is then discussed with faculty and supervisors and can be used to evaluate what the student has accomplished to date and what ongoing or future academic, personal, and professional needs might be addressed.

Hatcher and Lassiter (2007) suggested that portfolios may also be structured to correspond with the "Practicum Competencies Outline" that was discussed in Chapter 1. Consistent with the competencies identified in the outline, the portfolio contents can be organized to provide material related to each of those competency areas. Hatcher and Lassiter pointed out that this not only helps the intern and supervisor have evidence of work that has been done and levels of performance achieved, it can also be a useful tool for programs to use in examining which internships provide what sorts of training opportunities to students.

Yet another variation on portfolios has been developed by Barnes, Clark, and Thull (2003) who utilize Web-based digital portfolios. These portfolios are organized and perform essentially the same functions as more traditional paper versions, but they allow electronic exchanges of information and may be especially useful for remote supervision and, eventually, employment applications.

Portfolios are also especially valuable as you accumulate clinical experience and want to keep track of the number of hours spent in various settings, types of and hours spent in clinical activities, numbers and kinds of clients seen, intervention techniques used, and hours and nature of supervision. If you have written any interview, assessment, or other reports, keeping copies of them as examples (with names and other identifying information deleted to protect confidentiality) will be helpful when you apply for further studies, internships, or professional licensing or employment. Some programs in counseling are now also using portfolio development as the central part of their overall doctoral examination practices (Cobia et al., 2005). As an aid to facilitate your own record keeping and documentation of your internship experiences, you may want to use the form I have provided in Appendix J.

By starting a portfolio early in your studies and training, you will accumulate a ready and organized record throughout your career. Unlike students, who can report only a grade point average and courses taken, you will have real, tangible evidence of your work product. This is a tremendous advantage and will help your internship supervisor and academic instructor have a much fuller and more accurate appreciation of your qualifications. As an additional benefit, the information you store in your academic portfolio will also be useful when you eventually apply for licensure, because many licensing bodies request detailed information about the types of clients you have seen,

reports written, supervision hours, and so on. Finally, portfolios, like journals, can one day be a way of looking back at your own training and education to reflect on where you started out and what you achieved.

REFERENCES

Alvarez, A. R., & Moxley, D. P. (2004). The student portfolio in social work education. *Journal of Teaching in Social Work, 24,* 87–103.

Barnes, P. Clark, P., & Thull, B. (2003). Web-based digital portfolios and counselor supervision. *Journal of Technology in Counseling, 3*(1).

Borders, L. D. (1991). A systematic approach to peer group supervision. *Journal of Counseling and Development, 19,* 248–252.

Cobia, D. C., Carney, J. S., Buckhalt, J. A., Middleton, R. A., Shannon, D. M., Trippany, R., & Kunkel, E. (2005). The doctoral portfolio: Centerpiece of a comprehensive system of evaluation. *Counselor Education and Supervision, 44,* 242–254.

Furr, S. R., & Carroll, J. J. (2003). Critical incidents in student counselor development. *Journal of Counseling and Development, 81,* 483–489.

Hatcher, R. L., & Lassiter, K. D. (2007). Initial training in professional psychology: The practicum competencies outline. *Training and Education in Professional Psychology, 1,* 49–63.

Huhra, R. L., Yamokoski-Maynart, C. A., & Prieto, L. R. (2008). Reviewing videotape in supervision: A developmental approach. *Journal of Counseling and Development, 86,* 412–418.

Kadushin, A., & Harkness, D. (2002). *Supervision in social work* (4th ed.). New York: Columbia University Press.

Miller, W. R., & Ross, G. S. (2009). Toward a theory of motivational interviewing. *American Psychologist, 64,* 527–537.

Romans, J. S. C., Boswell, D. L., Carlozzi, A. F., & Ferguson, D. B. (1995). Training and supervision practices in clinical, counseling and school psychology programs. *Professional Psychology: Research and Practice, 26,* 407–412.

Sobell, L. C., Manor, H. L., Sobell, M. B., & Dum, M. (2008). Self-critiques of audiotaped therapy sessions: A motivational procedure for facilitating feedback during supervision. *Training and Education in Professional Psychology, 3,* 151–155.

Wilbur, M. P., Roberts-Wilbur, J., Morris, J. R., Betz, R. L., & Hart, G. M. (1991). Structured group supervision: Theory into practice. *Journal for Specialists in Group Work, 16,* 91–100.

CHAPTER 4

ETHICAL AND LEGAL ISSUES

The first rule of all health care and helping professions is "do no harm." As simple as that rule is to state, the implications and applications in practice are by no means always self-evident. One of the ways professions have sought to ensure quality treatment and reduce the potential for harm to clients is through the establishment of professional codes of ethics. Because internships represent a key step in the process of becoming a professional, as an intern it is vital that you understand and adhere to established standards of professional ethics.

Each of the major helping professions has its own code of ethics, but the essential elements and functions of the codes are consistent across professions. These functions include promoting the welfare of the people you serve, avoiding harm, maintaining your professional competence, protecting confidentiality and privacy, avoiding exploitation or conflict of interest, and upholding the integrity of your profession (Knapp & VandeCreek, 2006; Koocher & Keith-Spiegel, 2008). For an understanding of the origins of these principles, Guttmann (2006) offers a fascinating and informative history of ethics from early philosophical and religious traditions to present-day clinical practice and codes.

Along with understanding ethics, you must also understand and follow the laws and regulations pertaining to your profession and your activities as a professional. Just as professional organizations have established ethical codes to protect consumers and the profession, the federal government and the states have worked to protect the well-being of consumers by enacting regulations and laws governing the licensing and practice of various professions. Unfortunately, research has shown that in certain instances, even though many professionals may feel confident they know their own state laws, the majority may be misinformed in spite of coursework and continuing education classes related to the topic (Pabian, Welfel, & Beebe, 2009).

This chapter discusses key ethical and legal issues relating to clinical practice and internships. The importance of this chapter to your work as an intern and to your development as a professional cannot be overstated. Read it carefully, discuss it with your instructor and supervisor, and study your professional organization's code and any applicable laws and regulations. Review these often and in detail, and keep up to date with changes.

ETHICAL GUIDELINES OF THE HELPING PROFESSIONS

Membership in professional organizations carries with it a commitment on the part of each member to know and adhere to the ethical guidelines of the organization. Ethics codes are not handed down as final truths from above, and being a moral or ethical person is not the same as practicing as an ethical professional (Behnke, 2005b). Professional ethics codes are arrived at through extended discussion and review among the organization's members. As conditions change, ethics codes are updated; even before a code has been officially published, debate may have begun on how the code may need to be modified and improved (Kaplan et al., 2009; Kocet & Freeman, 2005). Once ethics codes have been established, professionals within the organization continue to discuss their strengths, applications, and shortcomings, and this discussion provides the basis for future revisions (Kocet, 2006). Even though ethics codes evolve over time, when they are in effect, members are expected to abide by them. Lack of awareness or misunderstanding of ethical principles is not a defense to charges of ethical misconduct; in many states, licensing and practice laws incorporate the professional ethics codes into law.

Not all ethical standards or state laws are identical for all professions, but most professional ethics codes share certain basic principles. Included among the principles shared by virtually all helping professions are respect for autonomy; avoiding harm; and promoting good, truthfulness, and justice. This recognition of the importance of underlying values is reflected in each of the major professional codes and is expressed explicitly in the preamble or general principles that begin the codes. For example, the National Association of Social Workers (NASW) code of ethics begins by articulating core values, including service, social justice, the dignity and worth of the person, the importance of human relationships, integrity, and competence (NASW, 2008). Similarly, the General Principles that begin the American Psychological Association (APA) code of ethics identify five key principles to guide ethical conduct: (1) beneficence and nonmaleficence, (2) fidelity and responsibility, (3) integrity, (4) justice, and (5) respect for people's rights and dignity (APA, 2010). Within the American Counseling Association (ACA) code

(ACA, 2005), core principles and values are articulated in the introduction to each major section of the code. Section A of the ACA code describes promoting client growth in ways that "foster the interest and welfare of clients." Section B emphasizes the importance of trust, boundaries, and confidentiality, and Section C addresses professional responsibility. These issues are also addressed in the Preamble of the American School Counselors Association (ASCA) ethics code (ASCA, 2010), which identifies fundamental rights to respect and dignity, to receive information, to understand educational choices, and to privacy, among other core rights.

Ethical guidelines for leading professional organizations can be found in the sources that follow. I encourage you to not only consult the ethical code for your own profession but also to review the standards of related fields so that you can see how different associations have dealt with similar issues. As you review the different codes, keep in mind that different professions may be treated differently in the laws of different states.

American Association for Marriage and Family Therapy. (2012). *AAMFT code of ethics.* http://www.aamft.org/imis15/content/legal_ethics/code_of_ethics.aspx

American Counseling Association. (2005). *American Counseling Association Code of Ethics and Standards of Practice.* Alexandria, VA: Author. http://www.counseling.org/Resources/CodeOfEthics/TP/Home/CT2.aspx

American School Counselors Association. (2010). *Ethical Standards for School Counselors.* http://www.schoolcounselor.org/files/EthicalStandards2010.pdf

American Psychological Association. (2010). Ethical principles of psychologists and code of conduct. http://www.apa.org/ethics/code/index.aspx?item=3

American Psychiatric Association. (2010). *The principles of medical ethics: With annotations especially applicable to psychiatry 2010 Edition.* Washington, DC: Author. http://www.psych.org/psych_pract/ethics/ppaethics.pdf

National Association of School Psychologists. (2010). *Principles for Professional Ethics 2010.* Bethesda, MD: NASP Publications. http://www.nasponline.org/standards/2010standards/1_%20Ethical%20Principles.pdf

National Association of Social Workers. (2008). *NASW code of ethics.* Silver Spring, MD: Author. http://www.socialworkers.org/pubs/code/code.asp

National Organization for Human Services. (1996). Ethical Standards for Human Service Professionals. http://www.nationalhumanservices.org/ethical-standards-for-hs-professionals

National Staff Development and Training Association. (2004). The NSDTA code of ethics for training and development professionals in human services: Case scenarios and training implications. http://nsdta.aphsa.org/PDF/Code_Ethics.pdf

Along with each discipline's code of ethics, you may also want to review accompanying books that have been written to expand upon the codes and give practical examples of their applications in clinical work. Examples include the following:

Dolgoff, R., Loewenberg, F. M., & Harrington, D. (2005). *Ethical decisions for social work practice* (7th ed.). Belmont, CA: Thomson/Brooks/Cole.

Guttmann, D. (2006). *Ethics in social work: A context of caring.* New York: Haworth Press.

Herlihy, B., & Corey, G. (Eds.). (2006). *ACA ethical standards casebook* (6th ed.). Washington, DC: ACA.

Jungers, C. & Gregoire J. (Eds.). (2012). *Counseling ethics: Philosophical and professional foundations.* New York: Springer.

Koocher, G. P., & Keith-Spiegel, P. (2008). *Ethics in psychology and the mental health professions: Standards and cases.* New York: Oxford University Press.

Knapp, S. J., & VandeCreek, L. (2006). *Practical ethics for psychologists: A positive approach.* Washington, DC: APA.

Nagy, T. F. (2005). *Ethics in plain English: An illustrative casebook for psychologists.* Washington, DC: APA.

Nagy, T. F. (2011). *Essential ethics for psychologists: A primer for understanding and mastering core issues.* Washington, DC: APA

Pope, K. S., & Vasquez, M. J. T. (2007). *Ethics in psychotherapy and counseling: A practical guide* (3rd ed.). San Francisco: Jossey-Bass.

Reamer, F. G. (2006). *Ethical standards in social work: A review of the NASW code of ethics* (2nd ed.). Washington, DC: NASW.

Zuckerman, E. L. (2008). *The paper office: Forms, guidelines, and resources to make you practice work ethically, legally, and profitably* (4th ed). New York: The Guilford Press.

SPECIFIC ETHICAL PRACTICE AND TREATMENT GUIDELINES

In addition to general ethical standards, some organizations have developed more specific guidelines that apply to clinical practitioners working in specified areas of practice or with certain client populations. Examples of such guidelines for the American Psychological Association, including guidelines for Forensic Psychology, Child Custody Evaluations, Practice with Older Adults, Multicultural Education, and others, can be found at http://www.apa.org/practice/guidelines/index.aspx. See also Arredondo and Perez (2006); Gallardo, Johnson, Parham, and Carter (2009); and the NASW's Standards for Cultural Competencies in Social Work Practice (NASW, 2001).

Still more specific guidelines for ethical practice include treatment or clinical practice guidelines. Closely related to the concepts of evidence-based practice and empirically supported treatment that were discussed previously, practice guidelines are designed to help professionals and clients make better decisions about the most appropriate interventions for specific clinical circumstances (Hunsley, 2007). Guidelines may also inform legal decisions and public policies (APA, 2005). Several guidelines clearinghouses have been established, including the National Guidelines Clearinghouse, which is sponsored by the Agency for Healthcare Research and Quality (AHRQ; www.ahrq.gov/), the National Institute for Health and Clinical Excellence (NICE; http://www.nice.org.uk/), and the Cochrane Collaboration (http://www.cochrane.org/).

Even though you are just beginning your work as a professional, you should know about and refer to practice and treatment guidelines for several reasons. The most important is that treatment guidelines are intended to represent the generally agreed-upon professional experience and scientific findings that can guide both practitioners and clients to make the most effective diagnostic and treatment decisions. You should also be aware that some treatment agencies and many insurance providers have expectations that professionals will adhere to specific guidelines in working with specific illnesses. Some insurers go so far as to specify that they will provide financial compensation only if specific treatment interventions are offered in specific ways by professionals who have received specified training in a designated treatment modality (Messer, 2003). Finally, treatment guidelines are important because they may be used as evidence in litigation if there are allegations of professional negligence or malpractice.

As you consider treatment guidelines, be aware that they are not without controversy. There are legitimate professional differences and conflicting empirical data about varying treatment approaches (Hunsley, 2007). What is more, parochial differences between professions may be reflected in the treatment standards proposed by one profession as compared with another (Messer, 2003). Thus, although it is good to be aware of the guidelines that may exist for your particular areas of practice or for specific client groups with whom you work, guidelines, just like any other source of information, should be considered critically and in the context of other information.

ENFORCEMENT OF ETHICAL STANDARDS

Ethical guidelines are established by professional organizations to govern the conduct of their members. Organizations have established procedures for investigating ethics complaints and disciplining members who are found to have violated ethical standards (APA Ethics Committee, 2012; Kocet & Freeman, 2005; NASW, 2005). The consequences of ethical violations can range from warnings and required educational efforts to dismissal from the organization.

Because ethical guidelines are established by organizations to govern member conduct, they do not formally apply to practitioners who are not members of the organization. Thus, social workers who do not belong to the NASW, counselors not members of the ACA, school counselors not members of the ASCA, and psychologists not members of the APA cannot be sanctioned by these organizations for violating their ethics codes. The same is true for members of other professions and organizations. This does not mean there will be no consequences for unethical conduct. Students, in particular, should know that violations of ethical standards for their profession can be considered grounds for academic discipline and possibly dismissal from a training program (Busseri, Tyler, & King, 2005). Furthermore, legal sanctions, both civil and criminal, apply regardless of organizational membership, and many courts may hold practitioners to the relevant organization's ethical codes whether or not the practitioner is a member of the organization (Kaplan et al., 2009).

ETHICS, LAWS, AND REGULATIONS

It is important to be aware that ethical standards exist and ethical practice must take place within a broader social and legal context that is constantly evolving. Ethical principles of leading professional organizations are often incorporated into the licensing and practice laws of individual states, and ethical standards of practice must also be followed in the context of various state and federal laws. To the extent that state laws incorporate or parallel professional ethical standards, practitioners who violate those laws face possible loss of license as well as possible criminal prosecution and even jail time for certain violations (Swenson, 1997). Civil actions for monetary damages may also result from unethical actions or from actions that are not considered unethical but nevertheless result in harm to a client or the client's family (Bennett et al., 2005). Also, remember that laws vary from state to state and are continually evolving as new cases arise.

Interns should also be aware that ethical guidelines may at times conflict with certain laws. This reality is acknowledged within many ethics codes, for example, in Section 1.02 of the APA code "Conflicts between Ethics and Law, Regulations, or Other Governing Legal Authority." Knapp, Gottlieb, Berman, and Handelsman (2007) offer an informative and thought-provoking review and a set of principles for decision-making under such circumstances. Keys to this process are (1) understanding what the law requires, (2) making sure one understands what the ethical guidelines require, and (3) determining if a real conflict actually exists and seeking ways of resolving it constructively. If such a resolution cannot be achieved, specific suggestions are offered on ways to determine other choices that will enable the practitioner to comply with the law while still adhering as close to the ethical principles as possible.

One of the most useful references I have come across to help you understand and deal with legal issues in general in the mental health field is Bernstein and Hartsell's (2013) *The Portable Lawyer for Mental Health Professionals*. This accessible reference covers virtually all of the key legal and ethical issues you are likely to encounter and offers a number of practical sample forms for common legal issues. Zuckerman (2008) is also a good reference that includes comparable forms to manage clinical, ethical, and legal matters. Bennett et al. (2005); Sales, Miller, and Hall (2005); Shapiro and Smith (2011); and Woody (2012) are all informative as well. In addition, the websites of each major profession's insurance plans offer a number of risk management suggestions and other valuable information plus online and phone help services to answer specific questions for policyholders.

A practical and useful source for information about state-specific laws is the "Law and Mental Health Professionals" series, published by the APA, which provides individual volumes addressing specific legal standards and issues relating to mental health professionals for each of more than two dozen states. You can also check with your state professional association for state-specific information and to find workshops and other educational material pertaining to your state laws. Finally, an excellent and concise primer on legal terms and concepts, plus an accompanying reference list, is provided by the APA Committee on Professional Practice and Standards (2003).

THE HEALTH INSURANCE PORTABILITY AND ACCOUNTABILITY ACT (HIPAA)

Without doubt, the most consequential and far-reaching law relating to ethical practice is the federal Health Insurance Portability and Accountability Act, or HIPAA (commonly pronounced like *hippo*, but with an *a*). Congress passed this law in 1996 as part of a broad effort to make sure that people could maintain their health insurance coverage even if they changed jobs or moved and in response to growing concerns about the confidentiality of electronically stored and communicated information (Benefield, Ashkanazi, & Rozensky, 2006; Knapp & VandeCreek, 2006; Richards, 2009; Schwartz & Lonborg, 2011).

Like many federal regulations, HIPAA rules are not impossibly complex, but neither are they simple. In this chapter, I highlight some of the areas in which HIPAA interacts with ethical principles and has an impact on your internship, but the discussion is far from complete for such a far-reaching piece of legislation. For further information, consider a training program designed specifically to teach HIPAA concepts for mental health professionals. A good place to start is by contacting your professional association. Most associations, including the APA, NASW, and ACA, have put together special training programs for their members. These can be accessed or ordered through the respective websites. At the very least, review the HIPAA guidelines provided by your internship site, and, as mentioned earlier, the HHS website also has extensive information to assist with HIPAA compliance.

For interns placed in university training clinics, an especially informative discussion of both HIPAA and FERPA (the Family Educational Rights and Privacy Act) is offered by Wise, King, Miller, and Pearce (2011).

ETHICAL AGREEMENT FORMS FOR INTERNS

Because it is so important for interns to adhere to ethical standards and follow the relevant laws and regulations, I require each intern I supervise to read and sign the Ethical Guidelines form presented in Appendix G. I keep this form in my class records for future information purposes. The form covers some of the essential guidelines that all professionals must know and follow. It also provides space for the intern, the field supervisor, and the instructor to sign indicating that the material has been addressed, along with any local or placement-specific ethical concerns. Because certain work settings (such as those involving children) and specific treatment modalities may present unique ethical issues, I also advise students to be aware of these issues and adhere to any relevant standards, including HIPAA, FERPA, and others.

ETHICAL DECISION-MAKING AND ONGOING ETHICS STUDY AND TRAINING

Reading and signing the ethics form should not be considered the last word on ethics. Rather, it is a fundamental starting point from which further discussion and ongoing evaluation should proceed. The importance of going beyond merely teaching about or memorizing ethics to a more internalized awareness and decision process was evident in the findings of Fly, van Bark, Weinman, Kitchener, and Lang (1997), who found that more than half of the interns who were reported to have committed ethical violations had previously completed a course in ethics.

Barnett, Behnke, Rosenthal, and Koocher (2007) have pointed out that ethical codes provide guidelines for conduct, but ultimately practitioners must make real-world decisions about how to apply those guidelines in different circumstances. Recognizing the essential function of reasoning and judgment in ethical conduct, Pope and Vasquez (2007) devote an entire

chapter to this topic, focusing extensively on the errors of judgment and decision-making that can lead to ethical lapses. Dodd (2007) offers useful additional insights from her survey of the most common ethical issues and conflicts encountered by MSW (master of social work) students in their field placements.

Knapp and VandeCreek (2006) asserted that an awareness and understanding of underlying principles is particularly helpful when ethical standards must be applied in ambiguous situations. Cottone and Claus (2000) offered similar observations. Consistent with this premise, Handelsman, Gottlieb, and Knapp (2005) and Bashe, Anderson, Handelsman, and Klevansky (2007) described an "acculturation model" they used to help students get beyond mere memorization of an ethics code and instead learn how to internalize thinking and decision-making about ethical conduct.

During your internship, you will discover that different stages and elements of your experience will involve different aspects of ethics codes and ethical decision-making. Zakutansky and Sirles (1993) identified six intern and supervisor relationships and discussed the ethical and legal issues relevant to each: "(1) student–client; (2) student–field instructor; (3) field instructor–client; (4) field instructor–field liaison (representing the social work program's field staff); (5) student–field liaison; and (6) field liaison–client" (p. 338).

As you deal with each of these relationships and the ethical challenges they may present, you will discover firsthand that ethical conduct requires a continuous process of self-monitoring; reference to the ethics code; reflection on underlying principles; and consultation with your supervisor, instructor, colleagues, and experts in the field. By understanding this and establishing a systematic process of approaching ethical decision-making early in your career, you are less likely to make ethical errors and more likely to be helpful to your clients.

EXERCISE

Before reading the discussion that follows, consider the case example presented here and identify any ethical concerns or violations you find. Remember to consider both the written code of ethics and the underlying principles that were just discussed. Keep in mind, too, that real situations often present conflicts between values, both of which may be good in themselves, and that sometimes conflicts will also arise between aspects of the same ethics code. When you have finished reading the chapter, review this case again and discuss it with your peers and instructor:

A therapist who specializes in work with geriatric clients also serves as head of a charitable organization. After a meeting of the organization, a woman who is both a personal friend and serves as vice chair of the charity's executive board approaches the therapist. The woman is having problems with her 15-year-old daughter, who has been skipping school and has been moody and depressed around the house. Because she trusts her, the woman asks the therapist to see the girl for therapy. The therapist agrees to do so without charge and suggests it would be less threatening to the girl if she stopped by the therapist's house and they talked. The girl comes to visit at the appointed time, but her mother has not told her the visit is for therapy. The therapist simply says that it has been a long time since she has seen the girl and explains that she just wants to talk. While talking, the girl tearfully and rather abruptly confides that she is having "problems" with an uncle who lives with the family and has been sexually abusing her. The girl says she has tried to tell her mother, but because the uncle is the mother's brother, she fears that her mother would not believe her. The girl is so upset about the experience that she has talked with a friend about wanting to kill the uncle by poisoning him. The therapist listens; then, after the girl has left, she calls the mother to tell her what happened in therapy.

COMPETENCE

One of the most important principles of ethical practice is to operate within one's level of competence. Consistent with the principle of "do no harm," knowing our limits means that no matter how much we may want to help others, we must recognize the extent and limitations of our abilities and seek assistance or supervision when we need it (Johnson, Barnett, Elman, Forrest, & Kaslow, 2012; Koocher & Keith-Spiegel, 2008; Pope & Vasquez, 2007).

The importance of knowing one's abilities and limits should make intuitive sense; but in the desire to help, it is easy to imagine that we are more capable than we actually are. We often learn this lesson the hard way, as we start something with the best of intentions only to wind up in a mess when the situation exceeds our abilities. A personal experience in a nonclinical setting may help to demonstrate both how easy it is to overestimate abilities and the possible consequences of making that mistake.

As a break from clinical work and teaching, I sometimes go whitewater kayaking. In kayaking, especially when learning, one must frequently exit the boat and swim for safety. There are also times when other boaters are swimming and need to be rescued. In these situations, the power and speed of rivers can be overwhelming, and one quickly learns that rivers are no place for the unprepared.

In river rescue situations, the first priority, even before trying to help a victim, is to not endanger yourself. As one river rescue expert explained it, "If you go jumping into a river to help someone, and you don't know what you're doing, the odds of your effecting a rescue are very, very small. Instead, the odds are high that you will become a second victim, and you may actually cause the victim and yourself to drown. Bravado and heroic intentions do not impress the river."

I observed this firsthand when an inexperienced kayaker tried to help a swimming boater by getting the swimmer to the apparent safety of a fallen tree that lay on the water surface. What neither the kayaker nor the swimmer realized was that trees in rivers, although they look safe, are actually among the most deadly hazards. The river pushes against the tree with incredible force, and even a relatively gentle current can easily entrap kayakers or swimmers. In this case, that is exactly what happened. When they reached the downed tree, the kayaker's boat overturned, trapping the would-be rescuer and the victim underwater, where they were unable to extricate themselves. Both would almost certainly have drowned had it not been for a more experienced boater who saw what was happening and managed to free them.

The purpose of this analogy is not to scare you away from your field placement (or from kayaking). Rather, it is to encourage you to be well aware of your limitations and not get in over your head. Just as beginners cannot fully appreciate the expertise required to run swift rivers or rescue swimmers, casual observers of clinical work often believe it consists of little more than listening to other people talk. The idea that anyone can do human service work without any training is not only wrong; it is also dangerous. Beginning trainees who try to provide treatment, assessment, or other services on their own without supervision are surely going beyond their limits. They might get lucky and do some good, but they might also get unlucky and do a great deal of harm to their clients and themselves.

One of the ways professional associations and educators have sought to address these issues is through the development of competency-based educational programs and competency certifications in areas of specialization. Typically, such programs emphasize core knowledge and training within a discipline, and then identify specific knowledge, skill sets, and personal qualities that must be developed and demonstrated in order to be considered competent in the specialty area (Rodolfa et al., 2005). For example, the National Council for Schools and Programs in Professional Psychology (NCSPP) lists seven core areas that are considered fundamental to entry-level psychology practice: relationship, assessment, intervention, diversity, research/evaluation, management/supervision, and consultation/education. Within each area, subdomains of skills and knowledge are identified. Also, competency expectations are identified for each of the core areas and subdomains at three different levels of training: beginning practicum, beginning internship, and complete doctoral degree. For examples of how specific disciplines within psychology are applying principles of professional competency to areas such as forensic psychology, neuropsychology, child psychology, and geropsychology, see the special issue of *Professional Psychology: Research and Practice* (2012, 43[5]).

Comparable initiatives are ongoing in social work. The Council on Social Work's Education (CSWE) Education and Policy and Accreditation Standards (2008–Updated August 2012) describe training and curriculum requirements for the baccalaureate and master's degrees in social work. Within these standards, 10 core competencies are identified along with descriptions of the skills, knowledge, values, and resulting practice behaviors that must be operationalized within curricula and assessment methods. Included among these 10 competencies are personal identification and conduct as a professional social worker, knowledge and adherence to ethical principles, applied critical thinking, engagement of diversity and difference in practice, and engagement of research-informed practice and practice-informed research.

Within the field of counseling, the Council for Accreditation of Counseling and Related Education Programs is, at the time of this writing, in the process of a multiyear revision of the CACREP standards, which guide the accreditation of programs in counseling and related fields (CACREP, 2013). Although the specific word *competency* is not featured as prominently in the draft of the CACREP standards, the effect is largely the same, that is, specifying in detail the specific skills, knowledge, experiences, ethical standards, and personal qualities that must be addressed and assessed in graduate counselor education programs.

The common element of all these efforts to promote and codify professional competence is to ensure that those who hold professional degrees and certification and who practice in the helping professions are in fact knowledgeable and well trained and will conduct themselves in the highest ethical and professional standards of the discipline. This training goes hand and hand with one of the key purposes of ethical codes: to remind us that as individuals we are not always the best judges of our own abilities and conduct. This point was highlighted by Johnson et al. (2012), who proposed a reconceptualization of competency as part of a "communitarian ethos" in which colleagues and the profession as a whole work together to promote and monitor competence as part of a broader ethic of care and professionalism. Hence, external standards and reviews must provide objective measures against which to weigh our competencies, and fellow professionals must simultaneously monitor and support one another to offer external feedback and observations of competency issues.

Simply because you want to believe you can help someone does not mean you are justified in proceeding. In all your clinical work, make it a practice to ask yourself as objectively and honestly as possible if you have any real training or experience in the skills required to work with a given individual or situation. Then go a step further and ask yourself how you would provide objective evidence of your competence if required to do so by an ethics review board or a court of law.

As you consider the matter of competence, keep in mind too that in the helping professions, competence is more than mere knowledge or technical skill (Rodolfa et al., 2005). Johnson et al. (2012) and Pope and Vasquez (2007) have pointed out that the work you will be doing requires both intellectual and emotional competence. Intellectual competence refers to knowledge and skill; emotional competence refers to one's internal emotional stability and ability to manage the emotional challenges of working with different clients. Not all therapists are equally emotionally competent to work with all types of clients or issues, and it is incumbent on therapists to recognize this. You must also recognize that competency in one domain of practice does not necessarily mean competency to practice in a different one (Johnson et al., 2012; Rodolfa et al., 2005). What is more, burnout, stress, personal issues, or other matters can all have an adverse impact on your emotional competence and your performance, regardless of your intellectual or technical skill. For suggestions on managing stress and burnout, see Chapter 8.

The principle of competence is so important that if you learn nothing else in your internship, you must at least learn how much you do not know. The fact is, no matter how much you study, there will never be a time when your knowledge is not vastly exceeded by your ignorance. From your first internship experience to the end of your career, you must continually strive to recognize when you need help and never be afraid or embarrassed to seek it. Until you have at least several years of experience, supervision should be an essential part of all your work and training (Rodolfa, Ko, & Petersen, 2004). Further, throughout your career, always seek supervision when you work with particularly difficult cases or if your own performance may be adversely affected by personal issues.

In my own practice, I read multiple professional journals, attend more than the required number of hours of continuing education each year, and regularly consult with other professionals about challenging cases. Even with these measures, there are still many times when I recognize that I am not adequately trained to deal with certain clients or issues. In such cases, one should not hesitate to seek supervision or to refer to other professionals with greater skills in the needed areas.

A final note about competence: Students sometimes believe that because they are students or interns, they will not be held accountable for their actions as they would be if they were professionals. This is not the case. Students who are at advanced levels of training and have primary responsibility for a client's care "are acting in a professional role, and with this status comes the responsibility to uphold the same legal, professional, and ethical standards" (Zakutansky & Sirles, 1993). Students who are found to have acted unethically in a training setting may be dismissed from their program (Fly et al., 1997). Students can be sued personally for malpractice, and supervisors and instructors may also be held accountable for a student's actions (Gelman, Pollack, & Auerbach, 1996). Thus, in considering your actions, recognize that part of accepting the role of intern means accepting the responsibility that goes with it.

EXERCISE

A good way to appreciate the importance of ethics and the principle of competence is to consider the matter from a client's perspective. Imagine that you are seeking a psychotherapist. What qualifications would you like the therapist to have for you to consider the person competent to help you with your particular situation? As you answer this, give some thought to such factors as academic degrees, professional licenses, years of experience in general, experience working with clients with the same concern, amount of supervised experience, specialized training in the areas of your concern, and continuing education. Most interns who do this exercise honestly find they have a greater sense of humility as they evaluate their qualifications and competencies for working directly with clients.

INFORMED CONSENT

The ethical principle of informed consent means that clients have a right to be informed about the treatment, assessment, or other services they will receive before they agree to participate in or receive those services. When applied in practice, this principle dictates that clients must be given certain information in a manner and language they can and actually do understand, clients must be competent to make decisions on their own behalf, and they must voluntarily give consent (Barnett, Wise, Johnson-Greene, & Bucky, 2007).

Barnett et al. (2007) reviewed the legal history of informed consent and offered recommendations for adapting informed consent procedures to the unique needs and circumstances of specific clients. Burkemper (2004) helped social work students understand this principle by using an informed consent template and inviting students to develop their own informed consent forms specific to their practice areas. Pomerantz and Handelsman (2006) and Harris and Bennett (2000) provided excellent examples of model informed consent contracts for psychotherapists. Harris (1995) also offered suggestions for what should be included in such documents, and Kennedy, Vandehey, Norman, and Diekhoff (2003) provided similar suggestions as part of a broader 10-point strategy for day-to-day risk management. Sample informed consent forms can be downloaded from the APAIT website (http://www.apait .org/apait/download.aspx). These forms can be customized for specific uses and settings, but keep in mind that it's a good idea to first consult an attorney who specializes in legal issues regarding clinical work.

At a minimum, clients should be informed about each of the following subjects:

1. They should know the qualifications of the person providing treatment. This includes the degrees, clinical experience, specialized training, and licenses the person has received.
2. In the case of interns, clients should know that the treatment provider is an intern and will be supervised. The intern's educational and training background should also be explained.
3. Clients should be given the name and qualifications of the intern's supervisor and should have an opportunity to meet with the supervisor if they desire to do so. Clients should also know how they can contact the supervisor if they have any questions or concerns in the future.
4. Clients should know the nature of supervision, including the frequency of supervision and the activities it will entail (e.g., reviewing case notes, listening to tapes of sessions).
5. Clients should be informed about the nature of the treatment or assessment to be provided. This includes a brief description of the approach to treatment or the purpose of an assessment and the instruments that will be used. Clients should also be informed about the empirical basis of treatment, and alternative approaches should also be described.
6. The frequency and duration of treatment sessions should be explained, as well as a reasonable estimate of the typical number of sessions to treat the given concern.
7. The client's responsibilities for participating in treatment must be made clear. For example, the client should be expected to attend scheduled appointments, notify the therapist in advance if appointments must be canceled or changed, and follow through with any assignments.
8. Medication issues should be addressed, including how the therapist works with medications and prescribing professionals.
9. Fees must be explained in detail, including the costs per session or per assessment and whether or not there are charges for missed sessions. How and when payments are to be made and the procedures that will be followed if payment is not made have to be explained. This discussion should also cover how insurance coverage will be handled, how provider contacts are made with the insurer, and how this impacts confidentiality.
10. If a client's insurance policy limits the number of sessions the insurance company will pay for, an agreement must be reached about how to proceed if more sessions are needed and the client is unable to pay without the assistance of the insurance.
11. Confidentiality must be spelled out clearly, including a specific discussion of any and all limitations to confidentiality of what is said in treatment, as well as what is contained in the client's records. This explanation should include how records are stored, how releases of information will be managed, and how government regulations (e.g., HIPAA) impact confidentiality. Also included in this discussion should be confidentiality issues relating to technology, that is, matters such as how electronic records will be managed and how electronic communications (e.g., email, text messages) should be handled.
12. Clients should know and agree on procedures for getting help in a crisis situation, including emergency phone numbers and contacts. This discussion may also include mention of how phone or Internet communication is handled and what sorts of billing or fees may be associated with such communications.
13. Termination policies should be described, specifying conditions under which either the client or the therapist may initiate termination.
14. When working with a client who is part of a managed-care arrangement, the therapist should review with the client any information that will be provided to the insurance company for purposes of utilization review or quality assurance.
15. Clients should know what options are available if complaints arise that cannot be resolved in the therapy process.
16. Provisions should be explained regarding how records will be handled in the event the therapist becomes incapacitated or dies.
17. Finally, there should be an opportunity to ask any questions before therapy begins or at any time during the treatment, and the client should indicate that he or she has been given that opportunity and understands the issues described here.

Although case law and ethical standards are still evolving on the issue of informed consent, at least one article and several court cases suggest that therapists should also disclose any financial or other conflicts of interest relating to treatment. There has also been discussion of the need to disclose any personal issues, such as substance abuse, on the part of the therapist that might have an impact on the client's treatment (Hafemeister, 2000). Item 16 was added to the previous list following a case in which a therapist was murdered and authorities suspected a client but were unable to explore this possibility because of confidentiality provisions (Bradshaw, 2006). Whether or not something so dramatic occurs, responsible practice and the realities of existence suggest that therapists should provide for continued care and the responsible management of client records if something were to happen to them during the course of their work with clients. A thorough discussion of this topic was offered by Pope and Vasquez (2007), who made comprehensive recommendations for establishing a "professional will."

When informing clients of the preceding issues, document that the information has been provided and understood. The best way to check understanding is to give clients opportunities to ask any questions they might have and give examples to illustrate what certain concepts mean in practice. It is good practice to document that this extra check on understanding was conducted as part of your informed consent procedure and practices. A sample form that addresses informed-consent issues is presented in Appendix H. This form covers each of the critical topics and provides a place for clients to sign indicating that they have read and understood the form and have asked any questions they have about the treatment they will be receiving.

Beyond the ethical requirements of informed consent, HIPAA has established extensive and detailed confidentiality requirements that must be scrupulously followed by health care agencies and practitioners (Knapp & VandeCreek, 2003; HHS, http://www.hhs.gov/ocr/privacy/hipaa/understanding/index.html; Schwartz & Lonborg, 2011). HIPAA also requires that patients be given written HIPAA Privacy Notices (separate from your other notice of confidentiality) that are written in "plain language" (the HHS website provides an extended guide to writing notices in plain language) and include the following specific elements:

- A mandatory header explaining the purpose of the notice
- Descriptions of the uses and disclosures of information that are permitted under the HIPAA for the purpose of treatment, payment, and health care operations, and an explanation of other uses of information for which the client's written authorization will be required
- Separate statements to explain certain uses of information (e.g., contacting the client to remind about appointments, a statement of the individual's rights under HIPAA, including the right to inspect his or her own health information and the right to receive accounting of any disclosures of information)
- A description of the duties of the "covered entities" (i.e., you and your agency) under the law
- Procedures the client can follow if he or she wishes to complain or believes that privacy rights may have been violated
- Contact information identifying a person or office the client can contact for further information
- The effective date of the notice
- Optional elements that the entity may wish to include, provided they are consistent with the rest of the HIPAA requirements
- Revisions to the notice

In most instances, your internship placement will have procedures in place for HIPAA informed consent compliance, but you should be aware of these requirements and follow them carefully, because both fines and criminal penalties can result from violations (Zur, 2003).

Documentation of informed consent serves several functions. First, and most importantly, it is the client's basic right to know what the terms of the relationship will be and what treatment or other service is being provided and why. Also, by scrupulously documenting that clients have been informed, therapists ensure that they are adhering to this ethical principle and are providing what is considered to be a key element of care. If questions arise later about treatment, fees, confidentiality, termination, or other matters, documenting that the client was informed about such

matters can be extraordinarily helpful, especially if legal issues, such as malpractice proceedings, arise. In many states, state ethical guidelines and/or laws require such documentation. Thus, developing the habit of completing informed consent forms is a wise, and in some cases legally mandated, practice for interns and professionals alike.

One final note about informed consent is that interns and their supervisors may want to consider establishing an informed consent agreement for the supervisory relationship. Barnett (2005) recommended that a supervisory informed consent agreement should include many of the elements of agreements with clients but should also address evaluation procedures, arrangements for emergency contacts, and any confidentiality issues that may arise between the internship site and the academic setting.

EXERCISE

Because informed consent is an ethical and legal obligation, this exercise is particularly important. If you are in an advanced setting and are seeing clients, informed consent may be legally mandated. If you are a beginner in your first placement, you should still complete this exercise because it will help you clarify your own qualifications and approach to therapy and your expectations for clients, and it will strengthen your knowledge of critical ethical principles. Tear out the treatment agreement and informed-consent form from Appendix H and use it to prepare a form tailored to your own circumstances. Then exchange your form with your peers and review it with your instructor. You will probably need to go through several revisions before achieving a draft that is satisfactory. In the future, as you gain additional experience or your approach to treatment changes, or as ethical or legal developments arise, you will need to adapt and revise your form.

CONFIDENTIALITY

Insofar as openness and honesty are essential ingredients of treatment, confidentiality is considered a necessary condition for effective therapy, and many clients insist that confidentiality is essential to their participation in treatment (Fisher, 2008; Koocher & Keith-Spiegel, 2008). All of the leading professional organizations recognize and share this value and have given it prominence in their ethical codes.

It was in large part due to the recognition of the importance of confidentiality, and in response to concerns about possible breaches in confidentiality, that the Privacy Rule of HIPAA (http://www.hhs.gov/ocr/privacy/hipaa/administrative/privacyrule/index.html) was established. The HIPAA Security Rule, which will be discussed shortly, was also implemented to address confidentiality issues, particularly as they apply to electronic information technologies (http://www.hhs.gov/ocr/privacy/hipaa/administrative/securityrule/securityruleguidance.html; Schwartz & Lonborg, 2011).

The essence of confidentiality is the principle that, except in special circumstances, clients should determine who will have access to information about them and their treatment. In clinical settings, clients need to feel that the information they share will stay with the professional and not be released without their permission. Without this assurance, clients are less likely to explore and express their thoughts and feelings freely. This, in turn, is likely to inhibit the client's willingness to share certain information and may distort the treatment process. At the same time, however, clients must be aware of the limits to confidentiality so that they can make informed choices (Fisher, 2008).

Despite, or perhaps because of, its importance, confidentiality is one of the issues most frequently identified as a source of ethical dilemmas for clinicians and educators (Bodenhorn, 2006; Dodd, 2007; Lazovsky, 2008; Wierzbicki, Siderits, & Kuchan, 2012). Violations of confidentiality are among the most common sources of malpractice claims against practitioners and the most commonly identified ethical breaches among students (Fly et al., 1997). Considering the high value placed on confidentiality and the ethical dilemmas it frequently poses, interns must fully understand the principle of confidentiality, know how to avoid violating confidentiality through carelessness, and appreciate the consequences of such violations. Interns also need to know that confidentiality is not fully guaranteed by their role or the clinical setting in which they work. What is more, laws concerning confidentiality and client–therapist privilege vary from state to state (Glosoff, Herlihy, & Spence, 2000; Glosoff, Herlihy, Herlihy, & Spence, 1997; Knapp & VandeCreek, 2006) and are addressed at the federal level by HIPAA. Also, I strongly recommend that all interns, supervisors, and practitioners consult the extremely informative and somewhat alarming article by Schwartz and Lonborg (2011), which details the many security risks inherent in electronic communication and the relative inattention that most practitioners give to understanding and managing those risks. Also recommended is a discussion by Devereaux and Gottlieb (2012) dealing with ethical issues and storage of electronic records in the "cloud."

It is particularly important as well that interns are aware of exceptions in which you may, and sometimes must, divulge information about clients. You need to know what such situations are, how to deal with them, and how to inform clients of these limitations to confidentiality.

The following discussion addresses general issues of confidentiality that apply to most settings. Although these guidelines should be helpful, certain therapy approaches pose unique problems, and some settings may follow specific approaches to protect confidentiality. For example, schools and other placements serving minors (Ellis, 2009; Lazofsky, 2008; Mannheim et al., 2002; Small, Lyons, & Guy, 2002), persons who are human immunodeficiency virus (HIV) positive (Anderson & Barret, 2001; Chenneville, 2000), persons in correctional institutions (White, 2003b), clients who are court-mandated to treatment (Regehr & Antle, 1997), persons in drug and alcohol treatment programs (Rinella & Goldstein, 2007), clients and service personnel in military settings (Murphy, 2005; Stall & King, 2000), seniors (Bergeron & Gray, 2003), rural settings (Helbok, Marineli, & Walls, 2006; Johnson, Brems, Warner, & Roberts, 2006; Schank & Skovholt, 2006), and other clients or settings may all call for special precautions and procedures. Group therapy and family therapy also pose certain unique ethical and legal issues with regard to confidentiality (Ellis, 2009; McCurdy & Murray, 2003; Rinella & Goldstein, 2007). In addition, HIPAA has special rules that apply to alcohol/substance abuse programs and to certain other clinical and research activities. Finally, as will be noted more than once in this text, computer communication and remote therapy also raise special ethical concerns, many of which are discussed later in this chapter and have also been addressed in the HIPAA security directives (Collins, 2007; Devereaux & Gottlieb, 2012; Heinlen, Welfel, Richmond, & Rak, 2003; Richards, 2009; Schwartz & Lonborg, 2011; Shaw & Shaw, 2006).

In all settings, at the beginning of the field experience, the intern should ask specifically about confidentiality policy and any unique issues that apply to the particular setting, client group, or other activity. If at any time questions arise pertaining to confidentiality, consult your supervisor and/or instructor.

RELEASE OF INFORMATION

To protect confidentiality, certain standards and guidelines must be followed scrupulously. First, the general principle to follow is that no one other than the client should be given any information—written, verbal, or otherwise—about the client without explicit written and signed permission from the client. Be aware, however, that within a treatment setting you are able to discuss the client with members of the treatment team. This is recognized in the HIPAA standards if the purpose is to provide quality of care (Benefield et al., 2006). Still, it is good practice to be careful about all communications, even within a setting. To help you deal with this issue, a suggested decision process is offered later in the chapter.

In contrast to information that is exchanged within a treatment team, there are standard "Release of Information" forms that can be used if a client wishes to authorize the release of information to someone outside the team or setting (Bernstein & Hartsell, 2004). These forms typically provide space to identify the person(s) who will receive the information, the purpose of the release, the specific information to be released, the form in which the information will be communicated, the date of the release, the period for which the release is to be valid, the name of the person authorized to release the information, the name of the client, and the signature of the client and the primary therapist or other professionals.

In practice, the requirement for written permission means that if someone calls or comes into an office claiming to have the client's permission to see records or discuss the case, do not acquiesce to this request or even acknowledge that the person is a client unless there is written permission authorizing such disclosure to the individual asking for the information. This may seem like a nuisance, but it is necessary.

If problems arise, you can cope with insistent or demanding people by saying something like, "I'm sorry, but I cannot share any information unless I have a signed release of information form. I'm sure you understand how important confidentiality is, and I'll be glad to provide you with whatever information I can as soon as a signed release of information is available." Note that this statement does not acknowledge that the individual in question is a client. It merely says that a release is necessary for any information to be shared. If the individual requesting the information does not accept this explanation or insists on being given information, refer the person to a supervisor. Under no circumstances should you let urgency, pressure, or inconvenience lead to laxity or carelessness about obtaining written releases.

SAFEGUARDING RECORDS AND THE HIPAA SECURITY STANDARDS

An important element of protecting confidentiality is the safeguarding of client records. In considering how records are to be safeguarded, in addition to the HIPAA Privacy Rule, which mandates what health care information can and cannot be communicated, HIPAA has also established a Security Rule, which outlines specific procedures for protecting the security of electronic information against inadvertent or unapproved access (Richards, 2009). Legally, the HIPAA Security Rule only applies to client information that is electronically stored, generated, communicated, or received. In practice, because so much of what is done involves computers and information technology, and because the HIPAA security principles are generally well founded, it is a good idea to know and follow these procedures even if you do not technically fall under the HIPAA mandates (APA Practice Organization, 2006). You should also be aware that for those who fall under HIPAA rules, one of the security rules requires that individuals and organizations conduct a formal risk assessment to evaluate and document measures taken to identify and minimize security risks.

The HIPAA Security Standard delineates a matrix of security standards that address administrative safeguards, physical safeguards, and technical safeguards. Briefly, administrative safeguards encompass staff selection and training, access-authorization procedures, contingency planning, and business contracts. Physical safeguards pertain to controlling access to records, workstation use and security, control of media devices, and methods for reuse or disposal of electronic devices or media. Finally, technical safeguards involve user identification and authentication, encryption, and security of data transmission and storage.

Again, whether or not you fall under the HIPAA requirements, common sense and sound practices suggest a number of measures that will help you stay in compliance with HIPAA. For example, all physical case notes, records, and other written or recorded information about the client should be kept in locked rooms and locked file cabinets. You should not leave notes, files, or other material with client names out in the open where others might see them inadvertently. As a further precaution, the words "Confidential Records" can be printed or stamped on all records and inserted at the top of electronic files.

Interns who keep class notebooks or journals should take care not to lose or misplace them. As an added precaution, interns should mark clearly on the outside of their notebooks that the material is confidential and should be returned unopened to the owner. I have all of our interns who keep journals write in bold letters on the front: "Confidential Personal Journal—If Found, Please Return to (intern's name and address)." In your writings for journals or classes, disguise the identity of clients by using pseudonyms or false initials, such as Mr. X or Ms. B. Avoid the use of real initials or first names only, as these can easily be connected to the actual individual.

NO CLIENT RECORDS should be kept on your regular personal laptop, tablet, computer, or other device as these can easily be lost or stolen or might be accessed at home or school. If case notes or any other clinical information is kept on computers, tablets, or other devices at your placement site, access to the device itself and to sensitive files should be restricted through not easily decoded passwords and firewalls, automatic log-off procedures should be operative, and you should have installed effective anti-virus and anti-spyware programs that are regularly updated and run. Fingerprint-secured thumb drives are far more secure and should be the only place such records are stored. Other electronic security measures are explicitly spelled out in the HIPAA standards. Most internship sites will have on-staff people who are trained in these matters, but I encourage you to familiarize yourself with the HIPAA standards and try to become personally proficient with key elements of computer and Internet security. Again, the article by Schwartz and Lonborg (2011) is highly recommended.

SHARING INFORMATION WITH COLLEAGUES

Guidelines for sharing information with outside sources are relatively clear, and, with the few exceptions to be discussed later, the rule can be summarized succinctly as "Not without written permission from the client." Questions about sharing information with colleagues and other professionals concerned with a case are not as easily answered (Behnke, 2005a). As each setting and situation is different, it may be helpful to offer a general framework you can use to make your decisions. The framework revolves around the question words: what, who, why, where, when, and how. Before sharing information about a client with anyone, you should ask yourself:

1. *What is the client's privilege, and what are the client's assumptions?* What has the client been told about confidentiality and its limitations, and what does the client know about how information will or will not be shared? What documentation is there that the client has been told these things?
2. *Who is receiving the information?* Has the client given permission for them to have the information? What is their role or authority within the clinical setting? What professional training do they have? What is their relationship to the client? What do you think of their clinical skills and ethical knowledge? Also ask yourself if they know about and respect the principle of confidentiality.
3. *Why do they want the information?* Are they involved in the client's treatment in some way? Are they just curious? Are they seeking information to understand the client, or are they likely to use it in some counterproductive way?
4. *What information is being requested?* Are these persons asking for data such as address, phone, and so on, or are they asking for clinical information about the nature of the client's concerns or background? Are they asking for general impressions from tests or interviews, or do they want specific scores or answers to specific questions? Remember that merely because someone is asking for a certain type of information does not mean you should provide the information requested. Depending on the circumstances, you may choose to offer summaries or general impressions rather than specific test results or interview responses. You may also choose to offer no information at all if there is a probability that it will not be used responsibly and professionally.
5. *Where are you?* Is the setting private, or are you in a public place where others could easily overhear your discussion?

Are the office doors closed? Could people in the waiting room hear you? Are other clients nearby?

6. *When should you discuss the information?* Is now the best time to share information? Will you have adequate time to discuss and explain things, or will you be rushed and not do an adequate job? Would it be better to schedule a specific time and place rather than sharing information in passing?

7. *How will you share the information?* Is it best to discuss it directly one on one, or can you accomplish the task over the phone? Should you formalize the exchange of information in writing, either by providing the information itself in written form or by keeping notes of the conversation? What are the relative pros and cons of direct verbal exchange versus written exchange?

8. *What are the laws and regulations, and have I complied with them?* Most important of all, you must be sure that you are in compliance with HIPAA regulations and any other state and local laws or regulations regarding what is shared, how, with whom, and under what conditions.

ELECTRONIC HEALTH RECORDS

Issues of sharing information with colleagues, the use of electronic information technology, and the HIPAA privacy and security standards all come together in the expanding application that is broadly referred to as health information technology (HIT). A central component of HIT is the use of electronic health records (EHR) or electronic medical records (EMR) systems (Steinfeld & Keyes, 2011). In an effort to increase efficiency, reduce medical errors, and improve communication and quality of care, a nationwide effort is underway to promote the use of EMR systems. A study by the RAND Corporation (Bower, 2005; RAND, 2005) estimated annual savings of $77 billion if HITs were fully implemented across the nation.

Thanks to the actions of Congress and the administration, a national coordinator of health information technology has been tasked with establishing standards and promoting the use and interoperability of HITs across the health care spectrum, beginning with all federally funded programs. In addition, economic stimulus legislation, the American Recovery and Reinvestment Act, passed by Congress in 2009, included $20 billion in funding for HIT.

Ideally, the use of EHRs will speed information entry, reduce errors caused by unrecognizable handwriting, allow instant access to records from across the country or even across the globe, enhance coordination with insurance providers, and facilitate quality-assurance measures. Electronic records also allow artificial intelligence systems to check for potential complications of treatments, for example, from unrecognized medication interactions. Intriguing ideas have also been put forward for ways in which EHRs can be used for both research and clinical efforts to enhance evidence-based practice initiatives (Drake, Teague, & Gersing, 2005).

Although potential benefits of EHRs exist, they also pose significant confidentiality issues, especially with regard to mental health treatment. Based on practical experience from a comprehensive health system using EMRs, Steinfeld and Keyes (2011) and Steinfeld, Ekorenrud, Gillett, Quirk, and Eytan (2006) offered helpful suggestions for how such systems can be implemented

and how mental health information can be incorporated. Central to this discussion is the interface between confidentiality issues, informed consent, and the technological capabilities of the EMR system. Within large, integrated health systems is a legitimate desire for other treatment professionals (e.g., primary physicians) to have some insight into any mental health or drug/alcohol issues that may be affecting their clients. On the other hand, clients may want to keep some of these issues absolutely private, particularly if a medical records system could be accessed by someone other than their immediate mental health care professional or their primary physician. Beyond client desires are legal guidelines for how such records must be treated. Steinfeld and Keyes (2011) pointed out that federal law explicitly prohibits sharing information about chemical-dependency treatment with anyone outside the specific treatment program except in cases of emergency.

From a technological perspective, this raises important issues about separating records and controlling access to information only to specified individuals for certain reasons and with specific permissions. Steinfeld and Keyes (2011) described a "split-note" structure in which portions of progress notes (e.g., those addressing medications or specific behavioral interventions) may be shared with other providers, but other sections (e.g., those describing personal issues or specific psychotherapy matters) are not accessible. This approach has merit, but I still have concerns about putting psychotherapy notes in any centralized electronic format that would be accessible to anyone other than myself. More will be said about this in Chapter 7, but I strongly recommend that, if possible, you put into an EHR only what other professionals must know in order to provide continuity of care. Furthermore, as Steinfeld and Keyes pointed out, informed consent is absolutely essential, and clients have a right to know how their information will be stored and managed and what will be included or excluded from any EMR.

If your placement site is using an EHR or EMR system, take the time to learn not only how to enter or retrieve data from the system but also to understand fully how access is granted or restricted, what informed consent procedures are in place, and what your options are in regard to entering notes about clients with whom you are working.

INADVERTENT CONFIDENTIALITY VIOLATIONS

To appreciate why so much attention is paid to protecting confidentiality, take a moment to consider the possible impact of a breach of confidentiality. Consider also how, even when scrupulous procedures are implemented within systems and institutions, breaches can nevertheless occur as a result of lapses in judgment by professionals (Fisher, 2008).

For example, I once observed a psychologist with 25 years of experience who was invited to a large introductory psychology class to discuss clinical issues. During his talk, he described a case study in which he mentioned that the client was a 50-year-old man, divorced, with two daughters. At this point, confidentiality was still protected. However, the speaker went on to name the town the client lived in, then said that he owned a local car dealership, was a past president of a well-known social organization, and had been struggling with a serious drinking problem for several years. The psychologist never actually divulged the client's name, but in the midsize community where this occurred, it was easy enough for several people in the class to realize who the client was.

As a second example, over lunch in a local restaurant, an intern and his social work supervisor were discussing a family the intern was seeing. At the end of the lunch, they arose to find that the same family had been sitting one booth away. Thinking about the discussion later, the intern realized he had criticized certain family members, and he was extremely troubled about how to deal with this in the next session.

In considering inadvertent confidentiality breaches, it should also be emphasized that clients play an important role, particularly with regard to electronic communications. Everything from voice or text messaging to email and regular mail can be sources of information leaks if not handled carefully. Schwartz and Lonborg (2011) point out that cybersecurity is "a 'two-way' street. Security protections at one end of a network or communication line may be only as good as those at the other end. Practitioners may establish adequate administrative, physical, or technical safeguards…but clients may not" (p. 422).

High-profile public instances in which email communications have revealed personal matters vividly illustrate this sort of risk, but there are abundant private cases in which individual information about therapy contacts or content has been inadvertently or intentionally accessed by family, coworkers, or individuals with malevolent intentions.

EFFECTS OF CONFIDENTIALITY VIOLATIONS

To appreciate the significance of breaks in confidentiality, imagine yourself as the client in the situations just described. How would you react to hearing your personal case discussed before a class in such a way that people would know your identity? What would be your reaction to the next therapy session if you overheard your therapist discussing your case over lunch? Would you even go to therapy, or would you simply terminate with no explanation? And what might be the implications if a family member or significant other read online communication with your therapist that you had thought would be private?

The clinical implications of confidentiality violations should be sufficient to promote caution, but there are also legal issues to consider. Violation of HIPAA confidentiality rules carries the possibilities of both monetary penalties and criminal prosecution for willful and serious offenses. In addition to the possibility of criminal prosecution, a client who is harmed in some way by a therapist's breach of confidentiality may well sue for damages (Bernstein & Hartsell, 2004; Sales et al., 2005). Because confidentiality is such a fundamental condition of therapy, a judge or jury would not be likely to look positively on an intern's or professional's carelessness in such matters.

EXCEPTIONS TO CONFIDENTIALITY

The matter of confidentiality is complicated by the requirement that certain information about clients may or must be shared with others (Bernstein & Hartsell, 2004; Fisher, 2008; Glosoff et al., 1997; Sales et al., 2005). This is further complicated by legal

uncertainties and differences in interpretation and statutes for different states (Pabian et al., 2009; Werth, Welfel, & Benjamin, 2009). HIPAA rules also describe permissible exceptions to confidentiality, which, in general, are consistent with established ethical standards and existing state and case laws.

Without attempting to provide specific guidance for each situation, five instances will be identified in which absolute confidentiality may not hold and information may need to be revealed. The main message in this discussion is that under no circumstances should you give a client the often-heard but erroneous assurance that "nothing you say or do will be shared with anyone else without your permission." That simply is not always true, and clients have a right to know the exceptions (Fisher, 2008).

Briefly, the five main exceptions to confidentiality occur in (1) cases of abuse, (2) cases in which clients are considered dangerous to themselves, (3) cases in which clients intend to harm others, (4) certain legal proceedings in which the case notes and other records can be subpoenaed, and (5) requests by insurance providers for case notes to assess the necessity for and benefits of services.

PRIVILEGED COMMUNICATION

Before discussing the exceptions to confidentiality, it will be helpful to introduce and explain the concept of privileged communications (Knapp & VandeCreek, 2006; Koocher & Keith-Spiegel, 2008). *Privilege* is a legal term referring to the right of individuals to withhold information requested by a court. Such privileges are established by law and pertain to professional relationships with clients, such as the relationships between attorney and client and between physician and client; communications with members of the clergy; and, in most states, communications between clients and officially recognized mental health practitioners, including psychologists, social workers, counselors, and others recognized by the states. As Swenson (1997) explained the rationale for such protections, "these are relationships in which the legislatures consider the benefits of confidentiality more important than a court's need for evidence" (p. 135).

It is important to understand that the legal right of privilege resides with the client, also referred to as the "holder" of the privilege. This means that it is the client's prerogative, not the therapist's, to decide to waive privilege and allow information to be disclosed. Except in certain circumstances to be discussed in a moment, the therapist's obligation is to protect the client's privilege whenever it is applicable. If therapists refuse to release information, they are doing so on behalf of the client's privilege, not because the therapist holds the privilege. Similarly, therapists must realize that apart from situations explicitly allowing or requiring confidentiality to be broken, the therapist cannot unilaterally waive a client's privilege. Unless the client has voluntarily waived privileges or the courts have specifically ordered otherwise, the therapist has a duty to assert the client's privilege and not release information.

The limits and protections of client–therapist privilege were clarified in an important U.S. Supreme Court decision, *Jaffee* v. *Redmond* (1996), in which the majority of the Court found that privileged communication between a client and a social worker was protected. This case was of particular significance because it specifically included social workers in the category of therapists who enjoy privileged communications, and it established a ruling at the federal level that could guide subsequent decisions by lower courts (DeBell & Jones, 1997). For updates on this case, and to get a deeper sense of how legal decisions in such matters continue to evolve, see http://www.jaffee-redmond.org/.

In essence, the court found in *Jaffee* v. *Redmond* that a therapist, in this case a clinical social worker, could not be compelled to reveal the private records of a client as part of a civil suit against the client by a third party. Specifically, the court held the following:

> Because effective psychotherapy depends upon an atmosphere of confidence and trust in which the patient is willing to make a frank and complete disclosure…For this reason the mere possibility of disclosure may impede development of the confidential relationship necessary for successful treatment. (p. 1928)

While noting that the Court's decision marked important progress toward defining privilege clients in therapeutic relationships, it is also important to emphasize again that certain legal exceptions apply (Glosoff et al., 1997). Just as courts have ruled that clients have a privilege to not disclose information shared with therapists, the courts have also determined that in certain circumstances, therapists must release information, whether or not the client would concur. Swenson (1997) explains that under normal circumstances, "a therapist is not liable for violating a client's privacy rights if the therapist discloses information covered by an exception or because a law mandates disclosure" (p. 135). Examples of such conditions are described in the following sections.

Again, I emphasize that the following material is intended to help you understand the issues you should consider in dealing with confidential material. Laws vary from state to state and change with time. Therefore, this discussion should not be taken as legal advice. You are responsible for understanding and abiding by the laws of your state and the practices of your agency. If you have any questions or specific concerns arise, consult your instructor, supervisor, state organization, professional insurance provider, or attorney. Throughout your training, it is also a good idea to attend periodic risk management workshops. In addition to providing updates and discussions of emerging trends in ethics and risk management, attendance at such workshops may also qualify practitioners for discounts on liability insurance with certain carriers.

ABUSE

In all states and the District of Columbia, specific laws require those in the helping and teaching professions to report instances of known or suspected child abuse (Bryant & Milsom, 2005; Mannheim et al., 2002; Small et al., 2002; Swenson, 1997). In most states, this principle also applies to cases of child psychological abuse or neglect (Marshall, 2012) and to abuse of disabled or elderly adults (Zeranski & Halgin, 2011). The core value involved is the need to protect vulnerable individuals from harm.

Under abuse reporting laws, if a child tells a therapist that he or she is being physically or sexually abused, or if the child has

bruises or other injuries that suggest abuse, or if the therapist has other clear grounds to believe physical, sexual, or emotional abuse is occurring, the therapist is obligated to notify agencies that will intervene to investigate the matter and protect the child. These agencies are generally referred to as Child Protective Services, Children's Services Division, or, more commonly in practice, by acronyms such as CPS, CSD, and so on.

In most states that require professionals to report abuse, the laws protect those who report from civil liability, provided the reports are filed in good faith and without malice, and, importantly, that the professional followed the statutory requirements (Small et al., 2002). Failure to report abuse may result in criminal penalties or in civil actions (Bryant & Milsom, 2005), and this can apply even if you fail to report because you believe someone else has already filed a report. In a number of states, there are criminal penalties for knowingly making false reports of abuse.

From a clinical perspective, abuse situations are further complicated by concerns about how clients or families will react if a therapist files a report with a protective services agency. The charge of abuse is very serious, and professionals must not be hasty in reporting cases. On the other hand, if there are sound reasons to believe that abuse is occurring, professionals or interns may be responsible to report the abuse, and they must know what their legal responsibility is. For useful guidelines about recognizing and dealing with psychological maltreatment of children, and for case examples of how to deal with these matters, see Marshall (2012).

In your own work as an intern, you should speak with your supervisor and instructor to be sure you are informed about the abuse reporting laws in your state. You should also know the procedures to follow if you have reason to believe a client is being abused or is abusing someone else. Such procedures must always include notification of confidentiality limits at the outset of therapy, careful documentation of information, and consultation with supervisors and instructors. Further, in all such situations, interns must inform and consult with their placement supervisors and faculty instructors whenever such questions arise and before filing any reports with authorities.

SUICIDE AND DANGEROUSNESS TO SELF

When clients are considered to be at risk of harming themselves, therapists are obligated to take measures to protect the client. Given the nature of the work and the clients served by helping professionals, this is not an uncommon situation. Indeed, surveys have shown that as many as one-quarter to one-half of therapists sampled reported that at some point in their careers, they lost a client to suicide (Sanders, Jacobson, & Ting, 2008).

Assessing for suicide risk is a particularly nuanced art and science and contains a significant risk for clients and helping professionals (Baerger, 2001; Jobes, Rudd, Overholser, & Joiner, 2008; Mishna, Antle, & Regehr, 2002; Paulson & Worth, 2002). As an intern, if confronted with a potentially suicidal client, your first obligation is to respect the ethical principle of competence and seek assistance. It would be unusual and unwise for someone still in training to have sole or primary responsibility for working with a client who presents a risk of suicide, and even highly experienced therapists often seek consultation when working with suicidal clients. McGlothlin, Rainey, and Kindsvatter (2005) provide helpful suggestions for how supervisors can assist interns who are working with potentially suicidal clients. Rudd et al. (2009) discuss the ethical issue of informed consent in working with potentially suicidal clients.

Whereas you should not attempt to manage a suicidal client by yourself, it is nevertheless important for you to have some framework from which to evaluate suicide risk in order to recognize when you may need assistance and when it may be necessary to inform others of the client's condition. A number of articles and books identify suicide risk factors and offer suggestions for working with potentially suicidal clients from both clinical and ethical/legal perspectives (Baerger, 2001; Berman et al., 2006; Bongar, 2002; Mishna et al., 2002; Oordt et al., 2005; Sanchez, 2001; Westefeld et al., 2000; White, 2003a). Sanchez (2001), Bongar (2002), and Oordt et al. (2005) have provided particularly useful reviews of both risk factors and protective factors along with practical guidelines and a checklist to record key elements considered in a risk assessment. Berman et al. (2006) focused on the challenges of understanding, predicting, and preventing adolescent suicide. Slovak, Brewer, and Carlson (2008) emphasized the commonsense, but often overlooked, advice to assess for a client's access to firearms.

Confidentiality matters are more complicated when the therapist has reason to believe the client is at serious risk of self-harm but is not willing to comply with treatment recommendations. In these situations, the therapist may have to take steps to seek involuntary commitment to a hospital unit or pursue some other treatment option to ensure the client's safety. Koocher and Keith-Spiegel (2008) advised that you should be thoroughly versed in the laws and procedures for commitment. Before a crisis arises, have information readily available about the relevant phone numbers and contact persons. If you are in a setting or role where this possibility might arise, I strongly encourage you to obtain this necessary information now and complete the form provided in Appendix F. Having the knowledge and information ready beforehand can save you a frantic and frightening search for it should a crisis arise. More importantly, it could save your client's life.

Procedures for obtaining involuntary treatment vary, but a common scenario is for the therapist to contact specifically designated mental health specialists who then evaluate the client and determine the need for commitment or other treatment. In general, as long as the therapist is acting in good faith and using sound professional judgment, pursuing such measures is protected by law, even though it means releasing information about the client to certain agencies or officials without the client's permission. This is a general rule, however, and you should check carefully about the procedures to be followed in each case and location (Jobes et al., 2008). Also be sure to carefully document the information on which decisions were made and the steps taken in response.

Two final points should be made before concluding this discussion of suicide risk and confidentiality. First, as in all of your clinical work, it is absolutely essential to adhere to the highest standards of care and document your actions carefully,

particularly when working with high-risk clients. Berman et al. (2006), Baerger (2001), and White (2003a) all emphasized that clinicians need not live in fear of client suicide or of being sued if a client commits suicide if the level of care provided was sound and is well documented. It should be emphasized, however, that if legal proceedings do result from a client's suicide, you will be expected to demonstrate through your written records that you acted responsibly and demonstrated reasonable care in the diagnosis and treatment of the individual. This means you must record both what you did to assess and treat the client and, if risk is present, the reasons for making certain treatment decisions given the information available to you and the client's needs at the time. Baerger offered a useful review of actual case law pertaining to client suicide and provided practical recommendations derived from those cases.

The second issue to keep in mind concerning suicide is the impact a client's death can have on you personally and emotionally. This will be discussed in more detail in a later chapter dealing with self-care for providers, but it is worth mentioning here because, as Knox and colleagues (2006) and DeAngelis (2001) pointed out, too little attention is given to supporting and caring for therapists after they lose a client to suicide.

EXERCISE

As noted in the text, being prepared by having the necessary information available and understanding the procedures to follow in the event of a crisis should be part of your training and practice. Whether or not you work in a setting where this issue might arise, it will be a valuable learning experience to review the process with your instructor or site supervisor. On the Emergency Contact and Procedures form in Appendix F, you will find a place to complete a step-by-step procedure to follow should it be necessary to consider commitment of a client. Review the procedures and complete the form now. Think of this as you would a life jacket on a boat. Chances are you may not need it; but if you do, you will be extremely grateful that you have it handy.

INTENT TO HARM OTHERS AND THE "DUTY TO PROTECT"

A second situation in which clinicians may be required to divulge information relating to danger arises when a client makes explicit threats or statements of intent to harm another person. This situation is now commonly known in the professions as a Tarasoff case, based on an incident in which a client told a therapist he wanted to harm a specific individual. The therapist believed the client was serious and took steps to pursue involuntary commitment, but the therapist did not manage to directly warn the intended victim. Several months later, the client, who had since dropped out of therapy, killed the young woman he had earlier threatened to harm. The therapist and the university he worked for were then sued for damages for not having warned the victim. Reviews of the Tarasoff case have been written by VandeCreek, Bennett, and Bricklin (1994), Fulero (1988), and Slovenko (1988), all of whom discussed in detail the initial case and the subsequent implications. Special Tarasoff-related considerations and implications for HIV-positive patients were reviewed by Chenneville (2000).

The "duty to warn," which developed from the Tarasoff case, has continued to evolve, with later rulings leading to the concept of "the duty to protect," which asserts that therapists must take measures to prevent possible harm, even if the information about a threat comes from someone other than a client's family member (Berger & Berger, 2005).

The key point is that if you have good reason to believe that someone seriously intends to harm another person, you may be required to take every reasonable step necessary to protect the intended victim, and this may include breaking confidentiality by warning the potential victim and advising responsible authorities such as the police.

You also need to be aware that there are substantial variations in state laws regarding the duty to protect. These variations are discussed in detail in Werth et al. (2009). Pabian et al. (2009) examined knowledge of these specific state codes among psychologists and found that in spite of having taken courses and continuing education in professional ethics, 76% of psychologists who responded to their survey did not have a fully accurate understanding of their state laws on this topic. What is more, some 41% of respondents gave answers that suggested they did not fully understand the principles of the APA ethics code as they apply to such cases. As these authors pointed out, failure to understand the laws of your state and the ethical codes of your profession can subject your clients, yourself, your supervisor, and your placement site to unnecessary risk and may effectively void any protections that would apply if you were following the laws as actually written.

Strategies for dealing with potentially dangerous clients have been described by Monahan (1993); Tishler, Gordon, and Landry-Meyer (2000); Tolman and Rotzien (2007); and others. Critical steps recommended include training and knowledge of risk assessment, examination of the client's past and current clinical record, direct inquiries of the client, and estimation of the risk and development of a responsible plan. Further discussion of this topic is provided in Chapter 9, which offers suggestions on how interns can reduce risks to themselves and others when dealing with potentially violent clients.

It is beyond the scope of the present chapter to go into more detail on this topic, but you are strongly encouraged to consult the references cited here; if you encounter such situations, you should immediately seek assistance from supervisors and instructors; from your professional organization; and, if necessary, from legal counsel. Also, be careful to document fully the steps you take and the information on which you base your decisions. This will help ensure that you follow sound clinical practice. If something unfortunate happens despite your best efforts, accurate documentation and sound consultation can help reduce your personal risks of liability.

LEGAL PROCEEDINGS AND COURT ORDERS

A fourth situation in which you may be forced to reveal information about a client is if you are ordered to do so by a court. This may come about through a variety of processes, but one of the more common reasons involves civil suits for damages (Glosoff et al., 2000). For example, if a therapist is seeing a client who sues someone else claiming the other person's actions caused psychological harm to the client, the attorney for the defendant may have the right to subpoena the plaintiff's psychological and medical records. When a client of a therapist is the plaintiff in a suit claiming mental or emotional damages, the client's records no longer fall under the protections of privilege discussed earlier. In these cases, the therapy records are considered to be evidence that is necessary and legitimate to help establish the nature and extent of the alleged damages.

In cases such as these, if someone other than the client requests your records, it is advisable to consult an attorney and do everything you can to avoid releasing information unless the client grants a release. Attorneys usually advise plaintiffs that their records may be requested in such proceedings and, therefore, to consider the possible review of clinical information in deciding whether to pursue a lawsuit. Nevertheless, a client may refuse to sign a release to share information with the opposition's attorney. In that event, the treatment professional may be ordered to comply with a court order to release the information.

Whether or not the client has signed such a release, if a court order requires it and state or federal law does not protect the client's privilege under the circumstances, the records must be released. Be sure, however, that before you release any records without the client's permission, a court has, in fact, ordered you to do so. Merely receiving a letter or subpoena from an attorney indicating that your records have been requested does not constitute a court order, and you are not, therefore, required to comply (Fisher, 2008). You should also know that a subpoena to appear before a court is not the same as a court order demanding records. If you receive a subpoena to appear without a specific order to produce your records, preserve the client's privilege and do not release records unless specifically ordered to do so, in writing, by the court. Further, you should never give information of any sort directly to a person who is serving you with a subpoena, no matter how insistent or aggressive he or she may be (Zur, 2006). Instead, accept the subpoena and send away the person who served it without even acknowledging that the individual is a client or that you have any involvement with the case. Then immediately contact an attorney and, of course, your instructor and supervisor. For a thorough review of dealing with subpoenas or court-compelled testimony, see the report by the APA Committee on Legal Issues (2006).

In light of the possibility for release of information through court order, three pieces of advice emerge. First, clients should be informed of this possibility at the start of therapy. This reduces the risk of a later lawsuit if the clinician makes an inaccurate comment such as "There is no way anyone can have access to your records without your permission." Second, clinicians need to be selective in what they put in their case notes. This matter is discussed in more detail in Chapter 7. Third, again, before releasing any information without a client's permission, consult with an attorney to be sure that the court order or other request has legal authority and cannot be refused, and always consult immediately with your instructor and supervisor.

INSURANCE COMPANY INQUIRIES, MANAGED CARE, AND ETHICAL PRACTICE

To understand issues of confidentiality in relation to health insurance, it is helpful to know a little about the concept of managed care. The term *managed care* broadly refers to efforts to contain the rising costs of health care by "managing" the health care services that are provided and the ways they are paid for. In a traditional "fee-for-service" model, clients seek care from largely independent health care practitioners who provide treatment and bill clients and insurers for services based on the practitioner's professional judgment of what is needed. By comparison, under managed-care arrangements, clients must receive care from a selected list or panel of professionals, and the services that will be provided are tightly specified and controlled by the managed-care insurance company.

Some managed-care organizations are essentially not-for-profit cooperatives, in which members participate voluntarily and share in the benefits of lowered insurance premiums as the result of the cost-saving measures. On the other hand, large for-profit managed-care companies provide health insurance to businesses and individuals as well as through government-funded insurance plans. These managed-care insurance companies are in business to make a profit and to return those profits to their stockholders or corporate owners.

The ostensible purpose of the managed-care approach is to control rising health care costs by limiting unnecessary or ineffective treatments or services. That effort, however, has also resulted in limitations on client choices (Kremer & Gesten, 2003); a loss of professional autonomy; and, many argue, health care decisions that are driven by economic concerns and profit motives rather than client care needs (Cooper & Gottlieb, 2000; Rupert & Baird, 2004). In addition, as managed-care insurers have set increasingly tight restrictions on what services they will pay for and which providers they will compensate for treatment, health care professionals have been forced to provide certain types of treatments, whereas other therapies have not been approved by managed-care companies (Braun & Cox, 2005). Further, in an effort to ensure that only the covered illnesses or treatments are being paid for, managed-care companies have increasingly forced therapists to divulge previously confidential information about their clients and their treatment methods (Acuff et al., 1999). Some insurers had even gone so far as to insist that therapists allow them to review the records of other clients who are not covered by the insurer in order to compare the kinds of treatment the insurance company's clients are receiving with those of other clients.

Regrettably, the intrusiveness of insurance companies has led to increasing reports of clients choosing not to seek needed treatment because they resent or are embarrassed by the intrusive questions of insurers. Some insurers have also begun to prescreen clients before authorizing therapy. In my judgment, this is unacceptable. For a suicidal client, a victim of sexual abuse, or anyone facing serious distress to have to discuss such issues with an anonymous insurance representative before meeting with a qualified therapist of the client's choosing is extraordinarily counter-therapeutic and potentially dangerous.

Although it is unlikely that you will be billing for services personally during your internship, it is highly likely that you will interact with these types of issues at some point in your future, either as a health care client yourself or as a provider (Daniels, Alva, & Olivares, 2002). To get a better sense of the ethical implications of managed care or other constraints on clinical practice, consider the following exercise.

EXERCISE

Refer back to the basic ethical values and principles discussed early in this chapter—for example, the values of service; social justice; dignity and worth of the person; and the importance of human relationships, integrity, competence, beneficence, and the like. With these values in mind, consider the ethical dilemmas that could be created by the following scenarios that can occur under certain insurance arrangements. Then, consider a second set of scenarios that could occur under a fee-for-service model and think about the ethical issues these raise. Finally, consult the code of ethics for your profession and others, and discuss these examples with your instructor or supervisor to determine how these matters are to be addressed in an ethical manner.

ETHICAL DILEMMAS THAT ARISE IN MANAGED-CARE ARRANGEMENTS

1. Research has shown that the relationship between therapist and client is often critical to effective therapy, but a managed-care company does not allow clients to select their own therapists; instead, it requires clients to accept therapists who are on a panel of approved providers. If you believe that a client will have difficulty forming a therapeutic relationship with any of the providers on the panel, what should you recommend to the client?

2. A client's insurance company will pay for therapy for one diagnosis but not for a different one. You are seeing a client who cannot afford to pay for therapy without the help of insurance. Although the client demonstrates some of the symptoms that are typical of a diagnosis that is covered for treatment, the most accurate diagnosis would be for a disorder that is not included in the client's insurance coverage. Which diagnosis should you give, and why?

3. In your best judgment and from your knowledge of the research literature, a client would benefit most from a treatment approach that is not included on the list of approved treatments covered under the insurance policy. If you treat the client with the approach you believe is most appropriate, you will not receive payment for the treatment from the insurance company. How should you proceed?

4. A client who is a prominent member of your community is seeing you for therapy regarding a delicate personal matter that could be detrimental to the client's reputation if it became public. In an effort to ensure that you are providing only approved treatments for approved disorders, the client's managed-care company demands to see your treatment records. The client has not given permission for you to release the records to the insurance company, but the company is threatening to withhold payments unless the records are released.

FEE-FOR-SERVICE DILEMMAS

1. You know of a colleague who practices a form of therapy that has not been shown by research to be effective and is highly expensive. The colleague's clients like the treatment approach and as long as their insurance company is willing to pay for the costs, they are happy to continue receiving the treatment for as long as they can. What are your ethical obligations, given what you know about the treatment, the costs, and the alternatives? How do broader social concerns (e.g., the overall costs of health care) relate to your decision and your ethical considerations?

2. A therapist believes that each session with a client should be considered a unique interaction in the moment and that keeping an ongoing record of psychotherapy notes tends to interfere with the ability to focus on the present moment of each session. As a result, this therapist keeps no ongoing notes other than a simple record of visits. When the client's insurance company asks the therapist to explain and document exactly what is being done in therapy to help the client, the therapist refuses to divulge any information, even though the client is willing to sign a release-of-information form.

3. A state agency contracts with a group of mental health therapists to provide services to children and adolescents in need. Because of budget constraints, the agency eventually determines that it needs to audit the treatments and outcomes to determine whether the money that has been spent has been effective in helping the children. The therapists maintain that their treatment has helped the children, and they resent any intrusion into or oversight of their practices. Do you believe state or federal agencies have a right or responsibility to review treatment practices and possibly limit services that they will pay for unless effective outcomes can be demonstrated?

Fortunately, thanks in part to the advocacy of the various professional associations, some of the ethical dilemmas raised by managed care have been addressed and clarified by HIPAA guidelines. Now, virtually every health care agency and provider will be required to give clients clear and specific information about precisely what information will or will not be made available to insurance companies and how the companies must handle the information.

What is more, in one of the more positive changes brought about by HIPAA, the confidentiality of psychotherapy notes is now explicitly protected by law, provided that the notes are kept separate from the rest of the client's record. As described in HIPAA, psychotherapy notes, which historically have been referred to as "process notes," are used by therapists to record ongoing therapeutic interactions, conversations, and observations of the client's dynamics. Not only are such notes protected, but also under HIPAA rules, insurers cannot refuse to reimburse providers for services if the client does not agree to the release of psychotherapy notes (Holloway, 2003). Keep in mind, however, that whereas psychotherapy notes may now have greater protection from disclosure to insurance companies, any writing or records regarding a client, including personal notes or process notes, may still be subpoenaed in a court proceeding.

CONFIDENTIALITY WITH MINORS

Our discussion of confidentiality concludes with a topic that is frequently raised by interns but has no simple answers. Confidentiality issues with minors can be especially complex because they involve the rights and responsibilities of at least two people, the minor and at least one adult, and because there are competing values, such as protecting the privacy rights of the minor and respecting the rights and responsibilities of parents or guardians (Behnke & Warner, 2002; Bodenhorn, 2006; Isaacs & Stone, 2001; Mannheim et al., 2002). In addition, as with other aspects of ethics and the law, standards vary across states, depending on the particular issues involved (e.g., alcohol and drug treatment, as well as sexual or reproductive concerns, may be treated differently from other health matters) and have changed over time (Maradiegue, 2003; Reamer, 2005b). For reviews of state laws pertaining to health care of minors, see Boonstra and Nash (2000) and the monograph from the Center for Adolescent Health and the Law (2003). Steinberg, Cauffman, Woolard, Graham, and Banich (2009) explore adolescent cognitive, emotional, and social maturation levels as they relate to the juvenile death penalty, access to abortion, and other matters. For a comprehensive and insightful discussion of research ethics and issues, including informed consent and confidentiality with regard to families and minors, see Margolin et al. (2005).

From a clinical perspective, research suggests, not surprisingly, that the promise of confidentiality increases the willingness of adolescents to reveal personal information and seek health care from a physician. Ford, Milstein, Halpern-Felsher, and Irwin (1997) compared the responses of adolescents exposed to three levels of confidentiality instructions. Their results showed that subjects who were assured of confidentiality were significantly more likely to express willingness to visit their providers again. This research also showed that 17% of the subjects said that concerns about confidentiality had caused them to avoid health care at some point in the past.

These issues can be particularly challenging in school environments, especially for school counselors. Huss, Bryant, and Mulet (2008) reviewed the key ASCA ethical principles involved and stressed the importance of involving parents or guardians in discussions about the role of school counselors and the importance of, as well as limitations to, confidentiality in that setting.

When working with children, it is also important to consider their cognitive ability to make decisions on their own behalf. Gustafson and McNamara (1987) reviewed both legal and developmental considerations relating to confidentiality with minors. They noted that in empirical studies (Belter & Grisso, 1984), 15-year-olds performed as well as 21-year-olds in assessments of their understanding of clients' rights. Other studies (Kaser-Boyd, Adelman, & Taylor, 1985) showed that therapy risks and benefits could be identified by minors, including those with learning and behavioral problems. In general, it appears that children older than about age 12 have a better understanding of confidentiality and related issues than do younger children.

Major professional organizations and their corresponding ethical codes recognize the complexity of confidentiality issues related to minors and families and urge professionals to address such issues by obtaining informed consent at the outset of treatment, clarifying who the client is, seeking specific releases of information when appropriate, and adhering to relevant laws. Huss et al. (2008) pointed out that within the ASCA code of ethics, all of Section A.2 deals with confidentiality and the term itself is found in 10 other places in the standards. Describing the relationship of counselors to parents, the ASCA code in Section B.2(a) advises counselors: "Inform parents/guardians of the counselor's role with emphasis on the confidential nature of the counseling relationship between the counselor and students."

Similarly, Section 1.07(f) of the NASW code advises that in their work with families, social workers should "seek agreement among the parties involved concerning each individual's right to confidentiality." The ACA code of ethics, Section B.5(a), advises that when counseling minor clients or adults lacking the capacity to give voluntary informed consent, counselors should "protect the confidentiality of information received in the counseling relationship as specified by federal and state laws, written policies, and applicable ethical standards."

The APA code of ethics is somewhat less specific about work with minor clients. For example, Standard 4.03 of the APA code of ethics states that when working with families, psychologists should "attempt to clarify at the outset, (1) which of the individuals are clients and (2) the relationship the psychologist will have to each person." Fisher (2009) made a compelling argument that the concept of identifying "who the client is" is actually better thought of as asking oneself, "Exactly what are my ethical responsibilities to each of the parties in this case?" The point of this reformulation is to recognize that especially when dealing with minors, families, or in other interactions in which multiple people plus multiple institutional entities may be involved, there may actually be multiple ethical duties, some of which may conflict with one another.

In addition to the guidance of ethical codes, HIPAA privacy standards also address the confidentiality of health records related to minors (http://www.hhs.gov/ocr/privacy/hipaa/faq/personal_representatives_and_minors/). HIPAA standards make important distinctions regarding when and how parents or guardians can access the records of minors. For example, disclosure requirements may differ depending on whether or not a parent or guardian initially authorized the relevant treatment. HIPAA also spells out specific conditions under which state laws protecting minors' rights must take precedence. As noted elsewhere, HIPAA standards also provide special provisions and protections for records from alcohol/drug abuse treatment.

Given the ethical and legal complexities of these issues, I find it helpful to follow the advice given some time ago by Gustafson and McNamara (1987), who recommended that therapists working with minors or families should establish a written professional-service agreement that explicitly states the conditions of confidentiality within which therapy will be provided. This should be reviewed with each person involved, signed, and made part of the client's permanent record. Reviewing conditions and signing an agreement beforehand reduces the possibility of later misunderstanding or conflict. This process also gives clients and therapists the right to decide whether they will participate in therapy under the established conditions. I would add that such contracts should be established for all clients, not just minors, and the contracts should reflect local, state, and federal laws.

Finally, let me add a special precaution for interns working with minors. In addition to the legal and ethical matters just discussed, interns should be aware that they may find themselves in particularly difficult situations while working with minors, especially adolescents. Because interns may be relatively younger than other professionals, they often experience a desire to befriend young clients. In turn, the young clients may confide in the intern with personal information and insist that the intern not share it with anyone else, including other members of the treatment team. I am familiar with instances in which trainees got themselves and their agencies into potentially serious legal and, indeed, possibly life- or career-threatening trouble by offering advice to minors contrary to the instructions of their supervisors and contrary to the wishes and legal rights of parents. Those trainees had good but misguided intentions, and their efforts ended up creating more problems than they were attempting to solve. By consulting carefully with supervisors and instructors, these students could have avoided the problems for themselves, their placement sites, and the clients and their families.

DUAL RELATIONSHIPS AND BOUNDARY ISSUES

The therapeutic relationship is unique. To protect the integrity of therapy, professional ethics prohibit the formation of dual relationships. Dual relationships encompass a wide spectrum of interactions, but the underlying principle is that the therapist must avoid becoming involved in relationships or roles that could compromise the therapeutic process for the client (Kagle & Giebelhausen, 1994; Kocet, 2006; Moleski & Kiselica, 2005; Reamer, 2003). Dual relationships can involve such things as serving as a counselor for a student who lives on your dormitory floor, agreeing to treat a coworker, or seeing your landlord's family member in exchange for rent reduction. In more malignant and destructive forms, dual relationships can involve romantic or sexual contacts between therapists and clients.

The danger of dual relationships lies in the possibility that therapists will in some way, consciously or unconsciously, let one aspect of their nonprofessional relationship with the client interfere with the treatment relationship. Kagle and Giebelhausen (1994) explained this as follows:

> Dual relationships involve boundary violations. They cross the line between the therapeutic relationship and a second relationship, undermining the distinctive nature of the therapeutic relationship, blurring the roles of practitioner and client, and permitting the abuse of power. (p. 217)

Barnett, Lazarus, Vasquez, Moorehead-Slaughter, and Johnson (2007); Gutheil and Gabbard (1993); and Younggren and Gottlieb (2004) delineated some of the most common areas in which boundaries may get crossed in therapy. These relate to the roles of therapist and clients, timing of therapy sessions, location of inter-actions, payment, attire, gifts, language, therapist self-disclosure, and physical contact.

Knapp and Slattery (2004) commented on how changes in service delivery, including the practice of providing service in the homes of certain clients, may raise new and challenging boundary and relationship issues. To help manage such situations, Knapp and Slattery, as well as Younggren and Gottlieb, offered valuable suggestions for questions to ask and risk management steps to undertake if contemplating such an approach. One area, however, in which there is universal agreement across all ethical codes, and for which serious legal strictures also apply, is the strict prohibition of sexual or romantic involvement with clients.

SEXUAL RELATIONSHIPS WITH CLIENTS

The most destructive and legally consequential forms of dual relationships are those involving romantic or sexual contacts with clients or with persons closely associated with clients (Pope, Keith-Spiegel, & Tabachnick, 2006). Recognizing this danger, the ethical codes of every major professional organization in the helping professions specifically prohibit sexual relationships with clients. Violation of this rule leads to almost certain sanction or dismissal from the professional organization and to loss of license. For interns and students in the helping professions, sexual misconduct will almost surely lead to dismissal from training, thereby ending one's career before it has begun.

In spite of ethical proscriptions and clinical concerns, Lamb, Catanzaro, and Moorman (2003) reported that 3.5% of respondents to a survey of professionals reported engaging in a prohibited relationship with clients, supervisees, or students.

Lest any therapist believe that having sex with clients is somehow beneficial to the client or that clients and therapists are just like any other adults and can freely engage in whatever relationships develop, the research and clinical evidence are clearly to the contrary. Bouhoutsos, Holroyd, Lerman, Forer, and Greenberg (1983) concluded that among those sampled in their research, the vast majority of cases involving therapist–client sex produced negative consequences for the client. At the very least, when sexual contacts develop, the therapy process is almost certain to be diverted from its original and legitimate goal and becomes obscured by or lost entirely in the sexual relationship. Therapists are also profoundly affected, with the majority of respondents to the Lamb et al. survey saying that their professional work was significantly impacted by the relationship, and 90% indicating that they would not do it again if the opportunity arose.

Survey data are further supported by the clinical experience of therapists who have treated clients whose former therapists engaged in sexual overtures or contact. Sloan, Edmond, Rubin, and Doughty (1998) reported that in a survey of social workers that 17% had at some point in their careers worked with at least one client who had been sexually exploited by a therapist. Pope and Bouhoutsos (1986) indicated that many clients who have formed sexual relationships with therapists find it extremely difficult ever again to trust a supposed "helping" professional. Such clients are described as suffering from what Pope and Bouhoutsos identified as "therapist–patient sex syndrome." Along with the feelings of

mistrust and guilt, many of the symptoms of this syndrome are similar to those of posttraumatic stress disorder (PTSD). Pope and Bouhoutsos also noted that there is an increased risk of suicide among clients who have been sexually abused by their therapist. This means that therapists who engage in such relationships with their clients are putting the clients at risk not only of psychological damage but also of death.

It should also be underscored that just as sexual intimacies with clients are expressly forbidden by ethical codes, such relationships with the cleints' relatives or significant others are also prohibited. Furthermore, it is unethical for therapists to accept as clients individuals with whom they have previously been sexually involved.

In addition to ethical standards and sanctions by professional organizations, many states have laws against such contact (Strasburger, Jorgenson, & Randles, 1991). This makes therapist–client sex not only an ethical matter but also a criminal one. The reason for such laws is that practitioners who are not members of professional organizations cannot be sanctioned by such organizations. Therefore, states have acted to make all practitioners responsible for ethical conduct, regardless of their membership status.

Along with criminal laws, in all states, the possibility of civil suits for damages exists (Jorgenson, Randles, & Strasburger, 1991), and malpractice insurance providers often limit protection against such suits. Thus, the costs of any damages would come directly from the therapist's financial or material assets.

Finally, the statute of limitations for sexual misconduct may offer therapists little protection. Unlike crimes such as theft or burglary, for which one cannot be prosecuted beyond a fixed period, in the case of sexual abuse, some states do not "start the clock" on the statute of limitations until the victim becomes aware of the damage. Thus, even if a client may have seemed a willing participant or may even have sought a relationship at one time, he or she might realize many years later that the relationship was harmful and sue as a result. It is also worth mentioning that there may be no statute of limitations in regard to disciplinary actions by licensing boards and professional organizations. There have been cases in which clients filed complaints with review boards for actions alleged to have occurred more than a decade earlier (E. Harris, February 3, 1995, personal communication).

MAINTAINING PROFESSIONAL BOUNDARIES AND DEALING WITH FEELINGS OF ATTRACTION

It should be clear from the discussion thus far that therapist–client sex is almost certain to have lasting and severe negative effects on the client, the therapist, and others, including family, friends, and professional colleagues, not to mention the profession itself.

These facts highlight the strictures against and consequences of therapist–client sex, but there is also a need to consider how to prevent sexual contact and how to train interns to deal with sexual issues in therapy more effectively (Clark, Rompf, & Walker, 2001; Reamer, 2003). This task is made at once more challenging and more important by the realization that it is not uncommon for therapists to feel attracted to clients. Indeed, Rodolfa et al. (1994) found that of the 389 survey respondents identified as working in university counseling centers, only 12% stated that they had never been attracted to a client. Similarly, Pope, Keith-Spiegel, and Tabachnick (1986) reported that among a sample of 575 psychotherapists, 87% of men and 76% of women reported having been sexually attracted to clients on at least one occasion.

Pope et al. (1986) emphasized several points that are particularly relevant to interns. Because it evidently is common for therapists to experience attraction to clients, it is essential to address this matter openly in training programs by recognizing the fundamental distinction between experiencing feelings of attraction and acting on those feelings. Students need to feel that it is safe to discuss feelings of attraction without fear that their instructors or supervisors will condemn, ridicule, or intrusively question them. In helping students understand and explore issues of attraction, instructors and supervisors must model the kind of professionalism they expect students to develop and exhibit as therapists.

In spite of such recommendations, a great deal of work still is needed in this area of training for supervisors and interns. Housman and Stake (1999) found that among students who had discussed their feelings of attraction to their clients with their supervisor, many did not develop an adequate understanding of the ethical boundaries regarding the attraction. On the one hand, a small but troublesome number (7%) apparently believed that sex with current clients could be ethical and therapeutic. On the other hand, 47% thought that any sexual feelings for clients were unacceptable. Whereas members of the former group may run into trouble because they have failed to understand ethical and clinical proscriptions on sexual relationships, the latter may have difficulty because they will be unlikely to deal therapeutically with any feelings of attraction that may arise.

Several authors have offered advice on how therapists can deal constructively with feelings of attraction that emerge in therapy. In the discussion of boundary violations alluded to earlier, Gutheil and Gabbard (1993) noted that role boundaries are fundamental to issues relating to boundary violations. They proposed a key question to help therapists understand and judge this issue: "Is this what a therapist does?" (p. 190).

Lamb et al. (2003), Gutheil and Gabbard (1993), Simon (1989), and Gabbard (1989) point out that in most instances, a common sequence of events leads to physical intimacy with clients. This sequence typically begins with apparently innocuous actions and then progresses to problematic levels. Referring to what they call the "slippery-slope" scenario, Gutheil and Gabbard described a

> transition from a last-name to first-name basis; then personal conversation intruding on the clinical work; then some body contact (e.g., pats on the shoulder, massages, progressing to hugs); then trips outside the office; then sessions during lunch, sometimes with alcoholic beverages; then dinner; then movies or other social events; and finally sexual intercourse. (p. 188)

Recognizing this sequence can provide an early-warning system for interns and therapists. If you find yourself dressing differently because you will see a certain client that day, if you are scheduling appointments late in the day or allowing sessions to run longer for some clients, if you are revealing more about your personal life than is typical, if you think about a client more than is normal for you when you are away from your office, if you are suggesting or accepting opportunities to meet outside therapy, or if other behaviors are beyond your usual conduct, you should recognize that something unusual is happening and should explore it in supervision.

Somer and Saadon (1999) offered further advice to help practitioners avoid actions that may lead, in small, seemingly insignificant increments, toward physical intimacy. Their suggestions include selecting office space in locations shared by other professionals, exercising special care in working with clients who are survivors of sexual abuse, limiting or avoiding physical consolation in times of crisis, maintaining careful records, and seeking consultation and supervision.

This issue is so important to the well-being of clients and therapists and to the integrity of the helping professions that it is incumbent on interns and professionals to deal with it responsibly and ethically. If during your internship, or at any time in your career, you find yourself crossing therapeutic boundaries and feeling sexually attracted to a client, or if a client is attracted to you, seek supervision. You will not be the first or the last person to find yourself in this situation, but it is essential that you deal with it professionally. Two excellent additional resources on this subject are Pope, Sonne, and Holroyd's (1993) *Sexual Feelings in Psychotherapy* and the APA video training guides, *Therapist/Client Boundary Challenges* and *Responding Therapeutically to Patient Expression of Sexual Attraction: A Stimulus Training Tape (2007).* The video format of these programs can be helpful because it shows ways in which clients might demonstrate sexual attraction to therapists and then offers responsible methods for dealing with such situations.

Nonsexual Dual Relationships

Because sexual relationships between therapists and clients can be so damaging, they have received the bulk of attention in discussions about the ethics of dual relationships. Less destructive, but still problematic, are dual relationships that do not involve sexual or romantic contact. Examples of such relationships were alluded to earlier; they include clients who are neighbors, fellow students, or coworkers (Reamer, 2003). Complex relationship issues can also develop when existing clients or close friends or acquaintances of the therapist refer new clients . It is not necessarily unethical to accept such referrals, but it is important to be aware of the ethical and clinical issues that can arise for both the client and the therapist (Moleski & Kiselica, 2005; Shapiro & Ginzberg, 2003; Younggren & Gottlieb, 2004).

In most instances, you can deal with ethically or clinically ambiguous situations by simply referring the individuals to other professionals. There are, however, conditions under which referral may not be practical. Campbell and Gordon (2003), Helbok et al. (2006), and Schank and Skovholt (1997) have all pointed out that few practitioners may be available in certain rural settings, where, sooner or later, practitioners are likely to have clients with whom they maintain some relationship apart from therapy. In rural settings, it is also likely that a practitioner who may not have known a client prior to beginning treatment will later encounter that person in some other role after treatment has begun. For example, a therapist might discover that a former or present client is a member of a service or social organization or is the coach of the opposing Little League or youth soccer team.

Barnett and Yutrzenka (1994) offered useful advice to professionals who, for reasons of geography or other factors, may treat persons with whom they have other relationships. Among other things, they recommended that professionals directly acknowledge their different relationships and seek to "compartmentalize roles, not relationships." In other words, professionals in rural communities must have their own identity and relate amicably to other community members, clients and non-clients alike. Compartmentalizing roles means that therapy issues should not be raised with clients outside the context of the therapy interaction, but issues outside therapy that might have an impact on the treatment process may need to be dealt with directly in therapy. This possibility should be addressed with clients at the beginning of treatment. Similar recommendations were offered by Schank and Skovholt (1997), who also addressed how overlapping relationships in small communities may affect members of the psychologist's family.

POST-THERAPY RELATIONSHIPS

A final area regarding dual relationships with clients concerns the nature of relationships allowed following therapy. With regard to romantic or sexual relationships after therapy has concluded, the ethical proscriptions vary somewhat across professions and are not as clearly stated as they are for such relationships during therapy. After much debate, the 2002 American Psychological Association's ethics code set a minimum time limit of two years, as did the American Association for Marriage and Family Therapy (2012), before a therapist could become romantically involved with a former client. The ACA ethics code (2005) sets a five-year prohibition on intimate relationships with former clients. Each of these codes also emphasizes that such relationships, although not prohibited under the codes, often have harmful effects, and even after the specified period they should only be considered ethical in extremely unusual circumstances and after careful consideration in which the onus falls on the professional to identify and prevent any potential harm. A similar approach is described by the NASW code of ethics, which states that social workers should not engage in sexual activities with former clients but then adds that if they do so and claim extraordinary circumstances, the burden of demonstrating that the client has not been harmed or exploited either intentionally or unintentionally falls fully on the social worker, not the client (NASW, 2008).

Given the ambiguity across ethical codes, the risks of harming a client, and the very real possibility of litigation, the current and safest advice in my judgment is to follow the same principles used with clients in therapy: There must not be a romantic relationship with a client ever—not before, during, or after the therapeutic relationship is established (for an extended and informative discussion, see Koocher and Keith-Spiegel, 2008). This principle was stated explicitly by the American Psychiatric Association, which voted in 1992 to declare sexual relationships with clients following therapy always unethical for psychiatrists (American Psychiatric Association, 1992). I concur with this position and believe it is the safest and most ethical position to take. Ruling

out any sexual relationship with clients at any time will help the therapist as well as the client avoid role or goal confusion during or after therapy and will help therapists recognize that their professional responsibility does not end when the formal therapy arrangement concludes.

Compared with sexual contacts, nonsexual and nonromantic relationships following therapy are less emotionally charged, but they nevertheless can pose important ethical and personal challenges for therapists and interns. Ethical codes provide less specific guidance regarding such contacts, but Anderson and Kitchener (1998) offered useful principles and decision-making criteria. They suggested considering four components in evaluating the ethics of a post-therapy relationship: (1) the nature and parameters of the therapeutic contract, (2) the dynamics of the therapeutic bond, (3) social roles, and (4) therapist motivation. Within each component, specific questions are presented to help the practitioner determine the issues involved and the proper course of action. Chapter 10 of this text also describes issues pertaining to closing cases and dealing with clients' desires to maintain contact after the intern leaves a placement.

RELATIONSHIPS BETWEEN EDUCATORS, SUPERVISORS, AND TRAINEES

The ethical guidelines for dual relationships identified in this chapter also apply to relationships among supervisors, instructors, and students (Congress, 2001; Gottlieb, Robinson, & Younggren, 2007; Kolbert, Morgan, & Brendel, 2002; Kress & Dixon, 2007). Much of the attention in this area has focused on sexual relationships between supervisors or instructors and students, but a number of other possible dual relationship issues can arise as well (Kolbert et al., 2002).

Just as sexual contact between therapists and clients breaks down the therapy process, sexual relationships between supervisors and interns are likely to interfere with the supervision process (Gottlieb et al., 2007). Recognizing this, the NASW code of ethics (2008), Section 2.07, explicitly states that social workers who "function as supervisors or educators should not engage in sexual activities or contact with supervisees, students, trainees, or other colleagues over whom they exercise professional authority." The 2010 APA code of ethics is also clear, stating in Section 7.07, "Psychologists do not engage in sexual relationships with students or supervisees who are in their department, agency, or training center or over whom psychologists are likely to have evaluative authority." Similarly, the 2005 ACA code, Section F.3(b), states, "Sexual or romantic interactions or relationships with current supervisees are prohibited."

In addition to impairing the direct supervisory relationship, the potential for sexual relationships between supervisor and trainee can also make open discussion about therapist–client attraction particularly difficult. At the conclusion of their 1986 article, Pope and colleagues stressed that in discussing issues of attraction, students must be safe from educators who might use such issues as openings to establish intimate relationships with the students themselves.

In spite of these clear proscriptions, research data suggest that sexual contacts between therapists and clients and between instructors and students are not uncommon. Pope, Levenson, and Schover (1979) reported that 16.5% of women respondents and 3% of male respondents reported that during their graduate training, they had sexual contact with their psychology educators. Among educators, 8% of women and 19% of men reported having engaged in sexual relations with someone they supervised. This survey also suggested that those who are involved in such interactions as students may be more likely to violate the comparable ethical standard as professionals. Comparable, though slightly lower, percentages were reported by Thoreson, Shaughnessy, Heppner, and Cook (1993).

Results similar to those of Pope and colleagues were reported by Robinson and Reid (1985), who found that 13% of women respondents indicated that they had had sexual contact with their educators during their graduate education. This research also indicated that 48% of the respondents had experienced some form of sexual harassment as graduate students. Consistent with studies suggesting that therapist–client sex is harmful to clients, 95% of those who had experienced sexual contact or harassment felt it was detrimental. In reviewing these and other studies of sexual contact or harassment, Bartell and Rubin (1990) noted that many respondents did not feel that sexual contact with instructors was coercive at the time it occurred. In retrospect, however, the majority saw some degree of coercion and considered it to be an ethical problem (Glaser & Thorpe, 1986).

Just as sexual contact between supervisors or instructors and students is prohibited by codes of ethics, sexual harassment is also considered unethical. Although such harassment is contrary to the ethical standards of the professions, the problems of educator–student sexual contact and harassment are real and ongoing. If you are placed in an uncomfortable position because of the unwanted comments or actions of an instructor, supervisor, coworker, or peer, you have the right to file a grievance and demand that the behavior be stopped. I suggest that students who are harassed file formal complaints with both their academic institution and any professional organizations or licensing bodies with which the harasser might be affiliated. For harassment to stop, everyone in the helping professions must understand the problem, adhere to the principles, seek supervision when necessary, and report violations whenever they occur. Then the consequences of violations must be certain, meaningful, and effective.

Though perhaps less volatile than sexual involvement or harassment, other forms of dual relationships can be problematic as well. Kolbert et al. (2002) and Congress (2001) described issues pertaining to social, business, and therapeutic relationships between supervisors and students. Kolbert et al. cautioned that faculty perceptions of which multiple roles are ethical may differ considerably from students' perceptions, with students expressing much greater concern about potential conflicts than faculty. For example, students expressed concern that friendships of some students with faculty or supervisors could lead to biased evaluations or jealousy among peers. There was also concern among students that in some instances the friendship might meet the instructor's needs rather than the student's. Students also feared that performance in nonacademic tasks, such as paid work for a faculty member, child care, and the like, could affect the faculty evaluation of the student's performance in an internship or in the classroom.

The key lesson from these findings should be that even though a faculty member or supervisor earnestly considers the ethical implications of involvement in nonsexual dual roles with students, the students themselves may experience those roles very differently but may be unlikely to express their concerns to the faculty or supervisor (Strom-Gottfried, 2000). Therefore, it is good practice to be aware of this possibility and to discuss it openly before any such relationships are entered into or at any point when they develop. For additional guidelines in dealing with multiple relationship issues in supervision, Gottlieb et al. (2007) offered a series of constructive and thought-provoking questions to help supervisors, administrators, and students evaluate the nature and consequences of any such relationships.

ETHICS IN CLASSES AND GROUPS

The preceding chapter described the potential benefits of internship classes or peer groups. As internship classes and groups often include case discussions, reviews of recordings, and role-plays, and since internship classes and groups deal with personal and sensitive issues, including those of the interns themselves, care must be taken to follow all of the ethical principles and practices that have been discussed thus far.

Prieto (1997) expressed concern about the dual relationship and "captive therapy" implications for students involved in group supervision that follows a group therapy model. Similar concerns were also addressed by Sklare, Thomas, Williams, and Powers (1996) and in the responses reported by Bogo, Globerman, and Sussman (2004). The essence of these concerns is that group supervision and learning can easily cross the line and become much like group therapy, with students feeling compelled to explore personal issues in front of their peers and instructor. Complications arising from this may include dual relationships when instructors function as both teacher and therapist. In addition, students legitimately fear that disclosing personal information might affect their grades. Sklare and colleagues recommended keeping a "here-and-now" focus in the group as a way of reducing these concerns. Prieto went a step further and advocated following a pedagogic, didactic construct as opposed to a therapeutic construct to guide group instruction and supervision. Whichever approach is chosen, it is important for instructors and students to be clear about the purpose of the activities and about their respective boundaries, roles, rights, and responsibilities.

Protecting client confidentiality is another area of concern that arises in class discussions. In most internship classes, it is standard practice for interns to review clients and clinical experiences as part of the class. Sensitive to issues of ethics, interns rightly ask if bringing case material to class is a violation of their client's or placement site's confidentiality.

This is admittedly a somewhat gray area, without a definitive answer. Measures, however, can and should be taken to lessen the possibility of confidentiality breaches. The first step is for each member of the internship class to know about the principle of confidentiality and agree to keep whatever occurs during the internship class strictly confidential. This means that students do not discuss class material with anyone beyond the confines of the class. Confidentiality is important because in addition to reviewing their cases, students and trainees must feel safe to acknowledge their own concerns, weaknesses, fears, and personal issues relating to their training. They must also be able to discuss cases and clients without fear that confidential information will go beyond the confines of the internship class or group.

Many institutional agreements with internship sites include a clause explaining that interns will be expected to discuss clients and clinical experiences with their instructor and during the class as part of their educational process. Interns are also instructed to tell clients from the outset that they may discuss the case with their instructor or supervisor and in the internship class. Interns are advised to tell clients that the client's identity will be protected in such discussions and that the discussion will be strictly for educational purposes.

Before recording therapy sessions or using recordings in class, you must obtain written permission from the client. The ethical principles of informed consent and confidentiality require that if a clinical session is to be recorded, everyone involved in the session must give permission. Written permission-to-record forms should specify precisely the purpose of the recording, how the recordings will be used, the period for which this use will be authorized, and what will happen to the recording at the end of the period. Clients must have the right to refuse recording clearly explained to them, and they must not be coerced into giving permission. Clients must be given information about the purpose of the recording and the confidentiality of the information. Clients should also be informed that the recordings will be shared only with the supervisor and class, that information will be kept strictly confidential, and that it will be erased by a specified date or immediately after the class use.

Another step to preserve confidentiality is that when interns discuss cases in class or write about them in a journal, they must protect the identity of clients. As discussed in previous chapters, interns may use a standard identification such as simply Mr. X or Ms. X to describe all clients. Interns are also instructed that if speaking about the details of a case might reveal the identity of the individual, even without explicitly saying the client's name, the intern should discuss the case with the instructor before raising it in class. This is particularly important if interns are working in a college counseling center or other setting where the identity of student clients might easily be discernible to other interns who also know the client. In such instances, caution is required, and on occasion it is better not to discuss a case in class if confidentiality cannot be preserved. For example, an intern might be working with a student body officer whose identity would necessarily be compromised in class simply because of the concerns being addressed in the case discussion. A similar situation might exist if recorded therapy sessions would reveal a client's distinctive voice and thus the identity of the person might become known to others in the class. Under such circumstances, the need to protect the client's confidentiality outweighs the educational benefit to the class.

Case material and information about clients is not all that must be protected by confidentiality. During internship classes, interns themselves often bring up highly personal material that must be accorded the same respect and protection. Because clinical work is so demanding and often touches on issues from the intern's own life, it is vital that interns feel they can trust their classmates enough to explore whatever arises. In other classes,

it might be acceptable for a student to tell a roommate something like, "You'll never believe what another student said in class today," but this is absolutely unacceptable for students in an internship class. Confidentiality is essential to your role as a professional, and the internship is the place to establish ethical standards that you will practice throughout your career.

LIABILITY AND INSURANCE

Just as you need to understand the principles of ethics and laws pertaining to your profession, you should also know about professional liability and liability insurance. As pointed out in Chapter 2, interns are less likely than practicing professionals to be the target of malpractice lawsuits, but they are by no means immune (Gelman et al., 1996). For this reason, VauPitts (1992) urged counseling programs to require liability insurance for all practicum and internship students. In addition to providing financial protection, VauPitts pointed out that obtaining such insurance acquaints students with "this reality of professional life" (p. 207).

Because many students will not be familiar with liability claims and the purpose of liability insurance, a brief review may be helpful. For a more extensive discussion, see Bennett et al. (2005).

ELEMENTS OF MALPRACTICE

Malpractice suits are special cases within the broader category of negligence. By virtue of their professional status and their relationship with clients, those in the helping professions have a responsibility to provide care that meets the standards of their profession. If a professional is sued for malpractice, plaintiffs must successfully prove each of four critical elements: (1) the existence of a professional relationship between therapist and client, (2) the existence of a standard of care and the failure of the practitioner to meet that standard in the care of the client, (3) the client suffered some form of harm or injury, and (4) the client's harm or injury was caused by the practitioner's failure to meet the standard of care (Bennett et al., 2005).

The best way to deal with lawsuits is to prevent them from happening by practicing within the standards of one's profession, scrupulously adhering to ethical codes, and thoroughly documenting what you do and why. To help reduce the risk of liability claims, leading association insurance programs have instituted risk management practices (Reamer, 2005b) and published guidelines and books with useful suggestions, checklists, and other resources. See, for example, the book by Bennett et al. (2005) and the Web-based program "Understanding Malpractice Risk: What Social Workers Can Do" (http://www.naswwebed.org/). In addition, some organizations, such as the American Association for Marriage and Family Therapy (AAMFT), have instituted comprehensive "Legal Risk Management Plans" that offer members legal consultation, resource material, and legal services.

LIABILITY INSURANCE

Bennett et al. (2005) emphasized that practitioners should have insurance for several reasons. Even if one's practice is perfectly within standards, there is no guarantee that a lawsuit will not be filed or that one would emerge unscathed from such a suit. A practitioner who is successfully sued could be required to pay damages as high or higher than hundreds of thousands of dollars and into the millions. Furthermore, regardless of outcome, the process of defending against the suit can be financially and emotionally expensive. An added benefit of insurance is that some providers, including each of the insurers in the list that follows, have begun to provide toll-free legal consultation. The goal of this service is to prevent problems from developing or to catch them as early as possible.

The cost of liability insurance for psychologists, counselors, social workers, and others remains low relative to some medical professions. Still, the frequency and size of claims have increased, as has the cost of insurance. Fortunately, liability insurance is available to interns for much lower rates than for fully licensed professionals, and organizations, for example, as discussed in Chapter 2, the AAMFT, ASCA, ACA, and others have begun to include access to liability insurance as part of student membership in the organization. Interns can obtain more information about such insurance by contacting their national organizations or insurance providers. Sources of information for key associations can be obtained at

http://www.aamft.org/

http://www.acait.com/

http://www.apait.org/

http://www.naswinsurancetrust.org/

http://www.schoolcounselor.org

When you look into liability insurance, you will discover two types of policies: (1) claims based and (2) occurrence based. Understanding the differences between policies is important because the type of policy you choose will influence how much you pay and how you are covered. In general, occurrence-based policies are preferable for interns for reasons that will be explained shortly, but let us first consider how claims-based policies function.

Claims-based insurance provides coverage for acts that occur during the time you are insured as long as you hold the policy continuously, but the coverage stops when you no longer carry the policy. This means that if you let a policy expire or choose to retire and no longer carry the policy, your insurer would no longer provide coverage even if you are sued for something that occurred when you did practice and did have the policy. In other words, when you discontinue the policy, your protection is also discontinued, regardless of when the event for which you are being sued occurred. As an intern, if you have a claims-based policy during your internship but then forget or choose not to continue your policy, once your policy is discontinued, you would have no protection should someone sue you retroactively for actions that occurred during your internship even if you had been covered by a claims policy at that time.

For practitioners planning long and continuous careers, the advantage of claims-based policies is that they are usually less expensive than occurrence-based policies during the first years

they are held. However, the cost increases with each subsequent year because the insurer is then providing protection for the year in which the policy is now held, as well as for events that may have occurred in previous years. You can, however, purchase special coverage called a *tail* or *rider,* which will insure you for a period following termination of your regular policy. Some policies also carry a clause that if one has held claims-based insurance for a number of years and then retires from practice, the tail coverage is applied free of charge.

An occurrence-based policy typically makes more sense for interns. The reason is that occurrence policies provide protection for events that occur during the time you held the policy, regardless of whether or not you are still carrying the insurance at the time you are sued and regardless of whether or not you may have gone for a subsequent period without coverage. As described by the APAIT: "An occurrence policy protects you from any incident occurring while the policy is in force. The policy then covers those incidents forever" (APAIT, http://www.apait.org/apait /products/professionalliability/faq/claimsmade.aspx#1).

This type of policy is typically more expensive to begin with, but once you purchase an occurrence policy, you are covered forever for the period in which you held the insurance. If someone sues you for an event that happened five years earlier, you will be covered under the terms of the policy as long as you held an occurrence-based policy at that time, even though you may not hold the policy at the time you are actually sued. With an occurrence-based policy, there is no need to purchase a tail.

In recent years, in an effort to manage risks and control costs, liability insurance companies have been shifting more toward claims-based policies and away from occurrence-based plans (Zuckerman, 2008). Again, however, because students may go on to other studies or careers and are likely to have periods in which they no longer participate in service delivery, occurrence policies generally make more sense even if they cost more initially.

As you evaluate different types of liability insurance policies, be sure to examine matters other than simply price and the surface differences between claims- or occurrence-based policies. Here are some other factors you should consider: What types of activities, situations, or expenses are not covered under the policy? Does the coverage include defense costs along with damages in the payment limits, or are these figured separately? What is the financial security and history of the company providing the insurance? (If your insurance provider goes bankrupt, you effectively become uninsured.)

This discussion has been intended to provide an introductory overview and should not be taken as constituting legal or financial advice. As with all insurance, it is essential to read the conditions of the terms carefully and to compare policies offered by different providers. This is particularly important in the case of malpractice insurance for interns. Such coverage may not apply to all internship placements or all activities of interns. Be sure that you understand the nature and limitations of any coverage your internship provides or you purchase for yourself, and consider these factors carefully in light of your own activities as a student, an intern, or an employee.

TECHNOLOGY AND ETHICS

Before concluding this chapter's discussion of clinical ethics, further discussion is in order about the use of technology and the ethical implications for interns and practitioners.

Clinically, technological advances have introduced new categories of presenting concerns, including Internet gambling, addiction to online pornography, identity theft, and failed Internet relationships (Mitchell, Becker-Blease, & Finkelhor, 2005). At the same time, technology has also become part of the treatment repertoire, with applications ranging from online counseling sessions (APA Task Force on Telepsychotherapy, 2011; Baker & Bufka, 2011; Harwood et al., 2011; Trepal, Haberstroh, Duffey, & Evans, 2007; Yuen, Geotter, Herbert, & Forman, 2012) and telephone-based interventions to automated computerized treatment protocols. The scope of this impact is reflected in proposals for specializations, such as the call by Parker-Oliver and Demiris (2006) for the establishment of "Social Work Informatics" as a specialty area within the field of social work.

From an ethical perspective, several areas are most relevant to our discussion in this chapter. We have already reviewed some of the issues relating to informed consent and electronic storage and communication of information, particularly as related to confidentiality, EMRs, and HIPAA rules. In addition to these issues, new ethical issues are raised by the increasing use of electronic media to provide clinical services through the telephone, the Internet, or specialized computer interventions (APA, 2011; Barnett & Scheetz, 2003; Collins, 2007; Ragusea & VandeCreek, 2003). Unique ethical and clinical issues are also associated with supervision, either computer based or provided remotely via the Internet (Barnett, 2011; Chapman, Baker, Nassar-McMillan, & Gerler, 2011; Clingerman & Bernard, 2004; Kanz, 2001; Kolmes, 2012; Vaccaro & Lambie, 2007; Wood, Miller, & Hargrove, 2005; Yuen et al., 2012). For comprehensive reviews of ethical and clinical issues pertaining to multiple aspects of telecommunication see *Professional Psychology: Research and Practice* (2012, *43*[6] & 2011, *42*[6]).

Particularly complex and fraught with risk is the fact that traditional regulation of health care delivery is based on a state-by-state regulatory and legal model. Harris and Younggren (2011) describe multiple ways in which this model is complicated by online service delivery across state and even national lines. These authors also offer a number of practical measures that can be taken to reduce risks in this evolving process.

For clinicians who are considering expanding their practice to include some form of telehealth or other technological intervention, Glueckauf, Pickett, Ketterson, Loomis, & Rozensky (2003) offered a framework of issues to be considered. Using the acronym STEPS, their framework addresses (1) state regulatory and licensure issues, (2) technology, (3) ethics, (4) personal relationship issues, and (5) specific training requirements, as they all pertain to the unique issues associated with technology. From the perspective of outcomes and efficacy, confidentiality, quality assurance, risk management, professional licensing, and regulatory oversight have all been identified among the issues

such services raise (Barnett & Scheetz, 2003; Koocher & Morray, 2000; Ragusea & VandeCreek, 2003).

Group work on the Internet also presents novel ethical and clinical issues (Humphreys, Winzelberg, & Klaw, 2000), as does family therapy and the training and supervision of therapists (Baltimore, 2000). Woody (1999) pointed out that technologies may also open some surprising and easily overlooked avenues for confidentiality breaches within families. For example, as noted earlier, voice, email or text messages may be retrieved by family members other than the client.

In response to these and other ethical concerns, the latest ACA code of ethics (2005) includes an extended section (A.12) specifically detailing ethical issues associated with technology, including the benefits and limitations of technology applications, determination that technology is an appropriate vehicle for services to specific clients, access to technology, application of state and national laws, guidelines for websites, and a detailed listing of informed consent practices including security and confidentiality issues. The National Association of Social Workers (NASW) code of ethics does not go into as much detail about technology but does contain specific references to electronic media, as in Section 1.03 (e), which advises that social workers providing services through electronic media must "inform recipients of the limitations and risks associated with such services." The introduction to the APA ethics code indicates that the code applies to activities including "telephone, Internet, and other electronic transmissions," but apart from this statement, the APA Ethics Committee has not yet incorporated technology issues directly into the APA code.

In an interesting but troubling empirical study of how well some of these ethical standards, notably those of the National Board of Certified Counselors, are being met by online "Web counseling" services, Heinlen et al. (2003) reported a host of shortcomings and generally low levels of compliance with ethical standards among the websites and services they surveyed. Of special concern, from both ethical and clinical perspectives, was their finding that more than a third of the sites they studied were no longer in operation just eight months later. Similar results were obtained by Shaw and Shaw (2006), who evaluated counseling websites based on a 16-item checklist reflecting the ACA ethical standards for online counseling (ACA, 1999). Their results showed that fewer than half of the websites studied were adhering to recommended practices on 8 of 16 items.

If you happen to become involved in some form of technological service delivery as part of your internship or later in practice, you can avoid some of these ethical pitfalls by following sound general ethical practices and by incorporating certain measures specifically geared toward technology. A good place to start would be to review the specific technology-related ethical guidelines mentioned earlier. You might also want to evaluate your activities in comparison with the checklists developed by Schwartz and Lonborg (2011) and Shaw and Shaw (2006). In addition, Maheu (2003) described a comprehensive clinical practice model that includes seven stages: (1) training, (2) referrals, (3) client education, (4) consent, (5) assessment, (6) direct care, and (7) reimbursement.

In many ways, the guidelines offered by these authors reflect the key principles addressed throughout this chapter, with the additional application to technology. For example, Koocher and Morray (2000) began with the principle of "competence" but pointed out that unique technical as well as clinical competencies are required for remote delivery of services. They also emphasized that, to date, there is no consensus on standards of care and that data concerning treatment efficacy may be limited. In order to ensure that liability insurance will protect a practitioner providing remote services, consultation with liability insurance carriers is recommended. Guidelines must also be established for crisis care or emergency situations, given that the location of the client might be far from that of the therapist. Confidentiality limitations must also be discussed with clients and documented, with particular attention to the limited confidentiality of online communications, computerized records, and cellular or other wireless phone conversations. Ragusea and VandeCreek (2003) give particular attention to website designs, with an emphasis on the unique demands of informed consent with technology, and on such matters as establishing and verifying client identities and locations.

The final topic to be discussed has to do with the use of social networking by interns. Of special importance in this context are the clinical implications of how your online presence and activities may impact your treatment work and the risks of violating confidentiality or other ethical considerations (Kolmes, 2012).

A particularly useful reference in this regard is the article by Meyers, Endres, Ruddy, and Zelikovsky (2012). As these authors point out, many interns have given little thought to how their online presence on social networking sites may be accessed by clients and the possible effects this will have on the treatment relationship. Not surprisingly, clients and for that matter coworkers, like anyone else, are increasingly likely to look on search engines or social networking sites for information about the people who are treating or working with them, and this includes interns. Potential personal safety and privacy concerns this raises are discussed in some detail in Chapter 9, but also consider how what you post or tweet online will reflect on your image and role as a professional and its possible impact on your treatment relationship.

For example, suppose an intern goes on a spring break vacation that involves drinking, possibly suggestive photos, and other rather common college activities and postings. For friends, this might be all in good fun, but if accessed by clients, it could seriously diminish respect for the intern as a professional. So too, suppose you circulate what you think is a funny joke, but it has racist, sexist, or other overtones that might be offensive. How would this look to a supervisor, colleague, or client?

Of special risk is the possibility that an intern would text, blog, or tweet messages about what is happening on his or her internship site or with a particular client. Imagine, for example, a tweet saying: "2 gross at wrk. Client made me sick and staff made me sicker. What am I doing here?" Riskier still would be an intern confiding in a friend about specific clinical issues with specific clients.

To help reduce such risks, it is always a good idea before posting anything online to recognize that NOTHING ON THE INTERNET IS PRIVATE!!! and imagine how what you say would look in a headline or if read personally by someone you are writing about without their knowledge or consent.

To help ensure that this discussion is not simply a discussion but a stimulus for action, I strongly encourage you to review and actually take the steps described in the exercise that follows.

EXERCISE: CHECKING, CORRECTING, AND MANAGING YOUR ONLINE PRESENCE

Consider the preceding discussion of social networking and online presence in the context of ethics and treatment considerations, and in light of the security issues discussed later in Chapter 9. Now, take some time to carefully and systematically review your own online presence. This should include checking your security and access settings and should also entail a review of the content you have posted. Provocative statements, photos, links, and so on are all worth revisiting with the following questions in mind: "How does this content reflect on me as a professional?" "How might this content impact clients, supervisors, colleagues, or others who might read it?" "Does my online presence and information create any personal security risks?" "Is there anything I have posted or am about to post that might constitute an ethical breach, particularly in regard to confidentiality issues?" In addition to conducting your own review, it is a good idea to ask a colleague or friend you trust to review the material independently to give you feedback about what is there and what might be removed, limited, or changed. Finally, it is sound practice after reviewing your online presence to not only change any existing problems but also carefully consider any future postings in the same light.

RESEARCH ETHICS

This chapter has primarily focused on ethical and legal issues pertaining to clinical practice, but interns who are involved in research activities, either as part of their thesis or dissertation or in some other capacity, must also be aware of the ethical principles and guidelines concerning experimental and clinical research (Wester, 2007). Extensive discussion of these guidelines is beyond the scope of this text, but many of the same principles that apply to clinical practice (e.g., informed consent, confidentiality) also apply to research. Each of the major ethical codes includes sections specifically dedicated to research ethics.

If you participate in any way in research as part of your internship, carefully study the ethical principles for research in your profession as well as any relevant laws or regulations. Perhaps not surprisingly, HIPAA also includes specific research guidelines and requirements that you should know and follow. You should also be aware that most academic and clinical settings conducting research have established review boards, often called "human participant review boards," that carefully study the ethical qualities of any research performed under their aegis or by their personnel. Before initiating any study, consult the research board of both your academic institution and your placement agency, and, of course, work closely with your instructor and your supervisor.

ETHICAL AND PROFESSIONAL CONCERNS ABOUT COLLEAGUES

Before concluding this discussion, it is important to raise a difficult topic that is part of all of our responsibilities as professionals but is too often neglected in training and in practice. I am referring to the matter of how one deals with clinical or ethical lapses by fellow interns or professionals (Forrest, Elman, Gizara, & Vacha-Haase, 1999; Johnson et al., 2012).

This issue is important for multiple reasons. First, colleagues who are acting unethically or not using sound judgment and clinical techniques are endangering the well-being of clients. Second, when one member of a profession violates rules or performs inadequately, the profession as a whole suffers in reputation, and that, in turn, harms not only the members of the profession but also other clients who might benefit from proper treatment but do not participate because of the effects of irresponsible practitioners. Professionals, clients, and society as a whole suffer in another way through increased liability insurance premiums resulting from malpractice claims against the few bad practitioners. These costs ultimately contribute to the overall increases in the costs of health care.

Later, in Chapter 8, we discuss the stresses facing interns and professionals and review literature examining the incidence of impaired or problematic students, as well as the mechanisms for self-care. For present purposes, it is sufficient to note, as many studies have indicated, that the factors impairing the ability of interns to perform adequately, whether academically or clinically, are by no means uncommon (Clay, 2012; Shen-Miller et al., 2011). Indeed, estimates of the incidence of impaired or problematic trainees range somewhere between 45% and 12%, depending on the study. What is more, interns generally believe that such issues are not dealt with well by training programs, and most interns apparently do not act affirmatively to notify training directors of their concerns (Oliver, Bernstein, Anderson, Blashfield, & Roberts, 2004; Rosenberg, Getzelman, Arcinue, & Oren, 2005).

These findings are troubling in many ways. In the context of our present discussion of ethics, all of the major ethical codes contain language explicitly addressing the importance of being alert to signs that we ourselves might not be functioning optimally. Interestingly, and to their credit, respondents in the Rosenberg et al. (2005) study indicated that if they were the subject of concerns by their peers or colleagues, they would want others to let them know of the concerns so that they could address them directly. This attitude is consistent with the previously described communitarian model advocated by Johnson et al. (2012).

The ethics codes also contain language indicating that professionals have a responsibility to deal with colleagues who may be acting unethically or non-therapeutically. In the studies by Oliver et al. (2004) and Rosenberg et al. (2005), this was unfortunately the exception rather than the rule. Behnke (2006) pointed out that although it may be difficult to confront the shortcomings or transgressions of a colleague, each of us accepts this responsibility and accepts that others may also hold us accountable, by virtue of having willingly signed up for the profession to begin with. Behnke emphasizes that the central principles of ethics, such as beneficence, dictate that we must not knowingly allow clients, our own or others', to be harmed. At the same time, however, Behnke identified a number of potential obstacles, such as uncertainty, fear of retaliation, the personal and time commitment required to see a complaint through, empathy for or personal loyalty to the individual in question, and other factors that may inhibit our willingness to take the necessary steps to address a problem.

What then should you do if you have concerns about a colleague? Wilkerson (2006) and Forrest et al. (1999) offered a series of suggestions for how faculty and supervisors can respond more effectively to the issue of problematic interns. How you proceed personally will depend on a number of factors, including the nature and severity of your concerns, your relationship with the individual in question, and the resources available to you. For simplicity, two broad categories of response are available—informal and formal. As always, consult with your supervisor and instructor before taking any action, unless, of course, your concerns happen to be with one of those same individuals. In such instances, consider consulting with another member of your academic department or another staff member at your training site.

Informal responses to ethical or professional concerns generally entail working either directly or indirectly with the individuals involved to address the matter. This route is usually most appropriate when there is some ambiguity about the concerns and when there is a basic level of trust and respect that allows for direct communication. One possible resource in this process is the increasing availability of colleague assistance programs in the different helping professions (Clay, 2012). These programs are typically established at the state level by professional associations, sometimes in collaboration with licensing boards, to provide assistance to practitioners who may be struggling with personal, ethical, or competence issues. Referring a colleague to such resources can be a caring and constructive way to help him or her receive needed assistance.

When considering informal resolutions, keep in mind that they are best chosen when the concerns do not represent severe breaches of fundamental ethics or gross violations of professional standards or performance that could endanger clients. If serious ethical transgressions have occurred (e.g., sexual relations with clients), it can be irresponsible to seek informal resolution because the alleged perpetrator can too easily pass the situation off with an apology and may well go on to repeat the offense in the future.

Severe matters call for more formal responses. Two primary elements of such responses would be the filing of formal complaints with the relevant professional association and with the state licensing board. One may also choose to make a formal complaint to the personnel office or board of directors of the placement site. Obviously, taking this step is a very consequential matter that could impact the career of the person involved. As such, it should not be entered into lightly. On the other hand, if a perceived violation or lapse is severe, neither should one lightly avoid filing formal complaints. Remember that although we have an obligation to our colleagues, we also have an obligation to clients and to the profession. This point was emphasized by Van Horne (2004) and Kirkland, Kirkland, and Reaves (2004), who reviewed data from state and provincial disciplinary boards and described how formal complaints are filed, investigated, and resolved.

I have rarely met a fellow professional who has not, at some time in his or her career, encountered a peer who seemed to be either incompetent or unethical. Behnke (2006) offered a similar observation. What is troubling is that when asked if these concerns were followed up on in any meaningful way, the answer, more often than not, is no, followed by some form of rationalization.

If we are truly committed to helping others, and if we are truly committed to our profession and the responsibility that entails, I believe more professionals need to step forward and make the tough decision to report and follow through when violations of ethics or practice are observed. If we fail to do this, we are letting down our clients, the rest of our colleagues, our interns and students, and ultimately ourselves. We are also, I should emphasize, violating our respective codes of ethics.

ESTABLISHING A PERSONAL, CORE ETHICAL IDENTITY AND A CENTRAL COMMITMENT TO ETHICAL CONDUCT

To conclude this chapter, one final and fundamental truth must be emphasized above all others. The truth is this: All of the material discussed in this chapter, and all of the information you receive from other coursework and training will ultimately have an impact only if you as an individual place ethical professional conduct central to who you are and how you conduct yourself as a person and as a professional.

This core truth about personal values, motivation, and conduct is vital because research and common sense demonstrate that a great many ethical violations occur not because people did not know what the standards were but because they knew the standards and for a variety of reasons chose to ignore them.

The question then is, "How do you develop your own strong ethical core values and conduct and how do you maintain, deepen, and strengthen that throughout your professional and personal life?" For guidance in answering this question, a number of sources offer useful insights. One of the more intriguing and thought-provoking studies of ethics and professionalism that I have come across is the extensive series of interviews conducted by Howard Gardner and colleagues and chronicled in *Responsibility at Work* (Gardner, 2007). Drawing on more than 1200 interviews with working Americans in nine fields, these researchers sought to identify the key elements and key exemplars of what they refer to as "Good Work," that is, work that is "socially responsible, ethical, and moral."

The entire book is relevant and of interest, but one of the most compelling essays is the chapter entitled "Taking Ultimate Responsibility," by William Damon and Kendall Cotton Bronk, who consider what makes some people accept and act on a sense of "ultimate responsibility," whereas others seem to disregard or avoid accepting responsibility. Damon and Bronk assert that the foundation for ultimate responsibility includes a strong sense of moral purpose that is the center of one's moral identity. Consistent with the writings of Johnson et al. (2012), they also emphasize the importance of institutional and organizational support from a group of respected peers and mentors.

From this foundation, a distinct difference emerges between the intellectual recognition of something as a moral or ethical issue and the deeply significant personal decision that "I myself must take this course" (p. 25). For this to occur, Damon and Bronk assert that people must make personal moral or ethical conduct central to their self-concept and to their life goals.

Within the workplace, Damon and Bronk's research distinguishes three types of responsibility: responsibility for the ethical conduct of the organization and workers, responsibility to the business goals and purpose of the organization, and responsibility to broader social and community interests. Applied to your clinical training and professional future, this means you must set high standards for your personal professional competence and conduct and must help create and participate in organizations that encourage, embody, and support such competence and conduct.

A number of elements can contribute to bringing about this personal and organizational development. Throughout this text, individual exercises encourage your personal exploration and understanding. This process of introspection is intentional. Ethical and personal development is an ongoing endeavor that advances only when we continually examine, evaluate, challenge, and enhance our awareness of how we personally embody ideals not only in our expressed values but in our actual behavior.

In addition to introspection and personal review, it is also especially beneficial to consider role models or exemplars of ethical professionalism. Hamilton and Monson (2012) emphasize this point in the realm of ethics and law by calling for a transformation in how legal ethics are taught. Rather than simply teaching the facts about ethical codes of conduct, these authors assert that trainees must be exposed to real-life examples of people who put ethics into practice in the real world and who make ethics core to their being and identity. Also important is the recognition that ethical development is not a static body of knowledge that is mastered but, rather, a dynamic and deepening awareness of the complexity of ethical principles and challenges. By studying how ethical exemplars develop as professionals, and by learning from how such individuals deal with difficult ethical situations, sometimes at great personal cost, we can gain not only greater personal understanding but also greater personal motivation to conduct ourselves in a similar fashion.

In your own personal approach to professional and ethical development, I encourage you to seek out exemplars from within your field and beyond who you believe embody a strong sense of ethical and professional integrity. This could be through reading biographies or, better still, by meeting with and really getting to know individuals you consider role models.

Throughout this process, a core question should underlie not only your intellectual study of ethics but also your personal examination of your values, knowledge, and actions: "Who am I as a professional and as a person, and how do my core values and understandings guide my decisions, choices, and conduct?"

If you keep this question present in your personal life and professional development; if you recognize that life and ethics are complex and dynamic; if you are guided by a deep sense of empathy and concern for the well-being of others; and if you are willing to listen to, study, and learn from the example and advice of others, your chances of becoming an ethical and professional exemplar yourself will be greatly enhanced.

SUMMARY

Ethical guidelines exist to protect the well-being of clients, practitioners, and the profession. As a trainee, it is incumbent on you to be well versed in the ethical principles established by your profession, by state and federal laws, and within your work settings. It is also essential to develop your personal understanding and commitment to ethical professionalism. This chapter has reviewed the key ethical issues that are most relevant to interns, but you are strongly advised to review the ethical standards of your profession as well as all relevant state and federal laws. Get to know these issues well, and discuss them with your peers, instructors, and supervisors. I suggest that you make it a personal habit to conduct a regular "ethics audit," as described by Reamer (2000). As noted throughout this chapter, ethical and legal standards evolve and change over time, and I fully expect that some of the issues addressed in this chapter will have evolved between this edition and the next one. Keeping up with such changes is part of the responsibility you are accepting in seeking to become a professional.

REFERENCES

Acuff, C., Bennett, B., Bricklin, P., Canter, M., Knapp, S., Moldawsky, S., & Phelps, R. (1999). Considerations for ethical practice in managed care. *Professional Psychology: Research and Practice, 30*(6), 563–575.

American Association for Marriage and Family Therapy (2012). AAMFT code of ethics. Retrieved from http://www.aamft.org/imis15/content /legal_ethics/code_of_ethics.aspx

American Counseling Association. (2005) ACA code of ethics. Retrieved from http://www.ncblpc.org/Laws_and_Codes/ACA_Code_of_ Ethics.pdf

American Psychiatric Association. (1992). Assembly takes strong stance on patient–doctor sex. *Psychiatric News, 1,* 20.

American Psychological Association. (2007). *Responding therapeutically to patient expression of sexual attraction: A stimulus training tape.* Washington, DC: Author.

American Psychological Association. (2005). Determination and documentation of the need for practice guidelines. *American Psychologist, 60,* 976–978.

American Psychological Association. (2010). Ethical principles of psychologists and code of conduct. Retrieved from http://www.apa.org /ethics/code/index.aspx?item=3

American Psychological Association Committee on Legal Issues. (2006). Strategies for private practitioners coping with subpoenas or compelled testimony for client records or test data. *Professional Psychology: Research and Practice, 37,* 215–222.

American Psychological Association Committee on Professional Standards and Practice. (2003). Legal issues in the professional practice of psychology. *Professional Psychology: Research and Practice, 34,* 595–600.

American Psychological Association Ethics Committee (2012). Ethics Committee: 2011 Annual Report. Retrieved from http://www.apa .org/about/governance/bdcmte/2011-ethics.aspx

American Psychological Association Practice Organization. (2006). Privacy compliance is not enough: Three things you should know about the HIPAA security rule. *Good Practice, 1,* 9–10.

American Psychological Association Policy and Planning Board. (2009). How technology changes everything (and nothing) in psychology. *American Psychologist, 64,* 454–463.

American Psychological Association Task Force on Telepsychotherapy. (2011) Report from the Task Force on Telepsychotherapy. Retrieved from http://www.divisionofpsychotherapy.org/report -from-the-task-force-on-telepsychotherapy/

American School Counselor Association. (2010). Ethical standards for school counselors. Retrieved from http://www.schoolcounselor.org /files/EthicalStandards2010.pdf

Anderson, J. R., & Barret, B. (2001). *Ethics in HIV-related psychotherapy: Clinical decision making in complex cases.* Washington, DC: American Psychological Association.

Anderson, S. K., & Kitchner, K. S. (1998). Nonsexual post-therapy relationships: A conceptual framework to assess ethical risk. *Professional Psychology: Research and Practice, 29,* 91–99.

Arredondo, P., & Perez, P. (2006). Historical perspectives on the multicultural guidelines and contemporary applications. *Professional Psychology: Research and Practice, 37,* 1–5.

Baerger, D. R. (2001). Risk management with the suicidal patient: Lessons from case law. *Professional Psychology: Research and Practice, 32,* 359–366.

Baker, D. C., & Bufka, L. F. (2011) Preparing for the telehealth world: Navigating legal, regulatory, reimbursement, and ethical issues in an electronic age. *Professional Psychology: Research and Practice, 42*(6), 405–411.

Baltimore, M. (2000). Ethical consideration in the use of technology for marriage and family counselors. *Family Journal, 8*(4), 390–394.

Barnett, J. E. (2005). Important ethical, legal issues surround supervision role. *National Psychologist, 14*(3), 16.

Barnett, J. E. (2011). Utilizing technological innovations to enhance psychotherapy supervision, training, and outcomes. *Psychotherapy, 48*(2), 103–108.

Barnett, J. E., Behnke, S. H., Rosenthal, S. L., & Koocher, G. P. (2007). In case of ethical dilemma, break glass: Commentary on ethical decision making in practice. *Professional Psychology: Research and Practice, 38,* 7–12.

Barnett, J. E., Lazarus, A. A., Vasquez, M. J. T., Morehead-Slaughter, O., & Johnson, W. B. (2007). Boundary issues and multiple relationships: Fantasy and reality. *Professional Psychology: Research and Practice, 38,* 401–410.

Barnett, J. E., & Scheetz, K. (2003). Technological advances and telehealth: Ethics, law, and the practice of psychotherapy. *Psychotherapy: Theory, Research, Practice, Training, 40,* 86–93.

Barnett, J. E., Wise, E. H., Johnson-Greene, D., & Bucky, S. F. (2007). Informed consent: Too much of a good thing or not enough? *Professional Psychology: Research and Practice, 38,* 179–186.

Barnett, J. E., & Yutrzenka, B. A. (1994). Nonsexual dual relationships in professional practice, with special applications to rural and military communities. *Independent Practitioner: Bulletin of the Division of Independent Practice, American Psychological Association, 14*(5), 243–248.

Bartell, P. A., & Rubin, L. J. (1990). Dangerous liaisons: Sexual intimacies in supervision. *Professional Psychology: Research and Practice, 21,* 442–450.

Bashe, A., Anderson, S. K., Handelsman, M. M., & Klevansky, R. (2007). An acculturation model for ethics training: The ethics autobiography and beyond. *Professional Psychology: Research and Practice, 38,* 60–67.

Behnke, S. (2005a). Cooperating with other professionals: Reflections on ethical standard 3.09. *Monitor on Psychology, 36*(3), 70–71.

Behnke, S. (2005b). Thinking ethically as psychologists: Reflections on ethical standards 2.01, 3.07, 9.08, & 10.04. *Monitor on Psychology, 36*(6), 86–87.

Behnke, S. (2006). Responding to a colleague's ethical transgressions. *Monitor on Psychology, 37*, 72–73.

Behnke, S. H., & Warner, E. (2002). Confidentiality in the treatment of adolescents. *Monitor on Psychology, 33*(3). Retrieved from http://www.apa.org/monitor/mar02/confidentiality.html

Belter, R. W., & Grisso, T. (1984). Children's recognition of rights violations in counseling. *Professional Psychology: Research and Practice, 15*, 899–910.

Benefield, H., Ashkanazi, G., & Rozensky, R. H. (2006). Communication and records: HIPPA [sic] issues when working in health care settings. *Professional Psychology: Research and Practice, 37*, 273–277.

Bennett, B. E., Bricklin, P. M., Harris, E., Knapp, S., VandeCreek, L., & Younggren, J. N. (2005). *Assessing and managing risk in psychological practice: An individualized approach.* Washington, DC: American Psychological Association.

Bernstein, B. E., & Hartsel, T. L. (2013). *The portable lawyer for mental health professionals: An A–Z guide* (3rd ed.). Hoboken, NJ: John Wiley & Sons.

Berger, S. E., & Berger, M. A. (2005). Duty to warn expanded by California Court. *AAP Advance,* Winter, 4. Retrieved from http://www.pfeifferphd.com/uploads/newsletters/aap_winter_2005.pdf

Bergeron, R. L., & Gray, B. (2003). Ethical dilemmas of reporting suspected elder abuse. *Social Work, 48*, 96–105.

Berman, A. L., Jobes, D. A., & Silverman, M. M. (2006). *Adolescent suicide* (2nd ed.). Washington, DC: American Psychological Association.

Bodenhorn, N. (2006). Exploratory study of common and challenging ethical dilemmas experienced by professional school counselors. *Professional School Counseling, 10*, 195–203.

Bogo, M., Globerman, J., & Sussman, T. (2004). Field instructor competence in group supervision: Students' views. *Journal of Teaching in Social Work, 24*, 199–215.

Bongar, B. (2002). *The suicidal patient: Clinical and legal standards of care* (2nd ed.). Washington, DC: American Psychological Association.

Boonstra, H., & Nash, E. (2000). Minors and the right to consent in health care. *The Guttmacher report on public policy.* Retrieved from http://www.guttmacher.org/pubs/tgr/03/4/gr030404.pdf

Bouhoutsos, J., Holroyd, J., Lerman, H., Forer, B. R., & Greenberg, M. (1983). Sexual intimacy between psychotherapists and patients. *Professional Psychology, 14*, 185–196.

Bower, A. G. (2005). The diffusion and value of healthcare information technology. RAND Corporation. Retrieved from http://www.rand.org/pubs/monographs/2006/RAND_MG272-1.pdf

Bradshaw, J. (2006). Crimes raise confidentiality questions. *National Psychologist, 15*(2), 1–2.

Brown, L. S. (1997). Remediation, amends, or denial? *Professional Psychology: Research and Practice, 28*, 297–299.

Bryant, J., & Milsom, A. (2005). Child abuse reporting by school counselors. *Professional School Counseling, 9*, 63–72.

Burkemper, E. M. (2004). Informed consent in social work ethics education: Guiding student education with an informed consent template. *Journal of Teaching in Social Work, 24*, 141–160.

Busseri, M. A., Tyler, J. D., & King, A. R. (2005). An exploratory examination of student dismissals and prompted resignations from clinical psychology PhD training programs. *Professional Psychology: Research and Practice, 36*, 441–445.

Campbell, C. D., & Gordon, M. C. (2003). Acknowledging the inevitable: Understanding multiple relationships in rural practice. *Professional Psychology: Research and Practice, 34*, 430–434.

Center for Adolescent Health and the Law. (2003). *State minor consent laws: A summary* (2nd ed.). Retrieved from http://www.guttmacher.org/pubs/tgr/03/4/gr030404.pdf

Chapman, R. A., Baker, S. B., Nassar-McMillan, S. C., & Gerler, E. R. (2011). Cybersupervision: Further examination of synchronous and asynchronous modalities in counseling practicum supervision. *Counselor Education & Supervision, 50*, 298–313.

Chenneville, T. (2000). HIV, confidentiality, and duty to protect: A decision-making model. *Professional Psychology: Research and Practice, 31*, 661–670.

Clark, D. (1998). The evaluation and management of the suicidal patient. In P. M. Kleespies et al. (Eds.), *Emergencies in mental health practice: Evaluation and management* (pp. 75–94). New York: Guilford Press.

Clark, J. J., Rompf, E. L., & Walker, R. (2001). Practicum instruction: Warning signs of boundary problems and what to do about them. *Journal of Teaching in Social Work, 21*(12), 3–18.

Clay, R. A. (2012). Determining your responsibilities when you believe a colleague may have behaved unethically. *Monitor on Psychology, 43*(9), 37–38.

Clingermen, T. L., & Bernard, J. M. (2004). An investigation of the use of e-mail as a supplemental modality for clinical supervision. *Counselor Education and Supervision, 44*, 82–95.

Collins, L. H. (2007). Practicing safer listserv use: Ethical use of an invaluable resource. *Professional Psychology: Research and Practice, 38*, 690–698.

Congress, E. (2001). Dual relationships in social work education: Report on a national survey. *Journal of Social Work Education, 37*, 255–267.

Cooper, C. C., & Gottlieb, M. C. (2000). Ethical issues with managed care: Challenges facing counseling psychology. *Counseling Psychologist, 29*, 179–236.

Cottone, R. R., & Claus, R. E. (2000). Ethical decision-making models: A review of the literature. *Journal of Counseling and Development, 78*, 275–283.

Council for Accreditation of Counseling and Related Educational Programs. (2013). Draft #1 of the 2016 CACREP Standards. Retrieved from http://www.cacrep.org/doc/Draft%201%20final.pdf

Council on Social Work Education. (2008; revised August 2012). Education Policy and Accreditation Standards. Retrieved from http://www.cswe.org/File.aspx?id=41861

Damon, W., & Bronk, K. C. (2007). Taking ultimate responsibility. In H. Gardner (Ed.), *Responsibility at Work: How leading professionals act (or don't act) responsibly* (pp. 21–42). San Francisco: Jossey-Bass

Daniels, J. A., Alva, L. A., & Olivares, S. (2002). Graduate training for managed care: A national survey of psychology and social work programs. *Professional Psychology: Research and Practice, 33*, 587–590.

DeAngelis, T. (2001). Surviving a patient's suicide. *Monitor on Psychology,* December, 70–73.

DeBell, C., & Jones, R. D. (1997). Privileged communication at last? An overview of *Jaffee v. Redmond. Professional Psychology: Research and Practice, 28*, 559–566.

Devereaux, R. L., & Gottlieb, M. C. (2012). Record keeping in the cloud: Ethical considerations. *Professional Psychology: Research and Practice, 43*(6), 627–632.

Dodd, S. J. (2007). Identifying the discomfort: An examination of ethical issues encountered by MSW students during field placement. *Journal of Teaching in Social Work, 27*, 7–19.

Drake, R. E., Teague, G., & Gersing, K. (2005). State mental health authorities and informatics. *Community Mental Health Journal, 41*(3), 365–370.

Ellis, E. M. (2009). Should a psychotherapist be compelled to release an adolescent's treatment records to a parent in a contested custody case? *Professional Psychology: Research and Practice, 40,* 357–363.

Fisher, C. B., & Fried, A. L. (2003). Internet-mediated psychological services and the American Psychological Association ethics code. *Psychotherapy: Theory, Research, Practice, Training. 40,* 103–111.

Fisher, M. A. (2008). Protecting confidentiality rights: The need for an ethical practice model. *American Psychologist, 63,* 1–13.

Fisher, M. A. (2009). Replacing "Who is the Client?" with a different ethical question. *Professional Psychology: Research and Practice, 40,* 1–7.

Fly, B. J., van Bark, W. P., Weinman, L., Kitchener, K. S., & Lang, P. R. (1997). Ethical transgressions of psychology graduate students: Critical incidents with implications for training. *Professional Psychology: Research and Practice, 28,* 492–495.

Ford, C. A., Milstein, S. G., Halpern-Felsher, B. L., & Irwin, C. E., Jr. (1997). Influence of physician confidentiality assurances on adolescents' willingness to discuss information and seek future health care: A randomized controlled trial. *Journal of the American Medical Association, 278*(12), 1029–1034.

Forrest, L., Elman, N., Gizara, S., & Vacha-Haase, T. (1999). Trainee impairment: A review of identification, remediation, dismissal, and legal issues. *Counseling Psychologist, 27,* 627–686.

Fulero, S. M. (1988). Tarasoff: 10 years later. *Professional Psychology, Research and Practice, 19,* 184–190.

Gabbard, G. O. (Ed.). (1989). *Sexual exploitation in professional relationships.* Washington, DC: American Psychiatric Press.

Gallardo, M. E., Johnson, J., Parham, T. A., & Carter, J. A. (2009). Ethics and multiculturalism: Advancing cultural and clinical responsiveness. *Professional Psychology: Research and Practice, 40,* 425–435.

Gardner, H. (Ed.). (2007). *Responsibility at work: How leading professionals act (or don't act).* San Francisco: Jossey-Bass,

Gelman, S. R., Pollack, D., & Auerbach, C. (1996). Liability issues in social work education. *Journal of Social Work Education, 32,* 351–361.

Glaser, R. D., & Thorpe, J. S. (1986). Unethical intimacy: A survey of sexual contact and advances between psychology educators and female graduate students. *American Psychologist, 41,* 43–51.

Glosoff, H. L., Herlihy, S. B., Herlihy, B., & Spence, E. B. (1997). Privileged communication in the psychologist–client relationship. *Professional Psychology: Research and Practice, 28,* 573–581.

Glosoff, H. L., Herlihy, B., & Spence, E. B. (2000). Privileged communication in the counselor–client relationship. *Journal of Counseling and Development, 78,* 454–462.

Glueckauff, R. L., Pickett, T. C., Ketterson, T. U., Loomis, J. S., & Rozensky, R. H. (2003). Preparation for the delivery of telehealth services: A self-study framework for expansion of practice. *Professional Psychology: Research and Practice, 34,* 159–163.

Gottlieb, M. C., Robinson, K., & Younggren, J. N. (2007). Multiple relations in supervision: Guidelines for administrators, supervisors and students. *Professional Psychology: Research and Practice, 38,* 241–247.

Gustafson, K. E., & McNamara, J. R. (1987). Confidentiality with minor clients: Issues and guidelines for therapists. *Professional Psychology: Research and Practice, 18,* 503–508.

Gutheil, T. G., & Gabbard, G. O. (1993). The concept of boundaries in clinical practice: Theoretical and risk management dimensions. *American Journal of Psychiatry, 150,* 188–196.

Guttmann, D. (2006). *Ethics in social work: A context of caring.* New York: The Haworth Press.

Hafemeister, T. L. (2000). Informed consent: Must a clinician disclose personal information? *Monitor on Psychology, 31*(8), 76.

Hamilton, N. W., & Monson, V. E. (2012). Ethical professionalism (trans)formation: Themes from interviews about professionalism with exemplary lawyers. *Santa Clara Law Review, 52*(3), 921–970.

Handelsman, M. M., Gottlieb, M. C., & Knapp, S. (2005). Training ethical psychologists: An acculturation model. *Professional Psychology: Research and Practice, 36,* 59–65.

Harris, E. A. (1995). The importance of risk management in a managed care environment. In M. B. Sussman (Ed.), *A perilous calling: The hazards of psychotherapy practice* (pp. 247–258). New York: John Wiley & Sons.

Harris, E., & Younggren, J. N. (2011). Risk management in the digital world. *Professional Psychology: Research and Practice, 42*(6), 412–418.

Harris, E. A., & Bennett, B. E. (2000). Psychotherapist–patient contract. In L. VandeCreek & T. L. Jackson (Eds.), *Innovations in clinical practice: A source book* (p. 18). Sarasota, FL: Professional Resource Press.

Harwood, M. T., Pratt, D., Beutler, L. E., Bongar, B. M., Lenore, S., & Forrester, B. T. (2011). Technology, telehealth, treatment enhancement and selection. *Professional Psychology: Research and Practice, 42*(6), 448–454.

Heinlen, K. T., Welfel, E. R., Richmond, E. N., & Rak, C. F. (2003). The scope of WebCounseling: A survey of services and compliance with NBCC standards for the ethical practice of WebCounseling. *Journal of Counseling and Development, 81,* 61–69.

Helbok, C. M., Marineli, R. P., & Walls, R. T. (2006). National survey of ethical practices across rural and urban communities. *Professional Psychology: Research and Practice, 37,* 36–44.

Holloway, J. D. (2003). More protections for patients and psychologists under HIPAA. *Monitor on Psychology, 34*(2), 22.

Housman, L., & Stake, J. (1999). The current state of sexual ethics training in clinical psychology: Issues of quantity, quality, and effectiveness. *Professional Psychology: Research and Practice, 30*(3), 302–311.

Humphreys, K., Winzelberg, A., & Klaw, E. (2000). Psychologists' ethical responsibilities in Internet groups: Issues, strategies, and a call for dialogue. *Professional Psychology: Research and Practice, 31,* 493–496.

Hunsley, J. (2007). Addressing key challenges in evidence-based practice in psychology. *Professional Psychology: Research and Practice, 38,* 113–121.

Huss, S., Bryant, A., & Mulet, S. (2008). Managing the quagmire of counseling in a school: Bringing the parents onboard. *Professional School Counseling, 11,* 362–367.

Isaacs, M. L., & Stone, C. (2001). Confidentiality with minors: Mental health counselors' attitudes toward breaching or preserving confidentiality. *Journal of Mental Health Counseling, 23,* 342–356.

Jaffee v. *Redmond,* 116 S. Ct. 95–266, 64 L.W. 4490 (U.S. Ill., June 13, 1996).

Jobes, D. A., Rudd, D. M., Overholser, J. C., & Joiner, T. E., Jr. (2008). Ethical and competent care of suicidal patients: Contemporary challenges, new developments, and considerations for clinical practice. *Professional Psychology: Research and Practice, 39,* 405–413.

Johnson, W. B., Barnett, J. E., Elman, N. S., Forrest, L., & Kaslow, N. J. (2012). The competence community: Toward a reformulation of professional ethics. *American Psychologist, 67*(7), 557–569.

Johnson, M. E., Brems, C., Warner, T. D., & Roberts, L. W. (2006). The need for continuing education in ethics as reported by rural and urban mental health care providers. *Professional Psychology: Research and Practice. 37,* 183–189.

Jorgenson, L., Randles, R., & Strasburger, L. (1991). The furor over psychotherapist–patient sexual contact: New solutions to an old problem. *William and Mary Law Review, 32,* 643–729.

Kagle, J. D., & Giebelhausen, P. N. (1994). Dual relationships and professional boundaries. *Social Work, 39,* 213–220.

Kanz, J. E. (2001). Clinical-Supervision.com: Issues in the provision of online supervision. *Professional Psychology: Research and Practice, 32*, 415–420.

Kaplan, D. M., Kocet, M. M., Cottone, R. R., Glosoff, H. L., Miranti, J. G., Moll, E. C.,... Tarvydas, V. M. (2009). New mandates and imperatives in the ACA Code of Ethics. *Journal of Counseling and Development, 87*, 241–256.

Kaser-Boyd, N., Adelman, H., & Taylor, L. (1985). Minors' ability to identify risks and benefits of therapy. *Professional Psychology: Research and Practice, 16*, 411–417.

Keith-Spiegel, P. (1994). The 1992 ethics code: Boon or bane. *Professional Psychology: Research and Practice, 25*, 315–317.

Kennedy, P. F., Vandehey, M., Norman, W. B., & Diehoff, G. M. (2003). Recommendations for risk-management practices. *Professional Psychology: Research and Practice, 34*, 309–311.

Kirkland, K., Kirkland K. L., & Reaves, R. P. (2004). On the professional use of disciplinary data. *Professional Psychology: Research and Practice, 35*, 179–184.

Kitchener, K. S. (1984). Intuition, critical evaluation and ethical principles: The foundation for ethical decisions in counseling psychology. *Counseling Psychologist, 12*(3), 43–56.

Kitchener, K. S. (1988). Dual relationships: What makes them so problematic? *Journal of Counseling and Development, 67,* 217–221.

Knapp, S., Gottlieb, M., Berman, J., & Handelsman, M. M. (2007). When laws and ethics collide: What should psychologists do? *Professional Psychology: Research and Practice, 38*, 54–59.

Knapp, S., & Slattery, J. M. (2004). Professional boundaries in nontraditional settings. *Professional Psychology: Research and Practice, 35*, 553–558.

Knapp, S., & VandeCreek, L. (1997). *Jaffee v. Redman:* The Supreme Court recognizes a psychotherapist–patient privilege in federal courts. *Professional Psychology: Research and Practice, 28*, 567–572.

Knapp, S., & VandeCreek, L. (2001). Psychotherapist's legal responsibilities to third parties: Does it extend to alleged perpetrators of childhood abuse? *Professional Psychology: Research and Practice, 32*, 479–483.

Knapp, S., & VandeCreek, L. (2003). An overview of the major changes in the 2002 APA Ethics Code. *Professional Psychology: Research and Practice, 34*, 301–308.

Knapp, S. J., & VandeCreek, L. D. (2006) *Practical ethics for psychologists: A positive approach.* Washington, DC: American Psychological Association.

Knox, S., Burkard, A. W., Bentzler, J., Schaack, A., & Hess, S. A. (2006). Therapists-in-training who experience a client suicide: Implications for supervision. *Professional Psychology: Research and Practice, 37*, 547–557.

Kocet, M. M. (2006). Ethical challenges in a complex world: Highlights of the 2005 ACA code of ethics. *Journal of Counseling and Development, 84*, 228–234.

Kocet, M. M., & Freeman, L. T. (2005). Report of the ACA ethics committee: 2003–2004. *Journal of Counseling and Development, 83*, 249–252.

Kolbert, J., Brendel, J., & Morgan, B. (2002). Faculty and student perceptions of dual relationships within counselor education: A qualitative analysis. *Counselor Education and Supervision, 41*(2), 193–206.

Kolmes, K. (2012) Social media in the future of professional psychology. *Professional Psychology: Research and Practice, 43*(6), 606–612.

Koocher, G., & Morray, E. (2000). Regulation of telepsychology: A survey of state attorneys general. *Professional Psychology: Research and Practice, 31*(5), 503–508.

Koocher, G. P., & Keith-Spiegel, P. (2008). *Ethics in psychology and the mental health professions: Standards and cases.* New York: Oxford University Press.

Kremer, T. G., & Gesten, E. L. (2003). Managed mental health care: The client's perspective. *Professional Psychology: Research and Practice, 34*(2), 187–196.

Kress, V. E., & Dixon, A. (2007). Consensual faculty–student sexual relationships in counselor education: Recommendations for counselor educators' decision making. *Counselor Education and Supervision, 47 (2)*, 110–123.

Kuhlmann, E. G. (2009). Competency-based social work education: A thirty-year retrospective on the behavioral objectives movement. *Social Work & Christianity, 36*(1), 70–76.

Lamb, D., & Catanzaro, S. (1998). Sexual and nonsexual boundary violations involving psychologists, clients, supervisees, and students: Implications for professional practice. *Professional Psychology: Research and Practice, 29*(5), 498–503.

Lamb, D. H., Catanzaro, S. J., & Moorman, A. S. (2003). Psychologists reflect on their sexual relationships with clients, supervisees, and students: Occurrence, impact, rationales and collegial intervention. *Professional Psychology: Research and Practice, 34*(1), 102–107.

Lazofsky, R. (2008). Maintaining confidentiality with minors: Dilemmas of school counselors. *Professional School Counseling, 11*, 335–346.

Maheu, M. (2003). The online clinical practice management model. *Psychotherapy: Theory, Research, Practice, Training, 40*, 20–32.

Mannheim, C. I., Sancilio, M., Phipps-Yonas, S., Brunnquell, D., Somers, P., Farseth, G., & Ninonuevo, F. (2002). Ethical ambiguities in the practice of child clinical psychology. *Professional Psychology: Research and Practice, 33*, 24–29.

Maradiegue, A. (2003). Minor's rights versus parental rights: Review of legal issues in adolescent health care. *Journal of Midwifery & Women's Health, 48(3)*, 170–177.

Margolin, G., Chien, D., Duman, S. E., Fauchier, A., Gordis, E. B., Oliver, P. H.,... Vickerman, K. A. (2005). Ethical issues in couple and family research. *Journal of Family Psychology, 19*, 157–167.

Marsh, J. C., (2003). To thine own ethics code be true. *Social Work, 48*, 5–7.

Marshall, N. A. (2012). A clinicians guide to recognizing and reporting parental psychological maltreatment of children. *Professionals Psychology: Research and Practice, 43*, 73–79.

McCurdy, K. G., & Murray, K. C. (2003). Confidentiality issues when minor children disclose family secrets in family counseling. *The Family Journal, 11*, 393–398.

McGlothlin, J. M., Rainey, S., & Kindsvatter, A. (2005). Suicidal clients and supervisees: A model for considering supervisor roles. *Counselor Education and Supervision, 45,* 135–146.

Messer, S. (2003). The controversy over empirically supported treatments. *National Psychologist,* September/October, 12–13.

Mishna, F., Antle, B. J., & Regehr, C. (2002). Social work with clients contemplating suicide: Complexity and ambiguity in the clinical, ethical and legal considerations. *Clinical Social Work Journal, 30,* 265–279.

Mitchell, K. J., Becker-Blease, K. A., & Finkelhor, D. (2005). Inventory of problematic Internet experiences encountered in clinical practice. *Professional Psychology: Research and Practice, 36*, 498–509.

Moleski, S. M., & Kiselica, M. S. (2005). Dual relationships: A continuum ranging from the destructive to the therapeutic. *Journal of Counseling and Development, 83*, 3–11.

Monahan, J. (1993). Limiting therapist exposure to Tarasoff liability: Guidelines for risk containment. *American Psychologist, 48*, 242–250.

Murphy, W. J. (2005). Military proceedings threaten therapy confidentiality. *National Psychologist,14 (5)*, 8–9.

Myers, S., Endres, M. A., Ruddy, M. E., & Zelikovsky, N. (2012). Psychology graduate training in the era of online social networking. *Training and Education in Professional Psychology, 6*(1), 28–36.

National Association of Social Workers. (2008) Code of ethics of the National Association of Social Workers: Revised 2008s. Retrieved from http://www.socialworkers.org/pubs/code/code.asp

National Association of Social Workers. (2001). NASW standards for cultural competence in social work practice. Retrieved from www.socialworkers.org

National Association of Social Workers. (2005). National Ethics Committee. Retrieved from http://www.socialworkers.org/governance/cmtes/ncoi.asp

National Board of Certified Counselors. (1998). A set of standards for on-line counseling [On-line], http://www.nbcc.org/ethics/wcstandards.htm

National Council of Schools and Programs in Professional Psychology. (2007). *Competency developmental achievement levels*. Retrieved from http://www.ncspp.info

Oliver, M. N. I., Bernstein, J. H., Anderson, K. G., Blashfield, R. K., & Roberts, M. C. (2004). An exploratory examination of student attitudes toward "impaired" peers in clinical psychology training programs. *Professional Psychology: Research and Practice, 35,* 141–147.

Oordt, M. S., Jobes, D. A., Rudd, M. D., Fonesca, V. P., Runyan, C. N., Stea, J. B.,...Talcott, G. W. (2005). Development of a clinical guide to enhance care for suicidal patients. *Professional Psychology: Research and Practice, 36,* 208–218.

Pabian, Y. L., Welfel, E., & Beebe, R. S. (2009). Psychologists' knowledge of their states' laws pertaining to Tarasoff-type situations. *Professional Psychology: Research and Practice, 40,* 8–14.

Parker-Oliver, D., & Demiris, G. (2006). Social work informatics: A new specialty. *Social Work, 51,* 127–134.

Paulson, B. L., & Worth, M. (2002). Counseling for suicide: Client perspectives. *Journal of Counseling and Development, 80,* 86–93.

Peruzzi, N., & Bongar, B. (1999). Assessing risk for completed suicide in patients with major depression: Psychologists' views of critical factors. *Professional Psychology: Research and Practice, 30*(6), 576–580.

Pollack, D., & Marsh, J. (2004). Social work misconduct may lead to liability. *Social Work, 49,* 609–612.

Pomerantz, A. M., & Handelsman, M. M. (2004). Informed consent revisited: An updated written question format. *Professional Psychology: Research and Practice, 35*(2), 201–205.

Pope, K. S. (1990). Therapist–patient sex as sex abuse: Six scientific, professional and practical dilemmas in addressing victimization and rehabilitation. *Professional Psychology: Research and Practice, 21,* 227–239.

Pope, K. S. (1993). Licensing disciplinary actions for psychologists who have been sexually involved with a client: Some information about offenders. *Professional Psychology: Research and Practice, 24,* 374–377.

Pope, K. S., & Bouhoutsos, J. C. (1986). *Sexual intimacy between therapists and patients.* New York: Praeger.

Pope, K. S., Keith-Spiegel, P., & Tabachnick, B. G. (1986). Sexual attraction to clients: The human therapist and the (sometimes) inhuman training system. *American Psychologist, 41,* 147–158.

Pope, K. S., Levenson, H., & Schover, L. (1979). Sexual intimacy in psychology training: Results and implications of a national survey. *American Psychologist, 34,* 682–689.

Pope, K. S., Sonne, J. L., & Holroyd, J. (1993). *Sexual feelings in psychotherapy.* Washington, DC: American Psychological Association.

Pope, K. S., & Tabachnick, B. G. (1993). Therapists' anger, hate, fear, and sexual feelings: National survey of therapist responses, client characteristics, critical events, formal complaints, and training. *Professional Psychology: Research and Practice, 24,* 142–152.

Pope, K. S., & Vasquez, M. J. T. (2007). *Ethics in psychotherapy and counseling: A practical guide* (3rd ed.). San Francisco: Jossey-Bass.

Pope, K. S., & Vetter, V. V. (1992). Ethical dilemmas encountered by members of the American Psychological Association: A national survey. *American Psychologist, 47,* 397–411.

Prieto, L. R. (1997). Separating group supervision from group therapy: Avoiding epistemological confusion. *Professional Psychology: Research and Practice, 28,* 405.

Ragusea, A. S., & VandeCreek, L. (2003). Suggestions for the ethical practice of online psychotherapy. *Psychotherapy: Theory, Research, Practice, Training. 40,* 94–102.

RAND Corporation. (2005). Health information technology: Can HIT lower costs and improve quality? Retrieved from http://www.rand.org/pubs/research_briefs/RB9136/index1.html

Reamer, F. G. (1995). Malpractice claims against social workers: First facts. *Social Work, 40,* 595–601.

Reamer, F. G. (2000). The social work ethics audit: A risk management strategy. *Social Work, 45*(4), 355–366.

Reamer, F. G. (2003). Boundary issues in social work: Managing dual relationships. *Social Work, 48*(1), 121–134.

Reamer, F. G. (2005a). Documentation in social work: Evolving ethical and risk-management standards. *Social Work, 50,* 325–334.

Reamer, F. G. (2005b). Update on confidentiality issues in practice with children: Ethics risk management. *Children and Schools, 27*(2), 117–120.

Regehr, C., & Antle, B. (1997). Coercive influences: Informed consent in court-mandated social work practice. *Social Work, 42,* 300–306.

Richards, M. M. (2009). Electronic medical records: Confidentiality issues in the time of HIPAA. *Professional Psychology: Research and Practice, 40,* 550–556.

Rinella, V. J., & Goldstein, M. R. (2007). Family therapy with substance abusers: Legal considerations regarding confidentiality. *Journal of Marital and Family Therapy, 6,* 319–326.

Robinson, W. L., & Reid, P. T. (1985). Sexual intimacies in psychology revisited. *Professional Psychology: Research and Practice, 16,* 512–520.

Rodolfa, E., Bent, R., Eisman, E., Nelson, P., Rehm, L., & Ritchie, P. (2005). A cube model for competency development: Implications for psychology educators and regulators. *Professional Psychology: Research and Practice, 36,* 347–354.

Rodolfa, E., Ko, S. F., & Petersen, L. (2004). Psychology training directors' views of trainee's readiness to practice independently. *Professional Psychology: Research and Practice, 35,* 397–404.

Rodolfa, E. R., Hall, T., Holms, V., Davena, A., Komatz, D., Antunez, M., & Hall, A. (1994). The management of sexual feelings in therapy. *Professional Psychology: Research and Practice, 25,* 168–172.

Rodolfa, E. R., Kitzrow, M., Vohra, S., & Wilson, B. (1990). Training interns to respond to sexual dilemmas. *Professional Psychology: Research and Practice, 21,* 313–315.

Rosenberg, J. I., Getzelman, M. A., Arcinue, F., & Oren, C. Z. (2005). An exploratory look at students' experiences of problematic peers in academic professional psychology programs. *Professional Psychology: Research and Practice, 36,* 665–673.

Rudd, M. D., Joiner, T., Brown, G. K., Cukrowicz, K., Jobes, D. A., & Silverman, M. (2009). Informed consent with suicidal patients: Rethinking risks in (and out of) treatment. *Psychotherapy Theory, Research, Practice, Training, 46,* 459–468.

Rupert, P. A., & Baird, K. A. (2004). Managed care and the independent practice of psychology. *Professional Psychology: Research and Practice, 35,* 185–193.

Sales, B. D., Miller, M. O., & Hall, S. R. (2005). *Laws affecting clinical practice.* Washington, DC: American Psychological Association.

Sanchez, H. G. (2001). Risk factor model for suicide assessment and intervention. *Professional Psychology: Research and Practice, 32,* 351–358.

Sanders, S., Jacobson, J. M., & Ting, L. (2008). Preparing for the inevitable: Training social workers to cope with client suicide. *Journal of Teaching in Social Work, 28,* 1–18.

Schank, J. A., & Skovholt, T. M. (2006). *Ethical practice in small communities.* Washington, DC: APA.

Schank, J. A., & Skovholt, T. M. (1997). Dual-relationship dilemmas of rural and small-community psychologists. *Professional Psychology: Research and Practice, 28,* 44–49.

Schwartz, T. J., & Lonborg, S. D. (2011). Security management in telepsychology. *Professional Psychology: Research and Practice, 42*(6), 419–425.

Shapiro, D. L., & Smith, S. R. (2011). *Malpractice in psychology: A practical resource for clinicians.* Washington, DC: American Psychological Association.

Shapiro, E. L., & Ginzberg, R. (2003). To accept or not to accept: Referrals and the maintenance of boundaries. *Professional Psychology: Research and Practice, 34,* 256–263.

Shaw, H. E., & Shaw, S. F. (2006). Critical ethical issues in online counseling: Assessing current practices with an ethical intent checklist. *Journal of Counseling and Development, 84,* 441–454.

Shen-Miller, D. S., Grus, C. L., Van Sickle, K. S., Schwartz-Mette, R., Cage, E. A., Elman, N.,... Kaslow, N. J. (2011). Trainees' experiences with peers having competence problems: A national survey. *Training and Education in Professional Psychology, 5*(2), 112–121.

Simon, R. I. (1989). Sexual exploitation of patients: How it begins before it happens. *Psychiatry Annals, 19,* 104–122.

Sklare G., Thomas, D. V., Williams, E. C., & Powers, K. A. (1996). Ethics and an experiential "here and now" group: A blend that works. *Journal for Specialists in Group Work, 21*(4), 263–273.

Sloan, L., Edmond, T., Rubin, A., & Doughty, M. (1998). Social workers' knowledge of and experience with sexual exploitation by psychotherapists. *Social Work, 43,* 43–53.

Slovak, K., Brewer, T. W., & Carlson, K. (2008). Client firearm assessment and safety counseling: The role of social workers. *Social Work, 53,* 358–367.

Slovenko, R. (1988). The therapist's duty to warn or protect third persons. *Journal of Psychiatry and Law,* Spring, 139–192.

Small, M. A., Lyons, P. M., & Guy, L. S. (2002). Liability issues in child abuse and neglect reporting statutes. *Professional Psychology: Research and Practice, 33,* 13–18.

Somer, E., & Saadon, M. (1999). Therapist–client sex: Clients' retrospective reports. *Professional Psychology: Research and Practice, 30*(5), 504–509.

Sommers-Flanagan, J., & Sommers-Flanagan, R. (1995). Intake interviewing with suicidal patients: A systematic approach. *Professional Psychology: Research and Practice, 26,* 41–47.

Stall, M. A., & King, R. E. (2000). Managing a multiple relationship environment: The ethics of military psychology. *Professional Psychology: Research and Practice, 31,* 698–705.

Steinberg, L., Cauffman, E., Woolard, J., Graham, S., & Banich, M., (2009). Are adolescents less mature than adults: Minors' access to abortion, the juvenile death penalty, and the alleged APA "Flip-Flop." *American Psychologist, 64,* 583–594.

Steinfeld, B. I., & Keyes, J. A. (2011). Electronic medical records in a multidisciplinary health care setting. *Professional Psychology: Research and Practice, 42*(6), 426–432.

Steinfeld, B., Ekorenrud, B., Gillett, C., Quirk, M., & Eytan, T. (2006). EMRs bring all of healthcare together. *Behavioral Healthcare, 26*(1), 12–17.

Strasburger, L. H., Jorgenson, L., & Randles, R. (1991). Criminalization of psychotherapist–patient sex. *American Journal of Psychiatry, 148,* 859–863.

Strom-Gottfried, K. (2000). Ethical vulnerability in social work education: An analysis of NASW complaints. *Journal of Social Work Education, 36,* 241–251.

Swenson, L. C. (1997). *Psychology and law for the helping professions* (2nd ed.). Pacific Grove, CA: Brooks/Cole.

Thoreson, R. W., Shaughnessy, P., Heppner, P. P., & Cook, S. W. (1993). Sexual contact during and after the professional relationship: Attitudes and practices of male counselors. *Journal of Counseling and Development, 71,* 429–434.

Tishler, C. L., Gordon, L. B., & Landry-Meyer, L. (2000). Managing the violent patient: A guide for psychologists and other mental health professionals. *Professional Psychology: Research and Practice, 31,* 34–41.

Tolman, A. O., & Rotzien, A. L. (2007). Conducting risk evaluations for future violence: Ethical practice is possible. *Professional Psychology: Research and Practice, 38,* 71–79.

Trepal, H., Haberstroh, S., Duffey, T., & Evans, M. (2007). Considerations and strategies for teaching online counseling skills: Establishing relationships in cyberspace. *Counselor Education and Supervision, 46,* 266–279.

Vaccaro, N., & Lambie, G. W. (2007). Computer-based counselor-in-training supervision: Ethical and practical implications for counselor educators and supervisors. *Counselor Education and Supervision, 47,* 46–57.

Van Horne, B. A. (2004). Psychology licensing board disciplinary actions: The realities. *Professional Psychology: Research and Practice, 35,* 170–178.

VandeCreek, L., Bennett, B. E., & Bricklin, P. M. (1994). *Risk management with potentially dangerous patients.* Washington, DC: American Psychological Association Insurance Trust.

VauPitts, J. H. (1992). Organizing a practicum and internship program in counselor education. *Counselor Education and Supervision, 31,* 196–207.

Werth, J. L., Welfel, E. R., & Benjamin, G. A. H. (Eds). (2009). *The duty to protect: Ethical, legal and professional responsibilities of mental health professionals.* Washington, DC: American Psychological Association Press.

Westefeld, J. S., Range, L. M., Rogers, J. R., Maples, M. R., Bromley, J. L., & Alcom, J. (2000). Suicide: An overview. *Counseling Psychologist, 28,* 445–510.

Wester, K. L. (2007). Teaching research integrity in the field of counseling. *Counselor Education and Supervision, 46,* 199–211.

White, T. W. (2003a). Legal issues and suicide risk management. *National Psychologist,* March/April, 12.

White, T. W. (2003b). Managing dual relationships in correctional settings. *National Psychologist,* September/October, 14–15.

Wierzbicki, M., Siderits, M. A., & Kuchan, A. M. (2012). Ethical questions addressed by a state psychological association. *Professional Psychology: Research and Practice, 43*(2), 80–85.

Wilkerson, K. (2006). Impaired students: Applying the therapeutic process model to graduate training programs. *Counselor Education and Supervision, 45,* 207–217.

Wise, R. A., King, A. R., Miller, J. C., & Pearce, M. W. (2011). When HIPAA and FERPA apply to university training clinics. *Training and Education in Professional Psychology, 5*(1), 48–56.

Wood, J. A. V., Miller, T. W., & Hargrove, D. S. (2005). Clinical supervision in rural settings: A telehealth model. *Professional Psychology: Research and Practice, 36,* 173–179.

Woody R. (2012). *Legal self defense for mental health practitioners.* New York: Springer.

Woody, R. (1999). Domestic violations of confidentiality. *Professional Psychology: Research and Practice, 30*(6), 607–610.

Younggren, J. N., & Gottlieb, M. C. (2004). Managing risk when contemplating multiple relationships. *Professional Psychology: Research and Practice, 35,* 255–260.

Yuen, E. K., Goetter, E. M., Herbert, J. D., & Forman, E. M. (2012). Challenges and opportunities in Internet-mediated telemental health. *Professional Psychology: Research and Practice, 43*(1), 1–8.

Zakutansky, T. J., & Sirles, E. A. (1993). Ethical and legal issues in field education: Shared responsibility and risk. *Journal of Social Work Education, 29,* 338–347.

Zeranski, L., & Halgin, R. P. (2011) Ethical issues in elder abuse reporting: A professional psychologist's guide. *Professional Psychology: Research and Practice, 42*(4), 294–300.

Zuckerman, E. L. (2008). *The paper office: Forms, guidelines, and resources to make you practice work ethically, legally, and profitably* (4th ed.). New York: The Guilford Press.

Zur, O. (2003). HIPAA WANTS YOU! Eleven reasons to become compliant: Eleven simple ways to achieve compliance. *Independent Practitioner, 23*(5).

Zur, O. (2006) How to respond to the dreaded subpoena. *National Psychologist,* March/April, 9.

CHAPTER 5

SUPERVISION

When asked to name the best part of professional training, a colleague said without hesitation, "Supervision. From one of my supervisors in graduate school, I learned more about therapy and working with people than I had learned in three years."

As such comments suggest, supervision can be a tremendous learning opportunity if it is managed well. The goal of this chapter is to familiarize you with some of the activities that are most commonly part of supervision so you understand their purpose and can make the most effective use of the opportunity. The chapter also considers how personalities and theoretical orientation play a role in the supervisory experience, and how interns and supervisors can manage differences or difficulties that may arise in supervision. As is the case throughout this text, research evidence is reviewed to promote an evidence-based practice approach to the supervisory process (e.g., Bogo & McKnight, 2005).

WHAT IS SUPERVISION?

Unlike academic coursework, in which the primary focus is on mastery of an established body of knowledge or skills, supervision involves ongoing work as it takes place in real time in a real-world setting. That is why supervision is so important and so valuable. Your field supervisor is the first person you will turn to if you have questions about what is happening at your placement site. Your supervisor also bears direct responsibility for your actions and your training while you are at the internship. Supervisors will help arrange for various learning opportunities, will review your work with you, may work directly beside you as you interact with clients, and will be involved in evaluating your professional development and performance.

HOPES AND FEARS OF INTERNS

Research in which interns have been asked to identify preferred characteristics of supervisors and supervision (Fernando & Hulse-Killacky, 2005; Fortune, McCarthy, & Abramson, 2001) indicates that desired supervisor qualities vary somewhat depending on experience, but across experience levels, the highest ratings are given to supervisors who are available and open to discussion and who are perceived as supportive and understanding (Falender & Shafranske, 2004). Within a supportive environment,

many interns feel it is valuable for their supervisor to help interns understand themselves and explore the interpersonal dynamics between interns and clients and between the intern and supervisor. Interns also express a need for direct observation and meaningful feedback and instruction about their work and therapeutic techniques (Henry, Hart, & Nance, 2004). Making connections between field activities and classroom work, help with problem solving regarding their own cases, feedback on process recordings, and opportunities to observe the supervisor in therapy are also rated highly.

Along with their hopes for supervision, interns also bring fears. Perhaps the two most common fears are "I am afraid I don't have a clue what I'm supposed to do or how to do it" and "I am even more afraid someone will find out I don't know what to do." Other authors (Gelman, 2004) have expressed similar observations. Harvey and Struzziero (2008) offered 11 practical strategies for reducing supervisee anxieties. These include such common sense, but easily overlooked, suggestions as providing greater structures in areas where interns lack experience, giving manageable assignments, and increasing positive feedback.

Awareness of the needs and concerns of supervisees has also been stressed by those who take a developmental approach to supervision (Deal & Clements, 2006). Stoltenberg (2005) has been a leader in modeling and research studies of the development of interns and how supervisors can effectively match the developmental stages of interns. Stoltenberg emphasized that beginning trainees are often so focused on concerns about their own knowledge and performance that it is difficult for them to give full attention to the client's concerns. Huhra, Yamokoski-Maynhart, and Prieto (2008) noted that this beginning anxiety can be particularly acute when new trainees are asked to review recorded therapy sessions with their supervisors.

I find it helpful to acknowledge at the outset that fears are perfectly understandable, not only for beginning interns but for experienced therapists as well. Any time we are learning something new, there are usually elements of both excitement and fear. Instead of disguising fears, interns are encouraged to acknowledge them so that the supervisor and the intern can work through the fear together. For this to succeed, interns must feel safe when they take the risk to speak about their fears. Interns must know that they will not be punished with poor evaluations or low grades if they are honest enough to speak about their insecurities.

HOPES AND FEARS OF SUPERVISORS

Interns are not the only ones who have hopes and fears in supervision. Supervisors have their own sets of wishes and trepidations when they accept interns. Phrases to describe the ideal intern would probably include "follows ethical principles," "is well-informed and eager to learn," "gets along well with staff and clients," "shows initiative," "follows through reliably," "communicates well," and "is attentive to detail." An intern should also be dependable, receptive to supervision, able to seek help when necessary, and willing to accept challenges.

Bogo et al. (2006) asked experienced field instructors to describe the qualities of both exemplary and problematic students. Exemplary qualities included the sorts of descriptors just mentioned. The problems of students included a number of troubling personal qualities, difficulty grasping and applying knowledge and skills, and ethically questionable conduct.

In my own experience and discussions with supervisors, the most common fear of supervisors is that an intern will do something that jeopardizes clients, the interns themselves, the institution, or the supervisor. In the clinical realm, supervisors get frightened when interns are not frightened. The supervisor's two worst nightmares are well-intentioned but overconfident or careless interns (Smith & Agate, 2004) and the occasional pathological intern who acts irresponsibly or is manipulative without concern for clients or the institution.

Concerns of supervisors about intern actions are not without foundation. Oliver, Bernstein, Anderson, Blashfield, and Roberts (2004) reported that doctoral clinical psychology students estimated that approximately 12% of their peers exhibited some significant degree of deficiency. Still more troubling levels of deficiency were identified by Gaubatz and Vera (2006) in a study of graduate counseling students whose estimates of deficiency rates among peers exceeded 21%. Gaubatz and Vera noted that this estimate was substantially higher than those given by the instructors in their survey. Gaubatz and Vera went on to discuss the implications of these findings for the "gatekeeper" role of supervisors and within the context of competence-based education. This will be discussed in more detail later in the context of evaluation methodologies for interns and practicum students.

Another common problem among not only interns but experienced practitioners as well is overconfidence. Citing multiple studies that suggest even experienced clinicians may express more confidence in the accuracy of their judgment than is actually warranted by the evidence, Smith and Agate (2004) recommended a training module specifically focused on reducing overconfidence and thereby improving clinical judgment among trainees. Elements of this module include analysis of a hypothetical clinical case along with presentation and discussion of the cognitive biases and faulty heuristics that can contribute to errors in judgment. Comparisons of students who completed this module with those in a control group demonstrated a positive effect of the training on reducing, though still not eliminating, overconfidence.

From a clinical perspective, overconfidence can not only lead to errors in judgment, it can also contribute to flawed assessments or interventions. This has the potential both to harm clients and to expose interns, their placement sites, and supervisors to liability risks.

SUPERVISOR LIABILITY RISKS

Pollack and Marsh (2004) and Harrar, VandeCreek, and Knapp (1990) described the concepts of "direct liability" and "vicarious liability" (Harrar et al., 1990, p. 39). These authors indicated that supervisors can be and have been sued for the actions of supervisees. They also noted that trainees are generally held accountable to the same standards of care as licensed professionals (see NASW Insurance Trust, 2004; Zakutansky & Sirles, 1993).

Because the supervisor is responsible for ensuring that interns meet professional standards of care, it should not be surprising that supervisors are intensely concerned about the quality of the work interns perform. For similar reasons, interns should not become defensive if supervisors insist on high standards of professionalism or are occasionally critical of an intern's performance. It is not the primary job of the supervisor to make every intern feel happy and comfortable. Rather, the supervisor's main task is to ensure that all interns are competent and apply themselves diligently and reliably to their responsibilities.

SUPERVISOR PREPARATION

Along with fears that interns will make harmful mistakes or are somehow unstable, supervisors also have many of the same fears as those of interns (i.e., "Do I know what to do in my own clinical work or in my role as supervisor?" and "What if someone finds out or suggests that I don't know what to do?").

The supervisory role is at least as complex as the role of therapist, and it is by no means easy. A professional who agrees to serve as a supervisor is accepting a position that will undoubtedly present a unique set of demands and vulnerabilities. Although some professionals have received specific training in supervision, many have not (Deal & Clements, 2006; Kaiser & Kuechler, 2008; McMahon & Simons, 2004; Riva & Cornish, 2008).

In recent years, training in supervision has increased. For example, McMahon and Simons (2004) presented a focused training program to enhance supervision skills, and they reported significant and lasting positive effects. Deal and Clements (2006) also reported positive effects from a developmentally based supervision training program for field instructors. Kaiser and Kuechler (2008) discussed similarly positive results from 10 years of experience at their "Supervision Institute," a program specifically developed to teach supervision skills to practitioners working in the field. Support of fellow supervisors can also be tremendously valuable, as demonstrated by the seminar for new supervisors developed and described by Finch and Feigelman (2008). Supervisors who have not had extensive training themselves or who feel a need for peer support may find it helpful to consult this article and perhaps replicate the model with their own peers. Another useful source for information about supervision is the special edition of *The Clinical Supervisor* (Vol. 24, 2005), which reviews theories and research across the helping professions, including *counseling* (Borders, 2005), *social work* (Bogo & McKnight, 2005), *psychology* (Goodyear, Bunch, &

Claiborn, 2005), and *school psychology* (Crespi & Dube, 2005). For trainees in school counseling or psychology, the book by Harvey and Struzziero (2008) is a particularly useful resource.

A final challenge that interns may not fully appreciate but supervisors struggle with is simply time. Globerman and Bogo (2003) reported that in many field placements, no workload credit is given for those who engage in supervision or student education. As interns have begun to appreciate the value of supervision and seek additional supervision opportunities, supervisors have found themselves pressed for time and struggling to manage complex and sometimes contradictory roles.

EXERCISES

At the very beginning, interns and supervisors should be open with one another about their mutual and individual needs, fears, and concerns. Just by acknowledging these factors up front, they can reduce a great deal of anxiety, crossed communication, and frustration. To start this process, I have listed some of the common needs of supervisors and interns. Interns and supervisors can check this list, modify or add to it, and then discuss individual and joint needs together.

- *What supervisors need from interns.* Honesty and integrity, ethical conduct, openness to suggestion, respect for the supervisor's experience, careful work, deep thought, hard work, and willingness to listen even if there is disagreement.

  Others: _____

- *What interns need from supervisors.* Support, patience, knowledge of the field, guidance, accessibility, modeling, direct teaching of information, involvement, some autonomy, trust, openness, and willingness to listen.

  Others: _____

CLARIFYING EXPECTATIONS

Clarifying at the outset the expectations of interns and supervisors will prevent later confusion and help achieve the most beneficial learning experience. Barnett (2005) and Thomas (2007) described the use of an informed-consent procedure comparable to the informed-consent forms described in Chapter 4 for use with clients. Among the expectations that should be delineated as clearly as possible between supervisors and interns are the following:

1. The frequency and timing of supervisory sessions.
2. The content of supervisory sessions (e.g., whether they will consist of case reviews via notes or tapes, didactic instruction in topic areas, informal personal exchanges, or some combination of techniques).
3. The theoretical orientation or techniques the intern is expected to learn and how specifically this learning will be demonstrated and assessed.
4. The extent to which personal issues of the intern or supervisor will be addressed as part of supervision.

5. Procedures for documentation, evaluation, feedback, and grading and how the clinical supervisor will interact with academic faculty or coursework.
6. Expectations for perfomring basic work requirements such as showing up on time, completing required paperwork, following instructions, and so on.

   Methods for dealing with conflicts should also be described and agreed upon.

Appendix C offers a form that can be completed by the intern and supervisor to address many of these issues and to establish specific learning goals and evaluation procedures. I encourage you to sit down with your supervisor early on to go over this form together and agree on each of the items.

FREQUENCY AND TIMING OF SUPERVISION

As noted in Chapter 2, supervisors and interns should establish formal agreements stating how often and when they will hold supervision sessions. Once they arrive at an agreement, interns and supervisors must make their best efforts to set aside as much time as necessary for supervision and hold to that time. When schedules get busy, people begin to sacrifice supervision time for seemingly more urgent tasks. Avoid this temptation. Except for rare crises or absolute emergencies, nothing should be thought of as more urgent than supervision. Interns and supervisors should schedule other events, projects, and meetings around supervision, not vice versa. If supervisors or interns begin to allow other things to take precedence over supervision, someone may need to gently call it to their attention, emphasize the importance of supervision, and explore ways of meeting reliably.

Exactly how frequently one should receive supervision and the level of the person providing the supervision depend on several factors, including the intern's activities; the level of the intern's experience or training; and the expectations of the instructor, the placement site, or, in some cases, the guidelines established within a profession. In the field of counseling, the Council for Accreditation of Counseling and Related Educational Programs (CACREP) has set supervision standards for both the practicum experience and the more extended internship training. These requirements specify 1 hour of individual or triadic supervisions per week and an average of 1.5 hours per week of group supervision on a regular schedule (CACREP, 2009, Sec. III, F & G). Internship policies for approved graduate programs in clinical psychology require a minimum of 1 hour of individual supervision for every 20 internship hours (Association of Psychology Postdoctoral and Internship Centers [APPIC], 2006). Comparable requirements have been described for social work field placements.

As a general principle, when specific professional standards are lacking or do not apply, the more interns are involved in direct services with clients, such as therapy or assessment, the more supervision they will need. Some programs suggest an initial ratio of 1 hour of supervision to every 4 to 6 hours of direct client contact. This is ideal, but experience indicates that in practice it is relatively unusual for supervisors of beginning interns to have sufficient time to meet this often. More common ratios are 1 hour of supervision for every 8 to 10 hours of clinical contact. In settings where interns are involved in three or four cases per day, this would amount to about 1 hour of supervision every 2 or 3 days. If supervision is less frequent than this, the interval between clinical interactions and supervision becomes too long, and important details or impressions are likely to be forgotten.

To the extent that interns have greater clinical experience or, at the other end of the spectrum, are less involved in direct clinical services, the frequency of supervision may be lessened. However, this does not mean supervision is unnecessary. Even therapists with many years of experience recognize the value of supervision and schedule it for themselves as part of responsible practice.

WHAT HAPPENS IN SUPERVISION

Most supervision involves a combination of activities, including didactic instruction, case discussions, role-plays, direct observation of sessions, joint therapy, review of audio or video recordings, and opportunities to observe the supervisor in therapy (Fortune et al., 2001; Huhra et al., 2008; Kadushin & Harkness, 2002; Romans, Boswell, Carlozzi, & Ferguson, 1995). I encourage interns to take an active role in discussing what kinds of learning experiences they believe would be most helpful in their own supervision.

SUPERVISION AS TEACHING

One approach to supervision is similar to the process instructors and students use in academic classes. Didactic, or teaching, supervision is best chosen when an intern wants to learn, or a supervisor wants to teach, specific information about a theory, technique, diagnosis, or some other topic relevant to the intern's activities. The goal of a didactic approach is to get information across as efficiently as possible so the interns can learn and apply the information directly to their work. Didactic approaches tend to be particularly appealing to beginning interns because they feel a need for concrete, practical information that will help them cope with the anxiety and ambiguity of starting something new.

If your supervisor does not initiate suggestions or assignments for readings, you may want to ask for specific information or for recommendations of useful books and articles. Supervisors sometimes take it for granted that the information they have studied or the references they use are known by everyone, and they forget that interns might not yet have studied a topic or know of a resource. A sincere request for information and references will typically produce resources that will help you understand your clients better and appreciate where the supervisor may have acquired his or her knowledge or approach.

Perhaps the main drawback to didactic methods is that over-reliance on them can cause supervision to become merely another venue for lecture-based instruction. Keeping supervision at the level of teaching content allows the participants to avoid more challenging issues, such as how interns feel about themselves or clients, how the supervisor and the intern are interacting, and how one deals with ethical dilemmas.

CASE NOTES AND DISCUSSIONS

Case discussions can take a variety of formats depending on the goals and preferences of the intern and the supervisor. Prieto and Scheel (2002) described the use of case notes as a basis for case discussions, but they noted that interns are often given relatively little instruction on how to write or use case notes in a format that is helpful clinically or for supervision. Systematically integrating case notes into supervision has the dual benefit of helping interns learn to record and use case notes more effectively and affording a source of information from which supervisors can get a glimpse of what occurred in sessions and how the intern processed that information. By using a specialized case note format, supervisors can help students better observe client behaviors, record and monitor what takes place in therapy, understand the significance of those interactions, formulate effective treatment plans, and identify any special issues of concern.

One of the more common approaches to using case notes in supervision is through "process notes," which include not only descriptions of the observable events in therapy but also the therapist's internal thoughts and observations about what is happening and why. Fox and Gutheil (2000) recommended that notes reflect background baseline information about the client and the treatment, observations about what is happening in a session and what may have changed since a previous session, the student's integration of his or her own knowledge into the understanding of the case, reflections about what went well or was difficult for the student in the session, and identification of specific skills the student used at different points of the session. Finally, they suggested that the notes include planning for the next session or next steps in treatment and any questions or issues the student wishes to raise in supervision.

Consistent with these suggestions, Sobell, Manor, Sobell, and Dum (2008) recommended the use of "motivational interviewing," focusing on the intern's self-reflection about what was done well and what could have been done better. By taking such a positive approach, even when the intervention may not appear successful, the supervisor can emphasize the intern's good intentions. Focusing on intern strengths in supervision can also remind interns to identify strengths and assets of their clients during supervision. This may increase the respect that interns have for client strengths.

EMPATHY AND EXPERIENTIAL CONSIDERATIONS IN CASE DISCUSSIONS AND MISTAKES TO AVOID

When using case discussions or questions, supervisors should give careful thought to the process. As noted, Falender and Shafranske (2004) and others (Bogo, 1993; Kaiser, 1992) emphasize that it is extremely important not to focus solely on the external events of therapy but also to consider the internal experience, concerns, and feelings of the intern and the relationship of the intern to the supervisor. Lambert and Beier (1974) reported in early research on supervision that when supervisors are acting as counselors, they tend to offer more empathic statements than when they are interacting with interns.

The role of empathy in supervision was studied empirically by Shanfield, Mohl, Matthews, and Hetherly (1992), who used a structured inventory to evaluate supervisor performance during videotaped supervisory sessions. Results of this research showed that the factors most closely related to ratings of supervisor excellence were the supervisor's empathy and attention to the immediate concerns and experiences of the interns. By comparison, supervisors who intellectualized and offered general elaborations with little attention to interns' concerns were rated as "low" in their facilitation of trainee learning.

Just as it can be a mistake for questions to predominate in a supervisory interaction, it is generally advisable to use questions sparingly in treatment interactions. Beginning interns are often prone to ask too many questions of clients in an effort to "solve" problems. When supervisors establish a model of supervision through questioning, interns may be inclined to emulate that approach in their therapy. This is inadvisable because much as interns need support and affirmation, clients also need more than just questions to experience therapeutic gains. This principle might not be modeled well in questioning-based supervision.

Perhaps just as important as discussing what constitutes good supervision is identification of problems that may interfere with effective supervision (Falender & Shafranske, 2004; Kadushin & Harkness, 2002; Magnuson, Wilcoxon, & Norem, 2000). Among the factors that have been identified as hindering supervision are failure to recognize the intern's developmental needs, inflexibility in supervision sessions, supervisors using the relationship to meet personal needs rather than the needs of interns, untrained or immature supervisors, too much focus on the technical or cognitive aspects of therapy, and general examples of inhumane actions of the supervisor.

VIDEO AND AUDIO RECORDINGS AND ROLE-PLAYS

Ways of using audio and video effectively were discussed in Chapter 3, and, if you have not read that chapter yet, you may find it helpful to do so now. Because most of what was said in Chapter 3 also applies to supervision, only a few key suggestions are reviewed here.

Perhaps the most important suggestion for using recordings is to select sessions in which you felt good about your work and sessions in which you felt confused or ineffective (Sobell, Manor, Sobell, & Dum, 2008). The successful sessions can help build your confidence and can also provide opportunities to identify what went well and why. Less successful sessions in supervision should also be reviewed so you can learn from your mistakes and expand your skills. If you do not feel comfortable revealing sessions in which your performance was not ideal, that feeling itself is worth exploring. You may want to consider the comments later in this chapter regarding how to deal with conflicts in supervision. If something can be done to increase your comfort in exploring your weaknesses with your supervisor, I encourage you to do it. For optimal learning and development, you must feel free, encouraged, and safe about revealing both strengths and weaknesses. For a discussion of how these issues can be addressed through developmental approaches to videotape use in supervision, see Huhra et al. (2008).

A safe, supportive relationship is also essential for effective use of role-plays in supervision. As discussed in Chapter 3, it is important to become deeply involved in the imagined roles and situations when doing role-plays. Interns may find this difficult in the context of supervision because the evaluative element of interacting with a supervisor can interfere with the ability to be open and involved. Much as you are encouraged to deal with issues concerning sharing of taped sessions, if your supervisor uses role-play techniques in supervision and you feel restricted by the evaluative component, talk about your experience with the supervisor. This may help bring out underlying issues relating to the dual roles of supervisor–evaluator and intern–student. Understanding your own difficulties in role-playing with a supervisor may also help you understand your clients in new ways.

LIVE SUPERVISION

As useful as case notes, recorded sessions, and role-plays can be, there is no substitute for directly observing therapy sessions. Interestingly, Romans et al. (1995) found that although training directors rated co-therapy and live supervision as the strongest learning activities for interns, these modalities were also among the least commonly used. Presumably, this is due to the difficulty of scheduling simultaneous times for the supervisor to directly observe or join the intern in therapy. This is certainly understandable; but, given the strength of this approach, if it is at all possible, you and your supervisor should include at least some live supervision or co-therapy in your schedules.

Several arrangements can be used for directly observing treatment. One way is for the supervisor to be physically present in the room with the trainee. Another possibility is to use a special observation room equipped with one-way mirrors. These allow the supervisor to remain unseen behind the glass during the therapy session.

By observing sessions as they occur, supervisors get a better sense of the process. They can listen to what is said, watch the nonverbal behaviors of the trainee and the client, note key moments in the session, and get a deeper awareness of the overall "feel" of the interactions. In some arrangements, supervisors can also instruct the trainee during the interaction. Using what is known as the "bug-in-the-ear" technique, supervisors observe the session from behind a one-way mirror and can speak to trainees through a microphone connected to tiny earplug-type speakers. This enables the supervisor to call the trainee's attention to certain behaviors or statements of the client. The supervisor might also point out the trainee's own behaviors or suggest specific things the trainee should say or do.

Although direct observation is an excellent way to learn therapy, it has some drawbacks. The most obvious is intrusion into the therapeutic interaction. Another potential problem is that many interns, who already feel anxious about the role of therapist, are now placed simultaneously in the role of therapist and student (Costa, 1995). Friedlander, Keller, Peca-Baker, and Olk (1986) commented on the role conflict that can occur in interns who are at the same time in the "subordinate" role of trainee and the "superordinate" role of therapist. This conflict can become acute when the intern receives instructions from a supervisor that contradict the intern's own sense of what should happen in therapy. One can imagine how this can play out with the bug-in-the-ear technique. If an intern is thinking about responding in a certain way but then is told through the bug to do something different, the intern must deal with the internal conflict while outwardly maintaining a composed demeanor for the client.

Because direct observation poses such problems, it is helpful for supervisors and interns to establish an agreement about how to proceed during these sessions. This agreement should clarify the expectations and goals for the therapy session, when or if a supervisor will intervene, whether the intern is expected to follow unconditionally the supervisor's lead or is allowed some discretion, and what the debriefing after the session will entail.

My own preference is to give interns a great deal of leeway and freedom to follow their own instincts. It is especially important for supervisors to keep in mind that they are teaching the interns, not doing the therapy themselves. Thus, although I occasionally offer suggestions, interns are generally given leeway over what to do. It is essential, however, to establish an agreed-on signal that tells interns if I have identified something important and they must follow my lead. I use this only rarely, but I make certain that the interns understand and respect the importance of this option. If the supervisor detects an issue of particular sensitivity, or if there is a possibility of significant risk, the intern must trust the supervisor's judgment and save explanations for later. The supervisor is ultimately responsible for the treatment, and interns must respect that responsibility. It is simply unacceptable for the intern and the supervisor to get into a conflict during a session.

One additional comment applies not only to direct observation but also to all forms of observing therapy. It is always easier for the observer to pick things up than it is for the therapist. This means the supervisor must be patient and not overly critical with an intern if the supervisor detects something in therapy that the intern may have missed. Calling things to the intern's attention is certainly useful, but the purpose must be to help educate the trainee, not to make the supervisor look good. The same principle applies when interns observe the work or are reviewing tapes of other interns.

OBSERVING THE SUPERVISOR IN THERAPY

Studies in which interns have been asked what their supervisors might have done differently have revealed that many interns desire more such opportunities to observe their supervisor in clinical work. Interns recognize that discussion about their own work can only take them so far. They also believe they learn a great deal when they can watch their supervisor in group or individual sessions, read reports written by the supervisor, and observe the supervisor in other actions such as staff meetings and conferences (Kaplan, Rothrock, & Culkin, 1999).

Levenson and Evans (2000) suggested that many training programs tend to underutilize video recordings for teaching and supervision. They also suggested that students could benefit from greater exposure to watching video of teachers and supervisors doing therapy. They noted, however, that this could raise touchy

issues for some supervisors: "If you think students are resistant to being taped, try asking a licensed professional to tape one of his/her sessions for teaching purposes" (p. 450). Students wishing to observe their supervisors either in person or on tape may wish to make this desire known, but in doing so they should be sensitive to the issues raised by Levenson and Evans.

If opportunities are provided for interns to observe supervisors at work, the experience will be more effective if the intern has some guidance and structure to work from. Kaplan et al. (1999) suggested a series of questions addressing the theoretical orientation being demonstrated, the stages of the counseling process being observed, key events that take place in the session, and the like. These authors also emphasize the ethical considerations of any observed therapy session, and they provide a helpful informed consent template that can be given to confirm client approval for the session to be observed either directly or on tape.

Another way for interns to observe supervisors in practice is for the supervisor and the intern to work together as co-therapists with clients. This is most commonly practiced in group or couples therapy, but it can also be used with individual clients.

If co-therapy is arranged, the same caveats described for observation techniques must be addressed. The supervisor and intern should agree on who will be the primary therapist and how to signal the intern if the supervisor needs to take the lead. It is also important to discuss the sessions afterward to explore what happened and share impressions of the interaction.

Although most supervisors are open to co-therapy if it meets with the needs of clients, many are not aware that interns would like such an opportunity. As a result, interns may need to ask whether they can observe supervisors in different settings. If this sounds obvious, it is, but often we neglect to do the obvious because no one thinks to ask.

EXERCISE

Many interns do not realize they can take the initiative by suggesting useful learning opportunities. Take a few moments to think of what opportunities your internship is providing and what additional experiences you might find interesting. If you had the opportunity to observe your supervisor in different aspects of clinical work, what would benefit you the most to observe? In order to better understand your supervisor's perspective, now ask yourself what concerns you might have if you were a supervisor being observed by an intern? Having considered these issues, you may want to speak with your supervisor directly about the kinds of learning experiences or opportunities for observation that you would find most helpful.

REMOTE SUPERVISION: INTERNET, TELEPHONE, AND OTHER TECHNOLOGIES

In most instances, your supervisor will be working in the same setting as you are, but it occasionally happens, particularly in rural settings, that your supervisor may not be physically present at all times or, in some instances, at all. In lieu of direct face-to-face supervision, online and telecommunication can enable remote supervisory interactions. This type of supervision can be economical, and in some instances, it is the only feasible way of providing any supervision to interns in remote locations.

Chapman, Baker, Nassar-McMillan, and Gerler (2011) describe research in which counseling practicum students volunteered to receive supervision online as part of a 14-week counseling practicum. Their research examined both asynchronous, that is, delayed time interactions such as email, versus real-time, synchronous modalities such as Web chats and Web camera communications. Results showed that trainees reported gains in self-perceived competence and confidence. Attitudes toward the supervisory methodology, including both synchronous and asynchronous methods, were positive, but differences were observed in individual comfort levels with the technology. With greater experience, however, all participants reported increased comfort with the technology and, by the conclusion, offered high ratings of the course and the supervision modality.

To assist with practical, clinical, and ethical considerations in using Web technologies, Abbas et al. (2011) reviewed the empirical literature on such techniques and then described in detail how they used Web cam and Web conference technologies to review recorded treatment sessions in a group format with participants in remote locations. Ethical issues, especially informed consent and confidentiality, are discussed with focused consent forms provided as examples. In addition, the importance of preparing trainees in both the technological and clinical aspects of these interactions is considered. Interns and supervisors interested in arranging such procedures would do well to consult this reference for helpful suggestions.

One particularly interesting advantage of remote supervision is the ability of trainees to study a particular approach to treatment or work with a recognized leader in a therapy or assessment method without having to travel personally to be physically present with the instructor. Indeed, as Manring, Greenberg, Gregory, and Gallinger (2011) pointed out, students from around the world can now simultaneously observe expert practitioners at work and in turn be observed in real time as they provide treatment themselves.

Whichever remote supervisory modality is chosen, there are trade-offs from direct supervision. For example, in remote, as contrasted with face-to-face, supervision, a supervisor may not be as able to pick up on subtle nonverbal clues from the intern, such as anxiety or frustration. On the positive side, however, electronic communication can also reduce some of the hierarchical tensions that exist between supervisor and trainee in face-to-face interactions.

Another potential limitation arises if urgent situations occur. In remote supervision, it may be more difficult for the intern to get immediate help from a supervisor who is physically distant. Remote supervisors also may not be acquainted with the other staff or even the basic physical location and layout of a placement site. This can be a significant shortcoming, as one of the ways a supervisor can assist interns is by helping them understand and appreciate some of the staff interactions that occur in all settings and can either enhance or detract from treatment and the intern's learning experience. If a supervisor has not been to a placement site personally and has not gotten to know the people there and developed a feel for the place, it will be more difficult for the supervisor to fully understand what the intern is experiencing and needs to work within that setting.

Several interesting ethical and legal issues are also raised by remote supervision. Confidentiality is an obvious and important concern if sensitive clinical material is being sent via the Internet. Less obvious, but nevertheless very important, are issues concerning the licensing laws and other requirements that apply if a supervisor is located in a different state from that of the intern's placement site. Because other legal issues (e.g., abuse reporting procedures, commitment laws) can also vary from state to state, it is important for both the supervisor and the intern to know that the laws from the supervisor's own state, which the supervisor may be most familiar with, may not apply in the same way in another jurisdiction. Finally, as with all supervision, clients should be fully informed about the nature of a remote supervisor–intern relationship, and they should be given some means of contacting the supervisor if necessary.

GROUP SUPERVISON

Much of the discussion thus far has focused on activities conducted during individual supervision, but it is also likely that at least some of your supervisory experiences will take place in a group format with other interns or coworkers. Group supervision presents a number of possible advantages as well as potential disadvantages relative to individual supervision.

Reviewing the literature on group supervision, Bogo, Globerman, and Sussman (2004) noted that one among the chief benefits may simply be efficiency and economics, with group work allowing a supervisor to meet with several interns at the same time and convey common concepts once instead of in each separate meeting. Riva and Cornish (2008) found that the most common activity of group supervision is case presentation, with 57% of the time described by their sample being spent in this activity. Case presentation in a group setting allows students to learn from the examples of their peers and from peer feedback. Peers can also provide emotional support to one another and, particularly when interns are involved in group therapy as part of their clinical duties, group supervision can involve "parallel process" observations, in which the supervisory group mirrors processes that might be observed by interns in their own therapy group work.

Kadushin and Harkness (2002) added to this list and pointed out that group supervision also affords an opportunity for the supervisor to observe interns in different interactions, and vice versa. In addition, there may be instances in which it is easier for a supervisor to communicate a point to an intern if group members are there to share, and perhaps reinforce, the concept or skill. Finally, group work provides a forum in which interns, through the process of observing peers and offering feedback, have an introduction to the tasks of supervision themselves. Kadushin and Harkness offer a number of suggestions on how to establish, prepare, and conduct supervision groups and how to deal with any problems that might emerge.

While recognizing the potential benefits of group work, disadvantages should also be acknowledged. Kadushin and Harkness (2002) pointed out that it could be harder to individualize an instruction or intervention in a group setting, especially if an intern's sensitive personal issue is involved. Groups can also pose problems if conflicts between members emerge or if group dynamics interfere with the learning opportunities. Of special importance in group work is how vulnerabilities, deficits, or "clinical errors" are dealt with. It is one thing to acknowledge a weakness or have a shortcoming pointed out in a one-on-one exchange with a supervisor. It is quite another to have such issues emerge in front of one's peers. Perhaps in recognition of this difficulty, group members may be reluctant to reveal potential weaknesses or to give honest, critical feedback to their peers. Group cohesion in supervisory groups can also create challenges, especially if the group begins in some way to work against a supervisor or if the group norms begin to reject a supervisor's input or theoretical approach.

Many of the issues identified by Kadushin and Harkness (2002) were also described by Enyedy et al. (2003), who studied what they described as "hindering phenomena" in group supervision as reported by counseling graduate students. Responses in this study addressed a number of potential problems that Enyedy et al. sorted into five clusters: (1) problems between members, (2) problems with supervisors, (3) supervisee anxiety, (4) logistical constraints, and (5) group time management. For each of these areas of concern, suggested strategies were offered to reduce problems before they develop and more effectively manage those that do occur.

Central to the findings of Enyedy et al., and to much of the literature in this area, is the primary importance of a supervisor who is skilled in group work. Bogo et al. (2004) examined the role of group supervisor by conducting systematic interviews with recent social work graduates to elicit their observations about their experiences in group supervision. Respondents in this study emphasized the fundamental requirement that supervisors be available and supportive. These qualities alone, however, are not sufficient to make for a quality group supervision experience. In addition, the supervisor needs to keep an educational focus, be able to maintain structure, manage group dynamics, and be skilled in dealing with "personal and shared experiences in a public space" (p. 204). The last issue mentioned earlier is of particular importance because the nature of clinical work so often and readily evokes personal issues that may be difficult to deal with and may be especially so in a group format with peers.

One final note about group supervision is that the supervisor is by no means the only key to success; the participants are at least as important. Chapter 3 of this text offered suggestions for making peer groups effective as well as more general suggestions for active participation and personal responsibilities as a learner. Those suggestions apply equally well to group supervision. The most important elements, in my experience, are that interns be open to giving and receiving feedback; that they do so in a positive, supportive manner; and that they maintain a constructive attitude that is focused on learning and professional development. Last, but by no means least, ethical strictures about confidentiality and other matters must be rigorously adhered to in group supervision as in all of your activities.

THEORETICAL ORIENTATION

One of the most common sources of confusion and conflict between interns and supervisors has to do with differences in theoretical orientation. In some instances, a supervisor believes a certain theoretical and technical approach to therapy or assessment is best, so interns must learn, practice, and demonstrate knowledge and skill in that approach. The advantage of this approach derives from the clarity of focus such training provides. Faced with many theoretical schools and techniques of therapy or assessment, interns sometimes feel at a loss to know how to proceed. A disadvantage of focusing on a single approach is that interns may conclude there is only one best way to do therapy and thereby ignore or even denigrate alternatives. It can also happen that an intern does not concur with the approach of the supervisor, and this leads to tension and conflict as the supervisor advocates a certain approach and the intern resists.

An alternative to emphasizing a single therapy approach is to adopt an integrative approach that focuses on core competencies across different theoretical orientations (Farber & Kaslow, 2010). In integrative approaches, supervisors may emphasize specific orientations but draw from multiple perspectives and skill sets and assimilate or integrate these into the training in case conceptualization, clinical skills, and so on. Ideally, in this approach, trainees are encouraged to think critically and reflectively on what may work best for which clients and conditions and why. Trainees are also encouraged to consider the research literature on treatment efficacy and effectiveness and take this into account in formulating their approach (Boswell, Nelson, Nordberg, McAleavey, & Castonguay, 2010). One of the advantages of an integrative approach to supervision is that it tends to reduce the problem of ideological conflicts and allows the supervisor and intern to focus more on skills and less on adherence to a fixed philosophy. An integrative approach also facilitates more open discussion of the relative pros and cons of different interventions.

It also happens in some internships that the supervisor takes a laissez-faire approach and offers too little guidance to trainees. With the exception of interns who have a great deal of experience, most interns need more structure and direction than a laissez-faire supervisor provides. It is an exceptionally rare intern who will receive optimum benefit without working from at least some structure and model. Whether the intern and supervisor agree or disagree on theory or technique, interns are usually helped by having supervisors who can articulate and demonstrate a coherent approach to treatment or assessment.

Whichever approach your supervisor adopts, you should consider the pros and cons of that approach as it relates to your own needs, the supervisor, and the setting. Do your best to understand the reasons for a supervisor's theoretical and supervisory approach and be willing to try new approaches. At various times in my own training, I believed certain therapy models were complete bunk until I had the opportunity to observe them and discovered that they offered valuable lessons. It has also happened that I wholeheartedly embraced one approach over others but gradually came to recognize both the shortcomings of the approach I had selected and the merits of alternative methods.

SUPERVISION AND THERAPY: DIFFERENCES AND SIMILARITIES

Because clinical work and the internship experience can evoke deeply personal and often difficult material for interns, clinical supervisors must not only help interns acquire specific skills, they must also help them manage the emotional and intellectual challenges and the personal issues that emerge in their training. This responsibility may place supervisors in a role that is very much like that of therapist for the trainee. This similarity of roles and processes is sometimes referred to as "parallel process" (Hebert, 1992; Kadushin and Harkness, 2002; Searles, 1955; Tracey, Bludworth, & Glidden-Tracey, 2012).

While recognizing the similarities between therapy and supervision, it must also be acknowledged that interns do not sign up for their internship as clients, and they have a right to work out personal issues on their own. Thus, for both supervisor and intern, there is a dilemma about how to deal with the intern's personal issues. This dilemma becomes quite acute if an intern's personal issues begin to interfere with his or her clinical work or development.

DIFFERENCES BETWEEN THERAPY AND SUPERVISION

Among the more important differences between therapy and supervision are the degree of choice involved in receiving therapy or supervision, the purpose and goals of therapy versus supervision, the role of the trainee compared with that of the client, the role of the supervisor compared with that of therapist, and the evaluative function of supervisors (Prieto, 1997; Sklare, Thomas, Williams, & Powers, 1996).

In therapy, clients have made a conscious decision to seek assistance for personal issues. They also have freedom to choose who will be their therapist and under what conditions the therapy will take place. By comparison, interns are often required to receive supervision as part of their education and training. They may or may not have a say in who their supervisor will be, but they are very likely not to have any say in whether or not they will receive supervision.

Another key difference between therapy and supervision is found in the purpose of the activity. Clients seek therapy primarily because they want to be helped personally in some way by the therapy. By comparison, training programs mandate supervision of therapists not so much to help the therapist as to protect the welfare of the client. Trainees can and should grow as individuals through the process of supervision, but the supervisee's personal growth is not the primary goal of many supervision arrangements with interns.

Closely related to the issues of choice and the purpose of therapy and supervision is the matter of dual roles for supervisors who would also engage in therapy with trainees. Because supervisors must perform many functions with trainees, including instruction; mentoring; support; and, of critical importance here, evaluation, their position in relation to the trainee differs markedly from that of the therapist in relation to a client. Interestingly, researchers have long recognized that although students are well aware of power differentials between themselves and their supervisors, supervisors may be relatively unaware of this issue (Doehrman, 1976; Kadushin, 1974).

A therapist may form positive or critical opinions about clients, but apart from certain institutional settings or extreme circumstances, the therapist is not in a position to take actions that would have substantial impact on the client's future outside therapy. This is not the case for supervisees. Supervisors may well hold the key to the supervisee's professional future. In the face of this power, interns may have good reason to choose information to disclose carefully and not be fully honest with their supervisors.

One manifestation of this dilemma was a student-drafted "bill of rights" described by Haley (1992), which stated that teachers were not to investigate students' personal lives unless the teacher could demonstrate the relevance of the exploration to the therapy task and could show how the personal exploration would help change the therapist's behavior in a positive direction.

Keeping in mind the differences between supervision and therapy and the differences across different approaches to therapy, certain conditions are nevertheless common to virtually all supervision and have important similarities to the therapy process. Because these intrinsic conditions cannot be avoided, interns and supervisors need to be familiar with them and learn to recognize and understand how they influence the supervisory relationship and process.

EXPLORING THE NEEDS AND PERSONAL QUALITIES OF INTERNS

Of the many reasons for interns to be aware of their own needs, two stand out most prominently. First, insofar as the therapist's self is "a therapeutic instrument" (Hebert, 1992, p. 131) it is necessary for the therapist to understand and be able to adapt the instrument (i.e., the self) as needed to assist the client (Falender & Shafranske, 2004). Second, if therapists are not aware of their own needs, they are more likely to use the therapy session to satisfy those needs, sometimes at the expense of the client.

If self-awareness is so important to therapists, and if lack of self-awareness can lead to trainees using therapy to satisfy their needs, how is a supervisor to promote self-awareness without serving as a therapist for the trainee? Hebert (1992) advocated self-examination on the part of interns. The goal of this self-examination is to increase the interns' awareness of such influences as sources of their anxieties, the struggle between wanting to change and wanting to stay the same, stimuli that trigger tendencies toward self-blame, authoritarian posturing, and other characteristics that could influence therapy.

Although Hebert (1992) stressed self-examination, he maintained that this examination should also involve the supervisor. Describing the responsibility of the supervisor, he emphasized the importance of supervisors showing confidence in the ability of interns to learn and change. Hebert's description of the supervisor's role sounds not unlike descriptions of the therapist's role and the necessary ingredients for helping relationships (cf. Rogers, 1961, pp. 50–57). Thus, although Hebert was keenly aware of the vulnerable position of trainees vis-à-vis their supervisors, he saw the task of self-awareness as primary to the development of therapists.

EXERCISE

This exercise has two parts. The first part asks you to explore your reactions to the ideas just presented regarding supervision and therapy. Do you think it is important to explore the needs and self of the therapist? Do you have any hesitations or concerns about this process for yourself? What would your reaction be to addressing these issues in supervision, and how would you like your supervisor to deal with this issue?

The second part of the exercise involves trying to identify any personal needs you are aware of that, if not managed well, could impede your functioning as a therapist. For example, you might consider your own needs for affection, approval, or power and ways in which these needs could influence your actions as a therapist. After thinking about these issues for yourself, you may want to discuss them with a peer or perhaps with your instructor or supervisor.

RESISTANCE TO SELF-AWARENESS AND CHANGE

Because self-awareness is so important in therapy training and supervision, it should not be surprising that some of the same processes that accompany self-awareness and change in therapy also emerge in the supervisory process. At least three types of resistance stand out in supervision. The first, resistance to awareness, relates closely to the preceding discussion of interns' needs. Resistance to awareness refers to the challenges associated with becoming aware of personal qualities or needs that are not easily acknowledged or owned:

> In learning about human behavior we are learning about ourselves, about our defenses, our motives, our unflattering impulses. In dispassionately examining the sources of our most cherished attitudes and illusions, we are throwing open to question the way in which we order our lives. (Kadushin, 2002, p. 228)

Resistance to this process is perfectly understandable and is probably to be expected of most trainees. A second source of resistance has to do with the reality that to learn, one must confess ignorance of what is to be learned. This is not easy for anyone, and it can be especially difficult for students who feel their competence is being tested at every turn. Kadushin (2002) described this dilemma particularly well:

> The learning situation demands an admission of ignorance, however limited. In admitting ignorance, supervisees expose their vulnerability. They risk the possibility of criticism, of shame and perhaps rejection because of an admitted inadequacy.
>
> Supervisees have the choice of being anxious because they do not know how to do their work or being anxious about confessing ignorance and obtaining help. (p. 229)

Because this paradoxical situation is inherent in the learning process, it can be difficult for interns to resolve on their own. As such, it is extremely important for supervisors to be sensitive to it and make every effort to allow interns to acknowledge their limitations in order to make learning possible. At the same time, interns should resolve that it is better to risk acknowledging their limitations than to feign knowledge at the possible risk of harming clients or the agency.

A third source of resistance in supervision is resistance to change. In a review of this and other topics in supervision, Rubinstein (1992) paraphrased similar comments by Kadushin (1985) and Rothman (1973) and explained that

> Change requires giving up old behavior patterns, which have helped the supervisee keep homeostasis in his or her personal life. Hence, a change of this kind evokes anxiety in supervisees, who are not sure they wish to change what has taken them so much time to learn. (Rubinstein, 1992, p. 99)

Interns may resist trying, learning, or sometimes even considering certain issues or techniques of therapy because they believe that their established ways of being and doing things as people are being threatened. Although the overt content of the verbal defense may be couched in language about what is good for the client, the source of the resistance is often found in the intern's need to defend what has worked well for him or her as an individual or as a therapist.

An example of this process comes from my own experience in the early stages of training. At that time I was very resistant to reflective techniques in therapy. Although I wanted to develop the skills of therapy, I was intent on not "sounding like a therapist." This desire gained support in my first practicum placement, in which the clinical staff followed a treatment model that was not at all consistent with the reflective approach. That same semester, during a classroom role-play exercise in which students were to practice reflective techniques, I offered verbal protest but went along with the exercise at the insistence of the instructor. After the exercise, I remained unimpressed with the technique, but the instructor patiently suggested that we review a tape of the role-play to identify the statements that had elicited the most response from the client. Much to my surprise, the tape revealed that the reflective statements, which I had been so critical of before, turned out to have produced the most extensive and useful exploration for the client. Along with demonstrating the potential of reflective techniques, this experience showed how resistance to a technique can sometimes reflect our own desires to meet personal beliefs or needs more than actual knowledge about what does or does not help clients.

Kadushin (2002) described a somewhat different, though undoubtedly related, interpretation of resistance. In a thought-provoking discussion, Kadushin suggested that change could create a sense of betrayal because the supervisee is being asked to give up behaviors or ways of thinking that were learned from parents and other significant people in the supervisee's past. Changing, therefore, implies disloyalty or infidelity to parents or other role models.

In these circumstances, resistance may take the form of arguing that a given concept or technique will or will not help clients, but the underlying issue is that accepting the new idea or approach implies that one's parents or other role models were somehow wrong. The intern resists that possibility because accepting it would introduce a host of other issues and anxieties with which most trainees are ill equipped to cope.

As this discussion demonstrates, resistance is a fact of life in supervision. How, then, can supervisors and supervisees deal with it most effectively?

Several principles may be particularly helpful. First, resistance to awareness and change should not be confused with legitimate self-protection deriving from the situational context of supervision. Students who appear to resist self-exploration may be seeking to avoid self-awareness, or they may be protecting their privacy against an unwanted and potentially damaging intrusion by their supervisor. As Rubinstein (1992) pointed out, one must be careful not to assign attributions without carefully considering the situation in which the behavior occurs. Before assigning a student's behaviors to resistance, supervisors would be well advised to consider how their own behaviors as supervisors or the atmosphere of a class might be contributing to the student's apparent resistance. Supervisors should also realize that just as interns may resist self-awareness, supervisors are not always the best judges of their own behaviors. Seeking an outside consult can sometimes help supervisors become more aware of their own actions.

Supervisors may also help students deal with their own resistance by explaining how resistance functions and appears in the therapeutic process and emphasizing that resistance applies in one way or another to all of us, not just to clients. So, too, supervisors can emphasize that although resistance processes are normal, developing greater self-awareness and openness to change is an essential process for students and therapists alike. Supervisors can facilitate this by creating safe and supportive environments that allow and encourage students to consciously express, identify, and explore their own resistance.

A final and extremely important point about resistance in supervision is that it provides a powerful learning opportunity for interns to understand something of what the process of change is like for clients. Studying concepts in the abstract is never as meaningful as experiencing them firsthand. If interns can become aware of their own resistance during supervision, that awareness may help them appreciate and respect the resistance clients display in therapy. Lacking such firsthand experience, interns tend to respond to client resistance as something that "interferes with therapy" or that shows clients to be "unmotivated." By comparison, after displaying and acknowledging resistance themselves, interns are more likely to go beyond the simplistic interpretation and appreciate resistance not as an obstacle to therapy but as a normal and important part of the process.

EXERCISE

Considering the three types of resistance (i.e., to awareness, to revealing ignorance, and to change), think about your education and training up to this point and try to identify instances in which you may have responded with each type of resistance. Next, try to imagine future situations that could evoke such reactions. Finally, because all of us are likely to show resistance in some areas, what matters most is that we learn to recognize and cope with the resistance productively. As you think of what might evoke resistance

and how you would recognize resistance in yourself, consider how you could learn to understand your resistance and be able to work with it to allow yourself to change.

TRANSFERENCE AND COUNTERTRANSFERENCE

In much the same way as resistance in supervision parallels resistance in therapy, transference and countertransference are also part of both therapy and supervision. These terms, which have their origins in psychoanalytic approaches, have been defined in various ways by different authors. For our purposes, it is enough to understand transference as a process in which clients, or in the case of supervision, supervisees, "replace" some other, typically earlier, person in their lives with the person of the therapist or supervisor, relating to the latter individual in ways that are similar to their relationship with the original person. For example, students may relate to supervisors much as they related to parents or other authority figures in their lives. If students happen to be older than their supervisors, it can also happen that the students will relate to the supervisors as they do to one of their own children.

Countertransference is somewhat the reverse of transference. In transference, clients relate to their therapists as if they were someone else. In the case of countertransference, therapists (supervisors) relate to the clients (supervisees) as if they were someone else. For example, a supervisor may relate to a trainee as if the trainee were one of his or her children or clients.

According to psychoanalytic explanations, both transference and countertransference take place unconsciously and are expressed behaviorally and emotionally. Kadushin (2002) pointed out that the supervisor–supervisee relationship tends to evoke the parent–child relationship and may, therefore, "reactivate anxiety associated with this earlier relationship" (p. 230).

As explained in regard to resistance, understanding transference and countertransference in supervision can help interns make the most of supervision, learn more about themselves, and gain greater awareness of processes they are likely to observe and experience in therapy. Recognizing and exploring transference reactions in supervision can also help interns develop greater self-understanding, which is critical to the therapist's development.

EXERCISE

Although transference is conceived to be largely an unconscious process, each of us has certain individuals in our lives who have represented authority figures in the past. Parents are perhaps the most likely to have filled this role, but others, such as older siblings, relatives, friends, or teachers, could also be such figures. The point of this exercise is not to circumvent the transference by trying to deal with it before it arises. Rather, it is to introduce a process of reflection and an understanding of transference that may be useful if or when transference occurs in supervision or therapy. To help you understand how transference might affect your own experiences with supervisors, consider this question: "If you were to anticipate a transference reaction toward a supervisor based on someone from your own past, who would the most likely person be?" "Why?"

SUGGESTED GUIDELINES FOR THERAPY AND SUPERVISION

Because of the similarities and differences between therapy and supervision, it is not easy to provide absolute demarcation between the two activities. On the one hand, as part of the training process, trainees need to explore personal needs and dynamics that may influence their work with clients. On the other hand, trainees are in a vulnerable position relative to supervisors and should have a right to choose how much personal information they wish to disclose.

The key here is that the focus must remain on the interns' actions in therapy. As long as their actions do not violate ethical standards, what trainees do outside therapy is not the concern of supervisors and should be left for the trainees to address on their own. According to Kadushin (2002), most supervisors report that they understand and respect these boundaries.

In my work with interns, I find that personal issues relating to an intern's clinical work can, and sometimes should, be identified by supervisors, but the process of working through those issues should best be left for therapy with someone other than the supervisor. I encourage interns to consider personal therapy as a valuable experience in itself and as an important, perhaps essential, step toward professional development. The benefits of individual therapy are very likely to carry over to the intern's clinical work and to supervision, but the supervisory work will not be confounded by the dual roles of supervisor–therapist or intern–client.

If an intern has access to a therapist, issues that arise in the intern's clinical work or supervisory relationship can be addressed in therapy. However, the goal of therapy should be to facilitate the intern's personal growth, not to vent frustrations or second-guess supervisors. The stresses of clinical work and benefits of personal therapy are addressed in Chapter 8 of this book.

EXERCISE

What are your personal attitudes toward seeking therapy or counseling for yourself? If you or your supervisor detected personal issues that were affecting your clinical work or training, would you be amenable to seeking therapy? If not, what are your concerns? What would the relative risks and benefits be if your supervisor also began to function as a therapist for you? How would you respond if you felt a supervisor was in some way stepping into the role of therapist and you were not comfortable with that?

CONFLICT IN SUPERVISION

FREQUENCY AND RESOLUTION OF CONFLICTS

Although most trainees have positive supervisory experiences, conflicts that interfere with learning are not uncommon (Grant, Schofield, & Crawford, 2012; Gray, Ladany, Walker, & Ancis,

2001; Nelson & Friedlander, 2001). In an early study, Moskowitz and Rupert (1983) surveyed 158 graduate students in clinical psychology and found that 38% reported major conflicts that made it difficult to learn from supervision. The three areas of conflict most identified by students were (1) theoretical orientation and therapy approach, (2) style of supervision, and (3) personality issues.

One of the most interesting findings of this research was that all the trainees who responded indicated that when conflict was present, they wanted the supervisor to identify it openly. Despite this desire, in the Moskowitz and Rupert sample, 83.8% of those who had experienced conflicts reported that it was trainees, not their supervisors, who had initiated discussion about the conflict. Gray et al. (2001) reported a similar finding, with most trainees wishing supervisors would recognize conflicts and bring them up to be resolved. At the same time, however, most interns indicated that they did not choose to bring up the issue of the conflict themselves, largely because of concerns about adverse reactions and even retribution from their supervisors. This finding suggests that if you experience a conflict in supervision and think it should be dealt with, you, the trainee, may have to be the one to raise the issue. Unfortunately, this also suggests that you may want to proceed with some caution should you choose to pursue this approach.

One other observation that is noteworthy from these studies is that interns rarely described conflicts resulting from supervisors not being sufficiently critical in their assessment or grading of interns' performances (Veach, 2001). I mention this here because it is easy to become upset if you feel that a supervisor has given you an unfairly low grade or is overly critical of your performance; however, an intern should actually have more reason to be concerned if a supervisor is not sufficiently attentive to areas in which the intern needs to improve. Remember that the purpose of your internship experience is to better your skills, not to have a supervisor simply tell you that everything you do is just fine. Keep in mind, too, that your supervisor is more likely to give you critical feedback, which may well be the most useful at times, if you are perceived to be open to such feedback and willing to learn from it (Hoffman, Hill, Holmes, & Freitas, 2005).

With regard to resolution of conflicts, Moskowitz and Rupert's (1983) findings revealed that outcomes relate significantly to the nature of the conflict. Overall, more than half of those who experienced conflict and discussed it with their supervisors reported that the discussion led to at least some improvement. However, 37% of the students who discussed conflicts indicated that there was no improvement or that the situation became worse. The most successfully resolved conflicts were those relating to supervisory style. In 90% of these cases, discussion led to improvement; in none of the reported cases did conditions worsen following discussion. Conflicts relating to theoretical orientation also showed improvement with discussion, but the effect, 55% improvement, was less impressive than that with supervisory style. The most difficult conflicts to resolve related to personality, with only 36% of students reporting improvement and 37% indicating that the situation became worse or led to a change in supervisors.

GUIDELINES FOR DEALING WITH CONFLICT

Because conflicts in supervision are not uncommon, several principles and useful tools may help interns and supervisors deal with conflict more effectively. To gain insights into how experienced supervisors manage conflicts in supervision, Grant et al. (2012) conducted in-depth interviews and reviews of recorded supervision sessions with 16 senior professionals recognized for their experience and expertise in supervision. Broadly speaking, conflicts included concerns about unethical conduct, competence, supervisee characteristics such as arrogance or defensiveness, and problems in the supervisory relationship. Among the strategies identified for managing conflicts, 4 overarching core themes emerged, with 23 categories and 4 subcategories of interventions identified. The 4 core themes were relational, reflective, confrontive, and avoidant.

Within the relational theme, interventions included naming the difficulty, validating and normalizing the conflict, offering support, anticipating challenges, modeling, addressing the parallel processes, and acknowledging mistakes when the supervisor had erred. Reflective interventions included efforts to encourage reflection on the part of both the supervisees and supervisors. Remaining patient and mindful, processing countertransference, reviewing case conceptualization, and seeking additional supervision from others were all identified within the reflective theme.

Confrontive strategies were more likely to be employed when relational and reflective approaches were considered to have been insufficiently effective. Typically, confrontive efforts would begin with a degree of intentional tentativeness that would progress toward more direct confrontation depending on the supervisee's responses and the nature of the conflict. Supervisors stressed the importance of carefully considering the qualities of the supervisee, the details of the conflict, alternative methods, and the likely impact of confrontation before engaging in this category of interventions.

Finally, though they were the least common of all reactions to conflicts, avoidant strategies were acknowledged by supervisors when they encountered cases that were intractable, or when issues were in some ways unsettling or personally challenging to the supervisor. Respondents indicated in these cases that they recognized the avoidant responses were not optimal, but they were honest in acknowledging that on occasion this was in fact how they dealt with certain conflicts and individuals.

As an intern, understanding how supervisors deal with conflict may give you insights into how you can approach conflicts if they emerge in supervision. In my experience, the first principle is to approach conflicts as opportunities for learning rather than as situations that can only interfere with learning. In managing a supervisory conflict, you may be able to discover how you react to conflict, what kinds of issues or interactions tend to promote conflict, and how you can more effectively cope with conflicts. In raising these possibilities, my intent is not to offer the simplistic aphorism that "everything is a learning experience," nor do I want to suggest, as one supervisor was fond of telling interns, that "conflict builds character." I do, however, suggest that one of the biggest blocks to resolving conflicts is the underlying idea that "conflicts should not happen, and I should not have to deal with this." If you take an attitude of learning from a conflict, rather than an attitude of anger, fear, or avoidance, you are more likely to deal effectively with the situation.

The second general principle is to identify what a conflict is really about before raising it with your supervisor. Are you at odds over issues of theory or technique? Do you believe that the supervisor is not giving you sufficient support? Are you having difficulty accepting a critical observation by your supervisor? What sorts of transference or countertransference issues might be present? Are logistics, such as timing of supervision, a problem? In thinking about the key subject of a conflict, recognize that often the surface content of a conflict does not reflect the real difficulty.

After identifying the nature of the conflict, ask yourself as honestly as you can what role you are playing in it. This does not mean that you should engage in self-blame, nor does it absolve your supervisor of responsibility, but it does suggest that you should explore your own actions and reactions to better understand your part in what is happening. If self-exploration is difficult, or if you find that it is hard to really recognize your role, you may want to get an outside perspective, perhaps from a peer or another faculty member. If you decide to get another perspective, do not approach the interaction by expecting the other person to reassure you that the conflict is all the other person's fault. There is a crucial difference between support and uncritical agreement. When you discuss a supervisory conflict with a third party, ask the other person to support you emotionally and to appreciate the difficulty of the conflict, but ask the listener also to evaluate the situation objectively and try to help you understand things you may not have been aware of. Remember in this process that the purpose of getting another opinion is to understand what is happening, not to prove you are right.

Trying to see the situation from the supervisor's perspective is another valuable step toward resolving a conflict. Is your supervisor doing or saying things for reasons that might not be immediately evident to you but that might make perfect sense from his or her position? Is your supervisor aware that a conflict exists? If so, would he or she define the conflict differently from how you would? Asking yourself these questions may help you resolve a conflict without speaking directly to your supervisor about it. If you do discuss the matter, this forethought will serve as preparation that should make the discussion more productive.

An especially important element in dealing with a conflict is to ask yourself what it is you want to be different and what you would like to happen to be satisfied. This might be a change in the way you and your supervisor interact, or it might be a modification of some arrangement, such as the hours you work, your caseload, or a similar matter. By thinking about your own desires, you will be better able to articulate both the present situation and your wishes for change. This clarity can help you and your supervisor identify specific steps for dealing with and resolving the conflict.

Keeping in mind the principles just described, it can also be helpful to have structured tools to identify and resolve potential conflicts. Falender and Shafranske (2004) presented two useful instruments for this purpose. The first instrument, the Working Alliance Inventory, was developed by Audrey Bahrick. This inventory provides forms on which the supervisee and and the supervisor can rate their impressions in response to statements indicating the level of understanding between them, feelings and attitudes toward each other, clarity of goals and purpose, the value of activities in supervision, and similar matters. If the supervisor and the supervisee both complete their respective forms and then discuss their mutual impressions, areas of commonality as well as differences can be identified and then worked on together.

A second instrument offered by Falender and Shafranske (2004) is the Role Conflict and Role Ambiguity Inventory, developed initially by Olk and Friedlander (1992). Role ambiguity refers to an intern's uncertainty about the supervisor's expectations and evaluations. Role conflict involves situations in which the role of student conflicts in some way with that of counselor or colleague. An example of an item from the Role Ambiguity Scale is "I was not sure if I should discuss my professional weaknesses in supervision because I was not sure how I would be evaluated" (Falender & Shafranske, 2004, p. 266). An example of a Role Conflict item is "I disagreed with my supervisor about how to introduce a specific issue to a client, but I also wanted to do what the supervisor recommended" (p. 267). For all items, interns are asked to respond on a five-point scale indicating the degree to which they experienced these difficulties. As with the Working Alliance Inventory, completing this tool can provide an externalized basis for discussion about how things are going in supervision. Because items in both inventories can raise issues that are difficult and may be perceived as criticism, it is important to establish an understanding that the purpose of using these or other such tools is to improve the quality of the supervisory experience for both the supervisor and the intern and, as such, that criticism should be offered, received, and responded to constructively.

Finally, while offering suggestions for identifying and resolving conflicts constructively, it must also be acknowledged that for a variety of reasons, this is not always possible. Under such circumstances, the best solution may be to invite in another person, perhaps one's instructor, another supervisor, or another professional, to help work through differences. If this is unfeasible or unsuccessful, it may be desirable in some instances to negotiate a change in supervisors or placements. If handled sensitively and professionally, this does not have to be a negative experience for the people involved, and it may well be more constructive than simply staying with a relationship that is clearly not constructive or conducive to learning.

COMPETENCY-BASED TRAINING AND EVALUATION

Perhaps the most difficult, ambiguous, and important task supervisors must perform is evaluation of the competence of trainees. Some students in internships present themselves as being "grade motivated," which means they focus on how they think they will be graded rather than on what they are learning or how they are performing. It is essential for you to understand that the internship experience is fundamentally different from the rest of your academic work. In a typical class, students receive a single overall grade at the end of the course and earn "credit hours" toward their degree, often with little if any explicit measure of specific competencies. In most academic classes, lacking a certain knowledge

or skill may lower one's grade, but otherwise little of any real consequence happens.

By comparison, at internships and in professional life, lack of knowledge or skill has real consequences that apply not only to the intern but also to the clients, the supervisor, and the agency. Indeed, lack of skill on the part of a professional can cost clients their lives. That is worth thinking about for a moment. As an intern, and as a professional, the stakes are much higher than in academic life.

This reality is part of the reasons most helping and many other professions today are increasingly embracing competency-based training and evaluation. Because professional training is moving away from credit hours and letter grades and to systematic and comprehensive assessment of competencies, it is important that you understand and embrace competency assessment as part of not only your training but also your practice as a professional.

There are naturally some differences in the competencies emphasized and measured by different helping professions, but in each profession an underlying goal of competency training and evaluation is to identify the key skills, knowledge, and personal characteristics that professionals must possess, then systematically develop and evaluate those elements at each level of professional training.

The American Psychological Association's Task Force on Assessment of Competence in Professional Psychology offers an example of how this task has been approached within psychology. The work of this task force is described in detail by Kaslow et al. (2007) and in other articles included in a special edition of *Professional Psychology: Research and Practice*, Volume 38, October, 2007. On the basis of extensive reviews of competency assessment models across diverse professions, the task force proposed 15 guiding principles for the assessment of competency within professional psychology. Many of these same principles have also been discussed in the context of competency assessment within other helping professions (see, e.g., Bogo et al., 2006).

Among the principles most relevant to our discussion here are that assessment of competence is a "career-long" endeavor and that it must take a developmental approach that recognizes different levels of competency at different levels of professional training. Assessment must be ongoing as well as summative and should be integrated with training techniques and goals. In addition, multiple traits and skills should be assessed using multiple methods and informants. Self-reflection and self-assessment should also be taught and incorporated into the assessment process. Along with specific knowledge and skills, interpersonal functioning and personal development as well as professional conduct and values must be addressed, and strategies must be put in place for remediation when deficiencies or concerns are identified. The subject of intervening when competency problems are identified is also discussed by several other authors who review procedures for intervening and legal implications to be considered when dealing with performance deficiencies (Behnke, 2008; Gilfoyle, 2008; Gillis & Lewis, 2004; McAdams & Foster, 2007; Wayne, 2004).

Building on the work just described, detailed models of competency benchmarks (Fouad et al., 2009) and related competency assessment tools (Kaslow et al., 2009) have been proposed with specific benchmarks and assessment tools designated for three stages of training: readiness for the practicum, readiness for the predoctoral internship, and readiness for entry to practice. Each of the benchmarks (Fouad et al., 2009) includes sub-components and each of these can be assessed by different methods and tools. Among the benchmarks identified are professionalism, including values and ethics, personal comportment, integrity, and responsibility; reflective practice, including self assessment, awareness of personal competencies, and self-care; scientific knowledge and methods, including understanding and ability to apply research methods and findings, awareness of biological aspects of behavior, knowledge of lifespan and cognitive factors; and relationship skills, including individual-, group-, and community-relating skills. As mentioned earlier, specific benchmarks are offered for each of the three stages of professional training.

To accompany the identified benchmarks, Kaslow et al. (2009) list corresponding assessment tools and review the relevance of each tool to different benchmarks along with issues such as the psychometrics, strengths, and limitations of each tool. Among the diverse and multimodal tools identified are case presentation reviews, annual/rotation performance reviews, client process and outcomes data, competency evaluation rating forms, consumer surveys, live or recorded performance ratings, role-plays, standardized written and oral examinations, and "360 degree evaluations." The authors emphasize that use of these tools is most effective when targeted to particular competency benchmarks, and different tools may be more or less well suited to different levels of training.

Incorporating many of the suggestions, Appendix D of this book contains an evaluation form that I ask supervisors to complete for our interns. Sections of the evaluation form address basic work behaviors (punctual, reliable, etc.), knowledge of clients and treatment issues, response to supervision, interactions with clients, and interactions with coworkers. Space is also provided for more specific comments, and supervisors are encouraged to offer constructive criticism. Depending on the nature of the internship and the goals of the intern, the instructor, and the supervisor, other areas will undoubtedly need to be addressed, and some areas currently mentioned may be deleted. For discussions of specific competencies in clinical specialties including neuropsychology, geropsychology, forensic psychology, and child psychology, see *Professional Psychology: Research and Practice* (2012, *43*[5]).

In addition to rating scales, it is helpful for supervisors to give specific behavioral feedback to interns. Being told one is below or above expectations can offer a general sense of how one is evaluated, but it does not provide information about what is being done well or how to improve performance. Insofar as evaluations are meant to not only rate past performance but also guide future development, evaluations should be part of a process of developing goals and action plans for the intern. This means that areas of relative weakness are not simply acknowledged and forgotten. Once identified, areas needing improvement should be addressed with specific strategies for making the necessary changes or acquiring the needed skill or knowledge. Thus, supervisors should offer, and interns should request, specific suggestions for continued growth.

An example of such feedback would be, "Tom demonstrates very good listening behaviors and develops rapport quickly with clients. He is less skilled at determining when and how to offer effective confrontations when clients have violated program rules." Another example might be, "Tom needs to work on writing more succinct reports with less jargon and more specific recommendations for the treatment team." Compared with rating-scale approaches, comments such as these focus on the individual's strengths and weaknesses without reference to an external standard of performance.

EVALUATION OF SUPERVISORS

Just as evaluation is an essential part of internship training, evaluation should also provide useful feedback to supervisors. As with intern evaluation, this process should not be limited to a single event at the end of the experience but should be part of an ongoing communication process. Throughout this chapter, it has been suggested that interns communicate with their supervisors about any concerns they may have or ideas for improving supervision. If trainees follow that advice, much of the work of evaluation will be incorporated as a natural part of the supervisory process. Nevertheless, it can still be helpful for interns to give more structured feedback at the end of an internship.

Kadushin and Harkness (2002) observed that compared with the availability of models for supervisee evaluation, relatively few examples have been published pertaining to supervisor evaluation. Although well-intentioned supervisors often engage in self-evaluation, self-evaluation alone may not be sufficient to produce substantial changes in supervisor behavior. A further drawback of self-evaluation is that supervisor self-ratings are not necessarily consistent with the ratings that would be assigned by their interns. Kadushin and Harkness (2002) offered a brief model of items from instruments for this purpose. Falender and Shafranske (2004) also provided useful forms for evaluating the process of supervision, assessing the qualities and performance of the supervisor, and providing feedback to supervisors at the conclusion of placements. On the basis of a review of the literature and comments of students, I have developed an evaluation tool that has been useful to both interns and supervisors. The form is presented in Appendix I. As with the form for evaluation of interns, this supervisor evaluation tool primarily serves as an example, but it is also printed on a perforated page so it can be easily removed for actual use. Modifications may be needed to better fit the specific needs of supervisors or interns. What matters most is not the precise detail of any form but the process of the evaluation and the spirit in which it is performed.

PLANNING FOR FUTURE SUPERVISION

Supervision is an important part of internships, but the value of supervision does not end when your internship concludes. In closing this chapter, I encourage you to think of supervision as an essential part of your work throughout your professional career as a therapist. Clinical work can be extraordinarily complex, and there will be many times when you are not able to understand a client or a situation on your own. At such times, you need to seek supervision and be open to the ideas and insights of a colleague. If you have positive experiences in supervision as an intern, the benefits will probably be evident, and continuing supervision as a professional will simply be a matter of remembering its value and making the needed arrangements with a fellow professional. If your supervisory experience as an intern was not positive, it might take some time for you to be willing to try supervision again. That is understandable, but do not let one or two unpleasant experiences dissuade you from something that has the potential to be among the most valuable learning opportunities.

In a real sense, the decision to enter a helping profession is also a decision to accept and seek supervision. The challenge is to find the right supervisor to meet your personal and professional needs, and then work with that person to ensure that you both make the most of the experience.

REFERENCES

Abbas, A., Arthey, S., Elliott, J., Fedak, T., Nowoweiski, D., Markovski, J., & Nowoweiski, S. (2011). Web-conference supervision for advanced psychotherapy training: A practical guide. *Psychotherapy, 48*(2), 109–118.

Association of Psychology Postdoctoral Internship Centers (APPIC). (2006). APPIC membership criteria: Doctoral psychology internship programs. Retrieved from http://www.appic.org/about/2_3_1_about _policies_and_procedures_internship.html

Barnett, J. E. (2005). Important ethical, legal issues surround supervision role. *National Psychologist, 14*(3), 16.

Behnke, S. H. (2008). Discussion: Toward elaboration and implementing a conceptualization of healthy, safe training environments. *Training and Education in Professional Psychology, 2,* 215–218.

Bogo, M. (1993). The student/field instructor relationship: The critical factor in field education. *Clinical Supervisor, 11,* 23–36.

Bogo, M., Globerman, J., & Sussman, T. (2004). Field instructor competence in group supervision: Students' views. *Journal of Teaching in Social Work, 24,* 199–215.

Bogo, M., & McKnight, K. (2005). Clinical supervision in social work: A review of recent literature. *The Clinical Supervisor, 24,* 49–67.

Bogo, M., Regehr, C., Woodford, M., Hughs, J., Power, R., & Regehr, G. (2006). Beyond competencies: Field instructors' descriptions of student performance. *Journal of Social Work Education, 42,* 579–594.

Borders, D. (2005). Snapshot of clinical supervision in counseling and counselor education: A five-year review. *The Clinical Supervisor, 24,* 69–113.

Boswell, J. G., Nelson D. L., Nordberg, S. S., McAleavey, A. A., & Castonguay, L. G. (2010). Competency in integrative psychotherapy: Perspectives on training and supervision. *Psychotherapy Theory, Research, Practice, Training, 47*(1), 3–11.

Chapman, R. A., Baker, S. B., Nassar-McMillan, S. C., & Gerler, E. R. (2011). Cybersupervision: Further examination of synchronous and asynchronous modalities in counseling practicum supervision. *Counselor Education & Supervision, 50,* 298–313.

Chapman, R. A., Baker, S. B., Nassar-McMillan, S. C., & Gerler, E. R. Jr. (2011). Cybersupervision: Further examination of synchronous and asynchronous modalities in counseling practicum supervision. *Counselor Education and Supervision*, 50, 298–313.

Costa, L. (1995). Reducing anxiety in live supervision. *Counselor Education and Supervision, 34,* 30–40.

Council for Accreditation of Counseling and Related Educational Programs. (2009). 2009 standards. Retrieved from http://www .cacrep.org/doc/2009%20Standards%20with%20cover.pdf

Crespi, T. D., & Dube, J. M. B. (2005). Clinical supervision in school psychology: Challenges, considerations, and ethical and legal issues for clinical supervisors. *The Clinical Supervisor, 24,* 115–135.

Deal, K. H., & Clements, J. A. (2006). Supervising students developmentally: Evaluating a seminar for field instructors. *Journal of Social Work Education, 42*(2), 291–306.

Doehrman, M. J. G. (1976). Parallel processes in supervision and psychotherapy. *Bulletin of the Menninger Clinic, 40,* 3–104.

Enyedy, K. C., Arcinue, F., Puri, N. N., Carter, J. W., Goodyear, R. K., & Getzelman, M. A. (2003). Hindering phenomena in group supervision: Implications for practice. *Professional Psychology: Research and Practice, 34,* 312–317.

Falender C. A., & Shafranske, E. P. (2004). *Clinical supervision: A competency based approach.* Washington, DC: American Psychological Association.

Farber, E. W. & Kaslow, N. J. (2010) Introduction to the special section: The role of supervision in ensuring the development of psychotherapy competencies across diverse theoretical perspectives. *Psychotherapy: Theory, Research, Practice, Training.* 47(1), 1–2.

Fernando, D. M., & Hulse-Killacky, D. (2005). The relationship of supervisory styles to satisfaction with supervision and the perceived self-efficacy of masters-level counseling students. *Counselor Education and Supervision, 44,* 293–304.

Finch, J. B., & Feigelman, B. (2008). The power of mutual aid in the educational process: A seminar for new field instructors of trainees. *The Clinical Supervisor, 27*(2), 191–214.

Fortune, A. E., McCarthy, M., & Abramson, J. S. (2001). Student learning processes in field education: Relationship of learning activities to quality of field instruction, satisfaction, and performance among MSW students. *Journal of Social Work Education, 37,* 111–125.

Fouad, N. A., Grus, C. L., Hatcher, R. L., Kaslow, N. J., Hutchings, P. S., Madson, M.,…Crossman, R. E. (2009). Competency benchmarks: A developmental model for understanding and measuring comptence in professional psychology. *Training and Education in Professional Psychology, 3*(4, Suppl.), s5–s26.

Fox, R., & Gutheil, I. A. (2000). Process recording: A means for conceptualizing and evaluating practice. *Journal of Teaching in Social Work, 20,* 39–57.

Friedlander, M. L., Keller, K., Peca-Baker, T. A., & Olk, M. E. (1986). Effects of role conflict on counselor trainees' self-statements, anxiety level, and performance. *Journal of Counseling Psychology, 33*(1), 73–77.

Gaubatz, M. D., & Vera, E. M. (2006). Trainee competence in master's-level counseling programs: A comparison of counselor educator's and student's views. *Counselor Education and Supervision, 46,* 32–43.

Gelman, C. R. (2004). Anxiety experienced by foundation-year MSW students entering field placement: Implications for admissions, curriculum, and field education. *Journal of Social Work Education, 40,* 39–54.

Gilfoyle, N. (2008). The legal exosystem: Risk management in addressing student competence problems in professional psychology training programs. *Training and Education in Professional Psychology, 2,* 202–209.

Gillis, H., & Lewis, J. S. (2004). Addressing the issue of psychiatric disability in social work interns: The need for a problem-solving framework. *Journal of Social Work Education, 40,* 391–403.

Globerman, J., & Bogo, M. (2003). Changing times: Understanding social workers' motivation to be field instructors. *Social Work, 48,* 65–73.

Goodyear, R. K., Bunch, K., & Claiborn, C. D. (2005). Current supervision scholarship in psychology: A five-year review. *The Clinical Supervisor, 24,* 137–147.

Grant, J., Schofield, M. J., & Crawford, S. (2012). Managing difficulties in supervision: Supervisors' perspectives. *Journal of Counseling Psychology, 59*(4), 528–541.

Gray, L. A., Ladany, N., Walker, J. A., & Ancis, J. R. (2001). Psychotherapy trainee's experience of counterproductive events in supervision. *Journal of Counseling Psychology, 48,* 371–383.

Haley, J. (1992). *Problem-solving therapy* (2nd ed.). San Francisco: Jossey-Bass.

Harrar, W. R., VandeCreek, L., & Knapp, S. (1990). Ethical and legal aspects of clinical supervision. *Professional Psychology: Research and Practice, 21,* 37–41.

Harvey, V. S., & Struzziero, J. A. (2008). *Professional development and supervision of school psychologists* (2nd ed.). Thousand Oaks, CA: Corwin Press.

Hebert, D. J. (1992). Exploitative need-fulfillment and the counseling intern. *Clinical Supervisor, 10*(1), 123–132.

Henry, P. J., Hart, G. M., & Nance, D. W. (2004). Supervision topics as perceived by supervisors and supervisees. *The Clinical Supervisor, 23* (2), 139–152.

Hoffman, M. A., Hill, C. E., Holmes, S. E., & Freitas, G. F. (2005). Supervisor perspective on the process and outcome of giving easy, difficult, or no feedback to supervisees. *Journal of Counseling Psychology, 52,* 3–13.

Huhra, R. L., Yamokoski-Maynhart, C. A., & Prieto, L. R. (2008). Reviewing videotape in supervision: A developmental approach. *Journal of Counseling and Development, 86,* 412–418.

Kadushin, A. (1974). Supervisor-supervisees: A survey. *Social Work, 19,* 288–298.

Kadushin, A. (1985). *Supervision in social work.* New York: Columbia University Press.

Kadushin, A., & Harkness, D. (2002). *Supervision in social work* (4th ed.). New York: Columbia University Press.

Kaiser, T. L. (1992). The supervisory relationship: An identification of the primary elements in the relationship and an application of two theories of ethical relationships. *Journal of Marital and Family Therapy, 18,* 283–296.

Kaiser, T. L, & Kuechler, C. F. (2008). Training supervisors of practitioners: Analysis of efficacy. *The Clinical Supervisor, 27* (1), 76–96.

Kaplan, D. M., Rothrock, D., & Culkin, M. (1999). The infusion of counseling observations into a graduate counseling program. *Counselor Education and Supervision, 39,* 66–75.

Kaslow, N. J., Grus, C. L., Campbell, L. F., Fouad, N. A., Hatcher, R. L., & Rodolfa, E. R. (2009). Competency Assessment Toolkit for Professional Psychology. *Training and Education in Professional Psychology, 4*(4, Suppl.), s27–s45.

Kaslow, N. J., Rubin, N. J., Bebeau, M., Leigh, I. W., Lichtenberg, J. W., Nelson, P. D., Portnoy, S. M., & Smith, I. L. (2007). Guiding principles and recommendations for the assessment of competence. *Professional Psychology: Research and Practice, 38*(5), 441–451.

Lambert, M. J., & Beier, E. G. (1974). Supervisory and counseling process: A comparative study. *Counselor Education and Supervision, 14,* 54–60.

Levenson, H., & Evans, S. (2000). The current state of brief therapy training in American Psychological Association–accredited graduate and internship programs. *Professional Psychology: Research and Practice, 31*(4), 446–452.

Magnuson, S., Wilcoxon, S. A., & Norem, K. (2000). A profile of lousy supervision: Experienced counselors' perspectives. *Counselor Education and Supervision, 39*(3), 189–203.

Manring, J., Greenberg., R. P., Gregory, R., & Gallinger, L. (2011). Learning psychotherapy in the digital age. *Psychotherapy, 48*(2), 119–126.

McAdams, C. R., III, & Foster, V. A. (2007). A guide to just and fair remediation of counseling students with professional performance deficiencies. *Counselor Education and Supervision, 47,* 2–13.

McMahon, M., & Simons, R. (2004). Supervision training for professional counselors: An exploratory study. *Counselor Education and Supervision, 43,* 301–307.

Moskowitz, S. A., & Rupert, P. A. (1983). Conflict resolution within the supervisory relationship. *Professional Psychology: Research and Practice, 14,* 632–641.

National Association of Social Work Insurance Trust. (2004). *Supervisor beware: Reducing your exposure to vicarious liability.* http://www.naswinsurancetrust.org/understanding_risk_management/pointers/pp%20Vicarious%20Liability.pdf

Nelson, M. L., & Friedlander, M. L. (2001). A close look at conflictual supervisory relationships: The trainee perspective. *Journal of Counseling Psychology, 48,* 384–395.

Oliver, M. M., Bernstein, J. H., Anderson, K. G., Blashfield, R. K., & Roberts, M. C. (2004). An exploratory examination of student attitudes toward "impaired" peers in clinical psychology training programs. *Professional Psychology: Research and Practice, 35,* 141–147.

Olk, M., & Friedlander, M. L. (1992). Trainees' experience of role conflict and role ambiguity in supervisory relationships. *Journal of Counseling Psychology, 39,* 389–397.

Pollack, D., & Marsh, J. (2004). Social work misconduct may lead to liability. *Social Work, 49*(4), 609–612.

Prieto, L. R. (1997). Separating group supervision from group therapy: Avoiding epistemological confusion. *Professional Psychology: Research and Practice, 28,* 405.

Prieto, L. R., & Scheel, K. R. (2002). Using case documentation to strengthen counselor trainee's case conceptualization skills. *Journal of Counseling and Development, 80,* 11–21.

Riva, M. T., & Cornish, J. A. E. (2008). Group supervision practices at psychology predoctoral internship programs: 15 years later. *Training and Education in Professional Psychology, 2,* 18–25.

Rogers, C. R. (1961). *On becoming a person.* Boston: Houghton Mifflin.

Romans, J. S. C., Boswell, D. L., Carlozzi, A. F., & Ferguson, D. B. (1995). Training and supervision practices in clinical, counseling and school psychology programs. *Professional Psychology: Research and Practice, 26,* 407–412.

Rothman, B. (1973). Perspectives on learning and teaching in continuing education. *Journal of Education for Social Work, 9,* 39–52.

Rubinstein, G. (1992). Supervision and psychotherapy: Toward redefining the differences. *Clinical Supervisor, 10*(2), 97–116.

Searles, H. F. (1955). The informational value of the supervisor's emotional experiences. *Psychiatry, 18,* 135–146.

Shanfield, S. B., Mohl, P. C., Matthews, K. L., & Hetherly, V. (1992). Quantitative assessment of the behavior of psychotherapy supervisors. *American Journal of Psychiatry, 149*(3), 352–357.

Sklare, G., Thomas, D. V., Williams, E. C., & Powers, K. A. (1996). Ethics and an experiential "here and now" group: A blend that works. *Journal for Specialists in Group Work, 21,* 263–273.

Smith, J. D., & Agate, J. (2004). Solutions for overconfidence: Evaluation of an instructional model for counselor trainees. *Counselor Education and Supervision, 44,* 31–43.

Sobell, L. C., Manor, H. L., Sobell, M. B., & Dum, M. (2008). Self-critiques of audiotaped therapy sessions: A motivational procedure for facilitating feedback during supervision. *Training and Education in Professional Psychology, 3*, 151–155.

Stoltenberg, C. D. (2005). Enhancing professional competence through developmental approaches to supervision. *American Psychologist, 60,* 855–864.

Supervision Interest Network, Association for Counselor Education and Supervision. (1990). Standards for counseling supervisors. *Journal of Counseling and Development, 69,* 30–32.

Thomas, J. T. Informed consent through contracting for supervision. *Professional Psychology: Research and Practice, 38*(3), 221–231.

Tracey, T. J. G., Bludworth, J., & Glidden-Tracey, C. (2012). Are there parallel processes in psychotherapy supervision? An empirical examination. *Psychotherapy, 49*(3), 330–343.

Veach, P. M. (2001). Conflict and counterproductivity in supervision—When relationships are less than ideal: Comment on Nelson and Friedlander (2001) and Gray et al. (2001). *Journal of Counseling Psychology, 48,* 396–400.

Wayne, R. H. (2004) Legal guidelines for dismissing students because of poor performance in the field. *Journal of Social Work Education, 40,* 403–415.

Zakutansky, T. J., & Sirles, E. A. (1993). Ethical and legal issues in field education: Shared responsibility and risk. *Journal of Social Work Education, 29,* 338–347.

CHAPTER 6
WORKING WITH DIVERSITY

One of the great opportunities and challenges of internships is encountering people who are different from you. Learning to understand and respond to those differences will be a central key to your internship success and to your development as a person and a professional. This task will not be easy because the issues can strike at the core of who we are as individuals and as a society, and they will sometimes touch sensitivities or biases that we did not know existed in us and that may be uncomfortable. Challenging though this may be, it can also be one of the most illuminating and rewarding aspects of your training and future work.

The goal of this chapter is to introduce some of the key ideas about working with diversity and encourage you to explore and understand your own background, knowledge, attitudes, and other factors that affect you personally and will impact your professional development and work. Understand, however, that as with other elements of this text, entire courses and countless books and articles are dedicated to these topics. Thus, whereas you are strongly encouraged to read this chapter carefully and complete the exercises for reflection, it is also advisable to engage in more extended and detailed study of these topics through dedicated courses and extended reading. Such focused coursework and training are required for graduation and certification in many professions.

BACKGROUND

Until relatively recently, helping professions and techniques developed from, and were largely directed by, a predominantly white Western European/American, male, college-educated, financially well-to-do perspective (Gelso, 2010). With a few exceptions, this perspective was taken for granted and was applied in research, training, diagnosis, and treatment (Constantine, Hage, Kindaichi, & Bryant, 2007; Kress, Eriksen, Rayle, & Ford, 2005; Smedley & Smedley, 2005; Sue, Arredondo, & McDavis, 1992). For example, research by Bernal and Castro (1994) revealed that 46% of the training programs surveyed had no minority faculty, and 39% of accredited clinical psychology programs had no minority-related classes. As a result, great numbers of people were left unserved or in many cases were disserved (Hall, 1997).

Lack of multicultural faculty and training may help account for results from studies described by Sue and Sue (1990), which showed that more than 50% of minority clients terminated therapy after just one contact with the therapist. In the case of clients

who terminated early, lack of cultural competence on the part of counselors was shown by Constantine (2002) to be related to client dissatisfaction with counseling.

Fortunately, things have changed and now all of the major helping professions explicitly address issues of cultural awareness and sensitivity in their ethical codes. What is more, professional associations have published specific guidelines for multicultural competencies and practice. Examples include the American Psychological Association (APA) Guidelines on Multicultural Education, Training, Research, Practice, and Organizational Change for Psychologists (APA, 2003), the National Association of Social Workers (NASW) Standards for Cultural Competencies in Social Work Practice (NASW, 2001), and the Multicultural Counseling Competencies and Standards (Sue et al., 1992).

In addition to professional guidelines, a host of books, specialty journals, and training programs have developed to promote research and training in cultural issues and practices. Arredondo, Tovar-Blank, and Parham (2008) and Arredondo and Perez (2006) offer informative and insightful reviews of the history of this movement, whereas Smith, Constantine, Dunn, Dinehart, and Montoya (2006) reported on a meta-analysis of studies on multicultural education, reporting that, overall, the results of such efforts have been positive. Looking at this trend from the perspective of treatment effectiveness, D'Andrea and Heckman (2008) reviewed 40 years of multicultural outcome research. An additional, and often overlooked, perspective is offered by Tseng and Strelzer (2004), who considered medical issues in mental health through a cultural lens, including differences in physiologic reactions to medications, cultural attitudes toward psychotropic medicines, traditional healing, and herbal remedies. Also along these lines, Gielen, Draguns, and Fish (2008) gathered fascinating and useful information about cultural approaches to therapy and healing from a variety of peoples, religions, and regions.

REASONS FOR DIVERSITY TRAINING

Proctor and Davis (1994) cited three critical reasons for addressing issues of diversity in clinical practice: (1) traditional segregation that limits the knowledge of different ethnic groups by persons outside that group, (2) the growing percentages of nonwhite persons in the population, and (3) the historical as well as present negative tensions that exist between groups. Other authors (e.g., Hage & Kenny, 2009) focused on social justice issues and the importance of social service professionals becoming informed about, and active in addressing, mental health issues beyond their clinical settings.

Although the literature just described has focused primarily on ethnic differences, similar principles apply to working with persons of differing genders, economic means, religious beliefs, sexual orientations, physical abilities, and geographic regions of the country (Cohen, 2009; La Roche & Maxie, 2003; Moodley, 2005). To the extent that our personal experience has not afforded contact with people who differ in significant ways from one's self, and in the context of past and ongoing social tensions and prejudices, we may have difficulty understanding the experiences, strengths, needs, and perspectives of others. Such difficulties notwithstanding, understanding diversity is essential to your development and work as a professional. As Speight, Myers, Cox, and Highlen (1991) posed the rhetorical question:

> If a counselor is unable to work with those she or he is different from, with whom will that counselor be able to work? (p. 30)

RESISTANCE TO DIVERSITY TRAINING

The importance and difficulty of coming to terms with diversity issues was illustrated well by the journal entries of a student whose initial response to a discussion of diversity was as follows:

> I think too much is made about race and all the other differences. We are all just people, and if we all just treat everyone alike, there wouldn't be all these problems. I'm not prejudiced myself, and I try to treat everyone the same.

This student's comments were made in all sincerity; from her perspective, she believed she had achieved an understanding of how best to deal with differences. Several weeks into her internship, a later journal entry revealed that she was beginning to gain deeper awareness of herself and others:

> I always thought that everyone was just the same and that I was not prejudiced at all. Working here I've started to understand that just because I think everyone is the same doesn't mean everyone else thinks that or everyone has had the same chances I have. I wonder what my life would be like if my family was as poor as the people I am working with. I always thought that people who were poor just didn't want to work hard. I think I was prejudiced and just didn't know it. Now I see this family working so hard and still not being able to afford the things I just take for granted. They can't even take the kids to the doctor. I'm beginning to understand why they seem angry. I'm getting angry myself. It isn't fair, but these people have to live with that every day and I get to go home to my comfortable dormitory. I'm starting to realize how sheltered I've been. This is opening my eyes, and it isn't easy.

This student was coming to understand that one cannot simply dismiss diversity issues by saying they are unimportant or by "treating everyone alike." A much deeper awareness of ourselves and others is required, and the internship is a good place to start developing that awareness.

Despite the evidence and arguments that have been offered for studying multicultural differences, resistance to such training is quite common. Deal and Hyde (2004) offered an especially thoughtful discussion of this topic and viewed both anxiety and resistance to multicultural training in the context of broader developmental challenges facing trainees. These authors identified three worries that emerge when students are faced with multicultural learning. The first worry pertains to the content of what students are learning, particularly as they are required to study the history and ongoing dynamics of oppression. A second fear is of self-revelation making the students feel "stupid" or "racist" or possibly forcing them to discover aspects of themselves that they had been unaware of and would not be comfortable realizing. The third concern centers on how other students may react. In this context, Deal and Hyde recognized that many students, particularly those who are new to these topics, are afraid they will "make a mistake" in what they say or that they will be subject to criticism or censorship by peers or faculty.

Recognizing the anxiety and resistance that can be evoked by multicultural issues and training, Deal and Hyde (2004) emphasized the fundamental importance of creating a supporting and safe environment in which these issues can be discussed. Deal and Hyde suggested that instructors need to assess the developmental level of students (e.g., Stoltenberg, 2005) and then help students understand that discomfort and risk taking are inherent elements of clinical education. Whatever the source of discomfort, one must learn to deal with the topic and the discomfort effectively rather than through avoidance. Building on a developmental formulation, Deal and Hyde offered a matrix that lists developmental stages across affective, behavioral, and cognitive components, identifying how multicultural issues and training experiences relate to each level and component. If you find yourself encountering some unexpected difficulties or reactions to multicultural issues, it may be helpful to step back for a second and consider your own developmental level in general and as it pertains to multicultural issues specifically.

STEPS TOWARD WORKING WITH DIFFERENCES—AWARENESS, KNOWLEDGE, AND UNDERSTANDING OF SELF AND OTHERS

Guidelines to help trainees learn to deal with people who are different from themselves have been offered by a number of authors. Among the most influential of these guidelines were provided some years ago by Sue et al. (1992). These authors began their analysis of multicultural competency in counseling with a three-characteristic by three-dimension matrix. The three characteristics they identified are (1) counselors' awareness of their own assumptions and biases, (2) understanding the worldview of the client, and (3) developing culturally appropriate techniques and intervention strategies. For each of these characteristics, the three dimensions identified are (1) beliefs and attitudes, (2) knowledge, and (3) skills (p. 481). Each of the nine competency areas is then elaborated upon, yielding a final total of 31 specific competencies.

The core principles elucidated by Sue et al. are reflected in the previously mentioned counseling guidelines of the key associations. Although the specifics of the guidelines vary somewhat, they all have several elements in common. These common elements include self-awareness on the part of the therapist; knowledge and appreciation of the cultures of clients, including within-cultural as across-cultural variations; an appreciation of historical issues and power dynamics that have accompanied issues of race and culture; development of specific culturally sensitive and relevant assessment and intervention skills; and finally, a commitment to organizational and social change. Let us consider each of these elements in more detail.

SELF-AWARENESS: KNOWING THE DIVERSITY WITHIN US

Guideline #1 of the APA Multicultural Guidelines (APA, 2003) states:

> Psychologists are encouraged to recognize that, as cultural beings, they may hold attitudes and beliefs that can detrimentally influence their perceptions of and interactions with individuals who are ethnically and racially different from themselves.

That this principle is the first of the guidelines highlights the importance of self-awareness in dealing with differences. Similarly, a number of authors (e.g., Toporek & Reza, 2001; Vasquez, 2007) have recognized that awareness of self is a vital first element for therapists learning to work with clients whose backgrounds differ from their own. Consistent with these ideas, as a step toward developing your ability to work with differences, it can be extremely beneficial to think at length about your personal experiences and perspectives. Unless you have given careful thought to who you are, it is difficult to be sensitive to differences or similarities in your clients.

In this context, it should also be kept in mind that as Atkinson, Morten, and Sue (1993) pointed out, most discussions about counseling "minority" clients assume that the counselor is from the majority group whereas the client is from a minority group. This assumption overlooks the reality that it may well be the counselor who is from a minority group and the client from the majority group. An extensive discussion of issues related to the diversity status of the psychotherapist can be found in the special issue of *Psychotherapy: Theory, Research, Practice, Training* (2010, *47*[2]), which addresses this issue of therapist diversity from a host of perspectives including ethnicity, gender, sexual orientation, and disability.

An African American intern in a rural community mental health center encountered this dynamic and wrote the following in his journal:

> It almost never fails. When people come in to the clinic the first time and see me, their first reaction is something like, "You're the counselor???" They may not always say that, but you can tell they're thinking it. Some even seem look around the room as if they're asking, "Isn't there someone else here I can work with?"

As an alternative to majority–minority distinctions, Atkinson et al. (1993) preferred the phrase "cross-cultural counseling," which, they suggested, "refers to any relationship in which two or more of the participants are culturally different" (p. 9). Cross-cultural counseling also includes counseling that crosses groupings based on economic factors, geography, religion, sexual orientation, and the like.

More obvious, but too often neglected, are differences in the experiences of men and women. In many ways, in fact, gender differences may be the most overlooked of all because men and women, at least in Western cultures, are around each other much of the time and may therefore fail to appreciate the many ways in which their worlds are different. Failure to appreciate and adapt one's approach in response to such differences can substantially decrease the chances of successful interactions and may increase the potential for iatrogenic effects.

Coleman (1997) took this issue a step further and pointed out that one must not only appreciate and understand ethnic and cultural differences per se, one must also appreciate differences in the ways individuals cope with those differences. Coleman hypothesized that conflicts in multicultural counseling relationships may develop either out of cultural differences or out of differences in how the therapist and the client approach their differences. Thus, a counselor who believes it is important to deal directly and explicitly with cultural differences may unwittingly clash with a client who deals with differences by choosing to overlook them and believes that all people are alike.

EXERCISE: KNOWING YOURSELF IN RELATION TO DIVERSITY

This exercise is designed to help you become more aware of your own cultural and personal backgrounds and characteristics. Because this understanding is a first step toward understanding how you will interact with others, it is perhaps more important than anything else in this chapter. I encourage you to spend substantial time on the exercise and, if you feel comfortable and safe doing so, to discuss it with your peers and instructor.

The list that follows identifies certain personal and cultural characteristics that have a profound influence on how people understand the world and interact with others. For each characteristic, begin by describing yourself, then take some time to seriously consider how each aspect of yourself taken separately, and how all the aspects taken together, affect your understanding of yourself and others. Also, give some thought to how these characteristics shape the assumptions you bring to your training as an intern. One way to enhance this understanding is to imagine how things you may have taken for granted about yourself are due, at least in part, to your ethnic or cultural background. For example, you might ask yourself, "Because I have [pink/brown/black/red/yellow] skin, I have experienced..." Or, "Because my family's economic status was..., I have experienced..." Another approach to enhance your understanding is to imagine how your life might be different if you had characteristics other than those you have. For example, you might consider, "If I were of (another) culture, I might..." "If my parents were very (poor/rich), I might..." "If I were a new immigrant, I might experience..." As a final response to this exercise, you may want to discuss your own responses with a peer or some other person. You may also find it helpful to discuss them with people who are much different from you in certain of the key areas identified. One other note, for convenience, items in this exercise ask about characteristics of father and mother in the singular sense. People from blended families may well wish to add people to this list, for example, stepmother or stepfather, as fits their circumstances.

1. My gender is _____, and this is how it influences my experiences and how I understand and relate to others:
2. My age is _____, and this is how it influences my experiences and how I understand and relate to others:
3. My physical appearance includes the following qualities (describe these as accurately as you can, and try to avoid oversimplifying or using racial terms):

   Skin:
   Hair:
   Facial features:
   Build:
   Other features:

   This is how those features influence my experiences and how I understand and relate to others:
4. The nationality and cultural background of my parents and grandparents are:

   My father's mother:
   My father's father:
   My mother's mother:
   My mother's father:
   My father:
   My mother:

   This is how the culture of my family influences my experiences and how I understand and relate to others:
5. With regard to economic resources, the family I was raised in was _____.
   This is how that background influences my experiences and how I understand and relate to others:
6. The religious orientation of my mother is _____.
   The religious orientation of my father is _____.
   This is how that background influences my experiences and how I understand and relate to others:
7. The political orientation of my mother is _____.
   The political orientation of my father is _____.
   This is how that background influences my experiences and how I understand and relate to others:
8. My mother's educational background is _____.
   My father's educational background is _____.
   This is how that background influences my experiences and how I understand and relate to others:
9. My own educational background is _____.
   This is how that background influences my experiences and how I understand and relate to others:
10. My physical health and abilities are _____.
    This is how that background influences my experiences and how I understand and relate to others:
11. My sexual orientation is _____.
    This is how that background influences my experiences and how I understand and relate to others:
12. Other characteristics that have influenced my experiences and understanding of others are _____.

CONFRONTING OUR BIASES AND ACKNOWLEDGING OUR IGNORANCE

Some interns come to training believing they have everything it takes to treat almost any client who comes to them. Others are not so confident, but very few are really aware of just how limited their own experiences or theories are.

In recognition of the importance of cultural awareness, a number of instruments have been developed to assess the beliefs, knowledge, and skills of therapists and counselors in relation to working with persons of different ethnicities and cultures. Reviews of such instruments have been offered by Hays (2008), Krentzman and Townsend (2008), and Green et al. (2005).

Based on the principles incorporated in these instruments, the exercise that follows is designed to encourage self-exploration of your preparedness to work with others from different backgrounds. In this exercise, you are invited to consider carefully and honestly the kinds of clients with whom you feel you have sufficient experience, knowledge, or understanding to interact in a way that will be genuinely helpful.

If you are like many of our interns, you may find that after completing the exercise, you are unsure whether you should try to interact with anyone other than yourself. If that feeling emerges, do not despair. The first step toward learning is acknowledging ignorance. Following the exercise, concepts and suggestions are presented to help build your awareness and abilities to work with differences.

EXERCISE: KNOWING WHAT YOU KNOW AND DO NOT KNOW ABOUT OTHERS

The following list includes some of the many characteristics that distinguish individuals and groups from one another. Consider these and try to identify where your knowledge, understanding, or experience would enable you to understand accurately and relate to their experiences, concerns, thoughts, emotions, or needs in a helpful way. For each group you think you know well enough to work with, give the reasons why. For example, what experiences, training, or personal knowledge do you have relating to this group?

Age groups:

Genders:

Appearance (e.g., skin color, facial features):

Ethnic or cultural background:

Generations lived in this country:

Economic status:

Education level:

Religion:

Sexual orientation:

Physical abilities or disabilities:

Geographical locations and related cultural issues:

THE HISTORICAL CONTEXT MUST BE ACKNOWLEDGED

A good starting point for beginning to understand groups or individuals who are different from you is assessing both your intellectual and emotional knowledge and ignorance of their history. However tolerant, open, understanding, or empathic therapists or interns might believe themselves to be toward others, those qualities cannot erase long histories and continued realities of racial, class, gender, and other discrimination or oppression. If a client, therapist, or both are from a group that has experienced historical or ongoing discrimination or oppression, that fact will unavoidably influence the clinical interaction. So, too, being from a dominant or privileged group or class will influence the interaction, albeit in different ways.

Another way to think of this issue is to consider that it would be irresponsible to treat a client without some knowledge of his or her individual history. That is why one of the first tasks on intake of a new client is to take comprehensive medical, psychological, and social histories. Taking this concept one step higher helps us understand that the individual's personal history takes place within a larger context that itself has a history. Although each individual's experience will be unique, that uniqueness nevertheless stands as part of the overall context of society, and having a sense of the overall context can help one interpret how the individual's experiences developed and what they may mean.

During discussions of this subject, one often hears such statements as "What happened to those people in the past is not my fault, and I can't change it. We need to get on with what is happening today." The problem with such statements is their suggestion that it is possible to somehow erase all that has gone before and all that is, in fact, still going on, without dealing with the cognitive, emotional, economic, social, and other effects that the past and present realities have created.

A colleague who teaches multicultural education suggests in regard to history that "we do not have to feel guilty for the past, but we must accept responsibility for the present" (R. Hardiman, personal communication, 1994). Her point is that those who feel overwhelmed with sorrow and guilt for what their ancestors did to others, as well as those who would prefer to ignore the past completely, need to find a realistic, constructive, and importantly a personal way to deal with the reality of the past within the context of the present. Others (Comas-Diaz, 2000) argue that it is incumbent on helping professionals to take an active role in the political process to help overcome existing racism and to correct the lingering effects of historical racism and prejudice.

Having advised that one must be aware of historical contexts while working with differences, it is unfortunate but true that very few interns or professionals are well informed about the historical treatment of persons from other groups. Most students know little about the histories of struggles for civil rights, women's rights, gay and lesbian rights, economic justice, or other long-fought battles to achieve fairness and respect for all peoples. If you are interested in learning more about these topics (and I believe that as part of your training you should be interested), I encourage you to immerse yourself in works describing the histories of the various groups with whom you work and the histories of the struggles for equality and respect. In addition to nonfiction works, I also strongly recommend studying poetry and fiction as well as other cultural works, including art, film, music, dance, and religion. Garcia and Bregoli (2000) give particularly useful suggestions for incorporating literary sources to help prepare counselors for multicultural practice.

TERMINOLOGY MATTERS

As you seek to better understand people from diverse backgrounds, be especially mindful of terminology and the implicit meanings that certain words can carry. For better or worse, the words we use shape how we view and understand people and the world, and this shaping often occurs without our conscious awareness.

You may not have noticed it, but up to now in our discussion of diversity, I have not referred to "race," whether of clients or of therapists, except in direct quotations or in the context of discussion of racism as a social phenomenon. There is a good reason for this. In a special edition of the *American Psychologist,* Smedley and Smedley (2005), along with Helms, Jernigan, and Mascher (2005), reviewed the use of the term *race* as it evolved in general usage and in psychological treatment and research specifically. They emphasized that the terms *race, culture,* and *ethnicity* are often used interchangeably and without appreciation of their different meanings.

Culture refers to the externally acquired set of beliefs, laws, customs, art, and other aspects of a society. *Ethnicity* is closely related to culture in that it describes external factors, including geographic location, language, and other characteristics that may distinguish one group from another, sometimes within a common overall culture or nationality. For example, within the same nation, there may be clusters of people of markedly different religious beliefs, countries of origin, linguistic patterns, food, dress, and so on (Cohen, 2009).

In comparison to these concepts, *race* has commonly been used to imply innate biologically based factors that distinguish people from others on such variables as body type and skin, hair, or eye color. These observed characteristics are then assumed to be associated with underlying abilities, tendencies, and personality traits. See, for example, Sternberg, Grigorenko, and Kidd (2005) for a discussion of the long-standing debate about race and intelligence.

Although the word *race* has been used widely in society and in research, it simply does not have scientific validity. As Smedley and Smedly (2005) explained the matter, racial distinctions fail on three counts: "They are not genetically discrete, are not reliably measured, and are not scientifically meaningful" (p. 16). Similarly, Helms et al. (2005) asserted, "Race has no consensual theoretical or scientific meaning in psychology, although it is frequently used in psychological theory, research, and practice as if it has obvious meaning" (p. 27).

Why is this important? It is important because, as Smedley and Smedley stated in the title of their article, "Race as biology is fiction, racism as a social problem is real." Attention to terminology is not a matter of being "politically correct." Rather, it is a matter of precision and accuracy in our thinking and our approach to research and treatment.

As a professional, one learns to understand the world differently and more precisely than one may have before. In the case of discussions about race, it is important for you to understand the imprecision of the term *race,* and to appreciate how its social applications in the past influenced people's lives and, for that matter, professional practice. To avoid repeating the conceptual and practical mistakes and the social consequences that have accompanied the uncritical use of the term *race,* let me encourage you to avoid racial distinctions and refer instead to differences in ethnicity, culture, or background. This does not mean that you do not talk about physical features such as skin color and the impact they have on individuals within our society. It does mean that those features are not used as if they describe a "racial" difference that has some specific innate significance or scientific meaning.

EXERCISE: OBSERVING YOURSELF DEALING WITH DIVERSITY AT YOUR INTERNSHIP

This is a challenging exercise because it asks you to go beyond the theoretical, intellectual understanding of diversity issues and look for subtle ways you might be adjusting or failing to adjust your behavior on a daily basis at your internship. During the next few days at your placement site, take a mental inventory of the people who are there, including not only clients but also staff at all levels. Then ask yourself honestly how your approach, behavior, impressions, cognitions, and emotional reactions to some of these people may be impacted by differences between yourself and them in terms of the issues we have been discussing. For example, are you more frightened, friendly, open, or intimidated with some clients or staff than with others? Do you have certain cognitions or formulate attributions about some people's behavior because of their skin color, language, or education? Now ask yourself the reverse questions. Do you think clients, other interns, or staff may be reacting to you differently because of diversity issues? Finally, and perhaps most difficult of all, take time to speak with some of the aforementioned people (e.g., selected clients, staff, or peers) and ask them the same questions, requesting that they be as open and honest as possible.

STRENGTHS MUST BE RECOGNIZED ALONG WITH PROBLEMS

Much of the literature on multicultural counseling has focused largely on issues of injustice and inequality among groups. As has been emphasized, it is essential for interns to understand these issues, consider them in their clinical work, and work to influence them in society. At the same time, however, it is just as important to recognize that stereotypical images may prevent us from seeing beyond repression to understand and appreciate the cultural richness and heritage of different groups.

It is not uncommon for interns to have at least some sense of the disadvantages faced by other groups but little or no awareness of the personal and cultural strengths of others. The roles of family, religion, school, art, and music may be very different for members of different groups and may be great sources of strength and pride that an intern may be unaware of. Understanding these and other institutions and traditions can help us appreciate our clients' experiences and can provide invaluable resources to help clients deal with their presenting difficulties.

UNDERSTANDING GENDER

Karen Horney, in her profoundly insightful work "The Flight from Womanhood" (originally published in 1927), wrote:

> Women have adapted themselves to the wishes of men as if their adaptation were their true nature. That is, they see or saw themselves in the way that their men's wishes demanded of them...If we are clear about the extent to which all our being, thinking, and doing conform to these masculine standards, we can see how difficult it is for the individual man and also for the individual woman really to shake off this mode of thought. (Horney, 1967, p. 57)

Horney's observations ring true in many ways today, in spite of several decades of feminist thought and activism and in spite of our society's belief that it has become somehow more liberated than in the past. Indeed, as Luepnitz (2002) argued with compelling evidence, many of our current therapy models are themselves based on and perpetuate gender-biased and sexist assumptions.

Just as it is important for clinicians to be aware of and purposeful in dealing with other areas of difference, so it is with gender differences. In countless ways that most of us take for granted, the existential worlds of men and women in our society are markedly different, and these differences have significant implications for all aspects of clinical training and work.

A male student described how he suddenly gained new insights into some of these issues as a result of a difficult interaction with his girlfriend:

> We were having a discussion about a sexual assault on campus, and I made some offhand comment that I thought was funny. All of a sudden my girlfriend started yelling at me with an anger I had never seen before. I had no idea at all what was going on or what I had done. Eventually after a few hours of talking, and me actually listening for a change, I realized how little I really knew about things. It had never really dawned on me that I take for granted things that women just can't do safely in our world. Something as simple as walking home from class is nothing to me but it can be a terror for a woman. I'd never even thought of that before. Really, never thought of it. Then I realized how much else I hadn't thought about before either, and I realized I've got some work, no, a lot of work to do.

Much of the emphasis on awareness of gender issues has grown out of feminist psychology and the psychology of women. For a comprehensive review of the history, recent thought and research, and multicultural aspects of this field, see Denmark and Paludi (2008). For a discussion of gender issues in supervision, see Heru, Strong, Price, and Recupero (2006) and Walker, Ladany, and Pate-Carolan (2007).

Although the example of the male student learning difficult lessons revealed how little he knew of the experiences of women, it is important to recognize that, as Horney observed, women may not have considered these issues either. Thus, it is not just men who need to study the literature on the psychology of women; women need to as well. The same holds true of the need for men and women to study the psychology of men. Useful resources for gaining insights into male gender issues as they relate to clinical work include the journal *Psychology of Men and Masculinity* and Englar-Carlson and Stevens (2006).

Take some time to have a discussion with your peers, and ask them to tell you how they think their world experience, from childhood up to the present day, has been influenced by and is different because of gender. Then, reverse roles and think about the same question from your own perspective. Next, build on this discussion to explore how the experience of men and women may differ in the role of therapist or client Finally, ask yourself how much study and reading you have done on this subject, particularly in areas that are beyond your traditional comfort zone.

DEVELOPING CULTURALLY SENSITIVE AND RELEVANT SKILLS

As if it were not enough to challenge students to better understand their own backgrounds and those of others, we must now confront another difficult reality: Many fundamental principles that underlie the leading techniques of treatment and assessment are antithetic to the values and practices of people from different cultures (Gielen et al., 2008).

The structure of the typical therapy interaction is, if one thinks about it, a rather strange arrangement. Two or more individuals who have not formerly known one another get together and talk about the most intimate details of the life of one of them. The strangeness is compounded by the assumption that part of the purpose of the interaction is to help one of the people become aware of, understand, and modify things that are not even accessible to that person's own consciousness. Strangeness can be transformed into harmfulness when the assumptions of a therapy model imply that an oppressed person's problems are the sole result of intrapsychic processes, with no attention to the social pressures and challenges the person faces (Priest, 1991).

Pedersen (1987) listed 10 common assumptions reflecting cultural bias in counseling, including assumptions about what constitutes normal behavior, the emphasis on individualism and independence, neglect of support systems, linear thinking, neglect of history, and a focus on changing individuals rather than systems.

Sue and Sue (1990) identified comparable issues, noting that even fundamental assumptions about counseling, such as verbal and emotional expressiveness, the value of insight, cause-and-effect orientations, and the process of communication itself, may differ across cultures. Sue and Sue also addressed the possibility that not only the techniques of counseling but also the goals may not be compatible across cultures. They delineated four conditions that may apply to culturally different clients.

The ideal situation, according to Sue and Sue, is one in which the therapist uses culturally appropriate treatment processes to help the client achieve culturally appropriate treatment goals. In contrast to this condition are situations in which processes are culturally appropriate but the therapy goals are not; situations in which the goals are culturally appropriate but the processes are not; and finally, but all too commonly, situations in which neither the goals nor the therapy processes are culturally appropriate.

In light of the four possible conditions identified by Sue and Sue and some of the cultural differences that have been described, select one or two of your preferred therapy models or techniques and consider how these might conflict with the values or traditional practices of people from other cultures. How might the goals you take for granted in therapy conflict with the cultural values of someone from a different background? If possible, after thinking about this for yourself, discuss the matter with someone from a different culture to learn about his or her impressions and ideas.

Two of the difficult questions raised by an awareness of diversity issues are these: "How can one possibly know everything there is to know to work with people from different cultural backgrounds?" "What is more, how can helping professionals make therapeutic use of the self as a tool in therapy when the self of the client has been influenced by so many cultural factors the therapist has not experienced?"

These questions take on added significance when one approaches them from the perspective of evidence-based practice or empirically supported treatments. D'Andrea and Heckman (2008) conducted a comprehensive review of multicultural counseling outcome research in the past 40 years. Their review identified some 211 studies that involved culture and outcome studies, but only 53 of these met more strict criteria for relevance. As the authors pointed out, the positive news is that the numbers of such studies have been increasing in recent years, but when one considers the multitude of multicultural groups and issues, plus the diversity of presenting clinical problems and possible intervention approaches, it is clear that relatively minimal empirical evidence is available to guide specific interventions with specific client groups.

How does one proceed while recognizing both the complexity of the issues and the limitations to the research data from which to guide interventions? There is no easy answer to this question, but several suggestions can provide useful guidance. Hansen et al. (2006) studied the degree to which the actual activities of practitioners corresponded to the values they reported regarding multicultural psychotherapy. Their results showed that almost all therapists reported that they often or very often engaged in efforts to respect the client's worldview, tried to be aware of their own personal and social biases, sought to establish rapport in "racially/ ethnically sensitive ways," and considered the impact of race/ ethnicity in diagnoses. On the other hand, 42% of the sample of psychotherapists had not implemented a professional development plan to enhance their competence in multicultural issues, 39% rarely or never sought culture-based case consultations, and 27% said they rarely or never referred clients to providers who were more qualified. More broadly, Hansen et al. reported that for 86% of the items that they identified as being recommended multicultural competencies, their respondents "did not always practice what they believed to be important" (p. 69).

Responding to these findings, Hansen et al. emphasized that it is not enough to simply study issues in the abstract; one must have a concrete plan for applying what one has studied and be diligent in that application. Hansen et al. suggested the use of their research checklist as a means of self-assessment for practitioners to evaluate the degree to which their personal practices correspond to recommended competencies. Roysircar (2004) also offered a self-appraisal checklist combined with group and individual activities to enhance awareness of and competence in dealing with cultural issues. Other considerations have been recommended by La Roche and Maxie (2003), who identified 10 suggestions for addressing cultural differences in psychotherapy.

The take-away messages from all these sources are that dealing with cultural diversity is best approached as an awareness and a process of problem solving rather than a formula to be memorized and applied automatically. Central to this process are many of the factors that have been discussed in this chapter. These include awareness of one's own background and biases, awareness and understanding of the backgrounds of other individuals and cultures, appreciation of the current context in which different people and peoples live, sensitivity to traditional healing models within other cultures and how those models may conflict with or complement more Western-based interventions, and a preparedness to address cultural and other differences as part of the treatment process itself.

Like all areas of professional development and practice, multicultural competence is not something one simply acquires and then maintains for life. Rather, it is an ongoing process requiring continued study, training, assessment, and supervision. In recent years, numerous books, special issues of journals, and individual articles have been written about working with clients from different populations. In addition, a number of journals focus specifically on diverse populations. Examples include the *Journal of Multicultural Counseling and Development, Journal of Black Psychology, International Journal of Intercultural Relations, Journal of Gay and Lesbian Social Services,* and *Journal of Multicultural Social Work.* I strongly encourage you to consult these resources as a regular part of your professional study and to seek out specific opportunities for training workshops and for supervision as part of your internship and your future professional practice.

CULTURAL AND ORGANIZATIONAL CHANGE

The final element of multicultural competence involves working within one's organizational setting and beyond to bring about greater sensitivity to diversity issues. This task is not always easy, and it requires sustained effort.

Tori and Ducker (2004) described a multiyear initiative to enhance inclusion of multicultural issues and training in a graduate training program. Elements of this effort included outreach to increase minority representation among all campus groups, specific training for faculty in faculty meetings and through continuing education, and requiring students to take courses and participate in experiential activities to increase their intercultural awareness.

Comparable initiatives were undertaken by Fouad (2006), who identified seven critical elements for a "multiculturally infused curriculum." These elements include making an explicit statement of purpose, actively recruiting and retraining students and faculty from diverse populations, reviewing course content for multicultural infusion, and annual evaluations of student cultural competence. Other authors, such as Resnick (2006), have described efforts to infuse multicultural awareness and skills in counseling centers and other applied settings. Ponterotto, Mendelowitz, and Collabolletta (2008) promoted the concept of a "multicultural personality" and offered recommendations on how this can be incorporated as an integral part of counselor education.

Beyond academic and clinical settings, I believe that members of the helping professions also have a unique role to play in contributing to broader social awareness and change. The issue of community and political involvement is addressed in more detail in Chapter 11, but for the present let me emphasize that multicultural awareness does not simply involve studying historical issues of discrimination or injustices. Those issues continue to be real and present today, and they continue to impact the lives of our clients as well as our own. Contributing your professional skills and insights along with your time and effort can help bring about these changes today and for the future.

REFERENCES

American Psychological Association. (2003). Guidelines on multicultural education, training, research, practice and organizational change for psychologists. *American Psychologist, 58,* 377–402.

Arredondo, P., Tovar-Blank, Z. G., & Parham, T. A. (2008). Challenges and promises of becoming a culturally competent counselor in a sociopolitical era of change and empowerment (Expanding cultural considerations). *Journal of Counseling and Development, 86,* 261–268.

Arredondo, P., & Perez, P. (2006). Historical perspectives on the multicultural guidelines and contemporary applications. *Professional Psychology: Research and Practice, 37,* 1–5.

Atkinson, D. R., Morten, G., & Sue, D. W. (Eds.). (1993). *Counseling American minorities* (5th ed.). Dubuque: Brown.

Bernal, M. E., & Castro, F. G. (1994). Are clinical psychologists prepared for service and research with ethnic minorities? Report of a decade of progress. *American Psychologist, 49,* 797–805.

Cohen, A. B. (2009). Many forms of culture. *American Psychologist, 64,* 194–204.

Coleman, H. L. K. (1997). Conflict in multicultural counseling relationships: Source and resolution. *Journal of Multicultural Counseling and Development, 25,* 195–200.

Comas-Diaz, L. (2000). An ethnopolitical approach to working with people of color. *American Psychologist, 55,* 1319–1325.

Constantine, M. G. (2002). Predictors of satisfaction with counseling: Racial and ethnic minority clients' attitudes toward counseling and ratings of their counselors' general and multicultural counseling competence. *Journal of Counseling Psychology, 49,* 255–263.

Constantine, M. G., Hage, S. M., Kindaichi, M. M., & Bryant, R. M. (2007). Social justice and multicultural issues: Implications for the practice of training of counselors and counseling psychologists. *Journal of Counseling and Development, 85,* 24–30.

D'Andrea, M., & Heckman, E. F. (2008). A 40-year review of multicultural counseling outcome research: Outlining a future research agenda for the multicultural counseling movement. *Journal of Counseling and Development, 86 (3),* 356–364.

Deal, K. H., & Hyde, C. A. (2004). Understanding MSW student anxiety and resistance to multicultural learning: A developmental perspective. *Journal of Teaching in Social Work, 24*, 73–86.

Denmark, F. L., & Paludi, M. A. (Eds.). (2008). *Psychology of women: A handbook of issues and theories.* Westport, CT: Praeger.

Englar-Carlson, M., & Stevens, M. A. (2006). *In the room with men: A casebook of therapeutic change.* Washington, DC: American Psychological Association.

Fouad, N. A. (2006). Multicultural guidelines: Implementation in an urban counseling psychology program. *Professional Psychology: Research and Practice, 37*, 6–13.

Garcia, B., & Bregoli, M. (2000). The use of literary sources in the preparation of clinicians for multicultural practice. *Journal of Teaching in Social Work, 20*(1/2), 77–102.

Gelso, C. J. (2010). The diversity status of the psychotherapist: Editorial introduction. *Psychotherapy, Theory, Research, Practice, Training, 47*(2), 143.

Gielen, U. P., Draguns, J. G., & Fish, J. M. (Eds). (2008). *Principles of multicultural counseling and therapy.* New York: Routledge-Taylor & Francis Group.

Green, R. G., Kiernan-Stern, M., Bailey, K., Chambers, K., Claridge, R., Jones, G.,…Walker, K. (2005). The multicultural counseling inventory: A measure for evaluating social work student and practitioner self perceptions of their multicultural competencies. *Journal of Social Work Education, 41*, 191–207.

Hage, S. M., & Kenny, M. E. (2009). Promoting a social justice approach to prevention: Future directions for training, practice, and research. *Journal of Primary Prevention, 30*(1), 75–87.

Hall, M. E., & Hall, T. W. (1997). Integration in the therapy room: An overview of the literature. *Journal of Psychology and Theology, 25*(1), 86–101.

Hansen, M. D., Randazzo, K. V., Schwartz, A., Marshall, M., Kalis, D., Frazier, R.,…Norvig, D. (2006). Do we practice what we preach? An exploratory survey of multicultural psychotherapy competencies. *Professional Psychology: Research and Practice, 37*, 66–74.

Hays, D. G. (2008). Assessing multicultural competence in counselor trainees: A review of instrumentation and future directions. *Journal of Counseling and Development, 86*, 95–101.

Helms, J. E., Jernigan, M., & Mascher, J. (2005). The meaning of race in psychology and how to change it. *American Psychologist, 60*, 27–36.

Heru, A. M., Strong, D., Price, M., & Recupero, P. R. (2006). Self-disclosure in psychotherapy supervisors: Gender differences. *American Journal of Psychotherapy, 60*, 323–333.

Horney, K. (1967). *Feminine psychology*, Ed. H. Kelman. New York: Routledge and Kegan Paul.

Krentzman, A. R., & Townsend, A. L. (2008). Review of multidisciplinary measures of cultural competence for use in social work education. *Journal of Social Work Education, 44*(2), 7–32.

Kress, V. E. W., Eriksen, K. P., Rayle, A. D., & Ford, S. J. W. (2005). The DSM-IV-TR and culture: Considerations for counselors. *Journal of Counseling and Development, 83*, 97–105.

La Roche, M. J., & Maxie, A. (2003). Ten considerations in addressing cultural differences in psychotherapy. *Professional Psychology: Research and Practice, 34*, 180–186.

Luepnitz, D. A. (2002). *The family interpreted.* New York: Basic Books.

Moodley, R. (2005). Outside race, inside gender: A good enough "holding environment" in counseling and psychotherapy. *Counseling Psychology Quarterly, 18* (4), 319–328.

NASW. (2001). NASW standards for cultural competence in social work practice. Retrieved from http://www.naswdc.org/practice/standards /NAswculturalstandards.pdf

Pedersen, P. B. (1987). Ten frequent assumptions of cultural bias in counseling. *Journal of Multicultural Counseling and Development, 15*, 16–24.

Ponterotto, J. C., Mendelowitz, D., & Collabolletta, E. (2008). Promoting multicultural personality development: A strengths-based, positive psychology worldview for schools. *Professional School Counseling, 12*(2), 93–99.

Priest, R. (1991). Racism and prejudice as negative impacts on African American clients in therapy. *Journal of Counseling and Development, 70*, 213–215.

Proctor, E. K., & Davis, L. E. (1994). The challenge of racial difference: Skills for clinical practice. *Social Work, 39*, 314–323.

Resnick, J. L. (2006). Strategies for implementation of the multicultural guidelines in university and college counseling centers. *Professional Psychology: Research and Practice, 37*, 14–20.

Roysircar, G. (2004). Cultural self-awareness assessment: Practice examples from psychology training. *Professional Psychology: Research and Practice, 35*(6), 658–666.

Smedley, A., & Smedley, B. D. (2005). Race as biology is fiction, race as social problem is real. *American Psychologist, 60*, 16–26.

Smith, T. B., Constantine, M. G., Dunn, T. W., Dinehart, J. M., & Montoya, J. A. (2006). Multicultural education in the mental health professions: A meta-analytic review. *Journal of Counseling Psychology, 53*, 132–145.

Speight, S. L., Myers, L. J., Cox, C. I., & Highlen, P. S. (1991). A redefinition of multicultural counseling: Multiculturalism as a fourth force in counseling. *Journal of Counseling and Development* [Special issue], *70*, 29–36.

Sternberg, R. J., Grigorenko, E. L., & Kidd, K. K. (2005). Intelligence, race, and genetics. *American Psychologist, 60*, 46–59.

Stoltenberg, C. D. (2005). Developing professional competence through developmental approaches to supervision. *American Psychologist, 60*, 855–864.

Sue, D. W., Arredondo, P., & McDavis, R. J. (1992). Multicultural counseling competencies and standards: A call to the profession. *Journal of Counseling and Development, 70*, 477–486.

Sue, D. W., & Sue, D. (1990). *Counseling the culturally different: Theory and practice* (2nd ed.). New York: Wiley.

Sue, D. W., & Sue, D. (2003). *Counseling the culturally different: Theory and practice* (3rd ed.). New York: Wiley.

Toporek, R. L., & Reza, J. V. (2001). Context as a critical dimension of multicultural counseling: Articulating personal, professional, and institutional competence. *Journal of Multicultural Counseling and Development, 29*, 13–30.

Tori, C. D., & Ducker, D. G. (2004). Sustaining the commitment to multiculturalism: A longitudinal study in a psychology graduate program. *Professional Psychology: Research and Practice, 35*, 649–657.

Tseng, W. S., & Streltzer, J. (Eds.). (2004). *Cultural competence in clinical psychiatry.* Washington, DC: American Psychiatric Publishing.

Vasquez, M. J. T. (2007). Cultural difference and the therapeutic alliance: An evidence-based analysis. *American Psychologist, 62*, 878–885.

Walker, J. A., Ladany, N., & Pate-Carolan, L. M. P. (2007). Gender-related events in psychotherapy supervision: Female trainee perspectives. *Counseling and Psychotherapy Research, 7*(1), 12–18.

CHAPTER 7
CLINICAL WRITING, TREATMENT RECORDS, AND CASE NOTES

WRITING SKILLS

Clinical writing is different from any other writing you have learned. The purpose, style, subject matter, and format of clinical writing require a new set of skills in which very few students are trained during their undergraduate education. This chapter is designed to help you understand the process and content of clinical writing so you can begin to develop skills that will serve you throughout your academic and professional careers.

One way to approach this topic is to assume that students have mastered basic writing skills and need to focus only on the unique aspects of clinical writing. My experience suggests this assumption is sometimes valid, but, more often than not, students have trouble with clinical writing because they have yet to develop their general writing skills. This is not surprising considering that, as shown in the landmark work, *Academically Adrift*, many students achieve their bachelor's degrees having done little if any writing in most of their courses (Arum & Roksa, 2011).

Within the helping professions specifically, Alter and Adkins (2001) reported that an assessment of first-year graduate social work students revealed fully a third who needed writing assistance, but only slightly more than half of those students actually took advantage of a program designed to improve their skills. The same authors (Alter & Adkins, 2006) found comparable results in a later study, with a quarter of the students in this cohort lacking adequate writing skills. Key areas of deficit included the inability to craft an essay with a persuasive voice and sufficient details.

There is no reason to assume that the results would be more promising for any of the other helping professions. My experience shows that even when students have relative competency in basic skills, they often need a great deal of assistance in adapting those skills to clinical, research, or policy applications.

This is tremendously important because, as Alter and Adkins observed, the lives of clients can be "significantly diminished by social workers' inability to write well, or significantly enhanced by strong writing proficiency" (2001, p. 497). A related point is made by Kahn and Holody (2012) who, following the writing across the curriculum model, emphasized that we must not just learn to write, we must also write to learn. This means that developing your writing skill is one of the best ways to develop your thinking and understanding about the work you do. If you cannot clearly and articulately write about a client or explain the rationale for an intervention, it is likely that the problem is not simply with your writing but with what you know or don't know and how clearly you think about what you are doing and why.

In light of these observations, this chapter offers suggestions both for improving your overall writing skills and for applying those skills to clinical uses. Even if you fancy yourself to be a skilled writer already, most students will be well advised to read the whole chapter carefully. As Fischer (1994) observed, many of the principles of writing good reports are "commonsensical...but not yet commonplace."

WRITING CAN BE LEARNED

It is sometimes said that writing is a gift and cannot be taught. That statement is false. Writing, like any other skill, can be taught and learned by most people. This does not mean we will all win Pulitzer Prizes, but it does mean most students can learn to write reports and notes that are accurate, clear, and in a style consistent with professional standards. If you are fortunate enough to have already developed good writing skills, this chapter will help you adapt those skills to clinical writing. If writing has never been a strong point for you, take heart from the following anecdote.

The summer before my first year of graduate school, I spent two months hiking and climbing in the mountains near my family home in Colorado. Much of that time, I hiked alone, and I often went for several days without speaking, hearing, reading, or writing a word. The experience was therapeutic, but it also posed a problem when graduate school began. Among the requirements for all first-year students was a course in psychological assessment. The course involved learning to administer, score, and interpret the major psychological tests. The course also involved writing two lengthy assessment reports each week.

As an undergraduate, I was an average writer, but considering the meager overall writing quality of undergraduate students, that wasn't really saying much. What is more, I had received no specific training in clinical writing, which, as you will discover, is much different from creative writing or typical college composition courses.

With such limited training, and after spending so much of the summer away from language itself, I found the task of writing in graduate school extremely difficult. Despite my best efforts, on embarrassingly frequent occasions, reports were returned with huge red Xs or "NO!" covering the entire first page. With innate clinical skill, I sensed that these messages were a sign of dissatisfaction on the part of my professor. I was right. Indeed, midway through the semester, I was told that if my writing did not improve I would have to retake the course or might even be dismissed. Faced with this disheartening news, I asked what I could do to improve my skills. The instructor replied that he did not know. He could teach assessment, but he could not teach writing. I would have to learn to write somewhere else.

Ultimately, with support and guidance from peers, extensive study of the writing process, the assistance of several field supervisors, and thousands of hours spent writing and rewriting reports, I eventually did learn to write well. That was not easy, but it was necessary to become a skilled professional and, as a result of all that work, I may have learned some things that will help the readers of this text develop their writing and clinical skills more efficiently. We begin with simple rules that apply to all writing, then proceed to discuss the specifics of clinical records and communications.

FOCUSED READING TO LEARN WRITING

One of the best ways to improve your writing is to change the way you read. Most of the time, when people read, they are interested primarily in the content of what they are reading. They want to know the news of the day, learn what the journal article concludes, or discover how a story turns out. This emphasis on content is a fine way to gather information, but it is not likely to improve your writing. For reading to improve your writing, you must focus on structure and style, not just on information. The focus of reading then changes from what the writing is about to how the piece is written.

A useful analogy may be to think about how a person who plays the violin will listen to a violin concerto much differently from a casual spectator with no aspirations of playing the instrument. The casual spectator merely enjoys the melody. The person learning to play attends closely to the technique of the musician. Similarly, most people who watch movies are interested primarily in the story line, the characters, or perhaps the special effects. Students of film, however, understand the importance of how the movie is made: what camera angles are used; how the lighting is constructed; what the editing transitions are; and through each of these elements, what the director was hoping to achieve.

If you want to learn how to write clinical reports, a good place to begin is by reading reports others have written (Kahn & Holody, 2012). When you do this, remember to change your focus. Merely reading the content of other reports will tell you little about how to write about clients you might see yourself. What really matters for this purpose is the structure and style of the reports and the ways in which words and phrases are selected and constructed. The specific content will change from client to client, but you can use structure and style again and again.

As an exercise to illustrate the distinction between content and style, consider the following sentence pairs. The contents of each pair are essentially the same, but the sentences differ in style and structure. The differences are intentionally subtle and you are not told which is "better." Your task is to note the differences and give some thought to how they communicate information. You may also want to try rewriting the sentences yourself to see if you can improve them. I will discuss these sentences further in a moment.

EXERCISE

SENTENCE PAIRS

1. A. During the interview, the client said that he had never before been seen in therapy by a therapist.
   B. The client indicated no previous experience in therapy.
2. A. Test results suggest the presence of mild to moderate depression, anxiety, and concerns about family matters.
   B. According to the results of the test, there is evidence of depression in the mild to moderate range, along with anxiety and apparent concerns about issues relating to family.
3. A. William Smith is an affable, energetic, 75-year-old male, who arrived neatly attired in a dark gray suit, spoke openly about his presenting concerns, and expressed a willingness to "do whatever it takes to get going again." Mr. Smith stated that he came to therapy out of concern that his sex life has begun to decline from a frequency of five to three times per week.
   B. William Smith is a 75-year-old male with a presenting problem of decreased sexual performance. At the time of the interview, he was well dressed and groomed and appeared to be well motivated.

PRACTICE AND FEEDBACK

Writing, like any other skill, is learned through practice, but practice alone is not enough. One also needs feedback and constructive criticism. Without feedback, there is a risk of practicing mistakes rather than learning new skills. As an intern, you have access to at least three sources of feedback on your writing. Your peers, supervisor, and course instructor can all offer input about both the style and content of your clinical writing. I encourage you to take advantage of each of these resources because they will offer different perspectives and because you may find it easier to work with one person rather than another. In my own experience, when my instructor was unable to help with writing, fellow graduate students were the most valuable source of feedback. Indeed, had it not been for their help, I might not have completed my degree. Later, supervisors at several internship placements offered further assistance. The importance of feedback continues to this day as colleagues, editors, and students offer their comments and criticisms. Indeed, before each new edition of this book, three to five reviewers offer extensive critiques and suggestions. This is not always easy to receive, but it is tremendously helpful, and many of the suggestions have made this edition better than the ones that preceded it. For that, I am extremely grateful to the reviewers and to the publisher and editor.

Just as you must read differently to improve your writing, you must also seek and accept a different kind of feedback. When people ask for comments on what they have written, they often ask with the hope of receiving positive statements. "Looks fine to me," "Very good," "Nice work," and so on can help us feel good, but such comments do nothing to improve our writing. To make feedback productive, you must be willing to invite and accept blunt criticism and suggestions. One student expressed this well when he circulated a draft of his report to several peers with a cover note that said, "Do me a favor and be as critical as you can. Rip this apart. I mean it. I need your honest criticism and suggestions."

Because people are used to asking for and giving only general and positive comments, you may need to take the initiative to ask for more specific and critical suggestions (Healy & Mulholland, 2007). The most important step is to go beyond global "grade-like" statements and solicit comments on specific parts of what you have written. For example, rather than simply asking people to read your work and tell you what they think of it, ask someone to read each sentence or paragraph and tell you how the writing could be clearer or more succinct. Invite your readers to suggest alternative ways of expressing what you have written. You may even ask them to write the same information in their own words, and then compare your work and theirs to see how each might be improved.

In our internship and assessment classes, I often instruct students to exchange their reports and offer critical feedback to each other. With students' permission, I also read reports aloud in class anonymously and ask for constructive group feedback on how the writing could be improved. Throughout the feedback process, you must be willing to wrestle with difficult phrases or passages until they come out the way you want. You may also have to throw out some of your favorite passages to make the overall writing work. This process of writing and revising helps develop the skills of the writer and of those who give feedback.

To enable your reader to give you the most useful suggestions, you may find the following instructions helpful:

> Please read this as carefully and critically as you can. I am not asking for you to tell me if it is good or bad. I want you to suggest how you think it can be improved. I welcome your comments and will appreciate whatever criticism you have to offer. As you read, please mark any sentences or phrases that are unclear, awkward, poorly worded, ambiguous, uninteresting, or lacking in some other way. If you have suggestions for improving sentences or passages, please feel free to write them. If there are problems with organization, please note them, and suggest alternatives. If any information is omitted or is not expressed clearly, please identify what should be added or expressed differently. Finally, if there are any other changes that you think would help, I would welcome your ideas. Thank you in advance for your help. Honest criticism is very hard to find, and I value your assistance.

Instructions such as these facilitate feedback in two ways. First, they give permission to your reader to be critical. Second, they suggest specific areas for the reader to focus on and ways of giving feedback on those areas. The next task is perhaps the most difficult. Having asked for honest criticism, you must be open enough to accept the criticism you receive without getting your feelings hurt or becoming defensive. Don't ask people for honest feedback then spend all your time telling them or yourself why their feedback is wrong.

REWRITING

Before this chapter was ready for publication, it went through perhaps as many as 20 revisions. Sometimes the changes were removal or replacement of single words to make sentences more succinct. Other times, entire sections were revised, moved, or eliminated. The idea of going through more than 20 revisions may come as a surprise to some readers, but it merely reflects a basic yet often unappreciated fact about the writing process: Writing skill develops through rewriting (Zinsser, 2006).

Quality writing depends on rewriting in two ways. First, to develop your skills as a writer, you must gain practice through revising whatever you write. Writing is like anything else you want to learn. You have to try, make mistakes, try again, make more mistakes, try again in a different way, make more mistakes, and so on, until your skills develop. The process of repeated revision helps you learn more efficient ways of writing and gradually enables you to write better first drafts.

Many students have not had experience rewriting because writing assignments in academic settings seldom require or allow for revision. As a result, students may have some practice in writing first drafts, and they may receive an evaluation of their writing skills, but such assignments do little to teach them how to write well. Students do, however, develop the bad habit of expecting to write something once and then be done with it. This experience often creates resistance when students are eventually told that they must rewrite a report or paper. It would be much better if every writing assignment in college and graduate school involved at least two drafts and feedback from multiple sources. This would help develop the habit of revision and would improve writing skills far more than would the predominant single-draft practice (Baird & Anderson, 1990).

COMMON WRITING PROBLEMS

As an instructor and supervisor, I have read several thousand papers and reports by students. This experience has taught me that most of the problems students have in writing can be grouped into a few categories. These include problems relating to clarity, choice of wording, grammar, transitions between topics, and organization. Students who do not write well produce sentences that lack clear meaning. Their writing often contains words that were chosen carelessly or mean something the student did not intend to say. Poor writers also have difficulty structuring the overall sequence of topics and connecting smoothly from one topic to another. These problems are all remarkably common and can lead to papers that are painfully difficult to read. The good news is that most of these errors can be corrected.

I have found several books to be useful in helping students learn to write well. Some of the books that address issues common to all writing are *On Writing Well* by William Zinsser (2006) and the classic *Elements of Style* by William Strunk Jr. and E. B. White (2000). *The Publication Manual of the American Psychological Association*, now in its sixth edition (2009), also contains, in addition to the standard style and formatting guidelines, many useful suggestions for improving writing.

Some of the excellent works geared specifically to clinicians are Norman Tallent's *Psychological Report Writing* (1997), Healy and Mulholland's *Writing Skills for Social Workers* (2007), Constance Fischer's *Individualizing Psychological Assessment* (1994), and Laura Glicken's *A Guide to Writing for Human Service Professionals* (2007). Tallent conducted extensive research on clinical reports and writing. Although his title addresses psychologists specifically, the book contains information that is useful to professionals and interns from many disciplines. In their books, Healy and Mulholland as well as Glicken not only provide advice on clinical writing but also offer valuable suggestions regarding grant writing, research reports, and writing for the popular press. Fischer's book, in addition to providing one of the clearest descriptions of the assessment and report-writing process I have found, offers extremely valuable writing tips and a host of examples of common student writing errors and ways to correct them. One other source that can help beginning clinical writers find suitable wording for reports is *The Clinician's Thesaurus, Seventh Edition: The Guide to Conducting Interviews and Writing Psychological Reports* by Edward Zuckerman (2010). An electronic version *Clinician's Electronic Thesaurus, Version 7.0* (2011) is also available.

Faculty and supervisors seeking to improve their students' writing may also want to review an informative article by Kahn and Holody (2012), who recommend 11 practical measures supervisors can take, including requiring writing from the beginning of the practicum, providing examples of professional writing, requiring writing about case assessments and interventions, setting expectations that revisions will be expected, and expecting professional-level language and communication.

Other useful and practical suggestions for teaching and improving writing in the helping professions are offered by Owens and Crum (2012); Brenner (2003); and Pelco, Ward, Coleman, and Young (2009), who present research-based guidance for improving the writing of psychological reports for use in education. Among the key points Pelco et al. emphasize are tailoring the readability of the report to the education level of recipients and avoiding technical terminology and psychological jargon that will be misunderstood by the reader. Their research also demonstrated the superiority of an integrated, thematic-based report approach that highlights specific relevant findings overall as compared to a test-by-test evaluation. Finally, and of particular importance, this research revealed that approximately half of the teachers who were recipients of sample psychological reports in this study were not able to translate the report findings into meaningful intervention strategies. Pelco and colleagues conclude that it is essential for professionals to write reports that are clear and readable and that offer tangible, research-based guidance for interventions based on the report findings.

Having identified these resources, I must now say something that should be obvious followed by something you may not want to but may need to hear. The obvious message is that all of the resources listed here will not help you at all if you do not use them. I know of a young staff member who wrote very poorly and to whom his supervisor made many of the recommendations just offered. Several months later, his writing had shown no improvement whatsoever and, after yet another very poorly written report, he was asked if he had read any of the books that had been recommended or taken any of the other steps suggested to improve his writing. He acknowledged that he had not done any of these things. The evidence of that was not only apparent in his inadequate reports but was sitting right on his desk in the form of the obviously unopened copy of one of the writing books he had been given to read.

Now for the hard part. That young man was asked to leave the organization shortly thereafter. Lest that sound harsh, understand that writing was a central part of what he was expected to do in his job, and the success of the organization's efforts depended substantially on his ability to produce quality written reports. If a specific skill is essential to your performance, if you are lacking in that skill, and if someone who is your supervisor gives you specific instructions and assistance to improve that skill but you take no action to do so, should any other outcome be expected?

CAUTION: TASTES, SUPERVISORS, AND INSTRUCTORS VARY

The next section reviews the suggestions of the authors previously mentioned as well as insights gained from my own experience as a clinician, supervisor, and instructor. Before I offer those suggestions, a brief caveat is in order. Although I will present examples and explanations of what I consider good and bad writing, other instructors and supervisors may have opinions and preferences that differ from what is said here. Healy and Mulholland (2007) placed particular emphasis on this point and described the "contextual approach" to writing that takes into account the institutional context of clinical practice and writing. If your instructor or supervisor offers alternative expectations or suggestions, you need not feel frustrated. Instead, try various approaches and examine their differences. As you continue your training, you can develop a style that works best for you, but always keep in mind the audience for your writing.

KEYS TO GOOD WRITING

SIMPLIFY YOUR WRITING BUT NOT YOUR CLIENTS

Strunk and White (2000) instructed the writer: "Use definite, specific, concrete language. Prefer the specific to the general, the definite to the vague, the concrete to the abstract" (p. 15). In a similar vein, "simplicity" is Zinsser's first principle of writing well. As he described it: "The secret of good writing is to strip every sentence to its cleanest components" (2006, p. 6). I strongly endorse these principles but add that the clinician's task is to simplify writing without simplifying the client. You must strive to write as simply and directly as possible, but you must also communicate accurately about your client.

The following examples demonstrate how simplicity and directness in writing can contribute to improved clinical reports.

EXAMPLE 1

A. At various occasions during the interview Mr. Johnson exhibited signs of nervousness and distress.
B. In response to questions about his family, Mr. Johnson began to shift in his chair, stammered slightly, and appeared to avoid eye contact.

Note how the first example may sound as if it uses clinical language and form, but it actually speaks in very general terms. Words such as "various occasions" and "signs of nervousness" do not really tell what the client did or when. By comparison, the second example directly describes Mr. Johnson's behavior and when it occurred. This lets the reader better visualize the client and connects specific behaviors with specific stimuli. Thus, by following the principle of preferring "the definite to the vague, the concrete to the abstract," the sentence is improved both stylistically and clinically.

The second example is one of the sentence pairs presented earlier in this chapter.

EXAMPLE 2

A. William Smith is an affable, energetic, 75-year-old male, who arrived neatly attired in a dark gray suit, spoke openly about his presenting concerns, and expressed a willingness to "do whatever it takes to get going again." Mr. Smith indicated that he came to therapy out of concern that his sex life has begun to decline from a frequency of five to three times per week.
B. William Smith is a 75-year-old male with a presenting problem of decreased sexual performance. At the time of the interview, he was well dressed and groomed and appeared to be well motivated.

Which of the two descriptions, A or B, do you prefer? Why?

This example is more subtle and might be subject to more dispute, but for most situations I would prefer the description offered in A. There are several reasons for this preference. First, although the second example is clearly more succinct, that quality alone does not necessarily mean it is more direct or that it better represents the client. Describing a "presenting problem of decreased sexual performance" does not tell the reader what the problem is. For some, decreased sexual performance might mean going from having sex twice a month to once a month. As the alternative version shows, for this man decreased performance has a much different meaning. The second reason I prefer Example A is that it gives the reader a better sense of who the client is as a person, again because the description is more specific. "Neatly attired in a dark gray suit" paints a clearer picture than "well dressed and groomed." Similarly, using the direct quote that the client would "do whatever it takes" brings the reader closer to the client than saying he "appeared to be well motivated."

Fischer (1994) offers advice consistent with this example:

Early in a report I provide physical descriptions of the client, in part so that the reader can picture the client throughout the written assessment. I try to describe the client in motion rather than statically, so the reader will be attuned to the ways the person moves through and shapes and is shaped by his or her environment. (p. 37)

Please note that although I would prefer the description offered in A for most situations, there are advantages to Example B, and there are instances in which it would be preferable. The main advantage of B is brevity. If time is at a premium and there is little need to convey a sense of the person beyond the clinical data that follow, the description can be shortened. Your task as a clinician and as a writer is first to make a choice about what matters, and then determine how best to include that in your report.

OMIT NEEDLESS WORDS

One way to simplify your writing is to leave out any words that are not needed. To appreciate this, compare the sentence you just read with the heading that preceded it. The heading, "Omit needless words," was borrowed directly from Strunk and White (2000, p. 17). It conveys the main idea in three words. By comparison, the sentence that followed took eight words (i.e., "leave out any words that are not needed") to say the same thing.

Zinsser (2006) observed that "writing improves in direct ratio to the numbers of things we can keep out of it that shouldn't be there" (p. 12). Strunk and White stated:

Vigorous writing is concise. A sentence should contain no unnecessary words, a paragraph no unnecessary sentences....This requires not that the writer make all his sentences short, or that he avoid all detail and treat his subjects only in outline, but that every word tell. (2000, p. 17)

To illustrate this point, let us return again to the examples offered in the discussion of focused reading.

EXAMPLE 3

A. During the interview, the client said that he had never before been seen in therapy by a therapist.
B. The client indicated no previous experience in therapy.

What unnecessary words has the second sentence eliminated? The phrase "During the interview" is removed because it can be assumed that is when the client spoke. The phrase "said that he had never before been seen in therapy," 10 words, is replaced by "indicated no previous experience in therapy," 6 words that mean the same thing. This cutting of words saves time and makes the report shorter but sacrifices no important information about the client. A similar process can be applied to another example from our earlier discussion. Read the two examples and identify where and how needless words are omitted.

EXAMPLE 4

A. Test results suggest the presence of mild to moderate depression, anxiety, and concerns about family matters.
B. According to the results of the test, there is evidence of depression in the mild to moderate range, along with anxiety and apparent concerns about issues relating to family.

Strunk and White offer similar examples of how everyday expressions contain many needless words. For instance, "This is a subject that…" versus "This subject…"; "I was unaware of the fact that…" versus "I was unaware that…"; "The reason why…" versus "The reason…." Common speech also unnecessarily places prepositions after many phrases or uses prepositions when other phrases would work better. Compare "Wake me up at seven" versus "Wake me at seven"; "Find out about…" versus "Learn…." In the helping professions, clinical verbiage can complicate simple matters. For example, "The subject was engaged in walking behaviors" versus "He was walking." Or, "He produced little verbal material" versus "He was quiet" or "He said little."

Just as dietary fat clogs your arteries, verbal fat will clog your writing. As shown in the preceding examples, learning to trim unnecessary words or phrases is a key step toward improving your writing. Zinsser put this well when he said, "Be grateful for everything you can throw away" (2006, p. 16).

As with the earlier recommendation to embrace rewriting, responding to the instruction to shorten your writing will take some adjustment. Students have learned that verbiage helps stretch papers to meet the 10-page minimum so often imposed by faculty. Now the message is to shorten those 10-page papers to the fewest pages possible and make every word count. Again, the requirements for professional writing may be much different than those you learned in English composition or other courses.

Tallent (1997) offered examples of lengthy reports to illustrate the merit of clarity and brevity. Following one example that failed this test, he quips, "Just glancing at this report one may wonder if it is too long. On reading it, one may be sure that it is" (p. 139). To avoid such statements about your own work, practice trimming away everything that is unnecessary. You will have much greater impact if you can express the most meaning with the fewest words, rather than the least meaning with the most words.

CHOOSE WORDS CAREFULLY

Along with limiting the number of words you use, be attentive to their meaning. As a clinician, you cannot afford to be careless or haphazard about what you say or write. In staff meetings, therapy sessions, and your written reports, the words you use will be crucial. You must be aware of all the subtleties of language and learn to say exactly what you mean. This is especially true of written reports because once a report is written, others may read it without your being present to explain, clarify, or correct mistakes. Careless use of words can also come back to haunt you if your records or reports are ever used in a legal proceeding.

Reamer (2005) advised practitioners to "use clear, specific, unambiguous and precise wording" (p. 330). Glicken (2007) offers similar advice and includes a catalog of some of the most commonly misused words. Zinsser advised: "You will never make your mark as a writer unless you develop a respect for words and a curiosity about their shades of meaning that is almost obsessive" (2006, p. 32). I agree and would expand this statement by substituting the word *clinician* for *writer*. You will never be a fully skilled clinician unless you are acutely aware of words, attend precisely to the words used by others, and think carefully about the words you use.

Tallent (1997) described a series of studies in which various groups of mental health professionals were asked to indicate what they liked and what they disliked in typical psychological

reports. Among the factors most often criticized, ambiguous wording was frequently cited as a problem. The use of vaguely defined clinical terms has also received criticism in the literature. Tallent cited a classic study by Grayson and Tolman (1950) in which clinical psychologists and psychiatrists offered definitions for the 20 words most commonly used in psychological reports. Reviewing the list of words and definitions, the authors of the study were struck by how loosely the professionals defined many of the words.

Seventeen years after the original study by Grayson and Tolman, Siskind (1967) replicated the design and found similar results. Although the specific words included in such lists might differ if the study were performed again today, there is no reason to assume the definitional ambiguities would be any less now than they were in 1950 and 1967. For students and interns, ambiguity can be quite challenging because many of the words that sound the most clinical are, in fact, highly ambiguous. Students may be eager to use technical terms as a way of demonstrating their knowledge to supervisors. The trouble is that a great deal of what passes for clinical wording may sound scientific but often obfuscates rather than elucidates. Harvey (1997) made a similar observation and advised students to shorten sentence lengths, minimize the number of difficult words, and reduce the use of jargon. Fischer recommended to writers: "Say what you mean in concrete terms rather than dressing up the text in professionalese" (1994, p. 125).

Tallent concurred:

> In our view words like *oral, narcissistic, masochistic, immature, compulsive,* and *schizophrenia* are often more concealing than revealing.
>
> Technical words do not cause, but readily lend themselves to, imprecise or incomplete thinking. There is the error of nominalism, wherein we simply name a thing or an occurrence and think we understand something of the real world. (1997, p. 69; italics in original)

Earlier in this book, I made similar observations about the overuse of the word *inappropriate*. Phrases such as *manipulative, dependent,* or *just doing it for attention* are used with similar frequency and with equal ambiguity. As an antidote to such jargon, Fischer asserted:

> Saying what one means, both in speech and in writing, requires one to anchor abstractions in concrete examples. Ask yourself how you would explain what you mean to a 12-year-old. If you can't figure out how to do that, then you do not yet know what you mean—what your technical information comes down to in terms of your client's life. (1994, p. 134)

Harvey (1997) took this advice one step further and actually subjected her student's reports to formal "readability" measures that assessed such things as word choice and sentence length. Harvey then used the measures to calculate a grade and difficulty level and asked students to rewrite their reports so they could be read at grade levels of 13 or below. Harvey explained this approach by pointing out that psychological and other mental health reports are increasingly being reviewed by parents and others who have less formal education than those writing the reports. Thus, making reports more intelligible to these consumers may enhance their usefulness and reduce misunderstandings.

EXERCISE

Read the following three sentences and ask yourself if the differences in wording might communicate subtle yet important differences in meaning.

A. Mr. Smith denied any abuse of alcohol or drugs.
B. Mr. Smith said he does not abuse alcohol or drugs.
C. Mr. Smith does not abuse alcohol or drugs.

In the first sentence of this exercise, we encounter another of the many misused clinical words. The word "denied" in this sentence is important. In psychological language, "denial" is a form of defense and implies that a person is not being fully honest or is unconsciously repressing information. In this case, it might be that Mr. Smith "denies" alcohol abuse, but we know or suspect that he, in fact, does. It might also be that Mr. Smith is genuine and does not abuse alcohol or drugs. If that is the case, the second sentence would be better because it avoids the subtle intimation raised by the word "denies." The third sentence is still clearer about whether or not Mr. Smith abuses alcohol or drugs, but it may suffer from a different problem. Do we really know the statement is true, or is it just something Mr. Smith has told us? The sentence as written implies that we know it to be fact, but if the source of information is Mr. Smith, we should indicate that.

This may sound like nitpicking, but it is not. To appreciate why, ask yourself what might happen if you gave a report containing these sentences to other professionals who based clinical decisions on a misunderstanding of what you wrote. Do other readers conclude from the first sentence that Mr. Smith really drinks but does not admit it, or do they conclude that Mr. Smith does not drink? Do they conclude from the third sentence that we are sure alcohol and drugs are not a problem, or do they assume that is just what the client has told us? If the scenario of clinical misinterpretation is not convincing, imagine trying to explain the meaning while testifying in your own defense in a liability suit.

One way to reduce ambiguity in reports is to read questionable passages to colleagues and ask them to tell you whether the passage is clear and what they think it means. In some cases, with names hidden to preserve confidentiality, I ask non-clinicians to read my reports and offer feedback. This is particularly helpful if a report might be read by family members or others who are not trained in the profession.

Another, and too often overlooked, tool is the dictionary. Students often become so dependent on word-processing spell checkers that they forget to look up the meanings of words. I encourage students to use both a standard dictionary and a dictionary of professional terms. Three specialty dictionaries that I highly recommend are the *Counseling Dictionary: Concise Definitions of Frequently Used Terms,* 3rd ed. (Gladding, 2011), the *Social Work Dictionary,* 5th ed. (Barker, 2003), and the *APA Dictionary of Psychology* (VandenBos, 2006). The standard

dictionary can help you understand what words mean and imply in ordinary usage. Be careful, however, not to assume that definitions offered in a general dictionary carry the same meanings when applied in clinical writing. If a word has specific clinical meanings, the professional dictionary will cite specific meanings within the clinical context. Time after time, students use words they think they know only to discover that the word means or implies something entirely different from what they thought. One student used the word *limpid* to describe how a brain-injured patient held his arm. Another spoke of a situation *attenuating* the client's anxiety when the situation, in fact, *exacerbated* the anxiety. I recently heard a colleague repeatedly use the word *duplicitous* when he clearly meant *duplicated.*

If you do not know the meaning of any of the words used in the previous paragraph, did you look them up? If not, why? One of my students answered a similar question in class by saying, "I already took the GRE." That student did not get the point, nor did he get a letter of recommendation.

Misuse of clinical terms is also common. Students frequently confuse "delusions" with "hallucinations," "obsession" with "compulsion," "schizophrenia" with "multiple personality," and so on. Certainly one of the most commonly misused terms is *negative reinforcement.* Even if you are sure you know what this means, look it up in a textbook. In one upper-division undergraduate class, out of 20 students who said they were sure they knew the definition, only 5 were actually right. Again, to appreciate the importance of precise wording, consider that misunderstanding the meaning of "negative reinforcement" in a report could lead to interventions that are exactly the opposite of what the writer intended.

CLARITY

Choosing words carefully is part of the larger issue of achieving clarity in writing and in clinical work. This demand includes both clarity of individual words and clarity in syntax and organization. If the organization of a report is not clear, the reader will have to search to find important information. If the syntax of a sentence is unclear, the meaning may be misinterpreted. For example:

The therapist told the client about his problems.

Whose problems is the therapist talking about—the therapist's or the client's?

Strunk and White (2000) cautioned: "Muddiness is not merely a disturber of prose, it is also a destroyer of life, of hope" (p. 72). In clinical work, this is not an overstatement. I know of a case in which one therapist told another he had an appointment to see a client "next Friday." As the conversation took place on a Wednesday, the listener assumed the appointment was two days away. The speaker, however, was referring to Friday of the following week. Because the client in question was experiencing a serious crisis, this difference of an entire week was of potentially grave consequence.

Although most people would agree that clarity is important in clinical reports, the difficulty lies in recognizing when our own reports are unclear. Because we think we know what we mean when we write something, we assume that what we have written adequately conveys our intention. Thus, we readily overlook passages that may be virtually incomprehensible or, worse, that may appear comprehensible but will be misinterpreted by others.

As suggested earlier, one way to limit misunderstanding is to have someone else read a report before it goes to the intended recipient. If this is not possible, it is often helpful to pretend you know nothing of the case yourself, then read the report out loud. Reading aloud brings out aspects of writing that we do not recognize when we read silently. If time permits, another extremely valuable technique is to set a report aside for several days and then read it again with an open mind. Along with helping to identify writing problems, this also allows one to think more about the case before sending the report.

I cannot overemphasize how important clarity is to your writing. Clinicians simply must learn to be extremely careful about their words. You must know and say precisely what you mean. It is not enough to defend with "C'mon, you know what I meant." That may work in everyday discourse, but it is unacceptable in professional work. If the reader does not know exactly what is meant, the responsibility falls on the writer, not the reader. Say what you mean, and say it clearly. I feel so strongly about this that I have on occasion told students bluntly, "If you do not want to learn to use words carefully and accurately, you should probably consider another profession."

KNOW YOUR AUDIENCE

The final recommendation about writing is to know your audience. Some instructors and articles about clinical writing dictate specific and fixed rules for the style and content to be included in clinical reports. I prefer an approach that offers suggestions but at the same time encourages you to choose and adapt your style and content with an awareness of your audience. This principle was also highlighted by Brenner (2003), who spoke of "consumer-focused" psychological assessment and the importance of making our writing relevant and useful to its readers.

Fischer (1994) said repeatedly in her book: "Reports are for readers, not for the author" (p. 115). Tallent stressed this principle as well and cited a report by Hartlage and Merck (1971) that showed that the utility of reports is primarily weakened by, as Tallent (1997) described it, a "profound...lack of reflection by report writers on what might be useful to report to readers, a simple failure to use common sense" (p. 20). Hartlage and Merck (1971) observed, "Reports can be made more relevant to their prospective users merely by having the psychologists familiarize themselves with the uses to which their reports are to be applied" (p. 460).

A report prepared for a fellow professional in your discipline may differ from a report prepared for an attorney, family members, or others with different backgrounds and needs. Similarly, if you believe others are overlooking certain aspects of a client, you may want to emphasize those in your report. The most important thing is for you to write with conscious awareness of how your style and content meet your clinical and professional purpose and institutional context (Healy & Mulholland, 2007; Pelco et al., 2009).

EXERCISE

As a way of enhancing your awareness of different groups to which your reports might be targeted, read the following list and list some of the concerns to keep in mind when preparing a report

for each of them. You might consider the readers' level of training or knowledge, how much time they have, and the style of reports they are accustomed to reading. How do these and other factors differ for each of the groups listed?

- The client
- Family members of the client
- Insurance companies
- Clinical psychologists
- Counselors
- Social workers
- Psychiatrists
- Non-psychiatrist MDs
- Schoolteachers
- Students
- Attorneys
- Judges
- Professional journals
- Newspapers
- Others for whom you might write

Reviewing the list should enhance your awareness of general factors to consider in writing, but you must also remember that regardless of their profession or role, individuals will have different preferences and needs. One schoolteacher may be well versed in diagnostic categories, but another may know nothing at all about them. One psychiatrist may prefer reports that are as brief as possible and that convey "just the facts." Another may appreciate more detailed reports that convey a sense of the client as a person.

If you know for whom you will be writing before you write a report, it is sometimes a good idea to contact the person and ask about his or her preferences for style and content and any specific requirement for the report. After you write a report, you can follow up by asking the recipient for feedback. Your role as an intern gives you a perfect opportunity to ask for such information, and many people will be glad to offer their suggestions.

THE FUNCTION AND MAINTENANCE OF RECORDS

One of the responsibilities of all health care professions is to maintain accurate records about the diagnosis and treatment clients receive. This responsibility is codified in all of the major organizations' ethics codes and in special record-keeping guidelines (e.g., APA, 2007). By understanding the function of clinical records and developing a systematic approach to their use and maintenance, you can make record keeping an integral element of your clinical training and, later, your practice.

Before talking about the specifics of how to write case notes, it is worth acknowledging that record keeping often provokes a great deal of frustration not only for interns but for established professionals alike. Comments such as "I entered this profession to help people, not to push papers" are not at all uncommon, nor is it rare to find practitioners who simply do not keep up with required records or reports. I knew of one colleague who got more than a month behind in his clinical records. Understandable though that was considering his busy schedule, it put him, his clients, and the institution in jeopardy in multiple ways.

In a concise but highly informative review of ethical and risk management issues pertaining to documentation in social work, Reamer (2005) emphasized that records serve multiple functions. They contribute to the quality of a client's current and future care, satisfy agency requirements, document care for the purpose of third-party reimbursement (i.e., payment for care by insurance companies), and protect against legal actions. These functions are also specified in organizational guidelines and codes of ethics of all the major professional associations (Knapp & VandeCreek, 2006; Koocher & Keith-Spiegel, 2008). In addition, medical hospitals and other health care institutions must maintain adequate records to receive approval from auditing agencies such as the Joint Commission on Accreditation of Hospitals and government agencies in charge of Medicare and Medicaid.

Knapp and VandeCreek (2006) considered the legal importance of records in our litigious society. On the basis of their review of existing case law, they emphasized that well-kept records can reduce the risk of liability, whereas the lack of good records may, in itself, be used as evidence that care was substandard. This point was also stressed by Reamer (2005) and Koocher and Keith-Spiegel (2008), as well as by Bennett, Bryant, VandenBos, and Greenwood (1990), who stated: "In hospital practice it is often said, 'If it isn't written down, it didn't happen'" (p. 77).

For these reasons, an essential part of your responsibility as a professional will be to maintain quality records. To do that, you should understand what goes into records, what stays out, and some of the models for organizing and writing progress notes. Reamer (2005) pointed out that depending on the setting in which you work, you should also be familiar with relevant state and federal laws relating to record keeping. These include the Health Insurance Portability and Accountability Act (HIPAA), which has been discussed in earlier chapters; the Family Educational Rights and Privacy Act (FERPA), which applies primarily to educational records; and, if you work with drug and alcohol involved patients, Federal Law 42 U.S.C. § 290dd-2 and regulation 42 C.F.R. Part 2, Confidentiality of Alcohol and Drug Abuse Patient Records (which applies to any program that involves substance abuse education, treatment, or prevention and is regulated by the federal government).

WHAT GOES INTO RECORDS

EXERCISE

Before reading the following discussion, give some thought to all the information you would like to know about a client. Organize this into categories, and create a simple form to use for an initial intake interview. When you have generated your list of key information, compare your ideas with those of your peers to see what their approaches are and what issues they have identified that you have overlooked.

When I refer to clinical records in this text, I am speaking of the totality of information pertinent to a client's treatment. The general rule for determining what to put in records is this: If something is important, document it and keep a record, but think carefully about what you say and how you say it.

Good records should include all present and previous relevant information about a client's history and treatment, current diagnosis, correspondence, releases of information, documentation of consultation, billing information, informed consent forms, and any other pertinent information. At the same time, however, psychotherapy notes should probably not go in general records because, as mentioned in Chapter 4, the HIPAA guidelines protect the confidentiality of psychotherapy notes, but only if those notes are kept separately from the rest of the client's health care records. More will be said about psychotherapy notes later in this chapter.

Different institutions and agencies have different record-keeping technologies. As discussed in Chapter 4, more and more settings are shifting to computerized electronic health records (EHRs) or electronic medical record (EMRs) systems, and these will eventually become the norm (Bower, 2005; RAND, 2005; Steinfeld, Ekorenrud, Gillett, Quirk, & Eytan, 2006). If you have not yet read Chapter 4, now would be a good time to do that because you will undoubtedly encounter electronic record systems at some point, either during your internship or later during your practice. As such, you need to have an understanding of the ethical and legal issues associated with such systems.

In more traditional settings that have yet to adopt an electronic system, typical physical materials involve either manila or metal folders subdivided into sections containing certain types of information. For convenience, subsections are often color coded and flagged with tabs identifying the contents. To ensure compliance with record-keeping guidelines, most institutions have some form of periodic record review that assesses the content, organization, clarity, and security of records. This has always been good practice but is now mandated under HIPAA rules.

Luepker (2003) offered a useful summary of what to include in records. She recommended that all records begin with a face sheet that includes basic personal data such as name, address, home and work phone numbers, date of birth, sex, family members' names, next of kin, and employment status. Also indicated here should be information about the date of initial contact, the reason for referral, and the names of other professionals (e.g., physicians, other counselors) who are seeing or have seen the client.

Most agencies use standard forms to gather the information in these categories at intake or first meeting with a professional caregiver. In some instances, the client completes the information; in other settings, intake specialists or the therapists themselves discuss the information with clients and record the data as the discussion proceeds. Interactive computer programs allow clients to enter this information themselves, but it should always be cross-checked through direct interaction.

Taking this type of information is a straightforward process with most clients, but in some cases, clients may not want to be contacted at their home address. For example, I have worked with abused spouses who did not want their partners to know that they were seeing a therapist. In these circumstances, you need to flag the record in some way to indicate precisely where and how a client should be contacted and billed.

Following the face sheet, Luepker places a section labeled "Evaluation." This information is typically collected at the outset of treatment for the purpose of developing treatment plans. In some approaches to records, this information might also be included in the initial intake forms mentioned earlier. Within the heading of "Evaluation," Luepker includes a description of the presenting problem; history of the problem; significant life history, including childhood history; medical history; substance abuse; observations from the interview; diagnosis; and treatment plan.

In some settings, particularly acute psychiatric or medical units, initial evaluations routinely incorporate a brief review of mental functioning known as the mini-mental status examination (MMSE; Folstein, Folstein, & McHugh, 1975). The MMSE is available in multiple languages and is so commonly used that it behooves interns to have some familiarity with how to administer and score the instruments and write the results (see Psychologist Assessment Resources Inc., 2010, for information about the recently revised edition).

As part of the assessment of health status and substance use, I advise interns to obtain, whenever possible, the requisite information releases and to establish close contacts with clients' physicians. I also suggest that clients who have not had complete physicals within the past year be encouraged to see a physician. A number of concerns that present with psychological symptoms may be caused by or related to underlying physical illnesses. Remember, too, as discussed in Chapter 4, federal guidelines require that information about treatment for drug or alcohol abuse must be provided special confidentiality protections, including special treatment in any record system accessible to others.

Another important point to make about evaluation is to not only consider information about the dysfunctional aspects of the client's life but also attend to the client's strengths and resources. Such information is particularly relevant to the client's life history and current functioning and should certainly include educational, vocational, or avocational strengths.

While gathering and considering any of the previous data, keep in mind also that some clients may be unreliable sources of information. Therefore, with required consent, it is advisable to obtain corroborating information from family or friends. Meeting with family members or friends at intake is virtually an essential for clients who, because of their presenting concerns (e.g., mental disorders, brain injury, certain personality disorders), may not be able or motivated to provide accurate data about themselves. Before making such contacts or conducting such meetings, however, you must be sure to have the client's specific written authorization.

Along with the information described thus far, as part of an initial assessment, I strongly recommend that you seek copies of the client's records if he or she has been or is being seen by other treatment providers or related professionals, provided you receive the client's authorization and signed release of information. A client's reluctance to allow you access to such records may serve as a red flag for making further inquiries about

the client's reasons. You should also be cautious in deciding whether or not to accept the client for treatment if you cannot obtain past records. From the perspective of managing liability risks, it is not advisable to treat clients without access to information about previous treatment. The reason is that such information can have a significant impact on how you understand the client's present situation and how you provide treatment yourself. If you have not made an effort to gather information about past or other ongoing treatment, and if you do not document that attempt and information in your own records, you could face added problems if legal concerns arise.

Once sufficient information has been gathered and evaluated, the clinician can and generally should include a treatment plan in the client's record. At a minimum, the plan should contain a statement of the problem, the goal of treatment described in behavioral terms, and the steps that will be taken to achieve the goal. Some clinicians advocate that the client and the therapist agree to and sign each treatment plan. As treatment proceeds, the client and the therapist should periodically review the treatment plan to assess progress and adjust the approach or goals as needed.

Managed care and other changes in health care are placing increasing demands on professionals in the mental health field to demonstrate the rationale for, and efficacy of, the work done with clients (Braun & Cox, 2005; Rupert & Baird, 2004). In some cases, if you have not formulated a sound treatment plan at the outset, and if you do not document through progress notes that your subsequent work with the client has followed your plan, you, the agency you work for, or the client may be denied compensation from the insurer. Thus, along with contributing to the quality of client care, well-formulated and clearly documented treatment plans can also contribute to your financial well-being and that of your clients.

Ongoing treatment and progress notes form the next major section of records, as described by Luepker (2003). In light of HIPAA protections for psychotherapy notes that are stored separately, I recommend that therapists simply include in the general record the time and date of the session, whether or not the client attended, a brief and general statement of what occurred in the session, and any relevant follow-up. Notes of the actual content of the session and the therapist's impressions should be kept separately from the general record.

At the conclusion of treatment, the therapist should write a brief synopsis of the case and include it in a termination summary that reviews the origin, course, and result of treatment. If the client will be referred to another professional, the termination summary should include mention of this or of other aftercare plans.

Following a termination summary, you will often find a general section of the records labeled simply "Other Data." Include here authorization for treatment, releases of information, copies of test results, and communications from other professionals. If you consult with other professionals about a case, make a record of the consultations to include here or in your case notes. Because this portion of records can become quite crowded with miscellaneous material, you may find it useful to organize the material with tabbed inserts.

WHAT STAYS OUT OF RECORDS

PROTECTING CLIENTS

Like all simple rules, there are caveats to the rule of documenting everything that is important. In the case of clinical records, the caveat arises because your case records are not strictly confidential. All ethical codes explicitly mention that information, including information in clinical records, may be required to be disclosed under certain circumstances. This reality was particularly emphasized by Reamer (2005) and is also clearly recognized in the APA (2007) Record Keeping Guidelines. Recognizing the possibility that records may be disclosed means you cannot afford to be careless, and it is your responsibility to protect records from disclosure, whenever legally required and permitted. When you keep any sort of record about clients or their treatments, keep in mind the possibility that others might have access to the record.

Institutional settings are an example of where confidentiality of records may be limited. If your treatment records are, or will become part of, a larger record to which other staff have access, it is obvious that your records can be seen by others. Under these circumstances, it would not be in the client's best interests to reveal in such accessible records information that was shared with you in confidence or that might be harmful to the client if disclosed. This is another reason it is a good idea to keep the psychotherapy notes separately. As an intern, it is especially important that you consult with your supervisor if you have any questions about whether or not something should be included in a record.

Another possibility that you should be aware of concerns computerized case notes and clinical outcome data. Jeffords (1999) reported that the National Research Council found the path of the typical medical record has changed with the proliferation of technology. Twenty-five years ago, records were held and used by a personal physician. Today, numerous individuals in more than 17 organizations may handle records. Recognition of this reality is part of the reason that the HIPAA guidelines about electronic data storage, communication, and security are so explicit and, along with specifying what information can and cannot be exchanged, include measures such as passwords and encryption to protect against hackers and other intrusions. Recommendations for secure handling of electronic records are offered by Schwartz and Lonborg (2011), whereas specific recommendation concerning cloud storage are given by Devereaux and Gottlieb (2012).

PROTECTING YOURSELF

Just as it is important to protect clients from the possibility that records may be viewed by others, it is also important to protect yourself. No clear-cut rules exist in this area, but interns and clinicians would do well to ask themselves how what they put in records might later sound in a court proceeding. Gutheil (1980) went so far as to suggest that trainees

> deliberately hallucinate upon their right shoulder the image of a hostile prosecuting attorney who might preside at their trial, and that to this visual hallucination they append the auditory impression of the voice most suited to it....

Having achieved this goal-directed transient psychotic state, the trainee should then mentally test out in that context the sound of what he or she is about to write. (p. 481)

This does not mean that you should be frightened about everything you write or that you should expect a lawsuit around every corner. At the same time, however, being aware that your records and notes can be exposed and analyzed in litigation serves as a helpful reminder and incentive to keep the quality of your treatment and documentation at the highest level possible.

Keep in mind, too, that under HIPAA guidelines, clients have access to their own records. Again, psychotherapy notes are protected under HIPAA if kept separately, but in the portion of the record that is accessible to clients upon request, it is advisable to avoid recording your own emotional reactions or opinions about clients if such reactions could be clinically harmful or litigiously consequential when read by a client. Be aware too that HIPAA does not afford protection for therapy notes if they are ordered by a judge to be produced.

From a liability risk management perspective, avoid (1) "raising ghosts" and (2) taking blame. By raising ghosts, I mean recording unfounded or unnecessary speculation. For example, if a client seems a bit down during a session but no reason can be found from the client's history, statements, or actions to suspect suicide potential, it would be unwise for a clinician to record "Client was down today, but I do not think suicide potential is high." If you mention suicide, you must also assess the potential carefully and document that you did so. If suicide risk is not elevated above normal, do not mention it at all. The same would apply to issues relating to dangerousness to others. Do not simply speculate about something so serious in your notes unless you followed up on that speculation during your session.

Also avoid taking blame. Do not write in your notes that you made a mistake in treatment. This might feel honest and cathartic, but it could get you into trouble later. If you are tempted to make such an entry, ask yourself what good it serves to write in your own notes that you made an error. You know it yourself, and that is sufficient. Remember the advice your auto insurance company gives you if you are in an accident. If something unfortunate happens and you have to defend an action in court, allow your attorney to advise you but do not put confessions in your records beforehand.

Finally, never falsify records (Reamer, 2005). If your records are demanded for a legal proceeding, you will be asked under oath if your records represent a true and accurate description of your treatment or have been altered in any way since they were originally written. If you alter records and do not so indicate, you may be guilty of perjury. It is far better to be careful in your treatment and in your records to begin with and then to be scrupulously honest if you are ever called to court. If at some point in your work with a client you realize that a previous record was deficient in some way, at the time you notice the deficiency you can make a note that you discovered something that needed to be added or changed in an earlier note. This does not mean you go back and actually change the note. It means you make a separate and later note that indicates the need to adjust, clarify, or correct the earlier note.

PROGRESS NOTES AND PSYCHOTHERAPY NOTES

EXERCISE

If you are working in a clinical setting, find out if you can obtain permission to review some of the client records. Then read the progress notes kept in the records and ask yourself the following questions: Can I detect differences in style or content in the notes of different staff members? What notes stand out as useful? What notes are not useful? What matters of style and information account for this difference?

STANDARD FORMATS

In an effort to standardize treatment notes, many agencies have developed or adopted specific guidelines for what should go where in notes. This is important in medical settings or group-care facilities where many treatment professionals interact with many clients and need to have ready access to key information quickly. Without a standard format, it is nearly impossible for members of a treatment team to find information in a record. Standardized notes also ensure that each member of the team is working consistently on an identified problem or goal for the given client and that each treatment team member follows a structured procedure in observing the client's status, recording information about that status, assessing the client's condition, and basing treatment on the assessment.

It is likely that your internship placement will have guidelines for keeping records and recording progress notes. If so, you must learn them, practice using them, and get feedback to be sure you are writing your notes correctly. As a check, interns should initiate their own records and progress note reviews with their supervisors. Supervisors tend to get busy and overlook such details, so it is a sign of responsibility if interns take the initiative to be sure they are keeping acceptable notes.

In your clinical work, you are likely to encounter two types of ongoing notes regarding treatment. For convenience, and consistency with laws such as HIPAA, we will refer to these as *progress notes* and *psychotherapy notes*. The former are records that are part of the documentation of treatments provided to clients and are available to other staff. By comparison, psychotherapy notes are your personal records of the events of specific therapy sessions or related interactions. Understanding the differences between these note types and learning how to use each effectively will help you become more efficient and effective in both your treatment and your record keeping.

PROGRESS NOTES

Progress notes are the core of most clinical records. They provide a record of events and are a means of communication among professionals. They encourage review and assessment of treatment issues, allow other professionals to review the process of treatment, and are a legal record. Progress notes have also seen increasing use by insurance providers seeking to determine whether a treatment is within the realm of services for which they provide compensation. In writing progress notes, you must keep all these functions in mind.

When I write progress notes, I find it helpful to ask myself several questions. First, I review the events in order to again assess and better understand what happened. This helps me process and check my treatment. Next, I ask myself: "If I read the notes several months or years from now, will they help me remember what happened, what was done, and why?"

Because I may not be the only one to read my notes, I also consider what would take place if something happened to me and another clinician picked up my clients. Though often overlooked, this consideration is specifically acknowledged in Guideline 13 of the APA (2007) record-keeping guidelines. This was also discussed by Pope and Vasquez (2007) in their suggestions regarding a "professional will." The key question here is: "If someone else takes over this case, would my notes enable him or her to understand the client and the treatment?" If I am in a setting where other professionals refer to the same record, I ask whether the notes I write will adequately and accurately communicate information to them. I include legibility in this consideration. If my handwriting is so poor that others cannot read it, the notes will not do them or the client much good. Finally, and very importantly, ask yourself: "What would be the implications and impact if these notes were used as a legal document in a court of law?"

TYPES OF PROGRESS NOTES

The two most common types of progress notes are problem-oriented and goal-oriented notes. As the names suggest, problem-oriented notes refer to one or more specific problem areas being addressed in treatment (Cameron & Turtle-song, 2001; Weed, 1971), whereas goal-oriented notes focus on specified treatment goals, with each entry relating in some way to a goal. In systems that use problem-oriented or goal-oriented notes, each therapist, or the treatment team as a group, identifies several key areas of focus in the client's treatment. For example, problems might be identified as follows:

1. Initiates fights with other residents
2. Does not participate in social interactions

Expressed as goals, these might be stated as follows:

1. Reduce incidence of instigating fights
2. Increase socialization

Once a list of the problems or goals is established, progress notes then refer to them by number or name.

The theory behind this approach is that it helps staff target their intervention to meet specific treatment needs or goals. Such notes may also help demonstrate to insurers that the treatment provided is systematic and is related to specific problems or goals for which compensation is being provided.

STYLE OF PROGRESS NOTES

In most progress notes, writing style is not important; clarity, precision, and brevity are. Your goal is to record all the essential information in as little space and time as possible. Because you may be writing and reading notes on many clients each day, you will want to save time by including only the essential details. By keeping your notes succinct, you will also save the time of others who may read them. This is especially important in settings where notes are shared among many professionals, each of whom has contact with many clients. When a clinician must read many notes, every minute saved in reading and writing adds up. As long as the notes are kept accurately and all essential information is provided, the time saved in charting can be better spent in direct clinical contact or other activities.

Using shorthand is one way to shorten progress notes. If you are taking notes primarily for your own use, any system of shorthand will do as long as you can decipher it later. However, if you are writing notes in a record that others share, it is essential that any shorthand be understood by everyone and accepted by your institution. If there is a possibility of misinterpretation, you are better off writing notes out in full. Also be aware that different settings may have different standards for using shorthand or abbreviations, and some may not allow any shorthand at all. If you take notes as part of your internship responsibilities, check to be sure before you write.

STRUCTURED NOTE FORMATS

SOAP NOTES

One of the most common formats for progress notes in health care is the SOAP format, which is part of the Problem Oriented Medical Records (POMR) system (Cameron & Turtle-song, 2002; Weed, 1971). The POMR system includes four components: clinical assessment, problem list, treatment plan, and progress notes (Shaw, 1997). The SOAP notes fall in the progress note portion of this system.

The letters in SOAP stand for Subjective, Objective, Assessment, and Plan. "Subjective" refers to information about the client's present situation from the client's subjective point of view. One way to think of this is as the client's presenting complaint or description of how he or she is doing and what he or she needs or desires. "Objective" information is the external data that are being observed. In a medical setting, this might be blood pressure, temperature, and the like. In a mental health context, observed data might include such things as pacing, speaking in a loud voice, fidgeting, and so on. The "assessment" portion of a note reflects how the therapist integrates and evaluates the meaning of the client's subjective report and the objective externally observable data in light of all the other information known about the client. From this assessment, the "plan" of treatment action is then recorded.

An example of how a SOAP note might be written for a client in a group home for adolescent runaways illustrates how SOAP notes might work in practice.

Dec, 15, 2012, 2 A.M.

S. Daniel J. came to the front room at 1:30 A.M. stating that he could not sleep because he was having nightmares about his family. He said he'd just had a dream in which his father was hit by a train and died.

O. Dan was somewhat teary as he described the dream. At the same time was hugging himself with a blanket around him and seemed to be at once frightened and angry. Asked if he wanted to go back to bed; he declined and opted instead to sit in the couch wrapped tightly in his blanket. I fixed him some hot tea and he sipped it for about a half hour while we talked about what his dream might mean and how he could cope with it. He then went back to sleep.

A. Dan has been talking about his family a lot lately in group sessions. This afternoon he for the first time expressed a great deal of anger about his father, who he said had been very abusive mentally and physically.

P. Report this event to Dan's therapist Mollie Jenkins. Monitor Dan's sleeping habits to observe for any changes or disruptions.

Although the concepts behind the POMR system, from which the SOAP system developed, are quite valuable, my experience with the SOAP format suggests that the terminology is rather ambiguous for use outside medical settings, and enforcement of the terminology can be paradoxically rigid, which can readily lead to needless debate about whether an entry should have been placed in the *S, O,* or *A* section (Cameron & Turtle-song, 2002). I have also found that efforts to conform to rigid SOAP guidelines tend to produce contorted writing that may obscure rather than clarify what happened and what was done about it. Nevertheless, many institutions use the POMR and SOAP systems, so you should be familiar with them and develop strategies for following these formats.

Cameron and Turtle-song (2002) offer useful suggestions for how the SOAP format can be used in mental health settings. If this system is used in your placement site, your supervisor will no doubt be familiar with it and can give you useful suggestions for putting your progress notes in the proper format for that institution. If you are interested in knowing more about SOAP, see the original work by Weed (1971) or the more general review of medical records by Avery and Imdieke (1984). Most settings that use SOAP or any of the other standard note formats will have training material or workshops that can teach you more about writing these notes.

If your internship does not require notes to be in the SOAP format, it is still helpful to have a structure to help guide your own note taking, particularly if you will be making entries in common log books or non-medical client charts. For those uses, I have found it helpful for interns to follow an approach that goes by the acronym DART. The *D* in DART stands for a "description" of the client and situation. *A* is for "assessment" of the situation. *R* is for the "response" of the clinician and the client, and *T* is for "treatment" implications and plan. One way to think of this system is that when you write progress notes, you must tell what happened, what you made of it, how you responded, and what you plan to do or think should be done in the future. This sequence of events is not only a useful way to conceptualize progress notes, it is also a useful way to approach a treatment interaction.

DESCRIPTION

The first part of any progress note should describe the basic *W* questions of journalism: when, where, who, and what. In practice, these W words are not actually used in the progress notes, but the notes must contain the information the words subsume. Some people prefer to put date and time at the end of a note, but I suggest you start the note with this information for ease of reference later. "Where" indicates the location of the event. If the location is always the same, such as a clinic office, this can be omitted. However, if many locations are possible, as in a school, hospital, or other large setting, it helps to note the exact location. Next, you should indicate "who" played a significant role in or observed the event you are describing. Noting who was present can come in handy later if there is a need to get additional information about a specific event or client.

Once you have provided the basic information, describe "what" is prompting you to write the note. The more significant the event, the more space will be dedicated to the corresponding progress note.

ASSESSMENT

The next step is to record your assessment of what it means. You do not always have to offer profound insights or explanations, nor do you always have to know what something means. Sometimes the most important notes are about behaviors that stand out precisely because their meaning is not exactly clear. For example, if a client who is normally rather quiet becomes very talkative and energetic, the meaning of the change might not be clear, but one could note it, suggest some possible considerations for what might be happening, or ask others to offer their insights.

To help guide your assessment, think about how the present event or behavior relates to other knowledge you have about the client and treatment. How does the present situation relate to previous behaviors, to recent events, to medical or medication issues, to family events, to the treatment plan, and to other factors? Remember that most events reflect a combination of both lasting and temporary factors within the individual and within the environment. Thus, you might observe a change in a client's behavior and note that it seems to reflect stresses over recent family conflicts and may also be a reaction to the overall level of tension in the treatment facility. The most important task is to give some thought to what you observed and try to relate it to your overall knowledge and treatment of the client. Again, this is not just good note taking; it is sound clinical practice.

RESPONSE

In good clinical work, you must first take in what is happening and what the client is doing and saying. Then you must assess what this means. Your next task is to respond in some way. Your progress notes should reflect this sequence. The description of your response need not be lengthy, but it must accurately note any important details.

Like your clinical response, your record should reflect a well-founded and rational treatment approach. Here it is sometimes helpful to consider how other clinicians might judge your response. It is also useful to think about the legal implications. As a legal standard, if something is not recorded, it is difficult to prove it was done. Learn to record scrupulously anything you do or do not do that might later be considered important. Be conscientious about noting such things as referring a client to someone else, administering formal tests or other measures, giving homework assignments or developing contracts, and scheduling future contacts. Also, keep notes if you consult with someone about a case. Include both the fact that you consulted and a summary of the consultation and results (Luepker, 2003).

To the extent that the severity of a client's concerns or the riskiness of a clinical decision increases, records should be more detailed. At the same time, however, Reamer (2005) advised against going into such extraordinary detail that red flags are raised or too much information is included. Bennett et al. (1990) suggested that records should describe the goal of the chosen intervention, risks and benefits, and the reason for choosing a specific treatment. It is also advisable to indicate any known risks, available alternatives and why they were not chosen, and the steps that were taken to maximize the effectiveness of chosen treatments. In some instances, documenting what you did not do and why you decided not to do it can be just as important as documenting what you did do. It is often useful to note any information provided to, or discussed with, the client and the client's response.

In essence, this process is tantamount to "thinking out loud" in the record. Gutheil (1980, p. 482) advised: "As a general rule, the more the uncertainty, the more one should think out loud in the record." In this process, the clinician is recording not only the action taken but the reasons for taking or not taking an action. If questions arise later, the explanation is already documented. In a legal context, Gutheil stressed that for liability reasons, this process reduces the possibility of a ruling of clinical negligence.

TREATMENT PLAN

Following the description of your immediate response, the final element of a well-written progress note is your plan for future treatment. This may be as simple as a note saying: "Schedule for next Monday" or "Continue to monitor condition daily," or it might be more complex, as in "Next session we will explore family issues. Client will bring written description of each family member, and we will complete family diagrams." Notes of this sort allow you to refer back to refresh your memory of what was planned.

If you are working in an agency where a daily log is maintained, it is often possible to leave notes there for other staff. For example, you might conclude a note by suggesting that the evening staff keep close watch on a client. If something is really important, be sure to highlight it in some way in your notes. Use stars, bold writing, or other methods to make the note stand out. If the matter is urgent or life threatening, do not leave the matter to progress notes alone; speak directly to someone responsible and document the conversation.

EXERCISE

If you are not already writing clinical notes, you may want to develop your skills by choosing a recent interaction with a friend or client and document it as if you were writing a progress note in a clinical record. If possible, review the note with your supervisor and request feedback on how you could improve the note.

TIME-SEQUENCED NOTES

As noted earlier in this chapter and in the discussion of HIPAA and ethics in Chapter 4, psychotherapy notes are different from progress notes and should not be kept in the client's general record. In contrast to notes written using the DART and SOAP approaches, which are used primarily to record specific events or interactions and are kept in the general record, a therapist's personal case notes from individual sessions typically follow a different format and serve a different purpose. Time-sequenced notes are the most common form of notation for therapy sessions. In time-sequenced notes, the therapy session is described as it progressed, with individual elements described sequentially in the order in which they occurred in the session. Some therapists make these notes during the therapy session. Others wait until the end of a session to record what happened.

The sequential approach is often used for records of therapy sessions because there are simply too many elements to address each separately following a more structured format. Sequential notes also enable the clinician to observe the order of events as they occur within a session. This can provide extremely useful clinical information. For example, it is probably not mere coincidence if a client begins by describing family conflicts and then shifts the topic to problems at work. Sequential notes follow this shift and enable the clinician to notice it in the record, even though it might have gone unnoticed during the session. An example of an abbreviated sequentially ordered progress note from a therapy session follows. Note the use of an informal shorthand to save time:

> 2/9/2004 2–3 P.M. JA began session by revu of 1st wks sesn. Said he had thought about it & did not understnd why he had felt so angry about his mother. We explored this more. JA cried again, remembered his mother being very critical when he made mistakes during a piano recital. Felt humiliated. Realized this was typical pattern. Gave recent example of visit during Xmas. His mother was critical of JA's job, an argument developed and JA returned home early. We explored pattern of seeking approval and fearing rejection. JA realized that anger is also there. This comes out in marriage as well. JA is often angry w wife if she disapproves of anything he does. He described two examples, when he cooks and in child care. He is not comfortable with his own behavior but is having hard time chnging. Agreed to explore this more nxt sessn.

In a one-hour session, there would obviously be more that could be recorded, but in this example, the therapist has chosen to note the events and topics she considered most important. This will vary from therapist to therapist and is also closely tied to theoretical orientation. Analytically trained therapists, for example, would be likely to make notes much different from those recorded by a behavioral therapist.

PROCESS NOTES

Process notes are yet another type of note with which you should be familiar. Process notes refer to notes in which the therapist includes personal reflections on not only the observable interactions in treatment but also the therapist's own thoughts and considerations of the unconscious dynamics of a client or the transference or countertransference issues in therapy. As contrasted with progress notes, which focus more on the externally observable, empirical events of treatment, process notes delve into the psyche of the therapist and the client. Notes of this type can be especially useful in training because they allow interns and their supervisors to review not only what was going on externally during the interaction but also what the intern was thinking (Fox & Gutheil, 2000). Professionals trained from a psychodynamic perspective will be quite familiar with process notes and may consider them essential to training and treatment.

Prior to the establishment of the protections now included in HIPAA, many professionals who valued process notes had legitimate concerns that insurance companies might seek such notes. Legally, clients also have access to their general medical records, and a client who reads a therapist's private speculations on the client's libidinal attachments, latent desires, or other potentially sensitive matters might not understand the purpose of such notes or the terminology involved. These concerns have largely been addressed by HIPAA protections, but, again, only if psychotherapy notes are kept separately from other records. HIPAA protections notwithstanding, however, be aware that process notes may also be problematic in legal proceedings and, as discussed in Chapter 4, HIPAA does not protect notes against court orders.

Given these concerns, many professionals have chosen to reduce substantially or eliminate the introspective and theoretical contemplation that was once standard in process notes. This is unfortunate because process notes can be tremendously valuable in clinical practice and especially in clinical training. For an excellent review of this topic and suggestions for effective use of process notes, see Fox and Gutheil (2000). Ultimately, what you choose to put in your notes is up to you and your supervisor, but keep in mind the benefits as well as the risks, and, again, be aware that other persons may read your notes.

SIGNING NOTES

The final step in writing progress notes is signing them. As an intern, you should check with your supervisor to be sure you understand exactly how notes or other documents are to be signed and how you are to identify yourself with your signature. Some institutions require interns to sign notes and identify themselves as "Psychology Intern," "School Counseling Intern," or "Social Work Student." It may also be necessary for your supervisor to co-sign any notes that you write. This might include daily progress notes, or it might apply only to more lengthy reports. Because different agencies or institutions will have different policies, the only sure way to know you are following procedures is to ask at the outset.

Along with being sure to list your status correctly, you should also consider the legibility of your signature. Mine happens to be almost totally illegible. With experience, secretaries, students, and colleagues all learn more or less how to decipher my scratchings, but those who have less experience and do not know me well are often at a loss. This can present a problem with regard to progress notes because sometimes there are questions relating to notes, and people need to know who wrote them. If no one knows who you are and your signature is illegible, it is going to be difficult to find you. My solution is to always print my name above my signature. Because most people will be less familiar with interns than with regular staff, it is especially important for you to be sure people can read your writing and identify your status clearly.

DICTATION

Whether you write or dictate your progress notes, their content and structure should follow the guidelines offered thus far. Dictation is in many ways like writing; both take practice to master. If you begin to dictate, it may help to work from a brief written outline. This is not as lengthy or redundant as writing the entire entry beforehand, but it does provide some structure and a reference point. It is also possible to use a general outline, such as the SOAP or DART format, and then make notes about the specific details for each client or event.

When you are dictating, keep in mind that the people who will transcribe your record have only what they hear on tape as a basis for what they will write. Remember to speak clearly, spell out unfamiliar names or terms, and verbally indicate where punctuation, paragraph breaks, or symbols should be placed. Do not be afraid to make corrections if you realize that you made a mistake or left out a detail earlier in your report. Rather than starting over, if you realize you made an error or omission, you can say, "I just realized I left out a sentence. Could you go back to just after…and insert…." When you have dictated the correction, you can continue from where you left off.

In most large institutions, you may never meet the staff who transcribe your dictated notes. Because I find this structure unfriendly, I make it a point to get to know the people who will be typing my notes. Building relationships with records and administrative assistants and other staff is not only rewarding interpersonally, it can also help prevent and more easily resolve a host of problems. As standard practice, it also helps to conclude your dictation by thanking the person who is doing the typing and acknowledging that person's work.

An increasingly useful and sophisticated alternative to human transcription involves voice recognition systems, in which one speaks directly to a computer, which then saves and prints out the dictated text. These systems are now remarkably accurate and can already manage complex clinical terminology and editing functions. However, such systems require the user to speak clearly and relatively consistently. This may take some getting used to, but with practice one can learn to interact effectively with such systems.

PROGRESS NOTES AND SUPERVISION

I have described the importance of progress notes for meeting agency standards, ethical guidelines, and legal documentation. In addition, progress notes can also provide useful material for clinical supervision. The general subject of supervision was discussed in Chapter 5, but a few additional comments are warranted in the context of notes.

It is a good practice for interns and supervisors to make reviews of progress notes a regular part of the supervision process. This review serves several functions. As noted earlier, reviewing notes with supervisors helps ensure that the intern's records are up to agency standards. Because record keeping is an important but often overlooked part of clinical training, supervisors may wish to offer advice about the content or the style of an intern's notes. Reviewing notes also allows interns the opportunity to ask about any issues pertaining to record keeping and note taking. Beyond the clerical aspects of note taking, reviewing notes and records helps supervisors observe what interns consider to be significant about a case or therapy session. Supervisors can monitor the intern's records of the content and process of therapy sessions, and the notes can be referred to as needed to supplement or guide case discussions.

USING YOUR NOTES

Having devoted this chapter primarily to how to keep records and progress notes, it should not be forgotten that the primary purpose of notes is to assist the treatment of your clients. It is surprising how often therapists take notes at the end of sessions but then do not refer to them again before the next session with their clients. This can easily happen as therapists with busy schedules shift from seeing one client to the next with little time in between. Understandable though it may be, this could result in lessening the quality of treatment.

I confess to having been guilty of this myself on occasion. I recall an instance in which a client said he had given a great deal of thought to what was said last week, and I found myself internally struggling to recall just what it was we had discussed. It has also happened that I "assigned homework" (i.e., suggested that a client do or write something between sessions), which I then forgot to discuss. Clients have called me on this and in some cases expressed their displeasure over what appeared to be a lack of concern or attention.

Beyond perceiving this as a matter of discourtesy or simple forgetfulness, many clients may actually consider such oversights unethical. In a survey of 96 adults, with or without experience as clients, Claiborn, Berberoglu, Nerison, and Somberg (1994) found that of a list of statements of about 60 possible hypothetical events that might occur in therapy, "Your therapist does not remember what you talked about in the previous session" was ranked the fourth highest among events considered ethically inappropriate. The mean ranking for this item on a scale of 1 to 5, with 1 being "completely inappropriate," was 1.32. Clearly, at least in this sample, recipients of clinical services placed a high value on therapists being aware of the content of previous sessions.

Given this finding, it certainly behooves the therapist to take the few minutes before a session to review the notes from the last visit. With heavy caseloads and busy schedules, oversights and lapses of memory are almost sure to occur unless clinicians take good notes and then make use of them. Clinicians who make efficient use of progress notes will be more aware of the sequence of events across sessions. This will lead to better therapeutic care and higher levels of satisfaction in clients.

OTHER GUIDELINES

This text has emphasized repeatedly that you must know your limits and be open to learning. This applies to records and notes as much as any other aspect of your internship. If you do not know how to write a note, or if you are unsure of the wording to use, ask for help. If you are describing an interaction with a client, do not write notes designed to impress everyone with your skills. While you are an intern, humility is a virtue, and hubris can get you into trouble. Remember the value of simplicity and objectivity.

Another principle of note taking is to be constructive. This is especially important if you are writing notes in a record that is accessible to others. Although part of your task is to assess and try to understand what you observe, your purpose is not to ascribe blame. Your goal is to facilitate treatment, not to be critical of clients or staff. For example, it would not be constructive to write a note such as "Dennis is up to his old tricks again. Found him masturbating in front of the television. Sometimes I think we should cut the thing off." This may sound shockingly callous, but I read precisely this note in staff records. Interns learn by example, but some examples are best not followed. Imagine the impact of such a note if read by an outside professional, by a family member, or in a court of law.

For similar reasons, if you are working in an institution where many staff members record notes in the same book, using the record to question or attack the conduct of other staff is not a good idea. Reamer (2005) referred to this as not "airing dirty laundry" in notes. Consider, for example: "The night shift is still not following through with last week's treatment plan. How is he supposed to get better if we are not consistent?" This note may stem from legitimate frustration, but a formal progress note may not be the best place to air those feelings. I have read record books that sounded more like a name-calling war between staff than a mutually beneficial discussion of treatment. Such notes cannot really be helpful to the clients or the staff. If you have concerns, address them with your supervisor, but keep the progress notes objective.

Finally, at the outset of your career, develop good note-taking and record-keeping habits. Make yourself write notes immediately or as soon after an interaction as possible. Schedule the time you need for note taking, and do not sacrifice this for other distractions. Keep your notes as thorough as they need to be, follow any required format, and establish a process of review to ensure that you keep everything up to date.

Faced with the many demands of clinical work, it is all too easy to become careless, or to let other tasks take precedence over note taking (Kagle, 1993). If you need 10 minutes for note taking between therapy sessions, schedule that in, and do not allow that time to be taken up instead by phone calls or other distractions. Unless they are urgent, save those other matters until you have finished your notes. You will be surprised how much gets forgotten, mixed up, or lost even by the end of the day. The longer you wait to record your notes, the less accurate and less valuable they will be. When it comes to clinical record keeping, a little compulsivity is not a bad quality to develop.

REFERENCES

Alter, C., & Adkins, C. (2001). Improving the writing skills of social work students. *Journal of Social Work Education, 37,* 493–505.

Alter, C., & Adkins, C. (2006). Assessing student writing proficiency in graduate schools of social work. *Journal of Social Work Education, 42,* 337–354.

American Psychological Association. (2009). *Publication manual of the American Psychological Association* (6th ed.). Washington, DC: American Psychological Association.

American Psychological Association: Committee on Professional Standards. (2007). Record keeping guidelines. *American Psychologist, 62,* 993–1004.

Arum, R., & Roksa, J. (2011). *Academically adrift: Limited learning on college campuses.* Chicago: University of Chicago Press.

Avery, M., & Imdieke, B. (1984). *Medical records in ambulatory care.* Rockville, MD: Aspen Systems.

Baird, B., & Anderson, D. (1990). A dual-draft approach to writing. *Teaching Professor, 4*(3), 5–6.

Barker, R. L. (2003). *The social work dictionary* (5th ed.). Washington, DC: National Association of Social Workers.

Bennett, B. E., Bryant, B. K., VandenBos, G. R., & Greenwood, A. (1990). *Professional liability and risk management.* Washington, DC: American Psychological Association.

Bower, A. G. (2005). The diffusion and value of healthcare information technology. RAND. Retrieved from http://www.rand.org/content /dam/rand/pubs/monographs/2006/RAND_MG272-1.pdf

Braun, S. A., & Cox, J. A. (2005). Managed mental health care: Intentional misdiagnosis of mental disorders. *Journal of Counseling and Development, 83,* 425–432.

Brenner, E. (2003). Consumer-focused psychological assessment. *Professional Psychology: Research and Practice, 34,* 240–247.

Cameron, S., & Turtle-song, I. (2002). Learning to write case notes using the SOAP format. *Journal of Counseling and Development, 80,* 286–292.

Claiborn, C. D., Berberoglu, L. S., Nerison, R. M., & Somberg, D. R. (1994). The client's perspective: Ethical judgments and perceptions of therapist practices. *Professional Psychology: Research and Practice, 25,* 268–274.

Devereaux, R. L., & Gottlieb, M. C. (2012). Record keeping in the cloud: Ethical considerations. *Professional Psychology: Research and Practice, 43*(6), 627–632.

Fischer, C. (1994). *Individualized psychological assessment.* Monterey, CA: Brooks/Cole.

Folstein, M. F., Folstein, S. E., & McHugh, P.R. (1975). Mini-mental state: A practical method for grading the cognitive state of patients for the clinician. *Journal of Psychiatric Research, 12*(3), 189–198.

Fox, R., & Gutheil, I. A. (2000). Process recording: A means for conceptualizing and evaluating practice. *Journal of Teaching in Social Work, 20,* 39–57.

Gladding, S. T. (2011). *The counseling dictionary: Concise definitions of frequently used terms* (3rd ed.). Upper Saddle River, NJ: Pearson.

Glicken, M. D. (2007). *A guide to writing for human service professionals.* Lanham, MD: Rowman & Littlefield.

Grayson, H. M., & Tolman, R. S. (1950). A semantic study of concepts of clinical psychologists and psychiatrists. *Journal of Abnormal and Social Psychology, 45,* 216–231.

Gutheil, T. G. (1980). Paranoia and progress notes: A guide to forensically informed psychiatric recordkeeping. *Hospital and Community Psychiatry, 31,* 479–482.

Hartlage, L. C., & Merck, K. H. (1971). Increasing the relevance of psychological reports. *Journal of Clinical Psychology, 27*(4), 459–460.

Harvey, V. S. (1997). Improving readability of psychological reports. *Professional Psychology: Research and Practice, 28,* 271–274.

Healy, K., & Mulholland, J. (2007). *Writing skills for social workers.* Los Angeles: Sage.

Jeffords, J. (1999). Confidentiality of medical information: Protecting privacy in an electronic age. *Professional Psychology: Research and Practice, 30*(2), 115–116.

Kagle, J. D. (1993). Record keeping: Directions for the 1990s. *Social Work, 38,* 190–196.

Kahn, J. M., & Holody, R. (2012). Supporting field instructors' efforts to help students improve their writing. *Journal of Social Work Education, 48*(1), 65–73.

Knapp, S. J., & VandeCreek, L. D. (2006). *Practical ethics for psychologists: A positive approach.* Washington, DC: American Psychological Association.

Koocher, G. P., & Keith-Spiegel, P. (2008). *Ethics in psychology and the mental health professions: Standards and cases.* New York: Oxford University Press.

Luepker, E. T. (2003). *Record keeping in psychotherapy and counseling: Protecting confidentiality and the professional relationship.* New York: Brunner-Routledge.

Owens, E. G. & Crum K. (2012). Teaching writing as a professional practice skill: A curricular case example. *Journal of Social Work Education, 49*(3), 517–536.

Pelco, L. E., Ward, S. B., Coleman, L., & Young, J. (2009). Teacher ratings of three psychological report styles. *Training and Education in Professional Psychology, 3*(1), 19–27.

Pope, K. S., & Vasquez, M. J. T. (2007). *Ethics in psychotherapy and counseling: A practical guide* (3rd ed.). San Francisco: Jossey-Bass.

Psychological Assessment Resources. (2010). *Mini-Mental State Examination* (2nd ed.). Retrieved from http://parinc.reachlocal.net /Products/Product.aspx?ProductID=MMSE-2

RAND Corporation. (2005). Health information technology: Can HIT lower costs and improve quality? Retrieved from http://www.rand .org/pubs/research_briefs/RB9136.html

Reamer, F. G. (2005). Documentation in social work: Evolving ethical and risk management standards. *Social Work, 50,* 325–335.

Rupert, P. A., & Baird, K. A. (2004). Managed care and the independent practice of psychology. *Professional Psychology: Research and Practice, 35, 185–193.*

Schwartz, T. J., & Lonborg, S. D. (2011). Security management in telepsychology. *Professional Psychology: Research and Practice, 42*(6), 419–425.

Shaw, M. (1997). *Charting made incredibly easy.* Springhouse, PA: Springhouse.

Siskind, G. (1967). Fifteen years later: A replication of "A semantic study of concepts of clinical psychologists and psychiatrists." *Journal of Psychology, 65,* 3–7.

Steinfeld, B., Ekorenrud, B., Gillett, C., Quirk, M., & Eytan, T. (2006). EMRs bring all of healthcare together. *Behavioral Healthcare, 26*(1), 12–17.

Strunk, W., Jr., & White, E. B. (2000). *The elements of style* (4th ed.). Boston: Allyn & Bacon.

Tallent, N. (1997). *Psychological report writing* (4th ed.). Englewood Cliffs, NJ: Prentice Hall.

VandenBos, G. R. (Ed.). (2006). *APA dictionary of psychology.* Washington, DC: American Psychological Association.

Weed, L. L. (1971). *Medical records, medical education, and patient care: The problem-oriented record as a basic tool.* Chicago: Year Book.

Zinsser, W. (2006). *On writing well: 30th anniversary edition: The classic guide to writing nonfiction.* New York: HarperCollins.

Zuckerman, E. L. (2010). *The clinician's thesaurus: The guide to conducting interviews and writing psychological reports* (7th ed.). Pittsburgh: Three Wishes Press.

Zuckerman, E. L. (2011). *Clinician's electronic thesaurus: Software to streamline psychological report writing* (Version 7.0). New York: Guilford Publications.

CHAPTER 8
STRESS AND SELF-CARE

When helping professionals tell others about their work, two common responses are "That must be so difficult, listening to people's problems all day. I don't know how you do it." Or, "Uh oh, I'd better be careful. You're not going to psychoanalyze me, are you?"

Although these comments typically come from people who are not involved in the field, both responses raise legitimate questions and concerns for interns. What does happen to people who work in the helping professions as a result of their work? How do we balance our professional roles with our personal lives away from work? And how can interns manage the demands of internships, school, family, friends, and work without falling apart?

This chapter discusses the stresses and rewards that interns and helping professionals experience and the ways those experiences affect our lives and work. The goal of the chapter is to help you understand the stresses and learn to cope effectively with them while maximizing the beneficial opportunities offered by your work and training.

EXERCISE

Before reading further, take a moment to write down some of your own thoughts about each of the following questions. If you do not have any actual clinical experience yet, answer the questions as you think you might be affected when you are working in a clinical setting.

1. In what ways—positive, negative, or otherwise—do you think your work as an intern affects you now?
2. Focusing on the emotional effects of your work and training, how does your internship work and study impact you emotionally? Consider all effects, including any stressors as well as beneficial impacts.
3. How does your internship influence your ideas about the clients you work with? About people in general? About people who are close to you? Society? Yourself?
4. How does your internship affect you physically? What kinds of physical demands or limitations do the activities of your work impose on you? Do you experience any physical responses to working with stressful clients, colleagues, or supervisors?
5. How does your internship affect your close personal, family, or social relationships?
6. Having considered how your internship is affecting you now, how do you think you would be affected if you were a full-time professional in your field?
7. What personal qualities do you think will help you in dealing with the stress of your work? What personal qualities do you think may make it difficult for you to deal with the stress of your work?
8. How will you be able to recognize if you are being affected adversely by your work?
9. How might you cope with a situation in which you come to recognize that you are under excessive stress and your professional effectiveness or personal wellness is being harmed?

However you answered the preceding questions, it is certain that you will be affected by your work. You simply cannot interact with people and not be changed in some way. At the same time, experiences and stresses in your life away from work will influence your performance as a professional (Baker, 2002; Barnett, Baker, Elman, & Schoener, 2007; Bride, 2007; El-Ghoroury, Galper, Sawaqdeh, & Bufka, 2012; Norcross, 2005; Norcross & Guy, 2007). As Guy (1987) observed in his book, *The Personal Life of the Psychotherapist*:

> Since their personality is the "tool" used to conduct this clinical work, who a psychotherapist "is" undergoes constant challenge, review, and transformation. One would certainly hope that the resultant changes are largely positive, improving the therapist's satisfaction with life and relationships. Regrettably...it may also be that certain changes have the potential to hinder interpersonal functioning in and outside of work. (p. 105)

Dealing effectively with potentially adverse impacts is not only important for your personal and professional well-being, it is also an ethical necessity as part of ensuring optimal care for your clients (Barnett et al., 2007). When one realizes that the work of therapy inevitably affects the therapist personally and that the therapist's own awareness and wellness are key elements of the treatment process, it is surprising that many undergraduate and graduate programs pay relatively little attention to this issue

(Barnett et al., 2007; Roach & Young, 2007). Fortunately, awareness of this subject appears to be increasing, and a growing body of literature deals with the effects of the helping professions on helping professionals and interns (Meyers et al., 2012). Perhaps the best news of all is that, overall, in spite of the demands and stresses, most practitioners report generally high levels of satisfaction and reward in their professional lives (Stevanovic & Rupert, 2004, 2009). What is more, many interns discover during their training that they learn a great deal personally from the clients they work with (Stahl et al., 2009) Let us look first at the challenges and stressors, and then explore coping strategies and the rewards of the profession.

CLIENT AFTER CLIENT, DAY AFTER DAY

Consider this scenario. You are a beginning professional working in a mental health center. On a Monday morning at 8 o'clock, your first client is a 25-year-old woman who has a physically and verbally abusive spouse. The woman has two children and a third on the way, recently suffered the death of her mother, and just found out that she will be laid off from work. The client is basically a caring, hard-working person who finds herself in a terrible situation and feels there are limited ways to get out of, or through, it. You feel very deeply what it must be like for this client and determine to work with her.

Your next client is a 15-year-old boy whose parents are getting a divorce. He has been experimenting with drugs and is afraid he is getting hooked on meth. He has also just been arrested for breaking into a car with some friends and stealing a stereo. He has never been in trouble with the law before, and his court date is coming up the following week. The boy is seeing you for help in dealing with the drug problem and with the upcoming court date.

The third case of the day is a man ordered by the court to seek therapy following an arrest for drunk driving. He makes it clear that he does not really want to be in treatment, has no intention of quitting drinking, and accepts no responsibility for his past actions or for change. He says he will come to meet with you only until the court-ordered period is up.

It is now just 11:00 on Monday. You will see four more clients today, and there are four more days to go until the weekend. Let us throw in as a background issue that your clinic's future is uncertain because federal and local funding for mental health have been reduced and third-party payments from insurers are also being lowered. What is more, there was a recent client suicide, and a series of staff meetings is taking place to review the incident. Finally, several of the staff members do not get along well with one another, so there is a prevailing state of tension among the staff at the clinic. How are you doing? Oh yes, I forgot to mention that your significant other is upset with you because you are on crisis duty and cannot get away for the weekend.

If this sounds like an atypical scenario, concocted just to present the worst-case picture of professional life, it is not. In fact, in many instances the actual cases and institutional issues are even more challenging than those presented here.

HOW COMMON IS STRESS AMONG INTERNS

Most interns are relatively new to the field and full of energy and dedication, so the stress of clinical work may not seem like an immediate concern. Be aware, however, that the demands of training and practice can be significant and, in some instances, can contribute to impaired functioning. This can be particularly challenging for many students who, in addition to their internship and academic responsibilities, are also trying to raise families and manage the demands of working at another job to help pay for tuition or student loans.

El-Ghoroury et al. (2012) surveyed graduate students in psychology and found that more than 70% of their respondents identified at least one stressor that "interfered with their optimal functioning." The most frequently identified stressors were academic/coursework, finances or debt, anxiety, and poor work/school life balance, all of which were identified by more than 55% of the sample. Additional stresses identified by more than a quarter of the sample related to family issues; research responsibilities; compassion fatigue; professional isolation; depression; physical health; marital/relationship problems; other interpersonal issues; and death, loss, or grief.

Hawkins, Smith, Hawkins, and Grant (2005) reported that nearly 80% of a sample of undergraduate social work students reported working at another job during their academic year, with the median number of hours worked reported to be 20 hours per week. Of those with outside jobs, a third indicated that their work interfered "much" or "greatly" with their academic studies. Impacts of work included reduced time for studying, exhaustion or fatigue, and added stress. Cumulatively, these effects correlated significantly with lower grade point averages (GPAs), as compared with nonworking students. Within this same sample, a subset of students also indicated that parenting responsibilities added to their time demands, with 57% of those who were parents indicating that family responsibilities interfered substantially with their studies.

IMPAIRED STUDENTS

One manifestation of the impact of stress on performance is seen in the subset of students who can be described as impaired in some way. Shen-Miller et al. (2011) surveyed trainees in master's and doctoral programs in clinical, counseling, school, or combined graduate programs and found that 44% reported having experience with a peer who demonstrated significant problems in professional competence. Oliver, Bernstein, Anderson, Blashfield, and Roberts (2004) surveyed students in graduate clinical psychology programs and asked respondents to estimate the percentages of students they viewed as impaired, describe the types of problems observed, and discuss the adequacy or shortcomings of the training program response. The results of this study were rather qualitative in nature, but overall estimates ranged from 0% to 21% of students considered impaired by their peers, with 12% being described as a typical number of impaired students across programs. The nature of impairments described by students ranged from emotional difficulties, such as depression or severe anxiety, to personality disorders, including narcissistic and antisocial personality traits. Students also identified deficits in basic academic abilities and in clinical skills.

Faced with these issues, students reported that they felt frustrated and confused about what to do and expressed concern that impaired peers were in some ways holding back the rest of the class and might also not be up to the task of becoming professionals. Unfortunately, many of the respondents believed that the training program did not deal well with these issues. Respondents indicated uncertainty about whether training directors even recognized the impaired students as having problems; if there was recognition, the respondents often reported a tendency to ignore or minimize the problem. One other interesting finding was a report by some students that attention needs to be given to "impaired training programs"—programs in which the faculty themselves or the inherent structure may be dysfunctional in some way.

Comparable findings were reported in a separate study by Rosenberg, Getzelman, Arcinue, and Oren (2005), who noted that use of the term *impaired* has come under criticism on conceptual and legal grounds. They suggested that "problematic trainees" would be a preferable descriptor. In their research, 85% of the respondents identified at least one problematic peer in their training programs, with the average number of problematic peers identified per program comparable with the numbers reported by Oliver et al. (2004). Also consistent were the kinds of concerns identified, including emotional and personality issues, academic deficiencies, and clinical deficiencies. Interestingly, when asked to indicate how they responded to these concerns about peers, expressing concerns to faculty was selected only 23% of the time. It was far more common for students to report talking among themselves or withdrawing from the peer in question. As with the students studied by Oliver et al., reasons for not dealing more directly with the issue ranged from poor relationship with and a lack of confidence in faculty to concerns about the impact on the problematic individual's emotional or professional well-being.

THE EFFECTS OF STRESS

It should be evident from the discussion thus far that there are numerous possible sources of work-related and personal stresses in the lives of interns and helping professionals. This raises questions about how such stresses may affect us as individuals and what impact stress has on our work with clients.

THE EFFECTS ON CLOSE RELATIONSHIPS AND FAMILIES

Perhaps problems of greater consequence arise in relationships with spouses, significant others, and family members (Hesse, 2002; O'Conner, 2001; Rupert, Stevanovic, & Hunley, 2009). The stresses that interns and the helping professionals face have contributed to the breakup of many couples, and it is not at all uncommon for therapists to find themselves doing exactly the things they advise their clients not to do.

We often work long hours and may not take enough time for recreation or private time with our families or significant others.

Tired of "communicating" in our work all day, we may resist talking about our own feelings or those of our partners at home. We may feel we do not need to hear our partner's problems on top of everything else we have been dealing with during the day. When concerned partners begin to express feelings about the relationship, we may deny the legitimacy of the concern or become defensive.

Rupert et al. (2009) found that family conflicts correlated significantly with burnout and, conversely, that family support tended to enhance well-being among their sample. They also found that the perceived level of control at work played an important role in this relationship, with those reporting greater levels of control at work also reporting less burnout and lessened impacts on family relationships.

Kottler (2003) described the transition from work to home in the following passage:

> We keep a vigilant eye on personal fallout to protect our family and friends from the intensity of our professional life. Yet with all the restraint we must exercise in order to follow the rules regulating our conduct during working hours, it is difficult to not be insensitive, surly, or self-indulgent with our loved ones. All day long we have stifled ourselves, censored our thoughts and statements, and disciplined ourselves to be controlled and intelligent. And then we make an abrupt transition to go home. Much of the pressure that has been building all day long as clients have come in and dumped their troubles finally releases as we walk through the door. If we are not careful, our families will suffer the emotional fallout. (p. 69)

EXERCISE

To help you assess some of the effects of your internship on your life and relationships, complete the following checklist by yourself and with your significant other:

1. How many days each week do you finish the workday feeling drained and lacking in energy or motivation to do much else?_____
2. How many days each week do you finish the workday feeling that you have been successful and have enjoyed your work that day?_____
3. When was the last time you and your significant other did something just by yourselves?_____
4. When was the last time you and one or more of your good friends did something just by yourselves?_____
5. How often in the past month have you not done something with your significant other because of work conflicts or effects?_____
6. How often in the past month have you not done something with friends because of work conflicts or effects?_____
7. Do you feel that you listen as well to your significant other or close friends as you would like to?_____
8. Do others feel that you listen as well to them as they would like you to?_____
9. What are you doing to take care of your physical health?_____
10. If you were a therapist and had yourself as a client, what would be your advice or exploration regarding self-care?_____
11. What forms of self-care are you not doing, and why?_____

12. In a typical week, how often do you find yourself thinking about your internship or clients when you are in other settings?_____

13. How often in your personal life do you experience anger or other feelings to a greater degree or with greater frequency than you would like?_____ Could this be related to stress at work?_____

14. How is your intimate relationship with your significant other?_____ Could work be affecting that?_____

After completing the checklist in the exercise, I strongly urge you to review your answers with the significant other in your life. If you identify areas of concern, you may want to evaluate together how your internship and personal life are affecting each other. Superb resources for further information about this and other topics of this chapter are Ellen Baker's (2002) *Caring for Ourselves: A Therapist's Guide to Personal and Professional Well-Being*, James Guy's (1987) *The Personal Life of the Psychotherapist*, and Norcross and Guy's (2007) *Leaving It at the Office*. See also Sussman's (1995) *A Perilous Calling: The Hazards of Psychotherapy Practice*.

Should you or your partner feel that your relationship is being adversely affected by your work or training, you may want to consider seeing a therapist. One intern I instructed maintained that his clinical training was having only positive influences on his life and relationships. However, when he completed the preceding exercise and discussed it with his partner, he was surprised to discover that from the partner's perspective, the relationship was, in fact, suffering a great deal. As a result, the couple decided to begin therapy together. Sometime later, they confided to me that entering therapy was one of the best decisions they had ever made. For further insights into the generally positive impact of therapists receiving therapy themselves, see Bike, Norcross, and Schatz (2009) and Geller, Norcross, and Orlinsky (2005). More will be said about self-care later in this chapter.

PHYSICAL EFFECTS

The mental as well as emotional toll probably comes to mind first when one thinks of the demands on the helping professionals, but in many ways the physical costs can be just as high. I have talked to therapists who spend 8 to 10 hours per day seeing clients, one after another, in windowless offices, sometimes taking only 10 minutes for lunch in the middle of the day, then starting right back up again with no other break. This simply cannot be healthy, and it cannot be sustained for long before the effects begin to appear. As one of these therapists said: "Every job has its occupational hazards. For us it's hemorrhoids." He might have added clogged arteries, atrophied muscles, weight gain, low back pain, and other physical ailments.

Psychotherapy and related activities are not aerobic exercises. In fact, if one watches video recordings of therapy, it is startling to see how little many therapists move during certain sessions. They may spend a great deal of mental energy, but their physical motion is minimal. This lack of motion contributes to what a colleague calls "hypokinetic disorders" (i.e., physical illness caused by inactivity).

Commenting on this aspect of therapy, Guy (1987) remarked that other occupations may be relatively sedentary; however,

> Few require that the individual stay riveted to a chair for 50 minutes at a time, without the opportunity to stand up, stretch, or walk around. If a therapist fails to appreciate the need for regular, extended breaks to allow for sufficient physical activity, his or her only exercise is likely to be an occasional brief stroll to the water cooler and restroom between appointments. Day after day of such a sedentary pattern creates a physical fatigue which can negatively impact both the professional and personal functioning of the individual. (p. 82)

In my own experience, I have found that I often store stresses in my neck and shoulder area. Other interns and colleagues have reported neck pain, aches in their jaws, headaches, tension in their forehead, and pain and tension in other areas. Physical consequences are by no means limited to muscle tension. To the extent that the role of intern creates additional demands, the risk of stress-related illness is increased. It is not uncommon for students to report severe stomach pains and other signs of physical reactions to stress. One colleague even believed he was having a heart attack the night before his dissertation defense. It turned out to be a combination of stress, attitude, and anxiety, but the experience reminded him to be more attentive and take better care of himself physically as well as emotionally.

Physical impacts have also been shown to be associated with symptoms of burnout, which will be discussed in greater detail shortly. Kim, Ji, and Kao (2011) conducted a three-year longitudinal study of social workers and found significant relationships between burnout symptoms and specific health problems as well as overall health. They interpreted the pattern of results to suggest that this relationship is due to causal factors of burnout worsening physical health with specific effects on self-reports of headaches, gastrointestinal problems, and respiratory infections.

EFFECTS ON SOCIAL RELATIONSHIPS

As mentioned earlier, every helping professional is probably familiar with being introduced to someone who responds with something like, "You're not going to psychoanalyze me, are you?" or, "Uh oh, now I better watch what I say."

While some people in social settings are worried about having casual conversations with therapists, it can also happen that social acquaintances will take the opportunity to seek advice outside the clinical setting. This is typically a sign of respect for you or your profession, and it is generally benign. A challenge in such cases is to avoid speaking as though you have knowledge if you really do not. More problematic still is the need to avoid dual relationships by providing clinical advice to casual acquaintances or even close friends without a formal therapeutic relationship.

EXERCISE

You may find it informative to think about how you might feel and react to meeting a client in another setting. What do your reactions suggest to you about your role and the therapy process? You might also put yourself in the role of the client and think how it would feel to meet your therapist in a public situation. Are there any settings where it would be more or less difficult to encounter clients? What are those situations, and what do the possible difficulties tell you about yourself or your role?

Another situation that many interns find awkward involves coincidental encounters with clients in nonclinical settings such as the grocery store, movies, or elsewhere. Oddly enough, in encounters outside the office, the awkwardness seems to come because both clinicians and clients are worried about being seen "as they really are."

Along with the issue of revealing different roles outside therapy, awkwardness in coincidental encounters is also created by the confidentiality of therapy and a sense of not knowing whether or how to greet and interact with the other person. Such coincidental interactions with clients can be dealt with much as you would if you met a friend in a similar setting. You might briefly ask how things are going, make small talk about the weather, and so on. If others are present and introductions seem called for, names alone are sufficient; one need not provide more information.

A final aspect of your professional role and social relationships is that, whether or not you like it, whenever you interact with other people, they may form opinions about both your personal qualities and your presumed qualities as a professional. What is more, based on their interactions with you, some people will form opinions about your profession as a whole. This does not mean that you should always try to present a certain impression in public. (It is okay to go out with paint or mud on your clothes on weekends.) It does not mean that all the helping professionals must at all times be models of "perfect mental health." It does, however, mean that you should be aware of the image you create and the effects it might have on others and on your professional role.

For example, if at a party you begin to tell stories about clients, you may preserve confidentiality by not revealing personal data, but the very fact that you are discussing clients publicly may be troubling to others and might be disturbing to your clients if they knew you were doing so. Even if no one could possibly identify the person you are talking about solely on the basis of a story told at a party, merely knowing that clients' lives are talked about publicly could prevent some people from seeking therapy or from being as open as they might need to be in therapy.

Apart from directly discussing clients, if in your life away from therapy you exhibit problems with substance abuse, controlling your anger, or other issues for which people might seek therapy themselves, you may create doubts about your credibility. If these or other behaviors are problems, you may want to consider seeking therapy yourself to work on them. Self-help workbooks, such as Kottler's (1999) *The Therapist's Workbook: Self-Assessment, Self-Care, and Self-Improvement Exercises for Mental Health Professionals*, may also be useful.

SECONDARY TRAUMA

Some of the effects of stress that have been identified thus far are seen in two recognized patterns of reactions that may develop among the helping professionals. These patterns are referred to as secondary trauma, also known as vicarious traumatization (Harrison & Westwood, 2009) and burnout (Freudenberger,

1974). In recent years, an important distinction has been drawn between vicarious traumatization and the concept of burnout, which will be described shortly. This distinction was described well by Trippany, Kress, and Wilcoxon (2004), who noted that whereas burnout may occur in some form in virtually any profession and tends to be gradual in onset, vicarious traumatization results specifically from work with traumatized clients, and the symptoms are directly related to trauma therapy. In contrast to burnout, which tends to develop gradually over time, secondary trauma can have an impact on a therapist after a single session with a traumatized client. Such a sudden onset can be particularly troubling and confusing, especially for beginning therapists or interns who have no frame of reference to help them understand the reaction. Trippany et al. (2005) also emphasized that vicarious traumatization is more likely to affect one's worldview and sense of trust. Finally, they and other authors (e.g., Harrison & Westwood, 2009) noted that vicarious traumatization and burnout are by no means mutually exclusive and, in fact, can and often do occur simultaneously.

Hesse (2002) offered a thorough and useful review of secondary trauma and noted that therapists can be impacted in a variety of ways, including effects on their sense of self and the world, feelings of trust and safety, relationships with others, and self-confidence as a professional. Cunningham (2004) particularly emphasized the impact of vicarious traumatization on the clinicians' worldview and suggested that one's belief system can be challenged as a result, and so, too, can one's sense of trust, personal safety, and even one's view of human nature.

In an effort to assess the frequency of secondary or vicarious traumatic stress, Bride (2007) surveyed 294 master's-level social workers. Among these respondents, 47% indicated that they worked with moderately traumatized individuals and 34.5% with clients who had been severely or very severely traumatized. Bride's results showed that 55% of respondents reported at least one of the core diagnostic criteria for PTSD, 20% met two, and 15% met three core criteria.

Most susceptible to secondary trauma are therapists who are new to trauma work and those with a personal history of trauma (Cunningham, 2004). Thus, interns may be especially vulnerable, both because they are new to the profession and because some percentage of interns will still be dealing with traumas in their own past that they have not yet worked through.

Therapists who are experiencing secondary trauma may find themselves reacting with remarkably strong emotions not only to the issues the client is presenting but also to matters within their own lives. If a client describes a particularly horrific incident, the therapist who experiences secondary trauma may have unpleasant dreams and intrusive thoughts and may react with fear, anger, grief, or other strong feelings. The therapist's worldview may also be affected, with the possibility of a lost sense of safety developing or perhaps a cynical view that everyone is corrupt or that no one can be trusted (Trippany et al., 2004). Relationships can also suffer, particularly if the secondary trauma triggers an awareness of fears, hurt, or other reactions toward someone in the therapist's own life.

Along with understanding how therapists can be affected personally by secondary trauma, it is also important to recognize the possible impact on the therapy process. For example, because of the challenging nature of the problems presented by traumatized clients, therapy may proceed slowly and with substantial difficulty. This can cause therapists to doubt their ability and may even lead to their trying to rush a client to a "cure," so that the therapist can both feel competent again and be relieved of the ongoing trauma of being present as clients work through the painful process. Other possibilities include the therapist's becoming so angry toward the person who perpetrated the trauma as to no longer be effective in treating the victim, let alone the perpetrator.

Hesse (2002) offered particularly valuable insights into the impact of secondary traumatization on therapy, and she emphasized the importance of the therapist's recognizing and dealing with those impacts effectively so that therapy is not compromised. This can include supervision, personal therapy, limiting the numbers of trauma clients seen at any one time, and finding other outlets for the stress of trauma work. Comparable suggestions are given by Trippany et al. (2004) and by Cunningham (2004), who underscored the importance of both advance preventive measures for students and dealing responsively and supportively if vicarious traumatization occurs. Harrison and Westwood (2009) also offered useful suggestions for preventing vicarious traumatization, including countering professional isolation, mindful self-awareness, active optimism, holistic self-care, maintaining boundaries and creating meaning, and empathic engagement.

Before leaving this topic to explore the related phenomenon of burnout, it is worth taking a moment to briefly look at three of the more profound experiences that may contribute to vicarious traumatization. The first, suicide, has been an issue in counseling and therapy for years; the second, responses to natural disasters or terrorist events, has gained special attention in response to the events of September 11, 2001, and the aftermath of Hurricanes Katrina and Sandy; and third, work with soldiers and civilians returning from conflicts in Iraq, Afghanistan, and elsewhere can profoundly impact service providers.

CLIENT SUICIDE

Of all the experiences that can confront interns, the loss of a client to suicide may be the most traumatic. Chapter 4 of this book described what to do if you are working with potentially suicidal clients in order to assess and reduce the risks of suicidal behavior. In spite of your best efforts, however, it may happen at some point in your training or career that you will be confronted with the suicide of a client. Surveys of practicing social workers (e.g., Sanders, Jacobson, & Ting, 2008) found that 55% of practitioners had experienced at least one client suicide attempt and 31% had experienced a client suicide. Surveys have suggested that as many as one in six psychology interns may experience a client suicide during their training (e.g., Kleespies, Smith, & Becker, 1990). Nevertheless, training in the assessment and treatment of suicide potential is by no means universal among internships, and systematic support for interns who have lost clients is less frequent still (Ellis & Dickey, 1998; Knox, Burkard, Jackson, Schaack, & Hess, 2006; Sanders et al., 2008; Ting, Jacobson, & Sanders, 2011).

I hope you will never have to face the loss of someone to suicide, but the incidence rates are such that you should at least be aware of the possibility should it befall someone with whom you are working. Many of the emotional impacts that have been described following client suicide are comparable with those associated with secondary trauma, though likely more acute. These can include intrusive thoughts, disbelief, sadness, fear, doubts about competency, and feelings of guilt and shame (Kleespies et al., 1990). On occasion, the strain of losing a client can be so great that a trainee will abandon professional training entirely.

Ting et al. (2008) distinguished between positive and negative coping behaviors in response to client suicide. In their study, 35.8% of social work respondents who had experienced client suicide described engaging in prayer or meditation, and 95% reported having available support from supervisors, peers, or family and friends. However, negative coping behaviors were indicated by 37.2% of respondents, with 16.2% reporting increased use of alcohol.

To assist trainees in dealing with this experience, Foster and McAdams (1999) recommended that internship sites and supervisors establish procedures to ensure that interns receive follow-up supervision and, if necessary, special help and support. They emphasized the need to review the case to understand what happened and to offer support and coping strategies. This need for case review was also highlighted by Ting et al. (2008). Knox et al. (2006) reported that having a supervisor provide a safe and supportive opportunity to process the experience was the single most important element in effective coping.

The intern's supervisor may also benefit from additional support (Dill, 2007), as may peers and coworkers who interacted with the client. Any legal implications should also be addressed, and it is important for interns to have assistance in this regard, as most will be quite unprepared to deal with legal matters of this magnitude. Finally, it should be kept in mind that although the acute effects of such profound experiences may diminish in a matter of weeks or months, lasting impacts may affect the intern's personal life and work with other clients for a long time thereafter.

NATURAL DISASTERS, TERRORISM, AND WAR

When the concept of vicarious traumatization was first introduced, the predominant focus was on the effects of working with clients on issues such as suicide, sexual abuse, violence, severe accidents, or serious illnesses such as cancer. As a result of the events of recent years, the helping professions have been called on to respond to traumas on a scale and type we have not seen in decades and, in some cases, ever before (Reyes & Elhai, 2004). It is increasingly important now to prepare mental health trainees to work with those who have experienced disasters and other traumas (Litz & Salters-Pedneault, 2008; Pfefferbaum et al., 2010; Yutrzenka & Naifeh, 2008). It is also essential to help trainees proactively prepare for self-care following disasters or work with disaster victims (Aten, Madson, Rice, & Chamberlain, 2008)

In many ways, people across the nation were subject to vicarious traumatization by the events of September 11, 2001, after that the tsunami in South Asia, then by the images and impact of Hurricane Katrina (see a special issue on Hurricane Katrina in *Professional Psychology: Research and Practice*, February 2008), and more recently Hurricane Sandy and the tragic school shootings.

On a personal level, during my tenure in Congress, my congressional staff and I saw from our window in the Longworth House Office Building the fireball explode from the Pentagon after it was struck by the passenger jet. We then initiated the evacuation of our building, wondering as we did if a second plane, truck bomb, or other event was imminent and would cause our own deaths. Just a few days later, recognizing the impacts of the experience on my staff and on others, I worked with our employee assistance program to initiate a proactive intervention program to help staff across the Capitol better prepare to assist constituents, some of whom had been in or near the World Trade Center or the Pentagon, others of whom had lost friends or loved ones, and all of whom had been deeply impacted by the event. The additional purpose of the effort was to help the staff themselves who, while responding to the needs of constituents and continuing to perform their other duties, had to also deal with their own losses; with the impacts of vicarious traumatization; and, in this instance, the awareness that, because of where they work, something more could easily happen and they might be in mortal danger themselves at any time.

Consistent with the research on vicarious trauma, I was struck by how the terrorist attacks profoundly shook the worldview of many and created a deeply unsettling sense of uncertainty and vulnerability. Also consistent with the research was a personal observation that one of the most important elements of helping was identifying and strengthening a sense of meaning or purpose to help people get themselves back together and keep serving the public. I am pleased to say that this process proved very helpful to many of the participants, several of whom confided to me later that they had been deeply shaken by the events of September 11 and were prepared to quit their jobs but decided to continue on because of the interventions we had offered.

If you work with individuals who have experienced these or other comparable events, be aware that a growing body of literature exists documenting the way such events affect people (Henry, Tolan, & Gorman-Smith, 2004; Meyers, 2006; Silver, Holman, McIntosh, Poulin, & Gil-Rivas, 2002), the responses of the various professional associations and individuals (APA Policy and Planning Board, 2006; Levant, 2002; Stoesen, 2005), and recommendations for intervention approaches (Cook, Schnurr, & Foa, 2004; Reyes & Elhai, 2004; Weaver, 1995). For an excellent review of the impact of trauma on clients and the history of interventions to treat trauma, see Gold (2004) and Courtois (2004). For useful insights into working with disaster victims, you may also want to visit the website eyeofthestorminc.com, which provides many practical tips from John Weaver, a practicing social worker who specializes in disaster response.

The final issue to mention here has to do with the impacts of war. The conflicts in Iraq and Afghanistan created a new generation of troops, families, and civilians who have been touched and, in many cases, wounded physically and psychologically by their war experiences. As of this writing, nearly 2 million troops and civilians had been sent overseas to the conflict areas. Given the numbers of people who have served in these conflicts, it is likely that you will at some point work with veterans or their families, and you should have some preparation for what you may encounter.

To ensure that these experiences are taken into account in clinical treatment, I strongly recommend that as standard practice when interviewing clients you ask (and encourage colleagues to ask) the simple question, "Have you or a family member been deployed to a combat area?" Please note too that this question does not specify military deployment alone because a host of civilians have been deployed during these conflicts, and many have experienced similar stresses to those experienced by uniformed personnel.

One issue you should be aware of when working with veterans of these or other conflicts has to do with how your own attitude or that of others about these conflicts may affect your clinical work. With strong public sentiments on various sides, it is especially important that treatment professionals know and are able to separate their political ideologies from their clinical work with clients. It is also very important to recognize that your personal reactions to such events may differ substantially from how members of the armed forces react to them. Do not assume that how you feel will be a good guideline to understanding how clients and families may feel.

A tremendously helpful resource regarding deployment issues is The Center for Deployment Psychology (deploymentpsych.org), which offers online and direct continuing education courses, links to a host of resources, and specialized certification in military and veterans' behavioral health. Special issues of *Psychological Services* (2012, *9*[4]) and *Professional Psychology: Research and Practice* (2011, *42*[1]) are dedicated to serving veterans, military service members, and their families. For a particularly useful summary of cultural and ethical issues encountered by interns working in the VA medical system, see the article by Strom et al. (2012). Evidence-based strategies for promoting mental health in the military are discussed in Adler, Bliese, and Castro (2011). Other works (e.g., Bowling & Sherman, 2008; Cook, Schnurr, & Foa, 2004; Creamer & Forbes, 2004; Gleisher, Ford, & Fosha, 2008; Mangelsdorff, 2006; Reyes & Elhai, 2004; Yutrzenka & Naifeh, 2008) also offer detailed information about these issues.

Perhaps the best, brief reference I have found comes from a psychologist who has served in the Iraq combat theater himself. Sammons (2007), a U.S. Navy captain, was deployed to Iraq from September 2006 to March 2007. He offered insights into what it is like working with troops while one is actually in the combat zone with them. I believe everyone who works with veterans of these conflicts should read what he has to say. Among other things, he observes that misconceptions about PTSD are

> far more likely to result in permanent disability than early and direct interventions. Treated early and well, PTSD and related disorders are completely recoverable problems. But in order to treat PTSD in combatants, it is vital to understand not only the context in which the trauma occurs, but the culture and training of warfighters. (p. 11)

Sammons goes on to discuss key treatment issues and goals for working with this population. Consistent with some of his observations, a number of other practitioners and researchers have begun to raise concerns about overuse and the possible iatrogenic effects of the PTSD diagnosis itself (Dobbs, 2009). Briefly, the concern is that too many people may be receiving erroneous diagnoses of PTSD and ineffective treatment. Giving a diagnosis of a disorder to the ways people cope with such events can create a tendency to cling to that diagnosis rather than seeking treatment to overcome the experience and move on. This can be especially problematic for veterans who can receive disability payments if they have the diagnosis of PTSD but could lose those payments if their symptoms abate. For further information, you may wish to review Dobbs (2009) as well as Rosen and Lilienfeld (2008).

BURNOUT

In contrast to secondary traumatization and reactions to acute traumatic events, burnout is a gradual progress in which the cumulative effects of working with difficult clients and in challenging settings slowly wears people down and can sap them of their energy, desire, and ability to function effectively as professionals. The term *burnout* is attributed to Herbert Freudenberger (1974), who introduced it to describe a pattern of responses shown by people who work in committed activities and begin to exhibit declines in personal involvement, effectiveness, or productivity (Farber, 1983b).

In addition to psychological changes, burnout has also been shown to have substantial physical impacts, including cardiovascular disease (Melamed, Shirom, Toker, Berliner, & Shapira, 2006). Since its introduction, burnout has been written about and studied in many populations, including schoolteachers, social workers, psychologists, police officers, nurses, physicians, business executives, and others who work in high-stress positions (Farber, 1983a; Golembiewski & Munzenrider, 1988; McKnight & Glass, 1995; Rupert & Morgan, 2005; Söderfeldt, Söderfeldt, & Warg, 1995).

SYMPTOMS OF BURNOUT

In an early review of theoretical writing and empirical studies, Farber (1983b) noted that burnout has been defined in several different ways. Some authors and studies emphasized the emotional features; others addressed physiological symptoms. The most commonly mentioned symptoms included emotional distancing from clients and staff, decreased empathy, cynicism, decreased self-esteem, physical exhaustion, sleep disturbance, stomach pain, and other stress-related physical complaints.

Maslach's (1982) description of burnout placed special emphasis on the importance of estrangement from clients and colleagues. Similarly, Pines and Aronson (1988) focused on the withdrawal process that is characteristic of burnout. They noted that professionals who are nearing or in burnout typically seek to withdraw, physically, emotionally, or mentally. Although this is an understandable response, it can adversely affect professionals and their clients. Withdrawal can also lead to further frustration and negative feelings as therapists recognize their reduced effectiveness and satisfaction but are unable to find more creative or constructive solutions.

STAGES OF BURNOUT

Many authors who have studied burnout have emphasized that it is important to view it as a process rather than an event. That is, one does not suddenly become burned out in a single day. Rather, a person typically passes through progressive stages on the way to burnout. Kottler (2003) underscored this distinction by suggesting that "rustout" might be a better term than "burnout." Kottler also emphasized that at varying times everyone experiences at least some symptoms of burnout in almost every job.

Edelwich and Brodsky (1980) described how people may pass through stages from initial enthusiasm through stagnation; frustration; and, ultimately, apathy. Edelwich and Brodsky emphasized an important difference between frustration and apathy, with burnout associated only with the latter stage. People who are frustrated are still involved, caring, and struggling to make a change. In the frustration stage, there is still a possibility of improving matters and returning to the more positive stage of enthusiasm. A person who becomes apathetic is burned out, and according to Edelwich and Brodsky, this substantially reduces the prospects for positive change.

In the context of the withdrawal process that Pines and Aronson described, apathy may be understood as a result of avoidant learning. Therapists who are burned out have learned that even when they try their best to do clinical work and empathize closely with clients, they are often frustrated by the inherent limitations of the task, the client's lack of change, organizational factors, or other elements that block success or pose excessive demands. This process produces a form of aversive conditioning in which therapists learn that one way to avoid negative consequences is to withdraw from the process. If the empathic sharing of a client's emotional suffering is aversive, the therapist may withdraw emotionally. If efforts to make cognitive sense of client issues or organizational processes do not yield positive results, the therapist may withdraw mentally and just go through the behavioral motions of the job. If the work setting itself becomes associated with unpleasant experiences, the therapist may withdraw physically from the setting. Awareness of this connection is clinically valuable because by identifying a person's pattern of withdrawal, one may gather clues about the key factors contributing to his or her burnout.

CAUSES OF BURNOUT

Causes of burnout have included factors within the individual, inherent features of demanding jobs, organizational structure, and managerial approaches (Rupert & Morgan, 2005). Collective self-esteem, that is, how one feels about one's profession, has been shown to relate to burnout in school counselors (Butler & Constantine, 2005), and work–family issues can also contribute to or substantially moderate burnout (Rupert et al., 2009). Broader social concerns, including worker alienation, have also been identified as contributing to burnout (Farber, 1983b). In addition to these general factors, several authors, including Farber (1983a) and Pines and Aronson (1988) have emphasized that the training and demands of the helping professions contribute in unique ways to burnout. In most cases, a combination of some or all these factors leads to burnout. Understanding their relative importance is useful; Pines and Aronson pointed out the following:

> How individuals perceive the cause of their burnout and attribute the "blame" has enormous consequences for action. If they attribute the cause to a characterological weakness or inadequacy in themselves, they will take a certain set of actions: quit the profession, seek psychotherapy, and so forth. However, if they see the cause as largely a function of the situation, they will strive to change the situation and make it more tolerable, a totally different set of remedial actions. (1988, p. 5)

Reviewing some of the more commonly identified contributors may help you recognize whether you or someone you work with is beginning to develop signs of burnout. On that basis, you may be able to cope more effectively with the situation. To draw again from Pines and Aronson: "The first and most important step would be to change the focus from "What's wrong with me?" to "What can I do about the situation?" (1988, p. 5)

INDIVIDUAL FACTORS

Some of the personality characteristics associated with burnout were alluded to earlier in this chapter as part of the discussion of the characteristics of stress and of the therapist. Among the characteristics often mentioned are lack of clear boundaries between self and work, extreme degree of empathy, exceptional level of commitment, and a fragile self-concept (Carroll & White, 1982).

Carroll and White also identified poor training as a contributing factor and noted that training deficits can lead to burnout in two ways. First, inadequate training for a job leaves one feeling unprepared, vulnerable and insecure, and fearing failure. Second, even those who are adequately trained in the skills of their job may not be trained to cope with its stresses. Thus, some people may face burnout because they were not adequately trained for the skills demanded in their job. Others may burn out because they have no training in coping with the emotional demands of the job.

Consistent with the results of Rodolfa, Kraft, and Reilley (1988), Farber (1983a) identified both the challenges of therapy itself and the supervision process as important stressors for trainees. Farber noted that the ambiguity of therapy, the difficulty of learning a complex new skill, and the mixed role of teaching and evaluation in supervision all make the training process highly anxiety provoking for most interns. As interns become aware of their own dynamics while beginning to fill the role of therapist, they must cope with two sets of issues that are fraught with ambiguity and anxiety. Either alone might be difficult enough, but the combination can be overwhelming.

ORGANIZATIONAL FACTORS

In addition to approaches that emphasize the individual's characteristics as contributing to burnout, organizational and managerial factors have also been studied. Pines (1982) observed that in studies that compared two treatment centers, higher levels of burnout were observed in one than in the other, even though the two were similar in clients served, location, staffing, and other variables. This difference suggested that organizational factors were involved in contributing to or reducing burnout in the two centers. A similar conclusion was reached by Arches (1991), who surveyed social workers and found that "lack of autonomy and the influence of funding sources are major contributors to burnout" (p. 202).

Managerial style has also been identified as a possible causative or preventive element in burnout. Murphy and Pardeck (1986) noted that burnout is probably best prevented by a managerial style that falls somewhere between authoritarian and laissez-faire. They explained that the authoritarian approach does not provide sufficient autonomy or self-direction to staff, does not involve staff in decision-making, and tends to give instructions without explanation. At the opposite extreme, laissez-faire approaches suffer from problems such as failure to provide staff with sufficient direction, guidance, or support.

THE STATE OF THE WORLD

Along with the stresses relating to clinical activities, field placements and clinical work often bring interns into contact with aspects of life that can be difficult to deal with emotionally and seem intractable or unsolvable. Kurland and Salmon (1992) commented on this and observed that social workers may

> soon fall prey to the perceived hopelessness of the situations and of these monumental social problems unless the teachers, supervisors, and consultants are able to help them go on. (p. 241)

Encounters with deep social ills are often the source of the most profound challenge not only for interns but also for experienced practitioners. If we care about others and are drawn to the professions out of a desire to help, how can we go on in the face of problems that seem so huge and that do real and lasting harm to so many people? There is no easy answer to this, and when we are unable to cope with the situation, burnout or other symptoms may result.

RECOGNIZING AND UNDERSTANDING YOUR OWN SITUATION AND BURNOUT

The literature on burnout is interesting from a theoretical perspective, but what really matters is how it relates to you personally, to your peers and colleagues, and to your work and life. There is great variability in the extent to which individual interns and internship settings reflect both the negative and the positive features that have been identified. Some interns are extremely dedicated and sensitive to their clients but are also remarkably fragile and susceptible to burnout. At the opposite extreme, I occasionally encounter interns who seem virtually immune to burnout because they distance themselves so much that they do not empathize or connect with their clients. Somewhere in the middle, one finds interns who exhibit a healthy balance of sensitivity to clients and dedication to the field but who are also able to keep a degree of objectivity and detachment that allows them to do good clinical work without excessively carrying the burdens of their clients' difficulties.

Similar variability can be found across internship settings. In the best settings, interns can feel the excitement, caring, staff support, and dedication to the profession and to clients. In other settings, there is a pervasive air of resignation, domination, or hostility.

Interns and their supervisors must be aware of both the individual factors and the situational factors that can lead to burnout. If interns are showing the symptoms described earlier in this section, that is a signal to explore what is happening and what can be done about it. As a relatively simple starting point, and as a way to help prevent burnout by understanding it before it develops, you may find it useful to complete the following exercise.

EXERCISE: PERSONAL AND ENVIRONMENTAL BURNOUT PRONENESS OR PREVENTION

In light of the material you have just read about burnout, answer each of the following questions:

1. What personal characteristics do you have that could contribute to burnout?
2. What personal characteristics do you think might help you prevent burnout?
3. What features of your current internship setting or possible future settings do you think would contribute most to burnout for you?
4. What internship-setting features could help prevent burnout?
5. What elements of your personal or family relationships may help prevent or exacerbate professional burnout?
6. What broad social issues impact your feelings about the world, and how might these impact your work as a professional?
7. Finally, what circumstances—clients, organizational, personal, social—do you think would be most likely to cause professional burnout, and how can you prepare yourself to recognize and cope effectively?

BURNOUT AS A COPING MECHANISM

In much of the literature and in professional discourse, burnout is viewed as a solely negative situation that should be prevented or avoided. One problem with this approach is that it overlooks the value and importance of burnout as an opportunity for the individual's learning and growth. If burnout is seen in only negative terms, interns or professionals may tend to deny their feelings to avoid acknowledging that they, too, are vulnerable to something that, because of its negative image, may be stigmatizing. The response may be, "I can't be burned out. Burnout is a sign of weakness or failure, and that just can't be me." Organizations may exhibit similar responses if employees begin to show signs of burnout, "No, our employees aren't burning out. That would mean there is something wrong with our organization, and we know that can't be true."

Interns, supervisors, and organizations would benefit from a perspective that views symptoms of burnout as valuable information that something is not working optimally and could be improved. It should also be emphasized that symptoms of burnout do not necessarily mean that the workplace is the only source of the problem. Other factors in the individual's life can also contribute to burnout.

In a particularly insightful and useful observation, Roberts (1987) explained:

> Burnout is perceived as an appropriate coping mechanism under the circumstances given the history of choices, experiences, and resources of the individual. The arena in which this form of coping (burnout) would surface—work, family, or friends—would likely be that one which offers the least resistance or least consequence to the expression of burnout. (p. 116)

In other words, just as the causes of burnout are not limited to the work setting, one can show signs of burnout outside the work setting as well. According to Roberts, burnout is a form of coping, and we are most likely to resort to it where it is safest to do so. This means we must be attentive to burnout not only on the job, but also in our relationships, school, and other aspects of our lives. In many cases, burnout may hit relationships well before work because it might be safer in some ways to burn out in our relationships rather than in our jobs. Thus, our relationships and our partners suffer.

If we recognize signs of stress wherever they appear, we can interpret them as a signal that our alternative coping mechanisms are being overwhelmed. From this painful realization, we can begin to explore where the stresses are in our lives and why our other coping mechanisms are not managing them. Thus, instead of viewing burnout and other signs of stress in solely negative terms, we can approach them as signals and opportunities for learning more about ourselves and our situations. How to deal with that awareness is the topic we turn to now.

SELF-CARE

Thus far, this chapter has described some of the stresses of internships and professional activities. Next, we will explore the importance of self-care and strategies for keeping oneself healthy while striving to assist others. By definition, the helping professionals seek to improve the quality of life of the people with whom they work. If you hope to be successful in that endeavor, taking care of yourself is one of the most important, yet sometimes one of the most difficult, tasks you will face as an intern or professional.

As described at the outset of this chapter, some authors (e.g., Barnett et al., 2007) argued that self-care is an ethical imperative to avoid practicing while impaired. Fortunately, increasing numbers of training programs appear to be addressing self-care and wellness as part of training.

Consistent with this text's earlier discussions of evidence-based practice (see Chapter 2), the ideas and recommendations that follow are based on research from a number of authors who have examined the issue of self-care among professionals and interns. For example, Meyers et al. (2012) and El-Ghoroury et al. (2012) surveyed psychology graduate students to assess how they cope with stress. Norcross (2005) conducted an extensive and insightful series of research studies on the use and impacts of personal psychotherapy for educating and training therapists. Osborn (2004) offered research-based suggestions for improving what she called "counselor stamina," whereas Harrison and Westwood (2009) gathered practitioners' input on how to avoid vicarious traumatization. Similarly, Stevanovic and Rupert (2004) described "career-sustaining" behaviors that help professionals deal with the stresses of their work. Turner et al. (2005) focused specifically on self-care strategies among interns, whereas Dearing, Maddux, and Tangney (2005) described study results identifying factors that predict help seeking among clinical and counseling psychology students.

Some may find that the suggestions that follow raise issues that are not often talked about in school or training. Others may resist or possibly even resent the suggestions to stay physically healthy or engage in some form of reflective meditation or prayer. The discussion of financial considerations may also come as a surprise. I am sensitive to such concerns, but I am convinced it is important to address precisely those issues that may be overlooked in academic training but are of critical importance in life and work beyond academia.

TIME MANAGEMENT

When interns are asked to list the sources of stress in their lives, having too much to do and time management are consistently identified among the primary concerns. Indeed, when El-Ghoroury et al. (2012) asked respondents to identify the barriers that prevented them from utilizing wellness strategies, 70% said lack of time.

This is not at all surprising. In the desire to do a good job on the internship while trying to balance school, work, family, and other demands, it is easy to feel that events control you. The problem is that if you do not manage your time well, you will eventually make inadequate notes, not take the physical and mental breaks you need, take work home, and probably regret it in the long run. If you do not take care of your time, you are probably not taking care of yourself in other ways as well. As a colleague of mine says, "If you're too busy to take care of yourself, you're too busy! Something's gotta change." The challenge, of course, is that lack of time is at once a major source of stress and one of the key obstacles impeding self-care among interns (Dearing et al., 2005).

Interns are not alone in feeling time-related stresses. Many experienced therapists feel overworked, and many professionals do not manage their time well. Especially common are the habits of not allocating sufficient time between sessions and not taking enough breaks from work to stretch or relax.

Some of the best recommendations I have encountered for dealing with these issues come from Osborn (2004), who identified "selectivity" and "time sensitivity" as two of her seven suggestions for counselor stamina. Selectivity, according to Osborn, is "the practice of intentional choice and focus in daily activities and long-term endeavors. It means setting limits on what one can and cannot do" (p. 322).

Time sensitivity, as described by Osborn, involves being constantly aware of, and thereby in charge of, time and the limitations on time. This means everything from ending therapy sessions on time to organizing and conducting meetings with fixed agendas and being cognizant of phone calls, email, texting, and instant messaging, all of which can eat unproductively into your time if not managed well.

As a starting point to managing your time better, you may want to explore some of the commercially available time management systems and training seminars. Companies such as Day-Timer and Franklin Covey offer an array of scheduling and time management products as well as various training options for these products. Students who have attended such courses generally report positive results. Software and mobile apps can also be tremendously helpful in planning, managing, and tracking your time and schedule.

If you use an organized scheduling and time management system, you may want to incorporate a concept that Fiore (1989) described as "unscheduling." Begin your scheduling by planning time for self-care. Once you have set aside this time to take care of yourself, schedule work and other activities around that. This might sound selfish, but if we do not take care of ourselves, we will eventually be unable to care for others. By scheduling self-care first, we are forced to rethink our priorities.

One reason many professionals have trouble managing their time is that they have not seriously examined how they actually spend their time. When I conducted an informal survey of colleagues in clinical practice, very few had kept precise track of how they spent their time and how long it took to complete various tasks. In a discussion of fee structure as it relates to professionals' time, Callahan (1994) noted that many therapists in private practice have a false understanding of how much they earn for their efforts because they have not accurately assessed the time they spend outside therapy in note taking, correspondence, and phone calls.

EXERCISE: TRACKING WHERE TIME GOES

To help develop your time awareness and management skills, during the next 2 weeks, keep careful track of all the activities you do each day for the full 24 hours. From 12:00 midnight each day to 12:00 midnight the next day, note when you start and end activities. This may feel like a nuisance or a waste of time, but, in fact, it is just the opposite. This is a way for you to begin to understand how not to waste time.

Keeping track of what you do will allow you to get a better sense of where your time goes and how long different activities actually take. For example, if you keep case notes for each session during a week, recording how long it takes you to write a case note will make you more aware of what writing case notes requires. You can then build that time into your schedule.

In this process, try to be aware not only of where your time goes now but also of how you are not spending time where you probably should be. Are you taking time to stretch, to get out of the office, and to recover between sessions? If your record reveals that comparatively little time is going to self-care, you may want to "unschedule" more of your time.

Along with budgeting time on a weekly basis for your regular activities, anticipate special time demands, such as preparation for exams, papers, and conferences. Also keep in mind key family or social activities that will be important for you to participate in. As you look toward these events, be sure to allow additional time in your schedule to prepare for them. Avoid the temptation to simply take that added time out of what you have set aside for self-care.

Putting time in our schedules is actually the easiest part of time management. Sticking to the schedule is the hard part. I advise trainees to include in their schedules a certain degree of open time that allows them to deal with unanticipated circumstances. I also advise trainees to make certain time inviolable. Except in extreme circumstances, do not let clients or staff intrude on this protected time. Do not use your note-taking time to make phone calls, do not let sessions run longer than they are scheduled, and do not treat time for exercise as a low priority that can easily be sacrificed.

SAYING NO

Keeping certain time for yourself requires the ability to say no. Interns are often overloaded with classes, other jobs, and family responsibilities. The task of meeting all these demands is exacerbated because many interns, as caring and dedicated people, have difficulty turning down worthy projects. The underlying principle that guides their decisions is to think first of the needs of others, then of their own needs, and almost never of the real limitations of time and the physical demands for rest or sleep. If someone at school needs a hand with a class, an intern offers to help. If volunteers are needed for a community service project, the interns are the first to lend a hand. If extra work needs to be done at internship sites, interns extend their hours.

All these activities are to be commended, and it is admirable that interns are willing to step forward. But it is also important to learn how to set priorities and make decisions. There is nothing wrong with setting realistic limits and standing by them. There will always be more work to be done than one person can do, and you do not have to feel that you must do it all.

SAYING YES

Learning to say no is an important side of self-care and time management, but learning to say yes to positive activities is just as important. Stevanovic and Rupert (2004) found that among the most common and important career-sustaining behaviors were spending time with partners and families and maintaining balance between professional and personal lives.

When I work with overstressed students or colleagues, the problem is not simply that they have a hard time saying no to extra work. It is also that they have a hard time saying yes to things they enjoy doing. A colleague who was working from 7:00 A.M. to 7:00 P.M. five days a week and half days on Saturday told me that one of his favorite things to do was to go sailing. Indeed, part of the reason he worked such long hours was to pay for a very expensive sailboat he recently purchased. When I asked how long it had been since he had gone sailing, he said he had gone once this year and two or three times each of the past two years. If sailing was indeed his favorite pastime, he was certainly not allocating a proportionate amount of time to it.

Rather than agonizing over every opportunity or request to do one more thing, I encourage you to sit down, alone or perhaps with your significant other, and think carefully about how you want to spend your time. It has been pointed out that the amount of time we give to something is one indication of how important we think it is. Yet, when people examine where they are really spending their time and why, they realize that some things are getting far more time than their real importance warrants.

EXERCISE: SETTING PRIORITIES

The previous exercise asked you to examine how you currently spend your time. Now consider where you would like to allocate time in the future. Make a list of the things that are important to you, and then identify how much time you would like to devote to them. Do not start with what you are doing and work from there. Instead, first list what is important to you, and then look at how you are actually spending your time. You may discover significant discrepancies between what you say matters to you and what you do. Based on this awareness, try to plan a schedule that would allow you to do more of what you have identified as top priorities.

CLOSING SESSIONS

The advice to keep sessions within the scheduled period is often particularly difficult for interns to follow. If clients are still talking about an issue when the session is about to end, interns tend to allow or encourage them to keep going. It also happens that some clients do not raise important issues until just before the session ends. This can happen for many reasons. Perhaps the issue is so sensitive that the client spent the entire session trying to gather courage to discuss it. Raising it at the end of the session provides a safety valve of sorts. Another possibility is that a client is testing the therapist; allotting extra time may seem to be a sign that the therapist really cares. Whatever the reason, if sessions run over, that is information the therapist should be aware of and seek to understand. Allowing overruns to occur repeatedly and without examination may mean the therapist is overlooking useful information.

There are several ways to bring sessions to an end constructively. To begin with, as part of the information provided to clients at the outset of therapy, it should be made clear how long sessions will last. If a clock is subtly but obviously visible in the background of an office, clients can monitor the time for themselves and most will be respectful of limits. During sessions, the easiest and most direct approach is for the therapist as the end of the session approaches to state, "We need to finish for now." If the client has just raised an important issue, the therapist might observe, "I think what you just spoke of is important and is something we should probably address in the next session. For now, we need to conclude for today." These methods will be well received and effective in most cases. If a client repeatedly runs sessions overtime, the therapist may need to address this. Here again, stating it directly in the form of a process observation can be helpful: "I have noticed that in the past few sessions we seem to raise important issues right near the end and then to run overtime. I want to be sure to give enough time to such issues, but it is important to be aware of the conclusion of our sessions. I wonder if there is a way we can address this more effectively."

In describing these techniques, it must be added that the therapist should, of course, use judgment. There are times when it is essential to run a little over. If a client reveals that he or she is in some danger, if a critical issue absolutely must be resolved, or if some other matter demands immediate attention, the therapist may elect to extend the session. This decision, however, should be made rarely; if it occurs repeatedly for the same client, the therapist should recognize and address the problem.

It is not only clients who extend sessions past the scheduled time. It also happens that clients are ready to conclude sessions on time, but the intern, perhaps wanting to feel needed or to "solve the client's problems," extends the session. This tendency is not only contrary to sound time management; it can also interfere with therapy. The reality is that the work of therapy is seldom "finished" by the end of any single session. There will always be more to do, and it is often a good thing to end a session with work still left to do. Clients are able to continue thinking about things on their own, and therapists need to be able to give them that opportunity. Interns must learn that sessions do not always end as neat or tidy packages, and clients do not, and probably should not, always leave a session feeling that everything has been resolved.

A colleague of mine uses the concept of "holding the question" to help interns understand that not everything is resolved in each session. Holding the question means accepting that some things are best pondered, and one should not expect an immediate answer to every question. Holding the question gives clients time to think about things between sessions. Because life does not always give neatly packaged solutions and we must be able to deal with that fact, developing the ability to hold the question is, in itself, highly therapeutic for clients as well as professionals.

COGNITIVE SELF-CARE

The normal stresses interns experience can often be exacerbated by beliefs they hold about themselves, their clients, the therapy process, and broader topics that might best be labeled "cognitions about the world." To the extent that these ideas create stress, recognizing and coping effectively with them can be a valuable element of self-care.

It is not uncommon for interns to approach their training or placements with unrealistic expectations about their own knowledge, efficacy, or feelings toward clients. For example, interns might believe they must not make any mistakes. Or they might fear that others will recognize their lack of experience. It is also common for interns to want to be liked, perhaps even loved and supported, by all their clients and coworkers.

Deutsch (1984) studied a number of ideas rated by clinicians as stressful and found that all of the three most stressful ideas dealt with therapists' needs for perfection. Other stressful ideas included the belief that the therapist is responsible for client change, that therapists must be constantly available to clients, and that therapists should be models of mental health themselves.

For interns, unrealistic expectations about themselves or clients add to the challenges of an already demanding position. At the same time, however, it is quite realistic and to be expected for interns to have some anxiety about their abilities as therapists. Engaging others in a relationship and seeking to help them make difficult changes is, indeed, a great responsibility. Interns who do not have at least some concerns about their abilities or about the therapy process are themselves sources of stress and anxiety for their supervisors.

In your own training, try to be aware of any beliefs or ideas that place unrealistic expectations on yourself. It may also be helpful to discuss these ideas with your peers, instructor, or supervisor.

Do not be ashamed to admit that there are times when you are unsure about what to do. Experienced supervisors will certainly understand this and would much rather an intern talk about such feelings than keep them inside and proceed without seeking assistance. The most important self-care cognition is probably "I do not have to be perfect, but I do need to get help when I need it."

COGNITIONS ABOUT CLIENTS

Just as unrealistic expectations of oneself can contribute to stress, inaccurate or unrealistic cognitions about clients are also a common source of stress for interns. Fremont and Anderson (1986) suggested that counselors carry a set of assumptions about how clients "should act and how counseling should progress" (p. 68). When these assumptions are not met, counselors may become angry or frustrated.

Despite, or perhaps because of such assumptions, in the course of your training you will probably find yourself thinking that clients are heroic, lazy, dangerous, suicidal, seductive, distancing, helpless, whiny, crazy, unmotivated, manipulative, passive-aggressive, logical, motivated, creative, suffering, or a host of other things. When you experience such thoughts and feelings, it may be helpful to keep the following ideas in mind.

First, the most stressful of all cognitions about clients is probably the notion that they should be different from who they are, and if they were, your own work would be much easier. This cognition can take many forms. You may think, "This client should be more open in therapy," or "This client should not be so angry," or "This client should not be so depressed," or "This client should be more appreciative of the service we provide."

However you finish the sentence, believing that clients should be different is a sure way to create unnecessary and unproductive stress for yourself and your clients. This is not to say that clients would not benefit from change. It is to say that wanting clients to be different and becoming upset because they are not is not treatment. Our task is not to determine what clients "should be" and wish that they were different from what they are. Our task is to help our clients determine what they want to be and then help them achieve that goal for themselves.

The second point to remember is that many interns add to their stress by overgeneralizing beliefs about specific clients to all clients. For example, some interns worry about the possibility of suicide with virtually all their clients. Because suicide is such a serious action and because it is possible for any person to take his or her own life, this concern is understandable. Most clients, however—even the most depressed clients—do not commit suicide. Thus, if you actively worry about suicide with every client, you will do a lot of worrying, and most of that worrying will be unnecessary. A large part of training involves moving from such overgeneralizations to more specific applications and more precise understanding. As this happens, you will develop a better sense of when you can relax and when you really do need to be anxious about clients.

COGNITIONS ABOUT THERAPY

Closely tied to the idea that clients should be different are ideas about the therapy process in general. As noted, one such cognition is the belief that clients should not be resistant to change.

Interns and beginning therapists often become upset with clients who "obviously need to change" but resist the therapist's best efforts to get them to do something different. In such situations, the problem and the source of the therapist's stress are not really the client. Rather, it is the therapist's belief that change is, or should be, easy for people. The reality is that change can be very difficult—sometimes it takes a long time to happen, and people (including interns and therapists themselves) tend to resist change because it is unfamiliar and uncertain. When resistance is understood and recognized as an expected and normal part of the treatment process, a therapist or intern is better able to respond to it effectively.

Another cognition that adds to stress is the belief that the helping professional is responsible for the client's life. Clients come to you or your agency because they want your help in understanding or altering something about themselves or their lives. You charge money for your time, and you have supposedly been trained in ways of helping, so there is at least an implied burden on you to do something useful. At the same time, as just discussed, clients often resist change and do not cooperate in the therapeutic work. This makes it easy to blame clients when progress is not achieved or does not come as rapidly as you or they might hope. Blaming clients for not changing is one way therapists deal with their own frustrations at not feeling successful or validated. But this response from therapists is ultimately an attempt to meet their own needs, not the clients'.

To deal more effectively with resistance, it helps to think of your role as a catalyst for change but not as the primary agent of change. You cannot, and should not, take full responsibility for solving your clients' problems for them. You must instead recognize that you play an important role in helping clients cope with their situations, discover resources within themselves, and make the changes they need to make for themselves. Ultimately, however, the clients themselves must make those changes; you cannot do it for them.

COGNITIONS ABOUT THE WORLD

Even when interns are away from their internship sites and clients, experiences in therapy can contribute to cognitions about the world that add to therapist stress. One of the ways this happens is through the development of a rather distorted sense of what constitutes "normal." If an intern spends much of the day dealing with people who are experiencing serious problems in their lives or who are hostile or severely impaired, the experience may cause the intern to begin to believe that most people have such problems. In some instances, this process can actually create or reinforce racial or other stereotypes.

One of our interns who worked for a semester in a juvenile detention center said, "I can't believe what those kids are like. I used to think I wanted to have children, but now, if they could turn out like these kids, forget it." Another intern who worked with abused children found herself "hating those parents and wondering if there are any decent people out there." Yet another intern worked with patients on the Alzheimer's disease unit of a nursing home. When she had the opportunity to do some intelligence testing with an elderly person who did not have dementia, she marveled at how intelligent the man was. In fact, he was in the average range for his age group, but he seemed to her to be a genius when compared with some others she had been working with.

Internship experiences also affect how interns think about systems. For example, an intern who worked in a social service agency first became angered, then frustrated, and eventually depressed by the inefficiency of the agency and the lack of dedication on the part of many employees. Another intern, also frustrated by systemic flaws, despaired of the helping professions entirely and concluded that she should "change my major, quit trying to help anyone, and just make money."

Interns should remind themselves that they are dealing with real people, real suffering, and sometimes with real dysfunctional systems. That is part of life, but it is not all of life. If you find yourself getting soured on life or work at your placement site, it can be extremely beneficial to seek experiences or information that will present the other side of the picture. Using a sports metaphor, Grosch and Olsen (1995) referred to the value of "cross-training" (i.e., varying jobs and activities to include other perspectives as a way of staying fresh). The interns described here might look for examples of youth who are contributing to their community; parents who are doing a thoughtful, caring job of raising their children; or senior citizens who are mentally alert and involved in programs that keep them healthy. Others might benefit by identifying systems that are successful and are staffed by dedicated, competent people. Such systems do, in fact, exist, but you may not have the good fortune to find them on your first or second field placement.

Making this effort helps interns come to grips with the reality of human suffering and shortcomings while not losing sight of the equally important reality of human joy, kindness, and health. It is essential for interns to understand that they have the potential to help change dysfunctional systems for the better. If everything already worked perfectly, there would be little need for the human service professions. Great strides have, indeed, been made toward making things better, and in each case these advances have occurred because one or more individuals dedicated themselves to a goal. As a student and as an intern, you have the opportunity to develop knowledge, experience, and insights that can help you make a real difference in the world. The task will not be easy, and it will probably not be completed in any one person's lifetime, but you can have an effect, and people's lives (including your own) can be more fulfilling because of your efforts.

EXERCISE: COGNITIONS REVIEW

On the basis of what you have read thus far and your own experiences, review your beliefs about your role as an intern, the treatment process, clients, and the world as a whole. What beliefs do you hold that may be causing unnecessary stress? What beliefs help you deal constructively with the stresses of your work or training? When you have written your own thoughts, discuss them with your peers and supervisor to get their ideas and feedback. If certain ideas are impacting you adversely, consider developing an active strategy to confront and change those ideas and their effects.

PHYSICAL SELF-CARE

We must all determine for ourselves how we define *physical health*. In my practice as a medical psychologist, I worked on a daily basis with people who suffered the psychological and physical effects of poor physical self-care. I was also involved in various efforts aimed at preventing illness and promoting physical wellness. Perhaps because of this background and because I know firsthand how physically draining internships and clinical work can be, I strongly urge interns to care for their bodies as well as their minds. Without becoming preachy, I want to help interns develop skills and habits that will serve them throughout their careers. Having seen the physical and emotional toll this line of work can take on people, I feel an obligation to at least raise the issue and perhaps offer some new perspectives.

PHYSICAL EXERCISE

As described earlier, the sedentary nature of clinical work and the tendency to internalize stresses place unusual demands on the body. Physical activity can help overcome some of the effects of sedentary work and can help you deal with stress more effectively.

When the subject of physical activity arises, some interns have no problem because exercise is already part of their daily routine. Others indicate that they are interested in exercising but cannot find the time. Still others respond as if I have suggested they do something abhorrent.

For those in the first group, one need only encourage continuing what is already in place and jealously guarding the time for daily exercise. For those who would like to exercise but do not find the time, it may be useful to reread the discussion on time management and unscheduling. For individuals who respond negatively to suggestions about exercise, I can offer a few thoughts based on what has worked with students and with clients wanting to change their physical activity levels.

First, do not feel you must start a rigorous exercise program right away. Take some time to think about what is or would be healthy for you. As you consider this, do not think in terms of *heavy workouts* or *strict diets* when you think of physical self-care. These terms do not really sound much like care, so it is not surprising that they are aversive. As an appealing and realistic alternative, you are more likely to succeed if you start small and consider your own needs and values. Without launching directly into a full workout regimen, you can find opportunities to incorporate less strenuous forms of exercise throughout the day. You can increase fitness by taking the stairs instead of elevators; parking a little farther from the office; or, better still, walking or biking to work. While at work, get in the habit of getting up and stretching between sessions. Similarly, if your work for the day involves long hours of reading, writing, or computer work, you can set a watch or other timer as a reminder to take a break to stretch your body and rest your eyes.

These changes can actually make a noticeable difference in health, but there may also be a need to structure some regular forms of aerobic activity during your week. When you reach this point, you may ask, as do many people, "So how much exercise do I *have* to do?" Specialists in the area of physical wellness suggest that a more constructive question is, "What level of physical activity will help me achieve noticeable health improvements?" This reframing removes the sense of obligation, and perhaps, along with it, a degree of resistance. The alternative question also emphasizes that in terms of reducing risk for such illnesses as coronary vascular disease, relatively little exercise can produce significant benefits.

For many people, even those who once thought of exercise as tantamount to self-imposed torture, the break they schedule for exercise soon becomes a highlight of the day, something they look forward to, enjoy doing, and appreciate throughout the day. Ideally, exercise should not be something we do "to ourselves." It should be something we do "for ourselves" to release tension and improve our overall well-being.

MASSAGE

For some people, physical exercise may not feel like self-care, but most would agree that therapeutic massage is pretty close to the epitome of self-care. Perhaps the best thing about massage for the helping professionals is that it allows you to put yourself quite literally into someone else's hands and let that person take care of you for a while. This is something many of us, particularly in the helping professions, do not do.

An example of the benefit of massage was quite immediate for me when I was writing this chapter for the first edition of this book. In the final stages of preparing the book, I was teaching full time, doing part-time clinical work, and putting in extraordinarily long hours of writing in between. My days often began at 5:00 A.M., and I stayed at it until I could go no further, often continuing until well past midnight. After many months of work when this intense effort had gone on with little respite, the effects were beginning to tell. Realizing I needed a break, but under pressure to meet deadlines, the idea of a massage came to me and seemed so appealing I almost called 911-MASSAGE. Fortunately, a massage therapist I knew was able to schedule an appointment for that same day. I explained my situation, lay down on the table, and let her do the work. During the entire massage I thought about work only once, and that was to make a brief mental note to add a word about massage to this chapter. It is not an exaggeration to say that an hour and a half later, I felt like a new person. I still had several long days ahead, but the massage had helped me weather a point of near-exhaustion and recharged the batteries to help me get through the rest of the way.

In addition to being a great way to release stress and help you relax, massage is also a good way of monitoring where and how you may be physically internalizing the emotional stresses of your work. Many of us tend to keep the accumulated emotions of our work somewhere in our bodies; headaches, backaches, and other pains may be the result. A skilled massage therapist will locate those places and, while helping to work them out, may give you some clues about where you keep your stresses in your body.

MONITORING STRESSES IN THE BODY

Few of us have the time or money to afford a massage every day or even every month. Lacking that luxury, we need to learn to deal with physical tensions as they arise during the course of our work.

Another useful suggestion offered by a colleague is to periodically run a "mental body check," noticing any signs of physical tension or other sensations that arise. Perhaps the easiest way to do this is to start at the top of your head and do a quick run-through of your posture, muscle tension, and other internal sensations. It may help to do this as you breathe in and out, thinking of letting go of any tension as you exhale. With practice, this self-check and relaxation can be done in a very short time and in a way that is not noticeable to others. I try to do such checks several times during each therapy session, meeting, class, or other event. This helps keep physical tensions from building and can reveal clues about how I am reacting to what is happening. When I work with clients, I also observe their physical posture and apparent tension levels. This awareness can provide valuable clues to what is going on clinically.

HEALTHY EATING AND HABITS

Along with a healthy amount of exercise and relaxation, healthy eating is also important. Just as internships can limit the time available for exercise, they often have an adverse influence on how, when, and what interns eat. Many interns are unaware of this until they think about it and realize that, in fact, the internship has affected their eating in several ways.

Some interns find that eating is one of the ways they cope with the stresses of the internship. A common experience is to come home from the internship site and feel a need to eat something to help settle down after a demanding day. Interns may also find themselves so rushed at their placement sites that they seldom take the time to relax and enjoy a meal that is really good for them. Instead, "lunch" becomes more like aerial refueling, consisting of a bag of chips and a soft drink or coffee (their third cup of five or more per day) from the vending machine or espresso stand.

If this description sounds a little too familiar, consider replacing the "foods" just described with more healthy choices, for example, fruits, grains, juices, or other items. The research in nutrition is increasingly clear that these changes affect our health in countless beneficial ways and the results are both immediate and lasting.

In my own life, my mother died at age 57 of a heart attack and several members of her family also passed away of heart disease at young ages. Studying the literature and consulting with my physician, I came to ask myself four questions about my dietary habits: (1) Do I love my wife and children and want to live as long as I can for their sake and mine? (2) Do I believe in scientific research as a basis for action? (3) Do I want to feel better physically and emotionally? (4) The fourth question logically followed from the first three—If I answered yes to those questions, which I did, then how can I justify not making significant changes in my diet for the better?

Faced with those questions and in light of the abundant evidence of the connection between diet and health, I made and have maintained changes that have indeed improved both my physical health and, hopefully, my long-term well-being as well. If you assess your own health and ask comparable questions, perhaps changes will make sense for you as well.

If poor dietary habits can be intrinsically harmful over the long run, the same point can and should be made about other habits that are also related to stress and coping. The use of alcohol, cigarettes, or other drugs is closely tied to stress, and the helping professionals are no less susceptible, perhaps even more so, to abusing these substances. In my clinical work and as an instructor and supervisor, I have come in contact with students, supervisors, and colleagues who had significant substance abuse problems. In most cases, these same individuals denied that they had a problem, even though virtually everyone who knew them was aware of, and concerned about, the situation. In addition to the damage and difficulties substance abuse causes the individuals themselves, the profession also suffers harm as members of the public look cynically at the helping professionals who do not appear able to deal well with problems themselves.

Once again, the goal here is to help interns become aware of signs that may indicate they are not coping well with personal or professional stresses. If you find your own use of legal or controlled substances increasing—if it sometimes feels you just have to have a drink, smoke, pill, or something else to cope with the stress of work—perhaps it is time to examine how work is affecting you or how the habits themselves are affecting your work.

EXERCISE: PERSONAL PHYSICAL HEALTH CARE REVIEW

As a step toward developing physical self-care habits, you may wish to conduct a simple personal physical health care review. This review involves taking stock of activities related to exercise, diet, and harmful habits. Write each of these headings on a sheet of paper: Exercise, Diet, Sleep, Habits. Under these headings, list items you think are conducive to self-care and those that might be harmful in some way. Ask yourself how your internship work or other activities relate to what you have written. Finally, give some thought to how changes in your self-care might benefit your internship, school, or other activities, and how changes in those activities could affect your physical care.

EMOTIONAL SELF-CARE

Two brief anecdotes illustrate the need for attending to one's own emotional self-care as an intern or clinician. The first happened to a young intern during his predoctoral internship at a psychiatric hospital. On the last day of work before the Christmas holiday, the intern was riding his bike home from an evening group meeting. As he rode, he was thinking about the contrast between his home where he would spend the coming week and the hospital facility where the patients would be. Quite unexpectedly, as the lights of the hospital faded behind him and he turned down a darkened road, he began to cry. In fact, he began sobbing so hard he had to stop his bicycle and sit beneath a streetlight, crying to himself for almost half an hour. He had been working at the hospital for four months and knew some of the patients very well; but until that moment, the full reality of their situation had not really struck him. When the realization hit, all of the emotions stored for months came out at once.

A second incident occurred more recently and demonstrates again how the emotional effects of clinical work can sneak up on us. As mentioned earlier, in addition to teaching, I practiced as a psychologist in medical settings. For a variety of reasons, including a difficult course load, challenging cases, seemingly endless and pointless political struggles within the institution, and numerous other factors, I was going through a series of rough weeks at just the time I was teaching the internship class about the topic of self-care. One day in class, I advised the interns to monitor their own emotional status. That same evening, a relatively small dispute with one of my children resulted in my shouting at, and criticizing, the child far more harshly than the situation called for. My wife noticed this and asked if perhaps the stresses at work were a factor in the reaction. Of course, I denied this vehemently (after all, I am writing a book on the subject), but after some reflection I realized she was right. Stresses at work had piled up, and although I did not think they were affecting me, I was carrying far more emotional tension than I realized.

It is probably not possible or desirable to try to be emotionally unaffected by one's clinical work, but it is vital that we learn to deal with those effects constructively. During a workshop on self-care and managing the stresses of work, several colleagues offered the following useful suggestions.

SELF-CHECKS

Perhaps the most important principle of self-care is to be aware of, and acknowledge, how our work affects us. One counselor said she makes a habit of doing a brief emotional self-check that is comparable with the physical self-checks described earlier. At the end of each session, after the client leaves, she takes a deep breath, closes her eyes, and asks herself how she feels emotionally at that moment and how she felt emotionally during the session. This process helps her be aware of what she is experiencing, and it provides new insights into what happened during the session. It also reminds her to relax.

CLEANSING RITUALS

Another colleague, a psychologist who often works with extremely challenging cases, makes use of what he calls "cleansing rituals" to help clear his mind and emotions between sessions. For example, if a session has been very demanding emotionally, he sometimes splashes a bit of cool water on his face afterward. This offers a refreshing break, and it reminds him to have a clear mind before meeting with his next client. He also uses stretching as a way to relieve physical as well as emotional tension. After each session, he makes a practice of taking several deep breaths while he stretches his back and legs. With each breath out, he imagines letting go of any stresses he might have stored during the session. With each breath in, he reminds himself to be patient and open to the next client's experience. He does not leave the office to invite the next client in until he feels he has sufficiently processed the interaction with the previous individual.

A different type of cleansing process was described by a social worker specializing in domestic violence. She uses the act of opening the door to her office as a signal to clear her mind for the next client. After finishing her case notes, she puts the client's folder away and says to herself that she will leave the client there until the next visit. This helps prevent her from "taking her clients home." Using the act of opening the door as a cue helps her meet the next client where that client is, rather than with emotional baggage from the previous session. At the end of the day, she uses the closing of her office door behind her as a reminder to leave the work of the day at the office. This allows her to go home to her family without carrying the day's accumulated feelings away from the office. Describing this practice, she noted that if she did not have some way of keeping what she dealt with at work separate from her home life, she would not last even three months in practice.

MEDITATION AND PRAYER

For therapists with religious backgrounds, prayer can offer another means of coping with the stresses of work. In a discussion of how child welfare workers cope with the effects of secondary trauma, Dane (2000) reported that many of her respondents said their spiritual beliefs helped them find meaning in their difficult work. Some also offered that they prayed before going on difficult field visits or after working with especially challenging cases. El-Ghoroury et al. (2012) also reported that many of the graduate students they surveyed identified spirituality as one of their effective coping strategies.

I have spoken with therapists who have said silent prayers during sessions both as a way of dealing with emotional stresses and in an effort to seek guidance for how best to help the client. It is important, however, to keep in mind that although prayer may be helpful to you personally, imposing prayer or religiously based interventions on clients who are not of the same persuasion would not be considered ethical or sound clinical practice.

Meditation has also been helpful to many therapists, with the approach of "mindful meditation" receiving increasing attention. Shapiro, Brown, and Biegel (2007) reported positive effects on therapist trainees who received a program of "Mindfulness-Based Stress Reduction," which was developed by John Kabat-Zinn (2005). Among the benefits reported by those who received this training were declines in stress, reduced negative affect, less rumination about cases, and increases in positive affect and self-compassion.

One of the foremost teachers of mindful meditation is a Vietnamese Buddhist, Thich Nhat Hanh. The practice of mindful meditation, which is perhaps best summarized in his book *The Miracle of Mindfulness* (1975), is accessible and easily incorporated into everyday life and can be of benefit regardless of one's religious beliefs. In essence, mindfulness entails being fully aware of what is happening in the present moment, whether one is walking, eating, or simply sitting quietly and being aware of one's own breathing. Taking a few moments before and after sessions to breathe quietly and mindfully can be remarkably beneficial, as can going for brief, mindful walks outside.

There are, of course, many other possibilities for emotional self-care, and you can probably find ways that work best for you. Whatever approach you try, it is worth developing some form of reliable practice that you can do between clients, meetings, or other activities and at the end of the day to finish the work and leave it where it belongs.

ORGANIZATIONAL MEASURES AND PEER SUPPORT

Self-care activities can go a long way toward helping clinicians cope with the emotional demands of their work, but proactive organizational activities and the support of other interns or clinicians are also important (Guy, 2000; O'Conner, 2001; Turner et al., 2005). If you find yourself feeling overwhelmed by work, or if you are carrying emotions away from your sessions, you may want to spend some time talking with your peers or supervisor about what you are experiencing. This advice, however, is easier to give than to follow. One way to make it easier to follow the advice of self-care is through activities sponsored by the institutions where you work. Another helpful approach involves the development of colleague assistance programs affiliated with state professional associations. Such programs provide peer-to-peer professional support for colleagues facing challenges ranging from personal stresses to ethical dilemmas to significant career changes (Munsey, 2006). You may want to reach out to your own professional association at the state or national level to find out if such programs exist in or near your area.

Organizational Factors and Structured Stress Management

In her discussion of the impact of secondary trauma, Hesse (2002) emphasized that agencies in which therapists must deal with victims of psychological trauma or other challenging cases should have organizational mechanisms in place to help them deal with the effects of their work. Sommer (2008) made a similar recommendation regarding the need for counselor training programs to prepare students for vicarious traumatization. Catherall (1995) recommended an organizational approach that includes identifying staff exposed to secondary trauma; developing a plan for educating staff about the effects of secondary trauma; training staff in ways of coping with those effects; and, finally, evaluating the success of these efforts and making changes as needed.

Dane (2000) described a program designed to help child welfare workers, who must deal on a daily basis with abused children and their abusers. Through focus group discussions, child welfare workers identified the most difficult elements of their work and the emotional and physical impacts these have on their relationships and on other areas. From that input, a two-day training program was designed to teach care workers about the stressful impact of their work, signs of burnout, secondary traumatization, countertransference, and ways of coping with these successfully. Results suggested that this approach was generally well received and helpful, but Dane emphasized the importance of follow-up through monthly discussion meetings, half-yearly booster sessions, and special provisions if highly traumatic events, such as the death of a client, occur.

Letting Off Steam

The process just described involves structured interactions that occur in private with other peers or colleagues. As helpful as these exchanges with professional peers may be, sometimes it is also incredibly helpful to just let off steam with people who know what the job is like. This is different from talking about one's day with a significant other, and it is different from clinical supervision. The goal is simply to relax and have fun, to do something with your colleagues that has as little to do with work as possible. Even if you are not the social type, it is important to interact with your peers and away from work.

If you do participate in such activities, without taking away the fun, keep three cautions in mind: First, be careful about the locations you choose and issues of confidentiality if the conversation is about clients. Everyone in your group may know about a given client, and there may be interesting or funny stories to share, but if the setting is public and the talking gets too loud, others may easily overhear you. Whether or not they personally know the individuals involved, merely hearing professionals talking, and perhaps even laughing, about clients in public could create a negative image.

A second concern is that there is a fine line between constructive stress release for staff and destructive derision of clients. It is one thing to say, "You'll never believe what so-and-so did today," followed by an anecdote that is funny without being demeaning. It is quite another to make the same opening statement in a harsh or critical tone, followed by a negative story about how bad the client is in some way. The same principle applies to stories about colleagues. Never forget that clients and colleagues, no matter how frustrating, are people who are doing their best to get by. If it helps you to laugh, by all means do so. But be sure you are laughing as much at yourself as at the wonderful, sad, and confusing thing it is to be human.

Finally, many TGIF (Thank God It's Friday) activities tend to take place in settings where alcohol is served. This is not necessarily a problem, but keep in mind that alcohol can easily become an external mood controller that one gradually comes to depend on for dealing with stresses. As noted, if this starts becoming a pattern for you or your peers, it is a good idea to explore how well you are coping with stress and if there are other, more constructive alternatives to alcohol.

Exercise: Emotional Coping

Having read the suggestions about coping with the emotional stresses of your work, this is a good opportunity to do an emotional self-check for yourself. As part of this check, identify what you currently do to cope with your own emotional reactions to your work. Also, identify things that might be helpful but that you do not currently practice. If you find some things you could and perhaps should be doing differently to take care of yourself, develop a plan to implement those changes. As a first step, discuss the issue with a peer and perhaps explore ways of working together to help each other.

MULTIMODAL SELF-CARE

Each of the various categories of self-care activities described earlier was integrated conceptually by Arnold Lazarus (2000) into what he referred to as "multimodal self-care." Consistent with his multimodal approach to therapy, Lazarus recommended asking yourself the following seven fundamental questions: (1) What fun things can I do? (2) What positive emotions can I generate? (3) What sensory experiences can I enjoy? (4) What empowering and pleasant mental images can I conjure up? (5) What positive self-talk can I employ? (6) Which amiable people can I associate with? (7) What specific health-related activities can I engage in?

Coming from a slightly different perspective, but offering a comparable multimodal approach, Norcross (2000) offers a list of self-care strategies that are "clinician recommended, research informed, and practitioner tested." The list begins by recognizing the hazards of clinical practice and then addresses a combination of cognitive, behavioral, and insight-oriented approaches for coping with stress. Norcross also recommends diversification of clinical activities and, finally, an emphasis on appreciating the rewards as well as the challenges of therapy.

PERSONAL THERAPY

It is often hard for interns or clinicians to acknowledge that they are having a hard time. The vulnerable moment in which one asks a friend or peer "Can I talk to you?" can be extraordinarily frightening. Yet that moment can also begin a dialog that will be of invaluable help. In my own career, there have been a number of times when I recognized that I needed help and had the good sense to ask for it. On other occasions, I needed help but was unaware of it or denied the situation. Fortunately, close colleagues who knew me well recognized that things were not right and gently offered an ear. At other times, I have done the same for them. In your own training, try to be aware of when you need support and to be sensitive to when other interns or professionals could use support from you.

Because all of us are limited in our ability to know ourselves and because we tend to be so exquisitely creative and effective in defending ourselves from awareness, we need outside information. One way to get such information is through therapy. Many practitioners, including myself, have found that personal psychotherapy is not only beneficial in helping deal with both personal issues and the stresses of practice, but it can also improve your understanding of the therapy process and thus make you a better therapist (Bike et al., 2009; Geller et al., 2005; Norcross, 2005).

If you choose to see a therapist, you will not be alone in that decision. Studies of factors contributing to professional development indicate that clinicians rank personal therapy among the three most important contributors, after direct client contact and formal supervision, to professional development (e.g., Orlinsky & Rønnestad, 2005).

In a comprehensive review of research involving a total of 8,000 participants, Norcross and Guy (2005) found that around 72% of therapists had participated in some form of personal therapy. Comparable results were described by Bike et al., who surveyed more than 700 psychologists, counselors, and social workers. In each of the professional groups, approximately 85% of the respondents reported having sought therapy at least once, with more than 90% of them reporting positive outcomes.

The benefits of therapy were demonstrated in research conducted by Andy Carey, Heather Giakovmis, and myself. Our survey of more than 500 counselors and clinical psychologists demonstrated that the majority of respondents, 79% of the sample, reported they had participated in personal therapy or counseling. Of that group, 93% categorized the experience as mildly positive to very positive. Results also showed that on an instrument designed to assess cognitions about clients, the therapy process, and the role of the therapist, 13 out of 38 items yielded statistical significance when therapists with personal experience in therapy were compared with those without such experience (Baird & Carey, 1992; Baird, Carey, & Giakovmis, 1992).

Despite the apparently widespread belief and empirical evidence that therapy is perceived as beneficial for trainees and professionals, this is an admittedly controversial subject. Although not recommending that therapy be required for all students or interns in training, evidence suggests that personal therapy can be a valuable experience for interns and therapists. In addition to helping us become more aware of ourselves, personal therapy also gives us a better awareness of what clients experience when they are in therapy.

Having said that, to be honest, I must now add that in the early days of training, I might have thrown away any book that recommended therapy for therapists or students. My feeling at the time was that one went into the field because one was pretty well put together to begin with and wanted to use this fortunate status to the benefit of others. That idea seemed to make good sense at the time, and it was certainly comforting to believe I was so well adjusted as to be able to help others without further work on myself. That this belief was held by someone who was still in his early 20s does not seem at all surprising. Indeed, it only served to support a belief that healthy personal adjustment and effective psychotherapy were not necessarily so difficult.

That is how I once felt. As I gained experience, and after a number of challenging events in my personal life, the awareness gradually emerged that even therapists (perhaps especially therapists) have issues that they need to work through. This realization led me to enter a group therapy experience with other professionals. The results were enlightening. Not only did I receive invaluable assistance in recognizing and working through some of my own issues, I also came to know firsthand how therapy can be helpful and how helpful it can be.

EXERCISE

If you have previously received therapy or counseling, this might be a good time to reflect on that experience and how it affected you as an individual and your work with others. If you have never been in therapy, you may want to consider whether you would be willing to seek therapy at some time. If you find yourself open to the idea, what benefits would you hope to receive? If you are opposed to the idea of entering therapy for yourself, give some thought to the reasons why. You may also want to consider what alternative methods you will establish and practice to cope with how your work affects you personally and how your own issues affect your work.

POSITIVE EFFECTS ON THERAPISTS

Thus far, we have focused primarily on coping with the stresses and potentially negative emotional and physical impacts that are encountered by helping professionals and interns. The intent has been to apprise you of some of the personal challenges you may face as an intern or professional. As important as it is to understand the challenges, it should not be forgotten that if stress were the only effect of this work, not many people would go into it. Therefore, it is equally important to recognize and value the positive effects of what you do (Berger, 1995). On this same theme, Kramen-Kahn and Hansen (1998) emphasized that it can be beneficial for stressed clinicians to keep in mind the often-forgotten rewards and seek out career-sustaining behaviors.

As one example of this, Stevanovic and Rupert (2009) found that psychologists who responded to a survey on the effects of work-to-family spillover were more likely to report positive spillovers that enhanced their family as compared with negative spillovers that somehow harmed the family.

EXERCISE: POSITIVE EFFECTS OF CLINICAL WORK

List the positive emotional effects you derive from your internship training.

List the positive cognitive effects you derive from your internship training.

List any other benefits you derive from the internship.

As you look toward the future, what benefits do you expect to receive in each of these areas as a professional in the field?

Finally, if you have the opportunity, discuss this question with those who have worked in your profession for some time. Ask them about both the benefits and the stresses, and how they have managed to balance the two.

I have asked numerous interns and experienced therapists about the positive effects they experience from their work. The most frequent response describes a sense of satisfaction in doing something to help others. As one clinician said, "Every now and then you work with a client, and it is just clear that you have been helpful to them. That really feels good to me, to know I made a difference like that." Berger (1995) reported similar statements from senior therapists describing factors that sustain their work. Stevanovic and Rupert (2004) found that therapists identified "promoting growth in clients/helping others" as their highest source of professional satisfaction, followed by intellectual stimulation and other intrinsic rewards.

Other rewards include the opportunity to continue learning, the pleasure of working with colleagues who share similar backgrounds and goals, the intellectual challenges of clinical work, and personal growth. Many professionals enjoy the relative autonomy and responsibility of the work, whereas others emphasize the interesting variety of tasks and clients they deal with. Your own list of benefits may have included those just described or others. Whatever you identified, it is important to recognize the positive elements of your work. If the positive elements begin to decline or are outweighed by the negatives, your motivation, effort, and effectiveness will eventually begin to suffer.

Being aware of the benefits of your training or profession can also influence the quality of your work itself. For example, if one of the benefits for most therapists is the satisfaction that comes when a client makes progress, it is easy for the therapist to become dependent on the client's changing, not for the client's own benefit but because it helps the therapist feel good. The helping professionals must maintain the fine balance between appreciating the rewards that come from feeling one has helped another person and not becoming dependent on that reward or allowing it to interfere with what one must do to, in fact, be helpful.

FINANCIAL SELF-CARE

The final self-care topic to be addressed here has to do with financial matters. Given the focus of this chapter on managing the stresses that come with internships and clinical work, it must be acknowledged that financial concerns are among the top-ranked sources of stress for people in virtually all lines of work, including the helping professions. Finances and debt were listed as the second most common stressor identified by El-Ghoroury et al. (2012), whereas the APA Center for Workforce Studies (Michalski, Kohout, Wicherski, & Hart, 2011) surveyed recent graduates in psychology and found that PhD graduates carried a median debt of $80,000, whereas PsyD graduates reported a median debt of $120,000 upon graduation.

Faced with these challenges, many interns and new professionals have received little if any direct instruction or support in learning how to manage their finances. Habben (2004), for example, observed, "We need to learn early on how to generate revenue, how to market ourselves, how to create a network—all of the things that we psychologists just don't like to do" (p. 54, quoted in DeAngelis, 2005).

In this text, I would not pretend to be able to offer advice on how you should invest your money, whether mutual funds are superior to money markets, or what the best retirement plan should be (though you should start and continue to invest in a plan as soon as you possibly can).

Instead, my goal is to suggest a way of thinking that may help reduce the stresses that so often accompany money matters. Much of what I have to offer in this regard is described well in the book *Your Money or Your Life* (Revised) by Vicki Robin, Joe Dominguez, and Monique Tilford (2008). Unlike many books that offer strategies to "get rich quick," these authors set out to help people determine when they "have enough." Their approach is centered on the simple yet profound truth that "money is something we choose to trade our life for."

From this awareness, it is possible to examine carefully not only the costs of spending money but also the costs of earning it. When one translates dollars earned and spent into life energy sacrificed, three questions naturally follow. Robin et al. suggested we ask ourselves the following:

1. Did I receive fulfillment, satisfaction, and value in proportion to the life energy spent?
2. Is this expenditure of life energy in alignment with my values and life purpose?
3. How might this expenditure change if I didn't have to work for a living?

Asking these questions of ourselves—seriously thinking about them in the short term as we go to work and make purchases and weighing them as we set goals and plan our lives for the long term—can have an enormous impact on the way we live. I know colleagues who establish their practices or take positions with agencies and then purchase homes and cars that demand virtually all of their incomes. These purchases are then followed by luxuries such as sailboats, vacation condominiums, or other "toys" for grownups. To meet these expenses, these individuals have to increase their practice or take on another position. In the end, they spend so much of their time earning money that they have almost no time to do anything but work to pay for the things they have bought. As Robin et al. (2009) remind us, the monetary cost in dollars is, in fact, paid in life energy—what we take out of life to put into "things" we can never reclaim.

Failure to think carefully about personal values and their relationship to financial matters can easily interfere with all other aspects of self-care. In extreme cases, as noted earlier, financial concerns can also interfere with sound clinical practice. Given this possibility, interns may wish to think seriously about the role of money in relation to their eventual goals and current practices. It can also be valuable to ask yourself what your purpose in life is and how your career and other activities fit within or compete with that purpose. Finally, you may find it enlightening to ask yourself what it means to have "enough" and if you are using your life energy wisely, whether you measure it in time or dollars.

REFERENCES

Adler, A. B., Bliese, P. D., & Castro C. A. (Eds.). (2011). *Deployment psychology: Evidence-based strategies to promote mental health in the military*. Washington, DC: American Psychological Association.

American Psychological Association Policy and Planning Board. (2006). APA's response to international and national disasters and crises: Addressing diverse needs. *American Psychologist, 61*, 513–521.

Arches, J. (1991). Social structure, burnout, and job satisfaction. *Social Work, 36*, 202–206.

Aten, J. D., Madson, M. B., Rice, A., & Chamberlain, A. K. (2008). Postdisaster supervision strategies for promoting supervisee self-care: Lessons learned from Hurricane Katrina. *Training and Education in Professional Psychology, 2*, 75N2.

Baird, B. N., & Carey, A. (1992, April). *The therapist cognition survey: Development, standardization, and uses*. Paper presented at the meeting of the Western Psychological Association, Portland, OR.

Baird, B. N., Carey, A., & Giakovmis, H. (1992, April). *Personal experience in psychotherapy: Differences in therapists' cognitions*. Paper presented at the meeting of the Western Psychological Association, Portland, OR.

Baker, E. K. (2002). *Caring for ourselves: A therapist's guide to personal and professional well-being*. Washington, DC: American Psychological Association.

Barnett, J. E., Baker, E. K., Elman, N. S., & Schoener, G. R. (2007). In pursuit of wellness: The self-care imperative. *Professional Psychology: Research and Practice, 38*, 603–612.

Berger, M. (1995). Sustaining the professional self: Conversations with senior psychotherapists. In M. B. Sussman (Ed.), *A perilous calling: The hazards of psychotherapy practice* (pp. 302–321). New York: Wiley.

Bike, D. H., Norcross, J. C., & Schatz, D. M. (2009). Process and outcomes of psychotherapists' personal therapy: Replication and extension 20 years later. *Psychotherapy: Theory, Research, Practice and Training, 46*, 19–31.

Bowling, U. B., & Sherman, M. D. (2008). Welcoming them home: Supporting service members and their families in navigating the task of reintegration. *Professional Psychology: Research and Practice, 39*, 451–458.

Bride, B. E. (2007). Prevalence of secondary traumatic stress among social workers. *Social Work, 52*, 63–70.

Butler, S. K., & Constantine, M. G. (2005). Collective self-esteem and burnout in professional school counselors. *Professional School Counseling, 9*, 55–63.

Callahan, T. R. (1994). Being paid for what you do. *Independent Practitioner: Bulletin of the Division of Independent Practice, Division 42 of the APA, 14*(1), 25–26.

Carroll, J. F. X., & White, W. L. (1982). Theory building: Integrating individual environmental factors within an ecological framework. In W. S. Paine (Ed.), *Job stress and burnout: Research, theory, and intervention perspectives* (pp. 41–60). Beverly Hills, CA: Sage.

Catherall, D. R. (1995). Preventing institutional secondary traumatic stress disorder. In C. R. Figley (Ed.), *Compassion fatigue: Secondary traumatic stress disorder from treating the traumatized* (pp. 1–20). New York: Bruner/Mazel.

Cook, J. M., Schnurr, P. O., & Foa, E. B. (2004). Bridging the gap between posttraumatic stress disorder research and clinical practice: The example of exposure therapy. *Psychotherapy: Theory, Research, Practice, Training, 41*, 374–387.

Courtois, C. A. (2004). Complex trauma, complex reactions: Assessment and treatment. *Psychotherapy: Theory, Research, Practice, Training, 41*, 412–425.

Creamer, M., & Forbes, D. (2004). Treatment of posttraumatic stress disorder in military and veteran populations. *Psychotherapy: Theory, Research, Practice, Training, 41*, 388–398.

Cunningham, M. (2004). Teaching social workers about trauma: Reducing the risks of vicarious traumatization in the classroom. *Journal of Social Work Education, 40*, 305–317.

Dane, B. (2000). Child welfare workers: An innovative approach for interacting with secondary trauma. *Journal of Social Work Education, 36*, 27–38.

DeAngelis, T. (2005). Things I wish I'd learned in grad school. *Monitor on Psychology, 36*(1), 54–57.

Dearing, R. L., Maddux, J. E., & Tangney, J. P. (2005). Predictors of psychological help seeking in clinical and counseling psychology graduate students. *Professional Psychology: Research and Practice, 36*, 323–329.

Deutsch, C. (1984). Self-reported sources of stress among psychotherapists. *Professional Psychology: Research and Practice, 15*, 833–845.

Dill, K. (2007). Impact of stressors on front-line child welfare supervisors. *The Clinical Supervisor, 26*, 177–193.

Dobbs, D. (2009). The post-traumatic stress trap. *Scientific American, 300*(4), 64–69.

Edelwich, J., & Brodsky, A. (1980). *Burnout: Stages of disillusionment in the helping professions.* New York: Human Science Press.

El-Ghoroury, N. H., Galper, D. I., Sawaqdeh, A., & Bufka, L. F. (2012). Stress, coping, and barriers to wellness among psychology graduate students. *Training and Education in Professional Psychology, 6*(2) 122–134.

Ellis, T. E., & Dickey, T. O. (1998). Procedures surrounding the suicide of a trainee's patient: A national survey of psychology internships and psychiatry residency programs. *Professional Psychology: Research and Practice, 29,* 492–497.

Farber, B. A. (1983a). Dysfunctional aspects of the psychotherapeutic role. In B. A. Farber (Ed.), *Stress and burnout in the human service professions* (pp. 97–118). New York: Pergamon Press.

Farber, B. A. (1983b). Introduction: A critical perspective on burnout. In B. A. Farber (Ed.), *Stress and burnout in the human service professions* (pp. 1–23). New York: Pergamon Press.

Fiore, N. (1989). *The now habit: A strategic program for overcoming procrastination and enjoying guilt-free play.* New York: St. Martin's Press.

Foster, V. A., & McAdams, Charles R., III. (1999). The impact of client suicide in counselor training: Implications for counselor education and supervision. *Counselor Education and Supervision, 39,* 22–33.

Fremont, S., & Anderson, W. (1986). What client behaviors make counselors angry: An exploratory study. *Journal of Counseling and Development, 65,* 67–70.

Freudenberger, H. J. (1974). Staff burn-out. *Journal of Social Issues, 30*(1), 159–165.

Geller, J. D., Norcross, J. C., & Orlinsky, D. E. (Eds.). (2005). *The psychotherapists' own psychotherapy: Patient and clinical perspectives.* New York: Oxford University Press.

Gleisher, K., Ford, J. D., & Fosha, D. (2008). Contrasting exposure and experiential therapies for complex post traumatic stress disorder. *Psychotherapy: Theory, Research, Practice, Training, 45,* 340–360.

Gold, S. N. (2004). The relevance of trauma to general clinical practice. *Psychotherapy: Theory, Research, Practice, Training, 41,* 363–373.

Golembiewski, R. T., & Munzenrider, R. F. (1988). *Phases of burnout: Developments in concepts and applications.* New York: Praeger.

Grosch, W. N., & Olsen, D. C. (1995). Prevention: Avoiding burnout. In M. B. Sussman (Ed.), *A perilous calling: The hazards of psychotherapy practice* (pp. 275–287). New York: Wiley.

Guy, J. D. (1987). *The personal life of the psychotherapist.* New York: Wiley.

Guy, J. D. (2000). Holding the holding environment together: Self-psychology and psychotherapist care. *Professional Psychology: Research and Practice, 31*(3), 351–352.

Hanh, T. N. (1975). *The miracle of mindfulness: An introduction to the practice of meditation.* Boston: Beacon.

Harrison, R. L., & Westwood, M. J. (2009). Preventing vicarious traumatization of mental health therapists: Identifying protective practices. *Psychotherapy: Theory, Research , Practice, Training, 46,* 203–219.

Hawkins, C. A., Smith, M. L., Hawkins, R. C. II, & Grant, D. (2005). The relationship between hours employed, perceived work interference, and grades reported by social work undergraduate students. *Journal of Social Work Education, 41,* 13–27.

Henry, D. B., Tolan, P. H., & Gorman-Smith, D. (2004). Have there been lasting effects associated with the September 11, 2001 terrorist attacks among inner-city parents and children? *Professional Psychology: Research and Practice, 35,* 542–547.

Hesse, A. R. (2002). Secondary trauma: How working with trauma survivors affects therapists. *Clinical Social Work Journal, 30,* 293–309.

Kabat-Zinn, J. (2005). *Coming to our senses.* New York: Hyperion.

Kim, H., Ji, J., & Kao, D. (2011). Burnout and physical health among social workers: A three-year longitudinal study. *Social Work, 56*(3), 258–268.

Kleespies, P. M., Smith, M. R., & Becker, B. R. (1990). Psychology interns as patient suicide survivors: Incidence, impact and recovery. *Professional Psychology: Research and Practice, 21,* 257–263.

Knox, S., Burkard, A. W., Jackson, J. A., Schaack, A. M., & Hess, S. A. (2006). Therapists-in-training who experience a client suicide: Implications for supervision. *Professional Psychology: Research and Practice, 37,* 547–557.

Kottler, J. A. (1999). *The therapist's workbook: Self-assessment, self-care, and self-improvement exercises for mental health professionals.* San Francisco: Jossey-Bass.

Kottler, J. A. (2003). *On being a therapist* (3rd ed.). San Francisco: Jossey-Bass.

Kramen-Kahn, B., & Hansen, N. (1998). Rafting the rapids: Occupational hazards, rewards, and coping strategies of psychotherapists. *Professional Psychology: Research and Practice, 29*(2), 130–134.

Kurland, R., & Salmon, R. (1992). When problems seem overwhelming: Emphases in teaching, supervision, and consultation. *Social Work, 37,* 240–244.

Lazarus, A. (2000). Multimodal replenishment. *Professional Psychology: Research and Practice, 31*(1), 93–94.

Levant, R. F. (2002). Psychology responds to terrorism. *Professional Psychology: Research and Practice, 33,* 507–509.

Litz, B. T., & Salters-Pedneault, K. (2008). Training psychologists to assess, manage, and treat posttraumatic stress disorder: An examination of the National Center for PTSD Behavioral Science Division training program. *Training and Education in Professional Psychology, 2,* 67–75.

Mangelsdorff, A. D. (2006). *Psychology in the service of national security.* Washington, DC: American Psychological Association.

Maslach, C. (1982). Understanding burnout: Definitional issues in analyzing a complex phenomenon. In W. S. Paine (Ed.), *Job stress and burnout: Research, theory, and intervention perspectives* (pp. 29–40). Beverly Hills, CA: Sage.

McKnight, J. D., & Glass, D. C. (1995). Perceptions of control, burnout and depressive symptomatology: A replication and extension. *Journal of Consulting and Clinical Psychology, 63,* 490–494.

Melamed, S., Shirom, A., Toker, S., Berliner, S., & Shapira, I. (2006). Burnout and risk of cardiovascular disease: Evidence, possible causal paths, and promising research directions. *Psychological Bulletin, 132,* 327–353.

Meyers, L. (2006). Katrina trauma lingers long. *Monitor on Psychology, 37*(5), 46.

Meyers, S. B., Sweeney, A. C., Popick, V., Wesley, K., Bordfeld, A., & Fingerhut, R. (2012). Self-care practices and perceived stress levels among psychology graduate students. *Training and Education in Professional Psychology, 9*(1), 55–66.

Michalski, D., Kohout, J., Wicherski, M., & Hart, B. (2011). 2009 doctorate employment survey. Washington, DC: American Psychological Association. Retrieved from http://www.apa.org/workforce/publications/09-doc-empl/index.aspx

Morgan, R. D., Kuther, T. L., & Habben, C. J. (2005). *Life after graduate school in psychology: Insider's advice from new psychologists.* New York: Psychology Press.

Munsey, C. (2006). Helping colleagues to help themselves. *Monitor on Psychology, 37*(7), 34–36.

Murphy, J. W., & Pardeck, J. T. (1986). The "burnout syndrome" and management style. *Clinical Supervisor, 4*(4), 35–44.

Norcross, J. C. (2000). Psychotherapist self-care: Practitioner-tested, research-informed strategies. *Professional Psychology: Research and Practice, 31,* 710–713.

Norcross, J. C. (2005). The psychotherapist's own psychotherapy: Education and developing psychologists. *American Psychologist, 60,* 837–851.

Norcross, J. C., & Guy, J. D. (2005). The prevalence and parameters of personal therapy in the United States. In J. D. Geller, J. C. Norcross, & D. E. Orlinsky (Eds.), *The psychotherapists' own psychotherapy: Patient and clinician perspectives* (pp. 165–176). New York: Oxford University Press.

Norcross, J. C., & Guy, J. D. (2007). *Leaving it at the office.* New York: Guilford Press.

O'Conner, M. F. (2001). On the etiology and effective management of professional distress and impairment among psychologists. *Professional Psychology: Research and Practice, 32,* 345–350.

Oliver, M. N. I., Bernstein, J. H., Anderson, K. G., Blashfield, R. K., & Roberts, M. C. (2004). An exploratory examination of student attitudes toward "impaired" peers in clinical psychology training programs. *Professional Psychology: Research and Practice, 35,* 141–147.

Orlinsky, D. E., & Rønnestad, M. H. (2005). *How psychotherapists develop: A study of therapeutic work and professional growth.* Washington, DC: American Psychological Association.

Osborn, C. J. (2004). Seven salutary suggestions for counselor stamina. *Journal of Counseling and Development, 82,* 319–328.

Pfefferbaum, B., Houston, J. B., Reyes, G., Steinberg, A. M., Pynoos, R. S., Fairbank, J. A.,…& Maida, C. A. (2010). Building a national capacity for child and family disaster mental health research. *Professional Psychology: Research and Practice, 41,* 26–33.

Pines, A. (1982). Changing organizations: Is a work environment without burnout an impossible goal? In W. S. Paine (Ed.), *Job stress and burnout: Research, theory, and intervention perspectives* (pp. 189–212). Beverly Hills, CA: Sage.

Pines, A., & Aronson, E. (1988). *Career burnout: Causes and cures.* New York: Free Press.

Reamer, F. G. (1992). The impaired social worker. *Social Work, 37,* 165–170.

Reyes, G., & Elhai, J. D. (2004). Psychosocial interventions in the early phases of disasters. *Psychotherapy: Theory, Research, Practice, Training, 41,* 399–411.

Roach, L. F., & Young, M. E. (2007). Do counselor education programs promote wellness in their students? *Counselor Education and Supervision, 47,* 29–45.

Roberts, J. K. (1987). The life management model: Coping with stress through burnout. *Clinical Supervisor, 5*(2), 107–118.

Robin, V., Dominquez J., & Tilford, M. (2008). *Your Money or Your* Life (Revised edition). City, State: Penguin Group (USA).

Rodolfa, E. R., Kraft, W. A., & Reilley, R. R. (1988). Stressors of professionals and trainees at APA-approved counseling and VA medical center internship sites. *Professional Psychology: Research and Practice, 19,* 43–49.

Rosen, G. M., & Lilienfeld, S. O. (2008). Posttraumatic stress disorder: An empirical evaluation of core assumptions. *Clinical Psychology Review, 28,* 837–868.

Rosenberg, J. I., Getzelman, M. A., Arcinue, F., & Oren, C. Z. (2005). An exploratory look at students' experiences of problematic peers in academic professional psychology programs. *Professional Psychology: Research and Practice, 36,* 665–673.

Rupert, P. A., & Morgan, D. J. (2005). Work setting and burnout among professional psychologists. *Professional Psychology: Research and Practice, 36,* 544–550.

Rupert, P. A., Stevanovic, P., & Hunley, H. A. (2009). Work-family conflict and burnout among practicing psychologists. *Professional Psychology: Research and Practice, 40,* 54–61.

Sammons, M. T. (2007). Letter from Camp Fallujah. *The National Psychologist, Sept/Oct,* 11.

Sanders, S., Jacobson, J. M., & Ting, L. (2008). Preparing for the inevitable: Training social workers to cope with client suicide. *Journal of Teaching in Social Work, 28,* 1–18.

Shapiro, S. L., Brown, K. W., & Biegel, G. M. (2007). Teaching self-care to caregivers: Effects of mindfulness-based stress reduction on the mental health of therapists in training. *Training and Education in Professional Psychology, 1,* 105–115.

Shen-Miller, D. S., Grus, C. L., Van Sickle, K. S., Schwartz-Mette, R., Cage, E. A., Elman, N.,…Kaslow, N. J. (2011). Trainees' experiences with peers having competence problems: A national survey. *Training and Education in Professional Psychology, 5*(2), 112–121.

Silver, R. C., Holman, E. A., McIntosh, D. N., Poulin, M., & Gil-Rivas, V. (2002). Nationwide longitudinal study of psychological responses to September 11. *Journal of the American Medical Association, 288,* 1235–1244.

Söderfeldt, M., Söderfeldt, B., & Warg, L. E. (1995). Burnout in social work. *Social Work, 40,* 638–646.

Sommer, C. A., (2008). Vicarious traumatization, trauma-sensitive supervision, and counselor preparation. *Counselor Education and Supervision, 48,* 61–72.

Stahl, J. B., Hill, C. E., Jacobs, T., Kleinman, S., Isenberg, D., & Stern, A. (2009). When the shoe is on the other foot: A qualitative study of intern-level trainees' perceived learning from clients. *Psychotherapy: Theory, Research, Practice, Training, 46,* 376–389.

Stevanovic, P., & Rupert, P. A. (2004). Career-sustaining behaviors, satisfactions, and stresses of professional psychologists. *Psychotherapy: Theory, Research, Practice, Training, 41,* 301–309.

Stevanovic, P., & Rupert, P. A. (2009). Work–family spillover and life satisfaction among professional psychologists. *Professional Psychology: Research and Practice, 40,* 62–68.

Stoesen, L. (2005). NASW responds to Katrina's impact. *NASW News, 50*(10). Retrieved from http://www.socialworkers.org/pubs/news/2005/11/katrina.asp?back=yes

Strom T. Q., Gavian, M. E., Possis, E., Loughlin, J., Bui, T., Linardatos, E.,…Siegel, W. (2012). Cultural and ethical considerations when working with military personnel and veterans: A primer for VA training programs. *Training and Education in Professional Psychology, 6*(2) 67–75.

Sussman, M. B. (1995). *A perilous calling: The hazards of psychotherapy practice.* New York: Wiley.

Ting, L., Jacobson, J. M., & Sanders, S. (2008) Available supports and coping behaviors of mental health social workers following fatal and nonfatal client suicidal behavior. *Social Work, 53,* 211–222.

Ting, L., Jacobson, J. M., & Sanders, S. (2011). Current levels of perceived stress among mental health social workers who work with suicidal clients. *Social Work, 56*(4) 327–336.

Trippany, R. L., Kress, V. E. W., & Wilcoxon, S. A. (2005). Preventing vicarious trauma: What counselors should know when working with trauma survivors. *Journal of Counseling and Development, 82,* 31–37.

Turner, J. A., Edwards, L. M., Eicken, I. M., Yokoyama, K., Castro, J. R., Tran, A. N., & Haggins, K. L. (2005). Intern self-care: An exploratory study into strategy use and effectiveness. *Professional Psychology: Research and Practice, 36,* 674–680.

Weaver, J. D. (1995). *Disasters: Mental health interventions.* Sarasota, FL: Professional Resource Press.

Yutrzenka B. A., & Naifeh, J. A. (2008). Traumatic stress, disaster psychology, and graduate education: Reflections on the special section and recommendations for professional psychology training. *Training and Practice in Professional Psychology, 2,* 96–102.

CHAPTER 9
ASSAULT AND OTHER RISKS

This chapter is admittedly a bit of a challenge because it addresses a topic that is not pleasant but must be dealt with. The unfortunate truth is some internship settings and the helping or health care professions in general may expose you to certain kinds of risks that are different from other professional settings and fields. Recognizing that reality can be troubling, but failing to recognize and prepare adequately can subject you, your colleagues, and clients to risks that can actually be managed if they are attended to properly. Consider two contrasting examples from my internship experience.

On the first day of my graduate internship at a Veterans' Administration (VA) hospital, the new interns took a tour of the wards, met the staff, and got a chance to talk with some of the patients. As soon as we came through the door on one of the wards, a man with wild, long, gray hair and wide, glaring eyes approached us rapidly. For some reason, the patient headed straight toward me, brought his face just a few inches from mine, and shouted some unintelligible words. Not knowing what else to do, I said "Hello." At that he smiled, then turned, and walked away mumbling to himself. That patient was acting very strangely, but he was not dangerous. Indeed, he had been diagnosed with schizophrenia some 20 years before, but he had never assaulted anyone in all that time.

Later in the same internship year, I was working with another patient whose behavior was by no means as unusual as that of the patient I just described. This man was in the hospital for treatment of depression and alcohol abuse. Throughout his stay, he had the habit of leaving the grounds on passes, visiting a nearby tavern, and returning to the ward in a highly intoxicated and belligerent state. After a series of these incidents, the staff decided he would not be allowed any spending money for a period of two weeks. When the patient, who was about 6 feet 4 inches and weighed well over 200 pounds, asked for money and a pass so he could go off grounds to purchase a watch, it was expected that he would, in fact, use the money to buy alcohol. I was given the task of explaining to him that because of his past actions, he would not be given any money.

Needless to say, the patient was not happy to learn he could not have his money that week. He argued and tried to bargain, but I insisted that he would have to wait a week. As I turned to go, he jumped over the chair, threw his hands toward my throat, and backed me against a wall. He then tried to choke me and smash my head against the wall. I was able to keep his hands away from my throat long enough for help to arrive, but it was a close call to say the least, and it left me bruised and shaken.

The possibility that you will be assaulted during an internship will depend heavily on the setting in which you work and the people with whom you interact. It will also depend on your own behaviors. Although it may be frightening to think about the possibility of an assault, the intent of this chapter is to help reduce that possibility by giving you some suggestions for preventing and responding to risks. The message is: Do not be afraid, but do be careful and prepared. I have included this chapter because it is important for interns to have an awareness of the risks involved in clinical work. It is also vital, literally, for supervisors and instructors to help students learn to reduce and cope with those risks. Unfortunately, this subject, as we will see in a moment, is too often neglected by academic programs and training sites (Lyter & Abbott, 2007).

RISKS OF ASSAULT

If the clients we worked with were all reasonable, self-controlled individuals, we would probably not encounter them in many of the settings where we work. Although most clients, even those with serious mental illness, are not dangerous, their behavior can be unpredictable. Those who work with people committed to psychiatric hospitals should be aware that in most states, the criteria for involuntary commitment specify that such individuals must be considered dangerous to themselves or others. Thus, in any setting where patients are involuntarily committed, or in group homes and other facilities for people who have previously been hospitalized, the possibility of violence must be taken seriously. Risks may be even higher if you are working in jails, prisons, or juvenile justice facilities with criminal offenders.

The potential for violence must also be taken into account when one is working with victims or perpetrators of domestic violence. Home visits can also pose an especially high risk (Lyter & Abbott, 2007). Finally, in whatever setting you work, keep in mind that you will encounter some people who, in addition to or as part of their mental illness, are simply mean and dangerous.

The federal Occupational Safety and Health Administration (OSHA) has produced a series of Guidelines for Preventing Workplace Violence for Health Care & Social Service Workers (http://www.osha.gov/Publications/OSHA3148/osha3148.html).

Included with these guidelines are statistics from the Department of Justice (DOJ) National Crime Victimization Survey for 1993 to 1999. According to these data:

> The average annual rate for nonfatal violent crime for all occupations was 12.6 per 1,000 workers. The average annual rate for physicians was 16.2; for nurses, 21.9; for mental health professionals, 68.2; and for mental health custodial workers, 69.

What is most striking about these numbers is that mental health figures are fivefold greater than the average across all occupations. The OSHA report goes on to note: "As significant as these numbers are, the actual number of incidents is probably much higher." This is due to underreporting, perhaps because assaults are considered "part of the job" in many mental health settings and thus are not reported. More recent government data come from the Bureau of Labor Statistics (BLS), which OSHA cites as indicating that in 2010 health care and human service workers were victims of approximately 11, 370 assaults by persons (OSHA http://www.osha.gov/SLTC/healthcarefacilities/violence.html).

Whereas the OSHA and BLS data report on broad categories of assaults within the mental health field, the professional literature provides insights into the frequency of assaults within specific professions. For example, Criss (2010) cites studies suggesting that between 65% to 85% of social workers have, at some point in their careers, encountered violence by a client. Ringstad (2005) found that among a national sample of social workers, 62% reported they had been the target of psychological or physical abuse.

The incidence of assault and violent experiences has been studied less frequently among trainees than among established practitioners, but the results are consistent and reveal that the risk of violence is real for trainees and may, in some instances, be even higher. Gately and Stabb (2005) found that among trainees surveyed from counseling psychology graduate programs, 10% of the respondents had been the victims of violence, and 26% reported that they had witnessed client violence. Criss's (2010) data from a national sample of social work students indicated that 41.7% of respondents had experienced some exposure to some form of violence, which in this study's definition included verbal abuse or observation of violence. Although the most common experience (37.5%) involved verbal abuse, 3.5% of respondents reported being physically assaulted.

Other dangerous and intimidating behaviors have been studied and are not uncommon in the mental health professions. Purcell, Powell, and Mullen (2005) studied the experience of stalking by clients of psychologists practicing in Australia. Their results revealed a lifetime prevalence of 20% among their respondents, with 8% experiencing stalking within the past 12 months. Romans, Hays, and White (1996) reported a somewhat lower but still troubling frequency, finding that out of a sample of 178 counseling staff members, 5.6% reported that they had been stalked, and 10% had a supervisee who had been stalked by current or former clients. Those findings are consistent with the research of Gentile, Asamen, Harmell, and Weathers (2002), who also reported an incidence rate of about 10% among their respondents and, interestingly, found no significant differences

in race, gender, or other variables between respondents who had been stalked versus those who had not been stalked.

Although less severe than stalking, 64% of the sample studied by Romans et al. (1996) had experienced some form of harassment by clients. Sexual harassment of female therapists by clients is also not uncommon, as reported by deMayo (1997), who found that more than half of the psychologists responding to a survey reported having experienced sexual harassment from clients at some point in their practice. Anecdotal reports of female interns indicate that sexual harassment and intimidation at internships are a particular concern, especially for younger women.

These findings should not be taken to mean that most clients are dangerous. In fact, most clients do not pose a high risk of assault, harassment, or other threatening behaviors. The frequencies just described derive more from the large number of clients that clinicians encounter during their careers. As a result, even though only a small proportion are likely to be assaultive or threatening, over time there is a good chance that a clinician will encounter numerous clients who are potentially assaultive. Despite the very real risk of assault during one's career, training for dealing with assault is seldom adequate (Lyter & Abbott, 2007).

INADEQUACY OF TRAINING

Notwithstanding the frequent incidents of violence experienced or witnessed by their respondents, Gately and Stabb (2005) found that trainees rated their preparation to deal with violence as inadequate on every topic presented, including assessment for violence, prevention strategies, safety at the workplace, intervention strategies, and self-defense. Spencer and Munch (2003) described similar gaps in training, noting that prominent social work programs they studied made no mention of safety issues in their curricula or their field placement manuals. Spencer and Munch found this disappointing in light of prior research showing the relatively high risk of assault and the comparative lack of adequate training.

Before continuing, one important caveat must be presented. The following discussion is intended to increase your awareness of how you can guard against violent assault. It does not claim to teach you how to identify or predict violence. As will be explained shortly, research on the prediction of violence suggests that the accuracy of such predictions tends to be low, even among those who believe they are able to assess the potential for violence well. Thus, while you seek to improve your understanding of violence, keep in mind the limitations of your own knowledge and those of the research within the profession.

COPING WITH AGGRESSION

Coping with the possibility of aggression involves a combination of knowledge and associated behavioral skills (Tishler, Gordon, & Landry-Meyer, 2000). Underlying all these suggestions is the basic principle that whenever you encounter a situation that is beyond your abilities or that poses significant risks, you must inform your supervisor and instructor. This is particularly important in the case of potentially violent clients. If you have reason to believe that someone you work with may be likely to harm himself or herself or may be dangerous to others, you must let your supervisor know so that staff can take appropriate action to prevent the client and anyone else from being harmed. Do not try to deal with such situations by yourself unless there is absolutely no alternative. In that case, one of your primary goals should be to obtain assistance as soon as possible.

With the awareness that you must contact your supervisor if you think a client or situation may be dangerous, consider the following factors in assessing, preventing, and coping with violence:

1. Understanding that strange and unusual behavior may be distressing but is not necessarily a sign of dangerousness.
2. Understanding developmental differences in clients and recognizing why clients of different ages may act aggressively.
3. Understanding and recognizing motivational factors that may contribute to aggression.
4. Understanding and recognizing situations in which clients may become assaultive.
5. Recognizing individuals who are more likely to be dangerous and assessing both the likelihood and the lethality of the risk.
6. Preventing violence through early establishment of relationships and expectations.
7. Preventing violence that appears imminent.
8. Coping with assault in a way that minimizes harm to yourself and to the client, staff, and setting.
9. Dealing with the emotional aftereffects of an assault.
10. Debriefing to understand why violence occurred and how it can be prevented in the future.

In addition to the discussion that follows, for excellent reviews of strategies for managing violent patients in mental health settings, see Gately and Stabb (2005); Lutzker (2006); Spencer and Munch (2003); Tishler et al. (2000); and Dunkel, Ageson, and Ralph (2000). For thorough discussions of violence risk assessment, I recommend Douglas and Skeem (2005); Haggard-Grann (2007); Quinsey, Harris, Rice, and Cormier (2006); and Skeem, Miller, Mulvey, Tiemann, and Monahan (2005).

STRANGE BEHAVIOR AND STRANGE PEOPLE ARE NOT NECESSARILY DANGEROUS

People with mental illnesses are sometimes described as "disturbed," but a more accurate description would be that they are "disturbing to others." There is something very troubling about individuals who say and do things that we do not understand and do not fit the norm. Most of us become uneasy when we see a man on a street corner talking in response to voices we cannot hear or a woman who sits staring and snarling at a vision we cannot see.

There are probably two reasons for this. First, we are afraid that if people are acting strangely in one way, all their behaviors may be unpredictable and possibly dangerous. Second, and equally important, we do not know how to respond to people who act so differently from the way we do.

In your experience as an intern, you will probably encounter individuals who are at least in some ways not like the people you

spend time with in your life away from the internship. Depending on how different the clients and the settings are from what you are familiar with, you may feel uneasy both about the clients and about yourself. This is normal and is nothing to feel bad or ashamed about. As you gain experience, you will gradually feel more comfortable, and by the end of your internship, you will take it for granted that you work in a setting and with people who may have once seemed strange or intimidating.

UNDERSTAND DEVELOPMENTAL DIFFERENCES

A 5-year-old throwing a temper tantrum, a 21-year-old starting a fistfight, and a 70-year-old with Alzheimer's disease may all engage in assaultive behavior, but the reasons for the assault and the consequences for the individual and the staff members are different in each case. Although much of the material in this chapter applies to clients of all ages, developmental differences require that we adjust our thinking and behavioral responses to match the age and developmental level of each client.

EXERCISE

Take a moment to think about the three clients just mentioned (i.e., the 5-year-old, the 21-year-old, and the 70-year-old). How do the individuals differ, and how do the differences influence what you would think and do about possible aggression? Among the factors to consider are the individual's peer group and peer-group norms regarding violence, the message that violence communicates for each person, the physical and mental capacity of the person to inflict serious harm to people or property, the person's understanding of and attitudes toward the consequences of a violent act, and the person's motivation. Many of these considerations will be addressed in a moment, but exploring them first yourself will deepen your appreciation of the causes of aggression in clients.

UNDERSTAND AND RECOGNIZE MOTIVATIONAL FACTORS

In his book *The Gift of Fear: Survival Signals That Protect Us from Violence,* Gavin DeBecker (1997) uses the acronym JACA to help explain and predict violence. DeBecker, who consults with celebrities, corporations, and others who might face violence, has studied hundreds of violent encounters and individuals. He explains that most people who engage in violence can be understood by considering their *j*ustification, *a*lternatives, *c*onsequences, and *a*bility. In other words, people who are likely to act violently typically feel their violence would be justified in some way, believe they have few alternatives to violence, can accept or in some cases even desire the consequences that might befall them for their actions, and have the ability to carry out the violent action against their victims. In the following discussion, each of these elements can be seen in the suggestions for assessing violence potential and the recommendations for reducing the risks of violence.

When students are asked why people behave violently, the most common response is that they are angry. This is often true, but it does not explain why violence is chosen as a behavior instead of some other response to anger. Focusing on anger as a cause of violence also ignores several other important motivational factors. These include violence as a response to fear, as a response to frustration, and as a way of controlling people. Dubin (1989) emphasized that many patients who become violent are in

> a desperate and panic-stricken struggle to prevent their imagined annihilation, either through the destruction of their physical selves or, even more frightening at times, through the destruction of their self-esteem. (p. 1280)

Dubin further observed:

> Paradoxically, clinical staff who are anxious and frightened by a patient whose behavior is escalating toward violence may react with an authoritarian or counteraggressive response that increases the patient's feelings of helplessness. (p. 1280)

If someone is angry and may become violent, it helps to first try to determine why he or she is angry, and then consider why violence is a possible response. Often, you can ask directly by saying something like, "I can see that you're upset about something and seem pretty angry. Can you tell me what's going on that has you so upset?" This message, which is not threatening or authoritarian, acknowledges that you recognize the person's present state and are interested in trying to understand it better.

If someone appears likely to become violent, it is probably not advisable to say directly that you are afraid of that possibility. It may, however, be worth asking how the person is feeling at the moment. One way of doing this is to simply address the person directly by name and in a calm but direct voice say, "Tell me how you're feeling right now."

This may bring the client's feelings out so that both of you can explore what to do with those feelings. If a client responds by shouting at you or making threatening comments, a possible response would be to say calmly, "I understand that you are upset, and I want to listen to what you have to say." This is much more likely to be effective than a command, such as "Calm down," when the person is obviously not interested at that moment in being told what to do or in calming down.

One reason it is important to try to begin a dialog with someone who appears angry is that we may not know or understand what he or she is upset about. Some clients become angry because they feel insulted by another client or a staff member. Others may respond with anger to frustrations at work or elsewhere in their lives. For another group, anger is a habitual response to any situation in which they feel insecure. The initial task facing the clinician is to try to understand the person in the moment, not to make a judgment about whether or not the anger is an "appropriate" response to a situation. That process may be useful later when a client is in a condition that makes exploration possible, but in a highly agitated emotional state, people are not likely to be open to exploring in the abstract whether their anger is justified.

As part of the process of trying to understand why a person may appear angry, it helps to recognize that what appears as angry behavior may not necessarily be a result of anger. As mentioned, violent behavior may be the result of fear, not anger. I have seen clients become violent when they were pressured too strongly to deal with an issue. A case that comes to mind involved a wheelchair-mobile, head-injured patient who struck a staff member who was attempting to transfer him to a toilet against his wishes. When the patient was asked about the incident later, he revealed that he was not so much angry as frightened that he could fall. When he did not feel anyone was listening or giving him an alternative, he panicked and struck out. Had his therapist recognized his emotional status and acknowledged the legitimate basis for it, the patient might have been able to express his fear verbally and thereby deal with the situation differently.

Whereas most beginning clinicians find violence that grows out of anger or fear understandable, violence displayed for intentional intimidation or manipulation tends to be more difficult to understand and manage. Some people have learned in their lives that violence is a way to get what they want, and they do not really care if it hurts others or even themselves in the process. In the case of these individuals, violence may be a response to anger or frustration, but it may also be a calculated means of achieving a desired end.

Again, whenever you are confronted by a situation that is beyond your abilities or that appears to pose a risk, you must seek help. If you find yourself faced with a client who threatens violence as a manipulative tool, your best choice as an intern is to seek assistance from someone in the setting who has more training and authority.

SITUATIONAL FACTORS AND VIOLENCE

Along with considering a person's developmental stage and motivations, you should also evaluate immediate situational factors and conditions that might increase the potential for violence. Douglas and Skeem (2005) distinguished between "risk status" and "risk state," with the former being largely static features of the individual's character, and the latter referring to dynamic situational factors within the environment and the individual. Using this approach, Douglas and Skeem advocated moving from violence prediction to violence prevention and reduction by recognition and manipulation of situational contributors to violence. They emphasized that "violence typically has no single cause. Instead, violence is a transactional process that likely reflects multiple causal risk factors and pathways; it is multiply determined" (p. 352).

In recognition of this reality, what are some of the dynamic situational factors that can contribute to or reduce the likelihood of violence? Important situational factors include similarities between the present situation and previous incidents, recent or immediate stress, the presence or absence of certain prescription medications (some of which may decrease assault potential, whereas others may increase it), alcohol or other drug intoxication, the client's cognitive functioning, the power differential between the client and responding staff, and obvious signs such as gestures or weapons that reveal violent intentions. Douglas and Skeem (2005) focused particular attention on the internal dynamics of individuals, including variations in negative affect, psychosis, and interpersonal relationships. These elements and others are addressed in the discussion that follows.

SIMILARITIES TO PAST SITUATIONS

A fundamental principle of psychology is that previous behavior is the best predictor of later behavior. If a person has a history of violence that follows certain patterns, be attentive to those patterns and any similarities to the present situation. For example, if an individual's history of violence is exclusively confined to assaults on women, the risk factor would be higher for women than for men. Although there are no guarantees that men are immune to assaults from such clients, female staff members should obviously use special care in dealing with them. Other factors to consider would be patterns in locations and times of assaults, weapons used, and specific stimuli that appear to have triggered assaults in the past. Recognizing such factors may enable one to control them and thereby prevent or at least anticipate and deal more effectively with the risk of violence.

STRESS

Stress is a situational factor that is often related to violence. In general, whether or not a person has a history of violence, the level of stress he or she has been experiencing may increase the likelihood of a violent act. A client may seem to be coping relatively well, but if several unfortunate events, such as a quarrel with a significant other, getting fired at work, a traffic accident, or some other event, all happen in proximity, the client might feel overwhelmed and act out violently in response.

Before or during interactions with clients, we should keep in mind the stresses they have been under and how they have coped with stress in the past. If a client has a history of responding violently when stressed, we should be particularly careful. We should ask what alternatives he or she has other than violence. Is this client able to deal with difficulties in any other way than through violence? Has he or she had success in the past doing so? To the extent that a client has a history of violence, lacks alternative behaviors, and is under stress, the potential for violence is likely to increase.

CONTROLLED SUBSTANCES AND MEDICATIONS

Along with situational factors, certain intoxicating substances and drugs can also increase the likelihood of aggression (Skeem et al., 2005). Alcohol continues to be the most commonly used and abused drug. Alcohol has disinhibiting effects that make some individuals feel invulnerable and that lessen their awareness of fear or pain. Other drugs, such as methamphetamines, tend to produce excitation; feelings of invincibility; and, in some cases, paranoia. This combination of energy, invincibility, and paranoia is extremely volatile. Phenylcyclohexylpiperidine (PCP), or "angel dust," is another drug well known for its ability to precipitate sudden and lasting psychoses, with violent, almost unrestrainable outbursts typical of the acute phase of intoxication. Trying to reason with someone who is influenced by any of these substances may bring little or no success, and the person has a relatively high potential for violence.

Certain prescription medications that may reduce the potential for violence are available; antipsychotic, antimanic, and antiseizure medications have long been used to control violent behavior both in inpatient settings and in the community. For clients taking medications to help control their behavior, the risk of assault may increase if the client fails to take the medications. One of the questions mental health crisis-response teams routinely ask is, "Are you taking your medications?" If a client has not been taking medications as prescribed, the potential for unpredictable behavior goes up. Keep in mind, however, that although correctly prescribed psychotropic medications may help reduce the risk of violence, there is evidence that some medications have the potential to increase the risk in certain client groups.

CLIENT MENTAL STATUS

Related to the effects of both prescription drugs and illegal substances is the more general question of the person's state of consciousness and awareness. Is the client capable of reasoning effectively and controlling his or her own behavior? Although it is possible to reason with many clients who appear to be at risk for violence, in some cases conscious awareness is so clouded that reasoning is not possible or practical. For example, some patients with brain injuries or illnesses and other neurologic impairments may not be in control of their own behaviors or capable of understanding what people say or do to them. These patients may act violently not out of an intention to hurt anyone but because they are confused and frightened and do not understand their situations or the people who are trying to treat them.

As noted earlier, people exhibiting certain severe psychiatric symptoms may also pose a risk of violence that is closely connected to their state of awareness. Clients in an acute phase of mania are not likely to listen well to calm discussion. Individuals with paranoid ideation may well interpret whatever is said to them as a sign of trickery. The problem each of these conditions poses for treatment staff is that it cannot be assumed that normal approaches to talking or reasoning will have any effect. In some instances, the client's mental and behavioral functioning may be so severely out of control that only physical or pharmacologic measures will be able to prevent them from hurting themselves or others. Failure to recognize or acknowledge such situations may place the helping professional or the client in danger of being injured.

Some clients, particularly those suffering from certain neurologic conditions or drug intoxication, may not be able to control their behavior regardless of the situation or consequences. There are, however, times when clients who seem to be out of control will be able to regain control if they recognize that they will not benefit from violence. To the extent that clients are capable of functioning cognitively and can recognize that they are in a less powerful position, the potential for aggression is likely to decrease. Even highly agitated and threatening clients with schizophrenia will often become cooperative without a struggle if enough staff members confront them with an overwhelming physical presence and provide an alternative to violence. It is therefore in the client's best interests that the staff be aware of the influence of this factor in dealing with potentially or actively violent individuals. Approaching a truly dangerous situation with too little power may indirectly encourage someone who is predisposed to act aggressively. Having insufficient support also tends to increase the likelihood of injuries to staff or clients if an altercation does ensue.

WEAPONS

Finally, as part of routine intake assessments, clinicians should ask clients and families about their access to and use of firearms. Slovak, Brewer, and Carlson (2008) emphasized the value of assessing the risk factor of firearms in suicide prevention, and this information is no less important in assessing the risk for violent behavior. Unfortunately, when these authors surveyed a large group of licensed independent social workers, they found that only 34% of respondents reported that they routinely assessed for firearm ownership or access.

Whereas routine assessment of firearm access should be standard practice, if a client's immediate behavior suggests that he or she may be dangerous and there is evidence or reason to suspect he or she is armed, one should be especially careful. There is a true account of a patient who entered a clinic carrying a gun and demanding to see a therapist. The therapist was called and was warned that the man had a gun, but the therapist nevertheless came out to talk with the him. As soon as the therapist entered the waiting room, he was shot and killed by the patient (Annis & Baker, 1986).

This tragedy perhaps could not be prevented, but it is easy to imagine a similar situation in which a therapist either overestimates his or her ability to manage a situation or fails to accurately assess the client's intentions. Without blaming the victims in such cases, we need to understand that if a person looks menacing and has the means to cause damage, we must take the risks seriously. If a client overtly threatens violence, either by announcing an intent to hurt someone or with physical signs such as clenching fists, holding a weapon, exercise extreme caution and summon help. Your task as an intern is to learn, but you do not have to lay down your life or be injured in the process.

RECOGNIZE POTENTIALLY DANGEROUS INDIVIDUALS

It is extremely difficult to assess dangerousness with any useful accuracy. In part, this is due to the "low-base-rate" phenomenon (Meehl, 1973). In essence, this means that because only a small percentage of individuals engage in violent assault, even a highly accurate test is likely to produce a substantial number of misdiagnoses of dangerousness.

Partly because of the low-base-rate problem, some studies suggest that our ability to identify the dangerous personality is not very good, so clinicians' predictions of which clients will or will not exhibit violence are often less accurate than chance guesses would be (Janofsky, Spears, & Neubauer, 1988; Monahan, 1988). More recent studies, however, have countered this conclusion, suggesting that mental health professionals may, in fact, be able to predict violence more accurately than chance, particularly if they use structured tools to assist in their predictions and, importantly, if those tools are applied to the types of client groups and settings for which the instruments were validated (Haggard-Grann, 2007).

McNiel, Gregory, Lam, Binder, and Sullivan (2003) studied the accuracy of three instruments designed to predict violence during acute psychiatric hospitalization. Their results showed that for purposes of predicting violence in the near term in acute treatment settings, measures of a client's current clinical profile are more likely to be accurate than historical information. Mossman (1994) utilized quantitative techniques for studying "receiver operating characteristics" and reviewed more than 40 studies of violence prediction. On the basis of this review, he concluded that although professionals may be able to do better than chance in predicting violence, the best predictor of all appears to be the client's past behavior:

> Past behavior alone appears to be a better long-term predictor of future behavior than clinical judgments and may also be a better indicator than cross-validated actuarial techniques. (p. 783)

The message from this research is that we may be able to do somewhat better than simply guessing, but we should be cautious about trusting our subjective impressions of who is or is not likely to be dangerous. At the same time, however, we may be able to reduce the uncertainty to a certain extent by considering a few things that are known about dangerousness. The goal here is not to give you the impression that you are competent to diagnose dangerousness. Rather, it is to provide a framework that will help you structure your thinking about dealing with clients and the issue of dangerousness. With this information, you may be able to assess clients and situations more carefully and reduce at least some of the risks.

What do we know, if anything, about predicting dangerousness in individuals? First, as mentioned, previous behavior is the best predictor of future behavior. Thus, a person who has a history of violent assaults, especially if those assaults are recent, presents a greater risk than someone with no record of assaults (Mossman, 1994). This seems like common sense, and it is, but we often forget to find out about clients' histories before interacting with them. The obvious way of reducing this risk is to include questions about previous violence or criminal acts as part of an intake history. Family members or friends can corroborate this information if they have accompanied the client to the intake. Wherever possible, it behooves the clinician to review intake notes and case histories before interacting with clients.

If a person has a history of violence, we should ask what the consequences have been and whether the client has learned anything from those consequences that would either increase or decrease the likelihood of further violence. For some people, violence has worked very well as a behavior choice. Although we tend to think of the downside of violence, it can also bring a person power, status, money, self-esteem, protection, momentary release of tension, and a host of other desirable consequences. We forget this at our peril. If someone has learned from experience that violence works, there is an increased likelihood that this person will resort to it again. There are also clients whose violence may have brought on negative consequences but who have failed to learn from their experiences. This diminished ability to learn from experience is characteristic of the sociopathic or antisocial personality.

Skeem et al. (2005) focused attention on the relationship between psychopathy and violence and the predictive power of certain aspects of the psychopathic profile. Their research suggested that the strongest relationship with violence exists for the "antagonism" component of psychopathic personalities. Antagonism was defined in their study as "a highly interpersonal construct that includes such traits as suspiciousness, combativeness, deceptiveness, lack of empathy, and arrogance" (p. 461). On the basis of this finding, Skeem et al. recommended that greater attention be given to personality factors, especially those of antagonism, as part of clinical assessments and efforts to predict and reduce violence.

Finally, although there is great variability among people in different diagnostic groups, certain diagnoses and symptoms may suggest an increased potential for dangerousness. In considering these groups, it must be emphasized that the majority of clients in each group are not likely to be violent. Although there may be an increased potential for someone with a given diagnosis to act aggressively as compared with someone who has a different diagnosis, just knowing a diagnosis provides little basis for concluding that a client is dangerous. With these caveats in mind, symptoms and diagnostic factors that may indicate increased risk of assault include clients for whom assault is a presenting problem, personality disorders (Haller & Deluty, 1990), delusions or hallucinations, manic disorders (Janofsky et al., 1988), and clients exhibiting both self-destructiveness during hospitalization and suicidal behavior before hospitalization (Hillbrand, 1995).

ASSESSING OURSELVES IN RELATION TO VIOLENCE ASSESSMENT

Doing a better job of assessing the risks posed by certain clients and situations is only part of the challenge. We also need to frankly assess how we deal with issues of violence. Even if we are aware of past violence, we sometimes disregard or discount the information and fail to deal with it realistically or strategically. In my own experience of assault by a patient, one mistake I made was to not fully appreciate the fact that the person in question was not given a pass precisely because of his belligerent behavior on returning from previous outings. A second mistake was to not have support available to deter or respond to violence if it occurred. Similarly, and with a more tragic outcome, the case notes of the patient described earlier who shot and killed the psychiatrist showed that the patient had previously made direct threats to kill his doctors.

The potential to ignore or discount past behavior may be due to carelessness, but it may also reflect our need to believe we are somehow more able than others to deal with people. Overestimating our own capacity, we confidently reason that merely because a patient is violent with others does not mean he or she will be violent with us. In some cases, this may be true, but most of the time we base this assumption more on ego than on real data, and it may take us into dangerous situations. In my own clinical and supervisory experience, I have found that this tendency is even more likely when one is dealing with people diagnosed with borderline disorders, who, paradoxically, may simultaneously be more dangerous and more likely to lead therapists to believe that they are immune from risk because they are somehow special.

Lyter and Abbott (2007), in their review of the risks posed by home visits, provided a particularly valuable discussion of what they called home visitor "styles." They identified five styles: (1) "frightened/avoidant," (2) "clueless," (3) "naïve/compassionate," (4) "bravado," and (5) "informed." These titles are almost self-explanatory, but the tremendously important message they carry is that we need to not only assess clients, we must also assess ourselves and, in some cases, our colleagues to understand how and why we may deal with different types of potentially dangerous clients or situations.

A tendency to overestimate one's own uniqueness or invulnerability was well illustrated by the following situation: A patient who had assaulted several people during the previous two-month period was being transported between wards by a nurse who had been well informed of the case but had never worked with the patient before. Despite the patient's recent actions and the nurse's lack of personal experience with him, she felt that he would not harm her because "she had a way with patients." On leaving the locked ward, the nurse, against policy, released restraints that had been holding the patient's hands to a belt around his waist. Seconds after he was released, the patient viciously attacked the nurse. Her life was saved only because of quick intervention by several coworkers who had witnessed the events from a nearby window.

There is a place for compassion, but there is also a place for caution, and the two are by no means mutually exclusive. If excessive self-confidence, an over-reliance on the protection of compassion, or simple cluelessness leads us to do something foolish, we are not acting out of compassion, we are acting out of egotistical needs that serve neither our best interests nor those of clients.

EARLY PREVENTION OF VIOLENCE

The best way to deal with violence is to prevent it. The importance of accurately assessing personal and situational variables has been discussed. Next we consider how what we say or do can lessen or increase the potential for violence.

The best prevention of violence is good clinical work. If you are skillful at understanding clients and building therapeutic relationships, you will lessen the likelihood of becoming the target of violence. This does not mean that people who are assaulted are therefore at fault or are, by definition, poor clinicians. Nor does it mean that because you assume you are above average in your clinical abilities (as most of us do), you are protected from harm. It does, however, mean that the way you interact with clients in any given situation will influence their behavior in later situations. It also means that by building positive relationships and a system of interacting that gives clients alternatives to violence, clinicians can reduce clients' potential to resort to violence.

This principle was modeled by a special education teacher who had some of the toughest, most disruptive students in the school together in one classroom. When other teachers heard of the combination of students in the class, they offered their condolences and remarked how awful it must be for the teacher. In fact, her classroom was surprisingly peaceful. This teacher's secret was not in some overpowering discipline technique. Instead, she treated the students in a way that showed she respected them and cared for them and that she expected the same treatment in return. She emphasized their accomplishments and got to know each one as an individual. When discipline was needed, she was firm, fair, and consistent. She also made it a point to touch each student in some way and to speak to each one by name every day. As a result, she did not have to deal with dangerous situations because she built a positive atmosphere that prevented such events from developing or escalating.

The setting of your internship or clinical work may not be identical to the classroom just described, but there will be parallels that relate to prevention. Whatever the situation, it is valuable for clinicians to ask themselves if they are paying enough attention to developing the positive side of relationships, setting and modeling expectations of respectful behavior, and setting limits and clear consequences for violent or aggressive behavior.

Prevention also involves being aware of settings and situations that might increase the risk of violence. Lyter and Abbott (2007) offered a particularly useful checklist for visit preparation, visit management, and crisis management for social workers making home visits. This list includes assessing the setting as well as the client, considering situational factors, not being alone with potentially violent people, knowing the community, and utilizing technology to enhance safety. I believe that this list, with situation-specific and client-specific additions as needed, should be standard operating procedure and a mandatory checklist used for all mental health professionals and interns who visit clients in field settings. If your internship involves home visits, I encourage you to ask if there is such a checklist that is used before each and every visit. If there is not, you may want to suggest that this practice be initiated and may wish to perform your own checklist review even if one is not required by your placement.

We tend to think of client interactions as occurring in homes or institutional settings, but they can also occur in automobiles, which can be another potentially high-risk setting. You should be especially cautious if asked to transport a client somewhere in a vehicle. The risks of something happening in a car are heightened, of course, because if one were assaulted, it would be especially difficult to defend oneself while trying to maintain control of the vehicle. What is more, it may also happen that a client would seek to gain control of the vehicle in order to effect some form of escape or for other purposes. Because of these dangers, I recommend that interns use extreme care if asked to drive a client somewhere. If you are at all concerned about safety, you should either insist on appropriate precautions such as the presence of other staff or the use of restraints if called for. If such precautions are not available, I encourage you to refuse the request. If this upsets someone, you can deal with that a whole lot easier than you can deal with a violent attack or a car wreck.

INSTITUTIONAL RESPONSES TO THREATS OF VIOLENCE

Given the clients and problems addressed in clinical work, it is neither surprising nor uncommon for clients to communicate threats directed either toward specific staff members or at an institution, such as a hospital or mental health center. As noted at the outset, the Occupational Safety and Health Administration has published detailed and useful guidelines for preventing workplace violence for health care and social service workers (OSHA, 2006). These guidelines note that all employers have a duty to provide a workplace free from recognized hazards. This implies that clinical settings must take proactive measures to reduce risks posed by violent clients or other hazards.

The OSHA guidelines suggest that the basis for efforts to reduce the risk of violence is an explicit written program with clear goals and objectives. Included within this program should be a zero-tolerance policy for workplace violence, protections for employees who report violence, a system for prompt reporting, a comprehensive plan for maintaining security, a strategy with individuals specifically responsible for appropriate training and skills, an affirmative management commitment to worker safety, and a comprehensive worksite analysis of risks. Employee responsibilities are also key to making any system work. The OSHA guidelines emphasize that employees must understand and comply with violence-prevention plans, actively participate in and apply violence prevention and response training, and report any violence they observe or experience. Other useful elements of the OSHA guidelines include practical suggestions for evaluating and modifying the physical aspects of institutions, such as locks, hazardous material storage, potential weapons, automobiles, security, and so on. Finally, there are also suggestions for what should be included in violence-response training and for establishing proactive programs to help workers who happen to experience an assault or violent act. To help ensure that all these measures are implemented, the OSHA website offers a number of useful checklists and self-evaluation instruments.

Recommendations comparable with the OSHA guidelines are also found in the professional literature. For example, Spencer and Munch (2003) provided an excellent review of the risks faced by social workers and offered comprehensive, practical suggestions and a self-assessment checklist that agencies can use to reduce the risk of violence. To deal with explicit threats, such as telephoned or mailed threats of violence, Burgess et al. (1997) referred to the process of threat analysis and suggested considering many of the elements already discussed in this chapter in response to threats. Motive, intent, duration, frequency, delivery style, and level of risk to victims were all considered in their analysis. The importance of taking every threat seriously and conducting careful, step-by-step analysis of severity was given particular emphasis. In addition, Burgess et al. recommended keeping careful records of threats and assigning a team to periodically review the threats, threat management, and outcomes.

Unfortunately, just as many clinical training programs do not have structured training to help interns anticipate and deal with violence, it is also true that many institutions have not implemented the procedures and recommendations just described. One practice I recommend that interns do at their placement site is inquire about what procedures, plans, and policies are in place. I also encourage you to see if any specific training opportunities are available, and if they are, to avail yourself of them. More will be said about such training later in this chapter.

PREVENTION OF IMMINENT CLIENT VIOLENCE

The first rule of interacting with clients who appear to be agitated is to remain calm and in control. Even if you are afraid a client is about to become violent, showing fear is unlikely to help the situation and may increase the chances that the client will become violent. This is easy to say, but the threat of violence automatically evokes our physiologic flight-or-fight response. The rush of adrenaline and other sympathetic nervous system changes may help us respond physically, but they tend to impede our ability to think clearly and calmly. To help you keep your wits about you despite fear, practice stepping back physically and mentally to evaluate the situation as objectively as you can and develop a personal safety plan (Tishler et al., 2000).

As you think about a dangerous situation, try to assess quickly what you might do if attacked. Mentally scan the environment; consider your options; assess what help might be available; and, as you are speaking, move to where you will be the least vulnerable. As you consider safety and protection, try to understand what the client's motivations for violence might be. Reviewing the earlier discussion of motivation may be helpful and can suggest possible responses to each of the different motivations. In what you say and do, try to acknowledge the client's distress but do not validate physical aggression as a response. It is important to not ignore threats but to convey that you have noticed and are responding to the client's distress.

For example, if a client is responding out of fear, you can seek to lessen the fear. Giving the client physical space, facing the client from the side instead of directly in front, holding your hands low and relaxed, speaking calmly, and reassuring the client that he or she is safe may all help lessen fear and the potential for violence. It may also help to say something like, "I can see you are upset, and I would like to help. What can I do?" This statement lets clients know that you are aware of their condition, and, by asking what they want to do, it offers them a sense of control that may lessen their fear.

In all cases of possible violence, it is important to speak clearly and simply. This is especially important if you determine that the client is confused or disoriented. Short, direct sentences that give specific information are advisable. Sometimes you may need to orient patients to who and where they are and who you are. For example, to a disoriented client you might say, "Mr. Smith, you are in a hospital. I am your therapist. Let's sit down and talk." Note how short the sentences are and how each expresses only a small bit of information at a time. In practice, each sentence might best be followed by a brief pause to allow the client to process the information before the next sentence is spoken. These sentences also give specific instructions, because in this instance the person's own thought processes may be so disrupted that he or she cannot determine what to do.

Along with remembering what you should do in dealing with clients, it is also important to know what not to do. Actions to avoid include arguing with the client, making threats that the client knows cannot be carried out, and challenging or daring the client to be violent. You may be able to argue with coworkers and friends without getting in a fight, but this does not always apply to your relationships with clients. Similarly, you might become angry if you are insulted or threatened physically when not in a clinical setting, but you must not respond to a client angrily and with violence. Although it may be useful to remind clients that there are known and sure consequences for violence, it is probably not a good idea to invent threats that have little probability of being carried out. Empty threats may only serve to remind clients that they can resort to aggression without consequences. For further suggestions about dealing with individuals who are armed and clearly intent on violence, see Burgess, Burgess, and Douglas (1994).

RESPONDING TO ASSAULT

Although the best way to deal with violence is to prevent it, even the best prevention efforts are not perfect. Therefore, you need to give some thought to what might happen if you are assaulted and how you would respond to minimize harm to yourself, the client, other persons, and property. Among the factors to consider in responding to assault are clothing, office layout, communications, dangerous and protective implements, and assault-response training.

CLOTHING

If you are working in a setting where assault might be a possibility, it is important to dress in such a way that your clothing cannot become an impediment to quick movement or a weapon that can be used against you. Take a moment to check out your personal attire and ask how it could aid or harm you if you were assaulted. Among the clothing elements that can increase risk are items worn around the neck. Ties, scarves, or strong necklaces all become tempting and dangerous items that people can grab and possibly use to strangle you in a struggle. Something around your neck can be extremely difficult, perhaps impossible, to release, and you will have only a very, very short time to get free before losing consciousness.

Ties and scarves present attractive targets to grab, and so do large earrings, particularly the loop kind. Regardless of your personal fashion tastes, think of a client grabbing a piece of jewelry or clothing and pulling hard. Then decide if that is really something you want to wear to your work or internship setting. If the dress code of the agency requires you to wear a tie or other such potentially dangerous items, you may want to discuss the safety implications with your supervisor or the setting director. If all else fails, wear a clip-on bow tie. Who knows, you may start a trend.

Also consider how your clothing might assist or impede your ability to avoid or escape an assault. For example, footwear should enable you to move quickly and offer a steady base of support during a struggle. High heels and slick-soled shoes are not recommended. Similarly, tight clothing should generally not be worn, as it may restrict your movement.

Finally, it is important, especially for women, to avoid clothing that might be deemed provocative in some way. In an ideal world, people should probably be able to dress however they like; however, in reality, at your internship, you must recognize the institutional needs and client characteristics and exercise good judgment about your appearance and the impression it creates. This is especially important for women who, as students on campus, may feel perfectly comfortable and think nothing of wearing short skirts, tights, and so on. If you or a fellow intern happens to dress that way from time to time on campus, take a moment to consider how such attire will impact your professional role as an intern and how it may be viewed by clients or professional staff. If you are assaulted, you do not want to become the target of criticism that you invited the assault by the way you dressed.

OFFICE LAYOUT

Escape routes are the first factor to think about in considering your office layout. If you were attacked or threatened with an attack, how readily could you exit? Similarly, could a client who is feeling pressured or cornered escape without having to go through you? The earlier discussion of situational assessment noted that dangerous clients should not be seen alone. If this cannot be avoided, try to find a room with two doors, so that you or the client can exit easily or help can enter in an emergency. If a room has only one door, be sure that the door cannot easily be locked in a way that would trap you inside and prevent assistance from entering quickly.

Office layout should also take into account the space between client and therapist. When working with potentially dangerous clients, leave sufficient space to give you time to react if the client moves to attack you. Although I generally avoid seeing a client "across the desk," the desk can provide an element of protection, and sometimes the space will help a client feel less pressured, thereby further reducing the likelihood of an attack. Make sure, however, that the desk cannot easily be turned over, trapping you beneath it. It would not be a pleasant experience to have someone overturn your desk and have it land on you, pinning you to the floor. This has actually happened to therapists.

Visibility is another factor that can increase safety but is often overlooked. If people can see into your office, the chance of assault decreases and the opportunities for quick help increase. You should situate yourself in such a way that you can see who is coming and going or who might be about to enter your office. The far wall may seem like a convenient location for your desk, but if it means you must sit with your back to an open door, it could leave you vulnerable. A bit of interior decorating creativity can make for a much safer working environment.

COMMUNICATION

If you are working with someone who might be dangerous, it is vital to have a way of letting others know if you are in trouble. There must also be a way for help to reach you quickly. This means you should establish an unmistakable and unambiguous signal that alerts coworkers when you need help. If you will be in the field, preprogramming emergency numbers and activating the location function on a mobile phone is a good idea. It is also useful to set up a way of activating this covertly if the situation become threatening.

Many clinics or institutions provide alarm buzzers on therapists' desks. Others have phone signals, and in some places a secretary or other staff member checks every few minutes to see how things are going. Leaving your door open may be a viable option, or you might tell the person in the next office to be aware that if sounds of a scuffle are heard, help is needed. If your office is away from others', it will be especially advisable to have a remote communication device, such as a buzzer or a phone.

As you think about how to signal to others that you need help, remember that research on bystander assistance indicates that ambiguity may substantially impede the likelihood of help being provided. If you need to send a person to get help, do not simply shout, "Somebody get help!" Chances are, no one will go. Instead, pick a specific person, call that person by name, and tell him or her exactly what to do: "Joe, go to the nurses' station, tell the first staff you can find that there is a fight in room 100, and we need help immediately. Go now and hurry." The importance of being specific applies not only to assault situations but also to any emergency situation you may encounter.

DANGEROUS AND DEFENSIVE IMPLEMENTS

To further enhance your safety, check your office for whatever potentially offensive and defensive implements may be there. Do not keep letter openers, spike-type message spindles, paperweights, and so on, in locations where clients could easily reach them. If you are not in your own office, consider whatever environment you are in and be aware of hazards. I remember once doing psychological testing with a client who had been convicted of a grisly murder. The testing was done in a high-security locked ward at a psychiatric hospital, but as the man used a newly sharpened pencil I had just given him to fill out the test I recalled, uneasily, that he was in the institution because he had stabbed someone to death with a screwdriver. In hindsight, it was not at all wise to put myself into that position and it would have been much smarter to find a different way of administering the tests.

ASSAULT-RESPONSE TRAINING

With all the precautions in place, you may still be wondering what to do if you are assaulted. Answering this question is not easy because every situation is unique, and every intern brings different resources to the situation. Recognizing these limitations, some suggestions may prove helpful.

The first suggestion, as mentioned earlier in this chapter, is that you seek specific training in dealing with assault (Gately & Stabb, 2005; Spencer & Munch, 2003). Many hospitals, mental health centers, and other programs offer such training, which typically involves a discussion of legal and policy issues, assessment of dangerousness, how to prevent assaults, and various means of physically protecting yourself without harming clients. In a study of the effects of such training, Thackrey (1987) found that staff who completed a training course reported significantly increased confidence in their ability to cope with aggression, but they would not be described as overconfident. These gains were maintained at an 18-month follow-up, suggesting that training can have lasting effects.

For interns who work with children and adolescents, specialized training can be particularly important because angry outbursts may be especially common with this age group and there may be specific institutional and legal guidelines for how such events are managed. Making sure you know what these guidelines are and gaining the requisite training should be a standard part of such internships whenever possible. Assault training is also of special importance for interns who work in placements involving persons convicted of crimes or in other settings where violent individuals are more likely to be encountered.

While recognizing the potential value, even necessity of assault training, it is important to weigh the quality of the training being offered. I am familiar with a widely distributed videotape series that purports to teach therapists how to deal with assaultive or belligerent clients. In my judgment, much of the advice and modeling in this series is extremely naïve and may actually be counterproductive.

If you do not have access to a high-quality program specifically designed around client assault, some forms of self-defense training may be helpful. Techniques of aikido are particularly adaptable. The nonviolent approach of aikido and the philosophy that accompanies it are useful training for interns and therapists. In addition to their value as training for responding to assaults, I have also found substantial clinical utility to the underlying concepts of aikido (see Tohei, 1966). Other so-called martial arts may also be useful, but for your clinical needs, you need to focus on the defensive techniques more than on the counterattacking, punching, and kicking skills. Knowing such skills may help boost confidence and could well help you in other situations; obviously you should not use them to harm or intimidate clients.

If you do not have experience or training in dealing with assaults, your best approach is to use common sense, be creative, do not be heroic, but do resist doing harm or being harmed. Common sense suggests that if you are assaulted, you need to protect the vital areas of your body, try to escape, and get help. At the same time, creativity can help you defend yourself. The comedian Steve Martin used to say that you could discourage robbery by throwing up on your money. He said it for laughs, but he is not far wrong. Try to rapidly assess the situation, identify options, and seek responses other than those that the assailant expects. This may give you the advantage of an element of surprise, and sometimes it can even stop the attack altogether.

The advice against heroics is meant to give you permission to run away if you must. If someone much larger or stronger than you poses a threat, you can try to deal with that threat verbally or in other noncombative ways, but if combat appears inevitable, you will probably lose. Under such circumstances, it may help to simply tell the person, "It is not necessary to try to fight with me because I am leaving."

AFTEREFFECTS

If you do have the misfortune to be assaulted, it is extremely important to deal effectively with the aftereffects. Some institutions have in place plans designed to help victims adjust after an assault. These plans include information such as who to notify and how to handle the assailant, documentation, and steps to help the victim deal with the emotional aftereffects. Gately and Stark (2005) and Spencer and Munch (2003) have also emphasized the importance of aftercare for assault victims.

The first thing to do if you are assaulted is to notify your supervisor so necessary records can be made. If you are injured, get medical help and be sure the events are well documented. You may also have to fill out certain incident reporting forms or other paperwork so you can receive compensation for medical expenses.

If you are not injured, after notifying your supervisor, go somewhere with your supervisor or a colleague and take time to deal with what happened. Immediately after an assault, you will probably experience the physical effects of the crisis. You may find yourself shaking, feel your heart racing, and perhaps feel sick to your stomach. These are normal responses and nothing to be ashamed of or hide. You probably do not want to go right back to what you were doing as if nothing has happened. Give yourself some time to let your body and mind get back to normal.

You will also need to work through the emotions that follow an assault. For example, you might be afraid to go back to the site of the assault (Criss, 2010). Or you may feel angry; you may want to get back at the client who assaulted you. Depending on the circumstances that led to the assault, you may try to think back to what happened. How did things develop, what might have been done differently, what was done well under the circumstances? All of these questions and feelings may strike at once, and it is not uncommon to find yourself replaying the event again and again in your mind. This process can often take at least several days and as long as a couple of weeks or more to work through.

If the aftereffects of an assault persist and are troubling you or interfering with your work, you may want to seek some form of counseling. You and your supervisor should also explore how the experience may affect your work and interactions with clients in the coming days and weeks. If others saw the assault, you may feel embarrassed about returning to work. A primary consideration must also be the possibility of recurrence of the assault. If your supervisor does not raise this concern but it is on your mind, be sure to express it. To feel safe returning to your position, you will need to consider this possibility and be assured that steps have been taken to prevent another assault. You will also need to have support to ensure that your clinical work will not be adversely affected by the experience (Criss, 2010).

You should not be afraid about going to your internship or interacting with clients, but you should be cautious. Knowing your limitations, developing your clinical skills, and seeking assistance when necessary are the keys to safety in your internship and in your future clinical work.

STALKING

Different from a direct assault, but potentially just as dangerous and emotionally difficult, is being stalked by a client. As noted earlier, several studies have indicated that being stalked is, unfortunately, not a rare experience among practitioners (Gentile et al., 2002; Purcell et al., 2005; Romans et al., 1996). Given this possibility, it is worth taking a few moments to discuss ways of preventing stalking and responding to it effectively if it occurs.

Purcell et al. (2005) reported that the most commonly cited reason for stalking by clients was resentment, often resulting from a practitioner's offering a professional opinion in a legal matter, such as at a child abuse hearing. Other reasons include unsatisfactory termination of clients who did not want treatment to end and infatuation. In 38% of the cases reported, some form of threat was associated with the stalking. These included threats of physical violence against the professional or family or staff, property damage, and threats of ruining the therapist's reputation or practice in some way.

Most respondents surveyed by Purcell et al. indicated that their training had not adequately prepared them to cope with these situations. In many instances, the experience caused substantial emotional stress and resulted in taking such actions as moving to a different location, delisting phone numbers, calling for assistance from police, and consultations with professional colleagues.

Purcell et al. reviewed a number of clinical issues that may be helpful in recognizing and reducing the potential risk of stalking. These include managing transference, dealing effectively with client attraction, maintaining professional boundaries, and careful diagnosis of potential personality disorders. In addition to giving greater attention to such clinical issues, Gentile et al. (2002) found that psychologists who had been stalked took other measures as well, including using an unlisted home address and telephone number, installing an office and/or home alarm system, and carrying mace or pepper spray.

Based on my own experience, I believe that virtually all of these measures should be standard practice not only for those who have been stalked but as common safety measures for all practitioners. In addition, these authors did not mention several other measures that I would strongly recommend, particularly for interns.

First is giving scrupulous attention to ensuring that personal contact information is not made available to clients either intentionally or unintentionally. You simply do not give out a personal phone number or address under any circumstances, period. The same rule should apply to other professional staff.

You may believe a person is completely harmless and think it could not hurt to give him or her your address to drop you a line from time to time. But keep in mind that the person who seems most benign and most interested in keeping in touch may well pose the greatest risk. It is simply easiest to have an iron-clad policy of scrupulously protecting your personal information. If someone wants to write or call, suggest writing to the internship site and arrange for a staff member there to pass the letter on to you. Lest this seem cold or impersonal, you can apologize and state that you are sorry but it is a strict institutional policy. If someone asks you or a staff member for contact information for a fellow staff member or other person, agree to pass along the request to the identified individual but under no circumstances should you give out someone else's contact information.

Along with preventing voluntary releases of your personal information, also be careful to avoid theft or other unauthorized access to such information. During one of my internship placements, a client told me up front that he was, in his own words, "a pathologic liar." We worked together for much of the year, and when it was time to conclude our treatment at the end of my placement, we had a final session together. For some reason, I was called away briefly during that session. As I attended to the other matter, I had left the client waiting in my office very briefly on his own; then I returned to conclude our interaction. Several hours later, I discovered that a special pen, given to me by my father, was missing. I could not prove that the client took the pen, but no one else had been in the office, and I am quite certain he took it while I was out for just a couple of minutes. The lesson here is that some clients, even after you have worked with them for a long time, still cannot be trusted.

Experienced professionals who have worked with sociopaths would all nod their heads at this story, most likely because they have had something similar happen to them. No matter who the client is, be safe. Do not leave your wallet, purse, credit cards, cell phone, or any other item that might have personal information anywhere so that someone could either steal it or take a peek at your information. Also, follow suggestions for avoiding identity or credit card theft by shredding critical documents and being sure not to leave credit card receipts, checks, or other items in the trash.

I also advise interns to adopt a heightened state of awareness when they are coming and going from their placement sites. Taking a second to see if anyone is watching you in an unusual way and looking back in the rearview mirror to see if you are being followed may sound like paranoia, but it really is simply a small and prudent precaution to protect your safety. Another helpful suggestion is to tell any roommates, family members, resident advisors, or others about the nature of your work, and advise them that if someone whom they do not recognize or who just does not seem quite right to them calls asking for you, they should not give out any information but should instead take down the person's contact information and pass it on to you.

This latter suggestion is especially important if you have a spouse/partner and children who could be in jeopardy if someone actually does seek to harm you. Take the time to discuss with your spouse/partner and with your children if they are old enough to understand any security procedures you want to follow as a family and any procedures that should be followed if someone unknown contacts them or something unusual occurs.

Another precaution that I have found helpful is to build a good relationship with local, neighborhood law enforcement personnel. For students, if any concerns arise about personal safety, stalking, or other matters, it is a good idea to let your campus safety officers and police know that you are an intern and have concerns just so they can keep that in the back of their minds and recall that information if something happens. The same applies in your community. Find out where the nearest police precinct is and stop by to say hello and get acquainted with the officers.

Finally, if you ever become concerned about your personal safety or are being followed, observed, or stalked, make sure you immediately notify your supervisor; your instructor; and, if necessary, the law enforcement. I strongly urge you to trust your guts on this, and do not feel embarrassed or ashamed to tell your supervisor that something just does not seem right or that you are worried, even if you are unsure. It is far better to be safe and take precautions beforehand than to regret later that something was not done.

SOCIAL NETWORKING, PERSONAL PRIVACY, AND SAFETY

The advice to protect personal contact information is made much more complicated by online communication and social networking. Most interns and students will probably be involved in some form of social networking, be it Facebook, Twitter, LinkedIn, or other variations. In ordinary academic life, this is usually not a problem, but you should keep in mind that clients may well look up information about you online. Consider, for example, that in one study of psychology graduate students (Lehavot, Barnett, & Powers, 2010), more than 80% of respondents had some form of online personal profile, and 67% of these students used their real name on their profile. Responses varied depending on the particular networking site in question, but among respondents between 15% and 34% indicated their privacy settings granted access to their profile to anyone, whereas roughly 5% were not sure who had access. When asked if they had posted information on their site they would not want faculty or clients to see, 29% indicated they had posted photos and 37% had posted personal information they would not want clients to see. This finding takes on added significance in light of the fact that 7% of respondents reported that at least some clients had told of seeking information online about the student (and that was just the number for whom a client had *volunteered* the information—the actual number of clients who check is likely much higher).

In many cases, this is simply a matter of clients legitimately trying to learn just who it is that is providing them services. In other instances, a client may be seeking personal information about you that could pose a threat. Regardless of the motive, significant clinical as well as personal safety issues are associated with your online presence.

To protect your privacy and safety, and to limit the possibility that personal information you post about yourself could adversely impact your clinical work, Lehavot et al. (2010) offer several practical suggestions. These include being thoughtful about who you accept on your friends list and using restricted access limits to your personal sites. Even with these measures, however, keep in mind that anything you post on the Internet has the potential to become public information or to be accessed by determined individuals. Lehavot et al. also advise that before posting anything you ask yourself, "What are the costs and benefits of posting this information?" And, remember when you ask this question that it takes on much different meanings now that you are a professional in training than it might have if you were a student in another field or role.

For a discussion of the ethical and clinical considerations of social networking and online communication, see Chapter 4 of this book. For an additional informative review of the benefits and risks of social networking as it pertains to your professional training and internship, see Meyers et al. (2012). The key point of these and other articles is that your public persona on the Internet must be managed with a thoughtful awareness that whatever you post may have ethical, clinical, and personal safety ramifications. Part of becoming a professional is accepting this responsibility and realizing that your professional persona extends well beyond the clinical setting and the classroom to encompass the online world as well.

COMMUNICABLE DISEASES

Just in case the discussion thus far has not been sufficiently disconcerting, I would like to add one final category of risks that go with human services but is often overlooked. Depending on your placement site, it is not at all unlikely that you will come in contact with individuals who have a higher risk of carrying communicable diseases. Institutions where many people live together are prime

breeding and transmission sites for colds and flu, and many who seek human services may have low personal hygiene standards.

To reduce your risk of contracting a communicable illness, several protective measures should be taken. First, be sure that all of your vaccinations are up to date. I recommend that interns make sure to have an annual physical, and the start of an internship provides a good opportunity to review with your health care provider what your vaccination status is for various illnesses. I also encourage all health care workers to get an annual flu shot. This is not only for your protection and that of the people you live with or around, it is also for the protection of clients who could get the flu from you. Many institutions will provide vaccinations, especially annual flu shots, free of charge to their treatment staff. Check with your placement site to see what is available. You may also want to touch base with your campus health service to find out what services of this sort it provides.

After vaccinations, your next and most important line of defense involves practicing excellent personal hygiene. More than once a client has sneezed into his hand just before extending it to me for a friendly handshake. It is telling that in most such instances the clients are completely unaware of what they are doing and of the risk of passing on their infection in this way. Less obvious, but perhaps more troubling, is the fact that many people who use public restrooms do not wash their hands after using the facility. Given how few people seem to attend to their own personal hygiene, it is all the more important that you attend to yours.

Even though you may not be in a medical setting as part of your internship, make it a habit to follow the Centers for Disease Control's "Standard Precautions" (http://www.cdc.gov /HAI/settings/outpatient/basic-infection-control-prevention-plan-2011/standard-precautions.html). These precautions include hand washing, using hand sanitizer, wearing safety items, and proper disposal of any contaminated material. I encourage you to wash your hands with disinfectant soap after seeing each client. Also, consciously avoid touching any part of your face, especially your eyes and mouth. For the protection of your family and friends, make it part of your departing ritual each day when you leave your placement site to wash your hands thoroughly one more time. It's also not a bad idea to keep a small bottle of hand sanitizer in your purse, backpack, or glove compartment.

Finally, as we discussed in the Chapter 8 about self-care and dealing with stress, one of the ways you can reduce the likelihood of contracting an illness is by taking care of your overall health. This is not always easy, given the demands of internships, families, dissertations, and work, but try your best to find time for sleep, exercise, and healthy meals. It is worth reiterating that if you do not have time to attend to these things, how much time will you have if you become sick, especially if you contract something serious?

SUMMARY

It would be easier and more pleasant to simply avoid talking about the issues that have been discussed in this chapter. Indeed, that may be precisely why research suggests that so many programs do not give much attention to either informing their students about these risks or preparing them to cope with them. Unpleasant though it may have been to read about them, I hope you can understand why I have given these matters so much attention. It is much better to go into your placement informed, aware of, and prepared to cope with any risks rather than pretending they do not exist. I also hope this discussion has conveyed to you that although we can never completely eliminate some of these risks, they are in most cases quite manageable with proper training and sound practice. It is the nature of this work that some level of exposure to danger may always be present, but your actions are the key to keeping the level of risk as low as possible and to coping effectively with any events that arise. Therefore, let me close by urging you to make a specific plan for yourself to implement the precautions recommended in this chapter, get whatever training is needed to enhance your safety, work closely with your supervisor and instructor to address any specific concerns, review your online presence and security, and scrupulously follow procedures to reduce the risk of violence, illness, or other hazards throughout your training and practice.

REFERENCES

Annis, L. V., & Baker, C. A. (1986). A psychiatrist's murder in a mental hospital. *Hospital and Community Psychiatry, 37,* 505–506.

Burgess, A. W., Burgess, A. G., & Douglas, J. E. (1994). Examining violence in the workplace: A look at work-related fatalities. *Journal of Psychosocial Nursing, 32*(7), 11–18.

Burgess, A. W., Douglas, J. E., Burgess, A. G., Baker, T., Sauve, H., & Gariti, K. (1997). Hospital communication threats and intervention. *Journal of Psychosocial Nursing and Mental Health Services, 35*(8), 9–16.

Campbell, J. C. (Ed.). (1995). *Assessing dangerousness: Violence by sexual offenders, batterers and child abusers.* Thousand Oaks, CA: Sage.

Criss, P. (2010). Effects of client violence on social work students: A national survey. *Journal of Social Work Education, 46*(3), 371–390.

DeBecker, G. (1997). *The gift of fear: Survival signals that protect us from violence.* Boston: Little, Brown.

deMayo, R. A. (1997). Patient sexual behavior and sexual harassment: A national survey of female psychologists. *Professional Psychology: Research and Practice, 28,* 58–62.

Douglas, K. S., & Skeem, J. L. (2005). Violence risk assessment: Getting specific about being dynamic. *Psychology, Public Policy, and Law, 11*(3), 347–383.

Dubin, W. R. (1989). The role of fantasies, countertransference, and psychological defenses in patient violence. *Hospital and Community Psychiatry, 40,* 1280–1283.

Dunkel, J., Ageson, A., & Ralph, C. J. (2000). Encountering violence in field work: A risk reduction model. *Journal of Teaching in Social Work, 20,* 5–18.

Gately, L. A., & Stabb, S. D. (2005). Psychology students' training in the management of potentially violent clients. *Professional Psychology: Research and Practice, 36,* 681–687.

Gentile, S. R., Asamen, J. K., Harmell, P. H., & Weathers, R. (2002). The stalking of psychologists by their clients. *Professional Psychology: Research and Practice, 33,* 490–494.

Haggard-Grann, U. (2007). Assessing violence risk: A review and clinical recommendations. *Journal of Counseling and Development, 85,* 294–303.

Haller, R. M., & Deluty, R. H. (1990). Characteristics of psychiatric inpatients who assault staff severely. *Journal of Nervous and Mental Disease, 178,* 536–537.

Hillbrand, M. (1995). Aggression against self and aggression against others in violent psychiatric patients. *Journal of Consulting and Clinical Psychology, 63,* 668–671.

Janofsky, J. S., Spears, S., & Neubauer, D. N. (1988). Psychiatrists' accuracy in predicting violent behavior on an inpatient unit. *Hospital and Community Psychiatry, 39,* 1090–1094.

Lehavot, K., Barnett, J. E., & Powers, D. (2010). Psychotherapy, professional relationships, and ethical considerations in the MySpace generation. *Professional Psychology: Research and Practice, 41*(2), 160–166.

Lutzker, J. R. (Ed). (2006). *Preventing violence: Research and evidence-based intervention strategies.* Washington, DC: American Psychological Association.

Lyter, S. C., & Abbott, A. A. (2007). Home visits in a violent world. *The Clinical Supervisor, 26*(1/2), 17–33.

McNiel, D. E., Gregory, A. L., Lam, J. N., Binder, R. L., & Sullivan, G. R. (2003). Utility of decision support tools for assessing acute risk of violence. *Journal of Consulting and Clinical Psychology, 71,* 945–953.

Meehl, P. (1973). *Psychodiagnosis: Selected papers.* Minneapolis: University of Minnesota Press.

Meyers, S. B., Endres, M. A., Ruddy, M. E., & Zelikovsky, N. (2012). Psychology graduate training in the era of online social networking. *Training and Education in Professional Psychology, 6*(1), 28–36.

Monahan, J. (1988). Risk assessment of violence among the mentally disordered: Generating useful knowledge. *International Journal of Law and Psychiatry, 11,* 249–257.

Mossman, D. (1994). Assessing predictions of violence: Being accurate about accuracy. *Journal of Consulting and Clinical Psychology, 62,* 783–792.

OSHA. (2006). *Guidelines for preventing workplace violence for health care & social service workers.* Retrieved from http://www.osha.gov/Publications/OSHA3148/osha3148.html

Purcell, R., Powell, M. B., & Mullen, P. E. (2005). Clients who stalk psychologists: Prevalence, methods, and motives. *Professional Psychology: Research and Practice, 36,* 537–543.

Quinsey, V. L., Harris, G. T., Rice, M. E., & Cormier, C. A. (2006). *Violent offenders: Appraising and managing risks* (2nd ed.). Washington, DC: American Psychological Association.

Ringstad, R. (2005). Conflict in the workplace: Social workers as victims and perpetrators. *Social Work, 50,* 305–313.

Romans, J. S. C., Hays, J. R., & White, T. K. (1996). Stalking and related behaviors experienced by counseling center staff members from current or former clients. *Professional Psychology: Research and Practice, 27,* 595–599.

Skeem, J. L., Miller, J. D., Mulvey, E., Tiemann, J., & Monahan, J. (2005). Using a five-factor lens to explore the relation between personality traits and violence in psychiatric patients. *Journal of Consulting and Clinical Psychology, 73,* 454–465.

Slovak, K., Brewer, T. W., & Carlson K. (2008). Client firearm assessment and safety counseling: The role of social workers. *Social Work, 53,* 358–367.

Spencer, P. C., & Munch, S. (2003). Client violence toward social workers: The role of management in community mental health programs. *Social Work, 48*(4), 532–545.

Thackrey, M. (1987). Clinician confidence in coping with patient aggression: Assessment and enhancement. *Professional Psychology: Research and Practice, 18,* 57–60.

Tishler, C. L., Gordon, L. B., & Landry-Meyer, L. (2000). Managing the violent patient: A guide for psychologists and other mental health professionals. *Professional Psychology: Research and Practice, 31,* 34–41.

Tohei, K. (1966). *Aikido in daily life.* Tokyo: Rikugei Publishing House.

CHAPTER 10

CLOSING CASES

Internships are time limited. Interns should keep this in mind throughout their placement and should plan well in advance for the time when they will leave the internship (Zuckerman & Mitchell, 2004). This chapter discusses some of the tasks that must be accomplished and issues that arise as one prepares for the completion of an internship. As in other chapters, I recognize that not all interns will be directly responsible for seeing clients or providing therapy. Nevertheless, even if you are primarily in an observational role or working as an aide, you are likely to form close bonds with people, and thus it may be difficult to leave the internship site. Understanding the issues involved in leaving the internship site and closing cases may help you deal with this process more effectively.

ETHICAL CONSIDERATIONS AND CLOSING CASES

All of the major professional ethics codes include a discussion of closing cases, sometimes referred to as termination, with principles established to ensure that (1) therapy is discontinued when clients no longer need or benefit from it, (2) clients are not "abandoned" (i.e., their case prematurely terminated without transition or follow-up provisions), and (3) transitions to new therapists are handled in a way that is sensitive to clients' needs and in the clients' best interests therapeutically (ACA, 2005; APA, 2010; ASCA, 2010; Behnke, 2009; NASW, 2008; Vasquez, Bingham, & Barnett, 2008; Younggren & Gottlieb, 2008).

For interns, these standards are especially important because it is common for internship placements to end before treatments for clients have successfully concluded. If adequate provisions and procedures facilitate transferring a client to another therapist, this does not constitute abandonment, nor is it an ethical breach. However, if an intern summarily announces to a client that the internship is ending and the intern will no longer be seeing the client, with no provisions for follow-up or transfer, that would be contrary to ethical standards and to sound clinical practice. As such, it is essential for interns to understand the clinical issues that are associated with termination and transfer and to make sure that this vital aspect of treatment is handled in a way that is as beneficial to clients as possible.

UNDERSTANDING CLIENT REACTIONS

For interns to deal successfully with either closing a case or transferring clients, it is important to understand how clients and interns alike are affected by this process. Walsh (2007), Schlesinger (2005), and Greenberg (2002) have pointed out that clients may experience many thoughts and emotions, both positive and negative, in response to termination, and it is important not to presume knowledge of these reactions.

Schlesinger (2005), in particular, gave a great deal of attention to the dynamics of termination in a training setting. Walsh (2007) reviewed termination issues from a variety of theoretical perspectives and offered numerous case study examples to illustrate the kinds of issues that could arise and how they could be dealt with constructively.

Roe, Dekel, Harel, Fennig, and Fennig (2006) also provided a useful review of the literature regarding termination, much of it from a psychodynamic orientation. They noted that when therapy has been successful and the relationship concludes as a natural result of having achieved goals, the experience is most often associated with many positive feelings.

When termination is imposed by events such as a therapist ending the therapy for his or her own reasons or, in our case, an intern leaving at the conclusion of training, reactions may be more complex but they are not necessarily always negative (Schlesinger, 2005). Some clients may perceive that they are being abandoned and feel that the therapist has betrayed their trust. This feeling can be reduced substantially, but not eliminated entirely, by interns if they notify their clients at the outset about the end date of their relationship and begin to prepare for it in the early stages (Zuckerman & Mitchell, 2004).

Anxiety is also common, as clients wonder if and how they will be able to manage without the assistance of the therapist. Many clients may feel a sense of loss with regard to the therapy relationship and the therapist.

In contrast to these responses, some clients may welcome termination as an opportunity to transition out of therapy. Others may appear to be enthusiastically happy for the intern who has completed his or her placement and now may move on to "bigger and better" things.

In responding to these reactions, the therapist should keep in mind that the initial or surface presentation, whether positive or negative, is likely to be only part of the client's overall reaction.

As part of appreciating the complexity of reactions to termination, be aware that a client's reaction to the end of the therapy relationship will be closely connected to the client's previous relationship and termination experiences. Also keep in mind that the way in which you conclude your relationship with clients has the potential to be therapeutic in itself, providing a model of a caring, thoughtful, and respectful transition, something that may be relatively unfamiliar to certain clients.

Schlessinger (2005) noted that clients' reactions to the termination process will be influenced by how they worked through earlier separation experiences in their lives and how they have dealt with conflicting feelings, such as dependence and independence or trust and mistrust. The same principle applies to interns. Although the immediate transition is of the relationship between you and the client, each of you will also cope with the experience based, in large part, on your previous experiences in other relationships. Awareness of this can be an invaluable aid in making the experience part of the overall therapeutic process.

EXERCISE

To further your understanding of client reactions to termination, consider the following questions:

1. How might the client's personality and presenting concerns influence his or her cognitive, emotional, and behavioral reactions to termination? In other words, how will different types of clients cope with the termination experience?
2. What kinds of previous termination experiences might influence how a given client will cope with terminating an interaction with you?
3. How will the approach one takes to therapy influence the way clients cope with therapy termination?

UNDERSTANDING INTERN REACTIONS TO TERMINATION

Understanding the client's reactions is only part of the puzzle. For the closing or transition of cases to be constructive, interns must also understand their own reactions. As with clients, the effects of this process will vary depending on the intern's personality and prior experience and the nature of his or her interactions with specific clients.

Unfortunately, relatively little research has specifically focused on intern or trainee reactions to forced termination. Zuckerman and Mitchell (2004) surveyed predoctoral psychology interns to assess the adequacy and nature of their training and supervision with regard to the termination experience. In response to open-ended questions, interns reported emotions including sadness and guilt, but also for many a sense of relief and feelings that the onset of termination had constructive effects, in many cases helping to focus and move forward the work of treatment. The

majority of respondents also described a strong sense of the need for more supervision in dealing with these issues.

Baum (2006) reported comparable findings from a survey of social work trainees at the end of their field placement year. Responses to open-ended questions indicated common feelings that the termination of treatment was untimely both for clients and for the trainees as professionals. Often expressed were concerns that treatment was just beginning to make progress and that the trainees felt they still had much to learn from the process with certain clients. Concerns about the impact on clients, a sense of guilt about "inflicting" a premature ending to a relationship, and worries about what would lie ahead for the clients were also common. There were also questions about how to best manage the process for the benefit of clients. Baum also noted significant differences between first- and second-year trainees, with the more experienced trainees generally expressing lower degrees of anxiety about how to manage the process and being less likely to indicate a desire to somehow continue the relationship with clients after the field placement ended.

In my experience, among the many emotions interns may experience as they conclude their relationships with clients, guilt is especially common. Having encouraged the client to trust, be open, and establish a therapeutic relationship, the intern is now ending that relationship, often before the work has been fully accomplished. This may be particularly difficult for interns, who are working with some of their first clients and are likely to establish especially close ties. Being forced to break those ties without realizing the completion of their joint labor with the client can bring both guilt and frustration.

Closely linked to guilt feelings may be a sense of omnipotence on the part of the therapist or intern. If a therapist feels he or she is the only one who really understands a client, it can be all the more difficult to transfer that client to another therapist for fear that no one else will be able to help as effectively. The reverse of omnipotent feelings is seen in an intern's fears that the next therapist the client sees may in some ways do a better job or will recognize that mistakes have been made. Owing to their relative inexperience, interns may be especially susceptible to concerns of this sort. The evaluation component of internship training is likely to heighten such concerns.

In contrast to feelings of guilt, loss, or concern about the client's well-being, interns also may experience a sense of relief at termination with some clients. Independent of reactions to specific clients, interns should also be aware of how transitions within their own lives and their personal future can influence their management of termination with clients. Gavazzi and Anderson (1987) contrasted the feelings of loss that clients may experience with the elation or relief that interns may feel as they look forward to completing an academic program or going on to other, perhaps more appealing, rotations. Interns who are glad to be done with a rotation or who can hardly wait to start something new may have a difficult time empathizing with clients who are experiencing loss, anxiety, anger, or other unpleasant reactions to termination.

Given what has been said about interns understanding their own reactions to termination, the following questions are designed to help you consider your own thoughts about terminating the internship or your relationship with specific clients. These questions might provide valuable material for discussing termination with your supervisor or instructor:

1. What concerns do you have for your clients as you think about concluding your work with them?
2. How are you dealing personally and in therapy with the concerns identified in the first question?
3. Are you giving equal attention to termination for all your clients, or are some receiving more of your energy than others?
4. How might your own thoughts about what lies ahead for you be influencing the way you are interacting with clients or others?

COMMON PROBLEMS IN TERMINATION

One of the reasons for reviewing client and therapist reactions is to help interns anticipate and avoid some of the problems that can contribute to or result from terminations that are not handled well. The key to many such problems is the failure of the therapist to approach the process therapeutically. To the extent that the therapist fails to use basic therapy skills, such as understanding the client, monitoring the therapeutic relationship, being aware of process as well as content, and watching for one's own issues, the termination process is likely to be difficult and possibly even counterproductive.

Therapists who fail to understand the possible origins and complexity of client reactions to ending the treatment relationship are unlikely to deal with those reactions effectively. Confronted by a client's anger, the therapist may become defensive; confronted by client anxiety, the therapist may be inclined to reassure the client with unrealistic promises. The potential for such responses is increased if therapists are also trying to deal with their own reactions (including perhaps guilt) or their needs to feel needed or competent.

Therapists who are conflicted about the process may also unconsciously pass some of their needs or fears onto the client. For example, therapists who feel themselves to have been the only one able to help a client might unconsciously communicate this and thereby sabotage attempts to transition the client to another therapist. Therapists may also try to make the client into a "good" client, both to ease the work of the colleague who will take the case and to make it appear that the therapy to that point had been more successful than it really was.

In my supervisory experience, I have noted that many interns subtly extract reassurance or perhaps even absolution from their clients. To ease the transition for themselves, interns may create opportunities for clients to tell them how much the therapy has helped or that they are happy for the intern's future opportunities. Such client statements might be perfectly legitimate and indeed therapeutic for the client, but if they are extracted covertly or to meet the intern's needs rather than the client's, they are less likely to be therapeutic.

Another approach to minimizing the difficulty of transitions is to leave little or no opportunity for clients to express any negative feelings. Some interns wait until the end of a session to tell clients that this will be their last visit. A less blatant approach is to give clients advance warning but then occupy the remaining time or sessions by reviewing only the positive elements of therapy. Such practices may ease the termination process for the therapist, and perhaps for the client as well, but they do not allow clients to work through their full range of feelings about the relationship or its conclusion.

TOWARD SUCCESSFUL TERMINATION OR TRANSFER

Although the focus of the discussion thus far in this chapter and, for that matter, in much of the literature has been on the difficulties associated with termination, if properly managed, the conclusion of a therapy relationship has the potential to be an extremely valuable therapeutic experience for clients and interns.

In a discussion of termination in short-term psychotherapy, Quintana (1993) argued that too much has been made of the notion that termination will inevitably be experienced as a crisis by clients. Referring primarily to planned termination (i.e., an ending that is mutually agreed on and not imposed by therapist departure), Quintana cited literature indicating that most therapists and clients handle termination well. Indeed, studies reviewed by Quintana showed that clients whose therapy was successful described the closing process in positive terms, focusing on the progress they had made and on the ending of therapy as a beginning of something new. For clients whose therapy was less successful, termination was less likely to be described in positive terms, with the focus placed instead on disappointment over the limited progress.

Based on his own research and review of the empirical literature, Quintana proposed that instead of focusing solely or primarily on the loss involved in termination, therapists should address termination as an opportunity for development and transformation. Of special importance is the process of helping clients internalize the therapeutic relationship, the gains that have been made, and a new image of themselves as the result of their growth in therapy. Quintana cited a valuable statement by Edelson (1963):

> The problem of termination is not how to get therapy stopped, or when to stop it, but how to terminate so that what has been happening keeps going inside the patient. (p. 23)

What keeps therapy going inside the client, Quintana (1993) asserted, is the benefit of recognizing and acknowledging the progress that has been made. Ideas similar to Quintana's were voiced by Siebold (1992) in relation to forced terminations. Greenberg (2002) offered a number of similar suggestions that can help facilitate therapeutic outcomes as the relationship concludes. Although Greenberg's principles are designed more for the "natural" course that occurs when therapy is completed, several of the principles are still quite useful when an internship concludes and the intern must leave. For example, Greenberg emphasized working with the client to underscore the client's strengths, review the changes the client has achieved, anticipate future challenges, and emphasize that change is an ongoing process with no fixed end point. Comparable recommendations were suggested by Vasquez et al. (2008), who listed 12 essential practices to ensure clinically and ethically responsible termination. These authors also included a number of sample letters that therapists can use to communicate formally with clients regarding termination under several different but common circumstances.

Fundamental to the points made by each of these authors is the assertion that the conclusion of the treatment relationship can present an opportunity for further growth if handled properly by the therapist. What are some of the key ingredients to a successful process?

CLIENT SELECTION

In Chapter 2 of this book, it was emphasized that internships are time limited, and this fact must be considered by interns and supervisors throughout their work with clients. Penn (1990) also stressed this point, recommending that clients who have a history of multiple losses should not be assigned to therapists who will likely need to terminate their treatment prematurely.

This point is repeated here for two reasons. First, an intern who has been working with clients for whom termination might be unusually difficult as a result of past experiences must consider that possibility and address it in the therapy process as termination nears. A second consideration should be careful selection of another therapist to take the case when the intern leaves. As Penn suggested, efforts should be made to avoid referring clients to other therapists or interns with whom the client is likely to experience another forced termination.

WORKING WITH SUPERVISORS TO PREPARE FOR TERMINATION

Before addressing termination in therapy with clients, interns should prepare themselves for the process. Self-preparation includes self-reflection, discussions with instructors and supervisors, and study of clinical termination issues and techniques.

Schlesinger (2005) advised therapists to explore their own feelings about leaving before raising the issue with clients. In my internship classes, we typically devote at least one or two class periods (or group discussions plus individual sessions) to discussing both general and personal issues faced by interns. This process often involves exercises such as those presented earlier in the chapter. We also use the group format of our classes to facilitate discussion about personal experiences of interns as they have concluded or changed in relationships in their own lives and as they consider the conclusion of not only the internship but of the internship group or class as well.

In addition to exploring termination in the academic context, interns should raise termination issues with their on-site supervisors. Interns and their supervisor must address two critical issues. First, interns should work closely with supervisors to understand their own reactions and possible approaches to termination with clients. Second, the intern and supervisor must also realize that the intern is simultaneously experiencing a termination with the supervisor.

Several authors have noted that the way supervisors address termination issues with their interns provides a model to help interns learn how to address termination with clients. Gavazzi and Anderson (1987) referred to the "parallel process" that occurs between supervisor and therapist, and between therapist and client. They suggested that supervisors and therapists should engage in a cognitive and affective review of their work together. The cognitive element would address the therapist's strengths and weaknesses, progress made during training, future directions, and so on. The affective review would entail talking about feelings toward each other, the supervisory experience, and termination itself. A similar review on both cognitive and affective levels is recommended as part of the termination work with clients.

One caveat should be mentioned about the supervisor–intern termination process serving as a model for termination with clients. In their study of trainees' impressions of the termination process, Geller and Nash (1987) found that many of the trainees they surveyed were disappointed with how their supervisors handled the termination process with them. Some supervisors were described as offering virtually no help with termination, whereas others focused solely on the clients' feelings about termination and neglected the reactions of the trainees.

This suggests that although the ideal supervisory relationship will address termination issues, it may also happen that supervisors neither help interns deal with client terminations nor effectively address termination of their own relationship with the intern. If supervisors do not introduce the subject of termination, interns may need to raise it themselves. If a supervisor seems uncomfortable dealing with the topic, interns may want to discuss termination with other experienced professionals or with their peers. It may also be possible for interns to observe how other practitioners manage termination.

A useful way to structure termination preparation is to follow a structured format that ensures key issues are addressed for each case. Fair and Bressler (1992) developed and tested a 55-item Termination Scale designed for use by supervisors and trainees before, during, or after the termination process. Though this scale was developed some time ago, the fundamental elements remain just as valid today.

The instrument includes two subscales: Termination Planning and Emotional Response to Termination. Items from the Termination Planning subscale address how the trainee and supervisor have worked to prepare for the termination process and how they conceptualize each case. Items from the Emotional Response to Termination subscale address the subjective emotional experience of the therapist as he or she prepares for and participates in the termination process.

Fair and Bressler suggested that their Termination Scale can serve several functions. Among these are helping to objectify termination despite painful elements, bringing out countertransference feelings, identifying areas for therapist improvement, and providing a structure to conceptualize termination. Use of the scale also helps supervisors encourage trainees to deal with a process that supervisors know can be challenging emotionally.

Whether you use Fair and Bressler's instrument or another, it is helpful to follow some format to be sure you cover all the bases and review your own responses to termination. Taking into account what has been said about termination in this and the preceding chapter, generate a checklist for yourself in which you identify key logistical details about termination. For example, your list might include details regarding notification of clients, arrangements for transfer, and so on. Then generate a second checklist that you can use to help monitor your own emotional reactions to termination and how you are coping with those reactions. It would also be helpful to review your ideas with peers, instructors, and supervisors for their feedback.

WHEN AND HOW TO NOTIFY CLIENTS

As stated earlier, because of the time-limited nature of internships, interns and supervisors should notify clients of the limited duration of their relationship at the beginning of an internship. Having done that, however, does not obviate preparation as the actual end date approaches.

In thinking about how and when to raise these issues during treatment, it is important that interns not let good intentions about advance notification become lost because of their own anxiety. If one is not comfortable about termination, it can be easy to run out of time in a session, forget to raise the topic, or generate a host of good clinical reasons for delaying the discussion.

I find that it is helpful for interns to work with their supervisor and set a fixed date by which all clients must be notified individually of the approaching departure of the intern. When that time arrives, there must be a point during sessions with each client in which the issue is raised and processed. I prefer not to start a session with the topic but to first get a sense of how the client is doing that day and what issues seem to be present. To begin a session by announcing that one is leaving, before knowing what is happening with the client, could obscure critical information that may affect how the client will react. My practice is to begin the session in the usual fashion, checking out what has happened since our last session and what issues the client is interested in addressing during the present session. After listening to these, I then set my mental clock to be sure to raise the issue of termination by at least mid-session. Sometimes this means changing the topic of discussion, but I do this to avoid the aforementioned temptation to avoid or delay telling clients.

One reason interns are reluctant to tell clients they are leaving is that they are not sure what to say or how to deal with clients' reaction. One intern told me he mentally practiced what to say, much as he had when he broke up with a girlfriend. Another said that she thought about handling terminations in the same way she handled leaving her family at the conclusion of holiday visits. "I just get on the plane and go," she said, "No long good-byes; no tears. I don't like to get emotional, or at least I don't like to show it." These examples reveal both the awkwardness of the subject and how therapy termination tends to evoke previous termination experiences for therapists as well as clients.

I do not have a fixed recommendation for what to say to introduce termination, but I suggest that you think carefully about what your choices may reflect about yourself and may imply for your clients. For example, one intern announced termination to all his clients by saying, "I have some bad news to discuss with you today." This statement assumes both that the intern knows what the client's reactions will be and that the news will necessarily be received as bad. Introducing the subject this way is likely to make it much more difficult to then review the positive gains the client has made or to explore the potential for further growth during the termination process.

My preference is, first, to be sure to address what has happened in the session up to that point. I then proceed in a more neutral, open-ended fashion to introduce the news about termination and offer a chance to discuss it. For example, an intern might say: "From what you've said so far today it sounds as though that is something we may need to talk some more about, but today I need to raise another issue, and I want to be sure we have time to talk about it. As we discussed when we first started working together, on (date) I will be finishing this internship, so we need to begin to discuss what that means and what you will want to do from that point. We should also talk about what you feel about the fact that we'll be finishing our work together and what is ahead for you."

At that point, I usually allow some silence, sometimes a rather lengthy silence, to give the client time to think about what has been said. Even though I may have some idea about how a client will react, I do not presume the client's immediate reaction, nor do I impose a plan of my own design. This practice allows clients to respond in whatever way they need, and it encourages them to be in control of their future. Although I discuss their responses and plans with them, I think it is important to let those responses and plans be the clients' own, not something I impose on them.

ISSUES TO ADDRESS IN TERMINATION

After taking the preceding preparatory steps and allowing sufficient time, termination should address these key topics: the progress the client has made, future directions for the client either in or out of therapy, and reactions to the termination process. Within these areas, it is important to address the cognitive, affective, and behavioral components of the client's reactions and plans (Walsh, 2007).

Quintana (1993) suggested:

> Termination is a particularly critical opportunity for clients and therapists to update or transform their relationship to incorporate clients' growth. For this transformation to occur, clients need to acknowledge the steps they have taken toward more mature functioning. Perhaps most important is for therapists to acknowledge and validate their sense of accomplishment. (p. 430)

Quintana further suggested that techniques for termination should help clients internalize positive images of themselves. Such images, developed from therapy and successful termination, could help clients cope with future crises.

Similar recommendations were offered by Penn (1990), who suggested that therapists "focus with patients on the therapeutic tools that they have grown to use over time and therefore take away with them" (p. 383). Penn suggested that therapists could facilitate this process by citing specific examples in which clients made connections, observed and questioned their own behaviors, or did other work in therapy for themselves. Therapists and clients may also review specific instances in which the client thought, felt, or acted differently from how he or she would have prior to therapy. Such concrete examples help strengthen the client's sense that changes have, in fact, occurred and will likely continue after therapy ends. In this process, however, it is important that the focus be on the gains the client has made using the client's own strengths, not on gratifying the interns needs by implying "look at how much you've achieved thanks to me." If this message is communicated, either explicitly or implicitly, it may make the intern feel good, but it tends to disempower the client and invalidate what he or she has achieved personally.

While recognizing gains is essential, it can be equally necessary to acknowledge any frustrations that may exist about ongoing problems or unrealized goals. This realistic appraisal helps clients and therapists recognize the reality that no treatment can "solve" all of a person's problems and no relationship is without its difficulties.

Acknowledging difficulties or unfinished work becomes especially important if clients will be transferred to other therapists. It may be that the outgoing therapist may not want to admit any shortcomings in therapy or identify unmet goals. Similarly, the client may not want to raise these issues, in part so that he or she will not appear disloyal to the therapist. Yet if therapy up to the present is not reviewed openly and honestly, subsequent treatment may be undermined before it begins.

The one caveat I would place on this is that therapists must be careful not to blindside clients by suddenly confronting them at the end of treatment with a list of shortcomings. One can imagine the deleterious effect it could have if a client has been encouraged to review his or her accomplishments and progress only to then be confronted by the therapist identifying all the things that have not been accomplished or the areas in which personal improvement is still wanting. Thus, although it can be important and valuable to acknowledge frustrations or shortcomings in therapy, this must be done with discretion and sensitivity.

In addition to evaluating the gains and challenges of therapy, termination work should also address the reactions of therapist and client to ending their relationship. Earlier in this chapter, we explored some of the feelings and thoughts therapists and clients might experience as therapy ends. The closing sessions of treatment are a time to discuss and work through those reactions. Penn (1990) pointed out that clients may be reluctant to discuss their feelings about termination. To help them do so, she recommended asking "what they are feeling" rather than "if they have any feelings." The first question assumes there will be some feelings without presuming what they are. This makes it less risky for the clients to begin to talk about how they are feeling about termination.

While encouraging therapists to provide opportunities for clients to verbalize their reactions, Penn also reminds us that clients may express their emotions indirectly. Apparent changes in attitude toward the therapist, missed or late appointments, sudden appeals for more help, or sudden denials of the need for further assistance, may all be manifestations of underlying reactions to ending the therapy relationship. Therapists need to be alert for such disguised responses and help clients recognize and understand them.

TECHNIQUES FOR TERMINATION

For interesting comparisons of how therapists from different theoretical schools approach termination issues, see Curtis (2002); Goldfried (2002); Greenberg (2002); Joyce, Piper, Ogrodniczuk, and Klein (2007); Wachtel (2002); and Walsh (2007). Beyond the usual methods of therapy, several authors have proposed specific techniques to bring out and help deal with issues relating to termination. Walsh (2007), for example, described a variety of "ending rituals" recommended by therapists of different perspectives. Common elements of rituals that Walsh saw as relevant to termination include the sense of specialness, connections to both past and future, dealing with contradiction, coping with emotions, and communication. Walsh also suggests that certain discussion questions can be especially useful in helping clients identify and voice their reactions to termination. These include asking the client to review how it felt to ask for help, what was most and least valuable in the work together, what will be missed, and what the client looks forward to.

EXERCISE

Think of relationships that have ended in your own life and any rituals that might have been part of that process. What functions did such rituals serve for you and the others in the relationship? What similar or different functions would need to be served by rituals to conclude therapy, and what types of activities might best serve those functions?

TRANSFERRING CLIENTS TO OTHER THERAPISTS

Unless the work of therapy is considered to be completed, therapists who must end their work with clients typically make arrangements with other therapists to take the case. Just as problems can arise when therapists terminate their own work with clients, the process of transitioning from one therapist to another also presents a number of therapeutic challenges.

A number of common pitfalls can impede effective case transfers. Several of these have already been alluded to. For example, if departing therapists do not deal effectively with their own issues about termination, they may undermine the possibility of the client building a therapeutic relationship with the new therapist. As Gavazzi and Anderson (1987) described this process in family therapy, departing therapists may attempt to make themselves "an absent but integral member of the client's system" (p. 148). This may feel comforting to the therapist, and perhaps to the family as well, but it can also block further work with a future therapist.

A second obstacle to effective transition is the tendency for the current therapist to allow too little time for transfer work with the incoming therapist. Just as therapists often allow too little time to work through their own termination with clients, they may allot insufficient time to work with the incoming therapist. I have seen many instances in which outgoing interns attempted to transfer their entire caseload to another person during a one-hour meeting. Such transactions typically involve exchanging case files, offering a few descriptive phrases about each client and his or her therapy, then moving on to describe the next client in comparably limited terms.

Another common obstacle to transitions is the failure of the outgoing therapist to ask or discuss with the client how the client feels about switching to a new therapist. Therapists may simply assume that their clients are still in need of treatment without checking with the clients to find out how they feel about the matter. Again, this practice may reflect therapists' attempts to assuage their own guilt about leaving. Whatever the therapists' motives, the results are not likely to be positive. At the very least, the client who is transferred without discussion or consent will not feel respected, and this feeling could undo much of the therapy work that has been accomplished up to that point. Further, if a client only reluctantly agrees to see another therapist, it is unlikely that the new interaction will be successful.

TOWARD EFFECTIVE TRANSFERS

The first task in relation to transferring clients is to determine which clients are in need of, and would likely benefit from, continued therapy. It is a mistake to assume that all clients will desire transfer to other therapists. It can also be a mistake for the therapist to unilaterally determine that a client does not need or want further treatment. If transfer is a viable option at a given placement, one recommendation is for interns or therapists to raise the possibility of transfer to all clients as part of the termination process. The option can then be discussed jointly between therapist and client.

Keep in mind as you consider this that a client's reactions to working with another therapist are not necessarily indicative of whether or not the client wants to make further changes. It is possible that a client feels a need for further work but is daunted by the prospect of starting over with a new therapist. Also, if termination with the current therapist is not handled well, the client may be reluctant to risk a relationship with someone new. This latter point highlights that transferring clients to other therapists in no way eliminates the need for the present therapist to deal effectively with termination issues. Indeed, if anything, the prospect of transferring only makes the termination more important because it will have a direct bearing on how well the subsequent therapy proceeds.

If clients are willing to work with another therapist, or are willing to consider the possibility but are unsure, the outgoing therapist's next task is to help orient the clients to the new therapist, and vice versa. The clients and the incoming therapist will have questions, and the outgoing therapist should help address these. This part of the process must involve more than a mere exchange of content information and case notes. The departing therapist should anticipate and explore client concerns, address these with the client, and communicate them to the incoming therapist.

The third phase of the transfer process involves the initial meeting between the incoming therapist and the client. Some therapists prefer that the outgoing therapist participate in these initial sessions. Others prefer to allow the new therapist and the client to meet separately. Whichever course is chosen, in this phase the outgoing therapist must begin to relinquish the role of therapist to allow the building of a new relationship.

Also important to this phase is exploring comparisons between therapists as individuals and their therapy styles. Clients will inevitably look for similarities as well as differences between the new and old therapists, and it may be helpful for the two therapists to discuss these differences openly and non-critically. Therapists should remember, and gently remind clients, that the real work of therapy resides with the client. Different therapists will have different ways of aiding this work, but clients can and should continue with the work that has already been initiated even though the therapists have changed. When I am in the role of incoming therapist, I encourage clients to let me know if something I am doing clashes in some way with their expectations or needs. By sincerely offering this opportunity, I hope to reassure clients that my aim is to assist their progress, not to compete in some way with their former therapist. This also takes some pressure off me because I do not have to worry that I am going to do something at odds with what has been happening in therapy. Should I, in fact, do so, clients have the chance to let me know so we can discuss the issue together.

One final note is in order about transfers. Although the focus here has been primarily on situations in which clients will be continuing in therapy, this does not mean that the issue of transfer should be ignored for clients who elect not to work with another therapist at the time. Many clients will, in fact, return later for additional therapy. In anticipation of this possibility, it can be useful to at least introduce them to another therapist and briefly discuss their case with that person. That way, both will be more prepared should the client choose to seek therapy sometime in the future.

If a client opts not to meet with a new therapist, it can nevertheless be helpful to explore with a client what considerations might play into the decision and how he or she might go about deciding at some point whether or not to seek additional help. The important point here is not to imply that they do or will need more help. Rather, it is to discuss a process by which the client can make that decision for him- or herself when and if the time comes.

GOOD-BYE MEANS GOOD-BYE •

As termination issues are worked through and the client builds a relationship with the new therapist or decides to go on without further therapy, it eventually becomes time for you to say good-bye. This should probably be done with just you and the client present. An important task of this meeting is to convey and process the reality that after you leave the setting and conclude the relationship, this will in fact be the end of the relationship and there will not be further contact.

Interns often find it difficult to accept and state that the ending of therapy is, indeed, the ending of the relationship (Baum, 2006). Because they may feel guilty about terminating and are concerned about what will happen after they leave, interns sometimes try to reassure clients by promising to visit, write, or in some other way maintain contact. Such promises may be made with the intent of helping the clients feel better, but generally the real function is to help interns cope with their own feelings. I recommend that interns avoid such practices.

There are several important problems with offering to stay in contact with clients after termination. First, if continued contact in fact occurs, it can inhibit the relationship of the clients with their new therapist. Second, despite their best intentions at the time of termination, the reality is that interns will rarely be able to maintain the kind of contact they may have promised. After an internship or rotation ends, interns move on to other activities and cannot find the time to keep in touch with former clients. The result is that interns feel guilty at not keeping their promises and clients feel let down.

Ethical problems can also arise if a relationship continues after therapy is terminated. As discussed in Chapter 4, romantic, sexual, or other conflicting relationships with former clients are to be avoided, and the therapist's responsibility to act with concern for the client's well-being does not end merely because the therapy relationship has been terminated. Finally, as discussed in Chapter 9, safety and security issues can be created if an intern offers to continue the relationship in some way and exchange personal contact information with clients.

Even though it may be difficult, the best approach is to deal with endings as precisely that: endings. If this is hard, working with peers or supervisors to deal with this may be helpful, but avoid the temptation to deny the reality of termination by making promises that will not be fulfilled. The following exercise may help you explore personal feelings about this process and practice ways of talking directly and honestly about both the reality of the finality of the termination experience and the way you and your client may feel about that reality.

EXERCISE

Unlike most personal relationships, in which the potential pain of leaving can be softened by saying, "Let's keep in touch" or "I'm sure we'll run into each other again soon," or similar comments, concluding your relationship with clients at your internship is much more final and that can be difficult. To help prepare for this, it can help to actually practice with your supervisor, peers, or even just by yourself how it will sound and feel as you say good-bye and how you can say it in a way that is emotionally valid for you and for your client. In this exercise, try different ways of saying this, and think about how these differences affect you and might affect your clients. Be especially attuned to what you are

feeling inside and, importantly, be aware of how those feelings may change as you practice and become more accustomed to and comfortable with saying a final good-bye in a way that is honest, sensitive, and at the same time true.

PREPARING TREATMENT OR DISCHARGE SUMMARIES

One final task that you will likely complete for each client before leaving is preparation of an end of treatment or case transfer summary for the client's records. When clients are leaving a treatment center entirely, you may also prepare discharge summaries. Whether you are writing a case transfer or discharge summary, the essential elements are similar.

In many settings, standard forms are used for preparing discharge or transfer summaries. You should inquire about such forms and seek guidance in preparing them if they are used at your placement. If standard forms are not used, you may wish to draw on more generally available models for guidance.

As one example of a mental health discharge summary, the Royal College of Psychiatrists (2012) has developed a collaborative model discharge summary designed to be used with electronic medical records systems. Without detailing all of the elements of this particular model and others, the most important categories of information for inclusion are the following:

1. Demographic information about the client and his or her family. This includes the client's date of birth; gender; ethnicity; location of residence; family members; living or deceased; marital status; children; siblings; religion; history of deployment or military service; and so on.
2. Information about the client's admission into the current treatment program or facility, including dates of admission, presenting concerns, assessments performed, and diagnosis.
3. Medical and mental health history. A summary of key prior and existing medical and mental health conditions including diagnoses, assessments, treatments provided, responses to treatments, and locations and names of prior treatment settings and professionals. Family mental health and medical history is also often included here.
4. Listing and summary of key psychological and medical assessment or diagnostic procedures performed in the current setting along with key findings. This section may also include information about allergies, injuries, or any other known risk factors that should be highlighted.
5. Listing of the key treatment modalities provided, including psychological and medical tests and interventions. Specifics of the types of therapy offered, including modality, duration, frequency, and identity of the specific providers. If medications are utilized, the names of the medications, dosage information, when started, current status, and description of the responses should be included. It can be especially important here to identify courses of treatment that were and were not deemed successful or that had adverse reactions so the successful measures are continued or repeated, whereas the ineffective or negative interventions are not used in subsequent care.

6. Diagnostic information about the mental and physical health status of the client at discharge or transfer.
7. Future care plans, including who will be in continued contact with the client, prescribed medical and mental health care follow-up, and ongoing treatment. Aftercare plans for some clients will also include residential planning, vocational training, and financial matters including disability status and support.

Although the list of key elements of discharge and transfer summaries is extensive, in practice these documents should be written as concisely as possible. The key question to ask in preparing them is, "What is most important to convey about this client to ensure quality of care in the future?" Remember that the rest of the detailed treatment record, including treatment notes, original diagnostic and assessment results, and so on will likely be available for review, so the summary is the quick, focused version.

In addition to the formal and standardized case information, it can also be helpful when transferring clients to provide the incoming therapist or treatment team with a brief summary of the major issues addressed in your work with the client, the treatment modalities utilized, and an assessment of how the treatment had progressed, what sorts of changes had or had not been made, and what recommendations might be offered for issues to address or approaches to be used in subsequent care.

If properly written and utilized, such summaries can be helpful to the incoming therapist. At the same time, however, if you do prepare such a summary, there are important caveats to keep in mind. The most important are informed consent and confidentiality. Clients have a right to know if you are preparing such a summary, what it will contain, and who will be receiving it. It is one thing to share a sensitive and detailed treatment summary with an individual professional with whom the client will be continuing primary treatment and with the client's approval. It is quite another if a summary is included in more broadly accessible notes or is made available to someone without the client's permission.

To appreciate this, imagine if a client had shared something deeply personal with you and you included that without the client's awareness in a transfer note to the subsequent therapist. If that therapist brings the topic up in treatment, and the client was unaware he or she knew the information, an experience of deep violation of trust could easily result.

Thus, although discharge summaries must by nature contain all of the key information that any subsequent treatment team member should know to understand prior care and provide informed treatment going forward, more personal summaries of psychotherapy should be crafted and shared with great care, with the client's specific knowledge and approval, and with close attention to sensitive information and who will be receiving it.

As you write discharge or transfer summaries, consult closely with your supervisor to ensure that the key information is being recorded in the proper format and language. Just as important, seek guidance to make sure information that should not be included is kept out and that any ethical or clinical implications of such summaries has been carefully considered before they become part of the client's record.

REFERENCES

American Counseling Association. (2005). *American Counseling Association code of ethics and standards of practice.* Alexandria, VA: Author. Retrieved from www.counseling.org/resources/ethics.htm

American Psychological Association. (2010). Ethical principles of psychologists and code of conduct. Retrieved from http://www.apa.org /ethics/code/index.aspx?item=3

American School Counselor Association. (2010). Ethical standards for school counselors. Retrieved from http://www.schoolcounselor.org /files/EthicalStandards2010.pdf

Baum, H. (2006). End-of-year treatment termination: Responses of social work student trainees. *British Journal of Social Work, 36,* 639–656.

Behnke, S. (2009). Termination and abandonment: A key ethical distinction. *Monitor on Psychology, 40*(8), 70–71.

Curtis, R. (2002). Termination from a psychoanalytic perspective. *Journal of Psychotherapy Integration, 12*(3), 350–357.

Edelson, M. (1963). *The termination of intensive psychotherapy.* Springfield, IL: Thomas.

Fair, S. M., & Bressler, J. M. (1992). Therapist-initiated termination of psychotherapy. *Clinical Supervisor, 10,* 171–189.

Gavazzi, S. M., & Anderson, S. A. (1987). The role of "translator" in the case transfer process. *American Journal of Family Therapy, 15,* 145–157.

Geller, J. D., & Nash, V. (1987). *Termination as experienced by therapists-in-training as viewed by psychiatric residents.* Unpublished manuscript, Yale University, Department of Psychology, New Haven, CT.

Goldfried, M. R. (2002). A cognitive-behavioral perspective on termination. *Journal of Psychotherapy Integration, 12*(3), 364–372.

Greenberg, L. S. (2002). Termination of experiential therapy. *Journal of Psychotherapy Integration, 12*(3), 358–363.

Joyce, A. S., Piper, W. E., Ogrodniczuk, J. S., & Klein, R. H. (2007). *Termination in psychotherapy: A psychodynamic model of processes and outcomes.* Washington, DC: American Psychological Association.

National Association of Social Workers. (2008). *NASW code of ethics.* Silver Spring, MD: Author. Retrieved from www.socialworkers .org/pubs/code/code.asp

Penn, L. S. (1990). When the therapist must leave: Forced termination of psychodynamic therapy. *Professional Psychology: Research and Practice, 21,* 379–384.

Quintana, S. M. (1993). Toward an expanded and updated conceptualization of termination: Implications for short-term, individual psychotherapy. *Professional Psychology: Research and Practice, 24,* 426–432.

Roe, D., Dekel, R., Harel, G., Fennig, S., & Fennig, S. (2006). Clients' feelings during termination of psychodynamically oriented psychotherapy. *Bulletin of the Menninger Clinic, 70,* 69–81.

Royal College of Psychiatrists. (2012). Mental health discharge summary. Retrieved from https://www.portal.nss.cfh.nhs.uk/sites/CDSA/MHDS /Lists/MHDS%20Approved%20Headings%20Final/Summary.aspx

Schlesinger, H. J. (2005). *Endings and beginnings: On the technique of terminating psychotherapy and psychoanalysis.* Hillsdale, NJ: The Analytic Press.

Siebold, C. (1992). Forced termination: Reconsidering theory and technique. *Smith College Studies in Social Work, 63,* 323–341.

Vasquez, M. J. T., Bingham, R. P., & Barnett, J. E. (2008). Psychotherapy termination: Clinical and ethical responsibilities. *Journal of Clinical Psychology: In Session, 64*(5), 653–665.

Wachtel, P. L. (2002). Termination of therapy: An effort at integration. *Journal of Psychotherapy Integration, 12*(3), 373–383.

Walsh, J. (2007). *Endings in clinical practice: Effective closure in diverse settings* (2nd ed.). Chicago, IL: Lyceum.

Younggren J. N., & Gottlieb, M. C. (2008). Termination and abandonment: History, risk, and risk management. *Professional Psychology: Research and Practice, 39,* 498–504.

Zuckerman, A., & Mitchell, C. L. (2004). Psychology intern's perspectives on the forced termination of psychotherapy. *The Clinical Supervisor, 23*(1), 55–70.

CHAPTER 11
FINISHING THE INTERNSHIP

The preceding chapter focused primarily on the process of termination with clients. This chapter addresses other important elements of finishing the internship and looking ahead. These include concluding the supervisory relationship, bidding farewell to staff members, expressing your appreciation, requesting letters of recommendation, and considering career options.

Internship opportunities are not easy to come by and the willingness of an agency or individual to accept interns depends on each intern doing quality work and leaving a positive impression. Because future interns depend on the good will of a placement site and staff for their opportunities, you must attend carefully to how you conclude your placement.

CONCLUDING THE SUPERVISORY RELATIONSHIP

Several tasks must be accomplished as part of concluding the supervisory relationship. Without reiterating material from the preceding chapter, a few ideas remain to be introduced in the context of termination with supervisors.

EXERCISE

Before reading about issues to address in concluding work with your supervisor, take some time to reflect on this yourself. You may want to review some of the issues addressed in the previous chapter regarding termination with clients, and you may want to focus specifically on the unique aspects of supervisory work and relationship. To help guide this process, consider the following questions, and generate new ones of your own that seem most important to your own experience:

1. As you anticipate termination with your supervisor, what kinds of positive experiences during your placement will be easy for you to discuss? What experiences may be more difficult or awkward for you to talk about?
2. Having considered positive experiences, what negative experiences or unfulfilled expectations are you aware of? What are your thoughts and feelings as you consider raising these with your supervisor?

3. Does considering the preceding questions enhance your appreciation of what your own clients might be experiencing as they address their own positive and negative feelings about their work and relationship with you?

REVIEWING THE INTERN'S PROGRESS AND AREAS FOR FURTHER GROWTH

Just as it is important at termination to consider the progress the client has made, a comparable process is equally important to the work of concluding supervision. In this process, interns and supervisors should allocate sufficient time to discuss both the development the intern has shown during the placement and any areas in which further growth is needed.

The topic of evaluation was discussed in some detail in Chapter 5. Dealing with evaluation so early in the internship ensures that students and supervisors alike will be aware of and agree upon the process at the outset so that expectations are clear throughout the internship and no one is surprised at the very end.

Building on the principles of competency-based education and evaluation, Appendix D presents a form that can be used for evaluations of interns by site supervisors. Although faculty instructors will often ask that such forms be sent directly to them as part of the grading process, the intern and supervisor should first review the evaluation jointly to directly exchange and discuss their ideas and impressions.

Other authors have created alternative evaluation forms and procedures. See, for example, the appendices offered by Falender and Shafranske (2004) with examples of separate forms for the evaluation of interns and the evaluation of supervisors. Also consider the "Competency Assessment Toolkit" described by Kaslow et al. (2009) and the "Competency Benchmarks" offered by Fouad et al. (2009). Applications of both the assessment toolkit and competency benchmarks as they relate specifically to internship training and evaluation have been discussed earlier in this text and by McCutcheon (2009).

Although we are discussing evaluation in the context of terminating the internship, it should be recognized that the competency evaluation methodologies just described should actually be an ongoing and strategic process that is incorporated throughout the internship, not simply conducted at the conclusion of training.

Perhaps the most difficult part of the evaluation process for interns is being able to give and accept critical feedback constructively. It is natural for interns to hope to hear nothing but praise from supervisors. It is equally understandable that supervisors would want to give all their interns glowing reviews. Praise is important, and one hopes that all supervisors will think carefully about and acknowledge the achievements and efforts of even their most challenging interns. At the same time, however, constructive criticism is essential if interns are to develop beyond their current levels. Whereas praise helps give one the strength and hope to carry on, constructive criticism helps show directions for further progress.

EXERCISE

One way to learn to receive criticism constructively is to write an evaluation of yourself identifying what you did well during the placement and areas in which you recognize a need for improvement. You can then imagine that your supervisor is not as positive about your strengths and raises a number of additional issues that need work. As you do this, notice any feelings of defensiveness, hurt, or other responses that could interfere with your ability to receive the comments constructively. If you detect such responses, practice relaxing and listening attentively without feeling a need to respond or defend. As part of this exercise, you might also imagine yourself receiving critical feedback and still thanking the supervisor for giving you his or her impressions. This may not be easy, and it does not necessarily mean you must agree with all the feedback, but it will help you be more open to at least hearing what your supervisor has to say. This process of self-evaluation also helps set a precedent of personal reflection that should be part of your regular practice throughout your career.

FEEDBACK TO SUPERVISORS

As a supervisor, I believe that feedback should be mutual. I encourage interns to tell me what they thought I did well as a supervisor and ways in which I could have done better or can improve in the future. This process helps me become a better supervisor, and it gives the interns an opportunity to practice giving honest feedback. Giving mutual feedback also helps bring better closure to the relationship. If the communication is only unidirectional, interns may be left with a feeling of unfinished business. Talking about their impressions of supervision helps reduce the feeling that something has been left unsaid or is incomplete.

To facilitate the process of giving feedback to supervisors, Appendix I in this text offers a structured format that addresses the key elements of supervision and gives interns a chance to express their appraisal of the supervision on each. If you use this form or have another opportunity to give your impressions to your supervisor, try to keep in mind the principles we have discussed about giving and receiving constructive feedback. Supervisors are human just like anyone else, and they are always glad to receive positive reviews. At the same time, well-intentioned and sensitively communicated criticism can also be welcome.

Because there is an inherent imbalance in the power structure of the relationship between supervisors and interns, interns should think carefully about how they deliver any negative comments to

supervisors. If a supervisor invites you to offer your impressions, it is probably a good idea to begin by getting clarification of what the supervisor is really requesting. You might tactfully inquire about the specific kinds of information the supervisor is interested in. The response to this question can help you determine how best to phrase your comments. Whatever the response, try to present your impressions in a way that is constructive and the supervisor is most likely to take well.

ENDING THE SUPERVISORY RELATIONSHIP

Even as they attend to all the tasks that have been described here and in the preceding chapter, the intern and the supervisor are also involved in the process of concluding their personal relationship. Depending on the level and nature of the relationship, this may be a simple matter, or it could be quite emotional. Whichever is the case, relationship issues should be addressed as part of concluding the supervisory relationship.

Unfortunately, in many cases, neither the supervisor nor the intern raises this issue. The reason probably is that it is not easy to do. It is also the case that little empirical research has been published regarding the issue (Baum, 2007). Discussing termination issues with clients, ensuring that case notes are in order, and even evaluating the intern's clinical performance are all easier than dealing with how the intern and the supervisor feel about each other and about the conclusion of their relationship. Nevertheless, to the extent that the supervisory termination is a model for therapy termination, and if dealing with relationship issues is a necessary part of terminating therapy, those same issues should also be addressed in termination.

The breadth of feelings expressed at termination ranges from bland to profound. I have supervised interns with whom lasting relationships were developed and with whom I still maintain contact. On the other hand, I am sorry to say that in some cases it seems I have scarcely known my interns, and they have known little about me. Similar experiences were described by Baum (2007), who surveyed field supervisors to assess their feelings at termination with interns. Among the most commonly described feelings was a sense of sadness at ending a close and productive relationship. Also common was an awareness of unfinished work, a feeling that some important issues or tasks were not completed during the time available. Then, too, a number of supervisors expressed a sense of relief from the time demands of supervision and, in some cases, from difficulties dealing with particularly challenging trainees.

All of these responses are perfectly understandable. In most instances, talking about these issues at termination can help bring a resolution to the supervision relationship that makes it easier for both intern and supervisor to move on. The exception to this, however, is in cases of exceptional conflict or difficult issues that have yet to be resolved. Raising such matters at the very end of the relationship is unlikely to yield positive results for the intern or the supervisor.

As you think about your own relationship with your supervisor and about discussing that relationship during termination, you might want to keep in mind a fundamental difference between your experience and that of your supervisor. It sometimes happens that an intern hopes to form a close relationship with the supervisor but is disappointed to discover that the supervisor maintains distance or relates primarily in an objective or didactic way, as opposed to a friendly or personal way. There may be many reasons for this. One of the most common is that although the supervisory experience is unique for the intern, in many instances the supervisor and staff will have worked with numerous interns before and will anticipate more in the future. Thus, an experience that stands out as unique and perhaps profound for the intern may, for the supervisor, be somewhat routine. This does not mean the relationship is unimportant, but it does mean that supervisors may not invest the relationship with the same emotional energy or sense of specialness as interns do.

Because students at internship placements often express frustration at not getting closer to their supervisors, understanding the dynamics just described can help the intern put those feelings into context. This may also help interns appreciate how clients might have different feelings about termination from those of interns or therapists. Once again, understanding the supervisory process helps one understand much about the therapy process.

LETTERS OF RECOMMENDATION ·

Interns who plan to go on to further studies or employment may want to request letters of recommendation from their instructors or supervisors. Even if you do not anticipate applying for a position in the near future, it is a good idea to request a letter at this time. After several years have passed, it is much more difficult for supervisors or instructors to write the kind of letter that they could compose when your work together is fresh in their minds. If you do not know exactly what you will be doing in the future, you can ask for a general letter of recommendation for either academic studies or work settings. These can then become part of your portfolio, as was discussed in Chapter 3.

Because letters of recommendation can be quite important, interns should think carefully about requesting them and should follow certain basic courtesies to make the instructor's or supervisor's task as easy as possible.

REQUESTING LETTERS

The most important thing interns must do if they plan to request a letter is be sure they did the best work possible at the internship. If your work was not of the highest level, you might want to think twice about asking for a recommendation letter. Positive letters can be the key to open doors, but negative letters may well lock them shut.

Even though you believe your work merits a positive letter, you should not take this for granted. Whenever you are thinking about asking someone for a recommendation on your behalf, and this applies to all settings, before requesting an actual letter or for someone to serve as a reference, it is a good idea to ask the person directly if he or she can write you a supportive letter. Take care to talk about your specific goals with your supervisor before asking how she or he would feel about writing a letter of recommendation. The reason is that your supervisor might feel comfortable about recommending you for a certain type of employment or educational program but less comfortable supporting other aspirations.

When you do ask for a letter, be attentive to the supervisor's first reaction. If it is immediately enthusiastic and supportive, you will probably receive a positive letter. If the supervisor thinks a long time, asks if you have thought about seeking letters from others, or otherwise seems reluctant, it is possible he or she has some hesitation about writing a supportive letter. If you detect such hesitancy, it is acceptable, indeed probably advisable, to ask about your impression in a tactful but forthright way.

Be aware, if you do this, that asking if an instructor or supervisor has any doubts or concerns about recommending you might put him or her on the spot, and this can be uncomfortable. At the same time, if you raise the question, it might be easier for the supervisor to express any reservations. Most supervisors are reluctant to be as blunt as they perhaps should be when they have reservations about a student. As such, they may speak in vaguely positive terms that would result in a rather lukewarm letter. It is better for you to know this in advance so you can make an informed decision and perhaps select an alternative reference.

Apart from trying to solicit positive letters, it can be extremely beneficial for you to hear any concerns your supervisor might have. You might want to take that into consideration in your deliberations about what jobs or positions to apply for or what you might wish to pursue as further training. If you respect your supervisor and believe she or he is caring and honest with you, it is worth listening carefully to feedback and advice. If a supervisor encourages you to pursue a chosen career or plan of study, that can be a heartening boost to your goals. However, if a supervisor expresses reservations or suggests alternatives, you may wish to reevaluate your aims or identify specific areas in which you need to work on new skills, knowledge, or personal qualities. Difficult though this might be, it can also be a stimulus for important personal development that might otherwise have gone unidentified.

GUIDELINES FOR SOLICITING LETTERS

If supervisors or instructors are willing to write a letter on your behalf, you can make their job much easier and increase the chances of a good letter by following a few simple steps. Whenever students request a letter from me, I give them the following set of guidelines that help ensure they do all they can to prepare forms, envelopes, and so on, and give me the information I need to write a strong letter of support.

PROCEDURES FOR THOSE SEEKING LETTERS OF RECOMMENDATION

The following describes my procedures for completing letters of recommendation requested by students:

1. *Advance notice.* As a general rule, I require a minimum of two to three weeks' advance notice between the time a letter is requested and the time the letter must be postmarked. Please plan ahead to allow at least this amount of time and preferably more. As it often happens, many students request

letters at the same time, and I may not always be able to get a letter out quickly. Therefore, it is advisable, wherever possible, to give me at least one month's notification.

2. *Preparation of forms.* Many programs request that specific forms be completed by reference sources. If you will be asking me to complete forms, please make my job easier by completing portions of the form that request the following information: my name; my address at the university; the amount of time we have known each other and the nature of our relationship; courses or internship setting in which you were a student or we worked together; my rank, which is _____ in the Department of _____ at _____ College/University. Complete this portion of every recommendation form prior to giving them to me. I suggest you type the information as it will be clearer for others to read. Also, be sure to sign your own name on forms where you are asked. This is mandatory. I will not send forms that are unsigned by students.

3. *Preparation of envelopes.* For each program for which you will request a letter, please provide a preaddressed and stamped envelope. Be sure you have enough postage for the envelope, the forms, and several pages of my letter. Submit the envelope and the aforementioned forms, paper clipped together such that it is easy for me to locate the form and the corresponding envelope for each program.

4. *Clear instructions.* If you have any special requests or instructions regarding letters or the completion of forms for different programs, clearly indicate those in a cover letter that you give me when you request letters of recommendation.

5. *Help me write the best letter possible on your behalf.* Please provide me with a brief summary of your academic achievements, internships or field experience, research, service, and other personal accomplishments. In this information, please clearly indicate the nature of our contact. In which classes or activities have we worked together? What did you do in the class or activity that was noteworthy? What other achievements stand out? Also, if there are any special points I should note (e.g., GPA in the major better than overall GPA), please let me know. Finally, if you have written a personal statement for the schools, it might help me to see a copy of that.

6. *Follow-up.* To ensure that requested letters are actually sent in a timely fashion, please take it upon yourself to contact me several days before the request is actually due to be sure I have completed and mailed the letters. My schedule is often very busy, and I would hate to become so tied up in other things that I fail to send a letter that was requested. You can help me avoid this by following up in a timely fashion.

7. *Notification of results.* Although it is not necessary, I would very much appreciate students for whom I write a letter letting me know the results of their application process. As faculty, we are interested in how our students fare, and it is a much-appreciated courtesy when students for whom we have written letters write to us and let us know how their applications went.

8. *Conclusion.* Thank you for your attention to the preceding details. If you have any questions, please feel free to ask me.

CONCLUDING RELATIONSHIPS WITH STAFF

Although interns will interact most closely with their immediate supervisors, they will also come into varying degrees of contact with other staff members at the internship site. As you prepare to conclude your internship, do not forget to inform those staff members that you will be leaving at a certain date. In most instances, this may simply involve letting people know a few weeks in advance, perhaps by making a brief announcement at a staff meeting or by posting some form of notice in a lounge. If closer relationships developed, more personal farewells are in order.

If you have been working with a client who is also being treated by a staff member other than your supervisor, you should schedule some time to meet with that person to discuss the case and your work to date. In this process, you must be careful not to violate confidentiality and to consider how information you share might influence the client's future treatment. In most instances, the other staff member will appreciate and make beneficial use of whatever information you provide. There may be occasions, however, when a client might feel betrayed if certain information were divulged to other staff members. If you are unsure about what information to share or how a specific staff member might use that information, consult with your supervisor to discuss the matter beforehand.

LETTERS OF THANKS

Most people who work with interns do so because they care about interns and the profession and want to contribute. Usually, they receive little or no compensation for their added responsibilities. Because of this, it is important that as part of concluding your placement, you express your gratitude and appreciation. Unfortunately, writing a thank-you note is a custom that is seldom taught and sometimes seems to have been lost. Even though one has said good-bye in person, taking just a few minutes later on to write a letter, a real letter not an email, of thanks is a simple gesture that will be much appreciated.

As a supervisor and instructor I can personally attest to how it can really make my day to receive a card expressing genuine appreciation for my work. It is not something I necessarily expect, but when I receive a card from a student or intern, the stress, the extra hours of work, and the time taken from other tasks all feel worthwhile.

I encourage our interns to write several thank-you notes after their internships. The first one should go to their immediate supervisors. These notes need not be lengthy, but at least a few lines acknowledging the supervisor's efforts, time, and what the intern learned as a result would certainly be welcome. If individuals other than the supervisor were particularly helpful, special notes of thanks to them would also be in order.

Interns sometimes ask if they should write a thank-you letter even when a supervisor was not "the best." Except in rare instances of extreme conflict, virtually all supervisors should be thanked. Even if supervisors were busier than they had hoped or other factors somehow diminished the experience, the supervisor still made it possible for the intern to have a real-world learning opportunity. That is valuable and merits an expression of appreciation.

In addition to the note sent to one's immediate supervisor, it is also courteous to drop a note of thanks to the overall agency director. Although an intern may have had no personal contact with the director, the director is ultimately responsible for what happens in the program, and it is through his or her good graces that interns are allowed to train in that agency. Recognizing this and acknowledging the work of your immediate supervisor will please both the director and the supervisor.

Next, I suggest writing a group thank-you letter to all the staff members the intern worked with at the placement site. These notes typically consist of one or two lines and are addressed "To everyone at…" This kind of note is often posted on a staff bulletin board for all to see. Again, it is a small gesture, but it helps everyone you worked with feel appreciated and acknowledged. Some interns have also left a flowering plant, box of chocolates, or other small gifts that can be enjoyed by everyone at the placement site.

Another person to whom you may want to send a note is your faculty instructor. Even if they do not have extensive contact with interns during the internship, faculty instructors do a great deal of work behind the scenes helping to arrange for placements, keeping in touch with site supervisors, resolving conflicts, and so on. Faculty, like anyone else, would certainly appreciate your thanks.

Finally, if someone was especially helpful to you, keep that person in mind down the road as you progress in your training or work. Just as thank-you notes right after an internship are much appreciated, people value learning what happens to their interns over the long run. It is gratifying to receive a letter saying that an intern has been successful in some way and that the efforts of supervisors, instructors, and others contributed to that. Because it is easy to get occupied with other things and let matters like this slip away, you may want to find a strategy to remind yourself to get in touch with the people who helped you in the past. Interns who keep personal schedule books might write a note in a yearly planner. Others might write in a memo on a date several months away on a calendar. Other creative possibilities are to leave notes in places where you might discover them later, such as dictionaries or other reference works. Whether or not and how you leave such notes is up to you, but some kind of follow-up correspondence is a gracious gesture. This is especially in order if you have asked someone for a letter of recommendation. He or she will want to know how things turned out for you, and it can be fun for you to fill them in.

LOOKING AHEAD ‣

So what's next? If you are planning to continue in your studies or go on to work in the field, you might give some thought to what lies ahead for yourself and for the helping professions in general. DeAngelis (2005) has written an interesting article on what recent graduates said they "wish they'd learned" in graduate school.

This included financial management, salary negotiations, workplace navigation, participating in professional associations, and professional diversification. Plante (1996) offered 10 "principles of success" for trainees embarking on their careers. These include staying on top of new developments; keeping abreast of changes in mental health; keeping in mind why you went into this profession to begin with; and taking pride in your efforts, achievements, contributions, and profession.

Expanding on Plante's list by highlighting the importance of being adaptive, Lopez and Prosser (2000) recommended that new professionals diversify their practice, be attentive to paradigm shifts in health care, learn more about the business side of care, strengthen their research and consulting skills, and be willing to break with tradition when needed. I would echo these recommendations and add that perhaps the most important key to success today and in the future is to have lots of keys. The internship experience that you are now completing constitutes one of the more valuable of those keys.

As you look toward a changing employment and service environment, keep in mind that in your academic work and your fieldwork, you have developed skills that can transfer from one setting or position to another. In the mental health workplace today and in the future, fundamental skills include writing well, verbal communication, research, critical thinking, mathematics, and technology skills. In addition to these academic and clinical skills, grant-writing and program- or outcome-evaluation skills are becoming increasingly valuable assets to job applicants in human services employment. More and more, professionals are involved in a combination of activities, including direct services to clients, teaching, consultation, and research. To the extent that you develop different skills, you will be more marketable and have alternatives to pursue if conditions or employment in one area change. One final tip about looking ahead is to reach out to former graduates of your institution. Thomas (2005) described the value of alumni peer-consultation groups for counselors. These groups serve a number of functions, including support and networking, continuing study and education, and practical advice for new graduates. It may be that such groups already exist for your academic institution, and if so, you can learn about them from your department or alumni association. If there is no group affiliated with your school, consider working with your department to start one. Getting started as a professional can be a real challenge, and having a friend or a ready-made group of colleagues to help guide you through can be a tremendous help.

PROFESSIONAL, COMMUNITY, AND POLITICAL INVOLVEMENT

Finally, I encourage you to become actively involved in your community, in your professional association, and in political activities. Although you are probably not aware of it, you are able to study and participate in an internship today because people in the profession before you worked to develop the profession and create the opportunities you now enjoy. So, too, the educational and professional environments of the future are being shaped by the current political and social systems and by people who are working hard and making personal sacrifices to ensure that clients are protected and your opportunities as a professional continue.

Beyond parochial matters of interest to our professional disciplines, broad social policy has a profound impact on other aspects of our lives and especially on the lives of our clients. As someone involved in human services, you will have a unique interest in the outcome of policy debates and can make substantial contributions to your community through community or political involvement

For those interested in becoming more involved, practical suggestions for effective policy advocacy at the state level were offered by Hoefer (2005), and Staller (2004) provided an excellent resource for students interested in understanding more about federal policy in particular, with a primer on how to access and understand information about federal legislation and regulations. Safarjan (2002) offered more general but practical suggestions for how social and psychological issues can be advanced in the public and political spheres. Included among Safarjan's 12 "principles for advocates" are the importance of educating policy makers about your profession and issues, choosing your battles wisely and not spreading yourself too thin, giving credit to others, being generous with time and political contributions to candidates and your association's political committees, understanding what is important to policy makers, and finally persistence.

Protecting and advancing your professional opportunities and interests and working to ensure that clients receive the services they need take tremendous effort, financial resources, and commitment. I encourage you to join your professional organization, contribute through dues and special contributions, and take an active role in the activities. As a student, you may also want to become involved in the national student association of your profession.

Finally, if you do become involved in political activities, you may at some point want to go beyond working on campaigns or advocating on issues to actually run for office yourself. Speaking from my own experience as a psychologist who served in Congress, I can tell you that elected public service is a tremendously rewarding opportunity. If you choose to pursue it, you will find that your academic and professional training will be helpful in countless ways.

Ultimately, the skills and knowledge you gain in your internship will serve you and others well in many settings, and your opportunities to contribute can and should extend beyond your school or workplace. Our overall goal as professionals, as individuals, as citizens, and as members of our community should be to contribute in whatever ways we can to help improve the lives of others. The sooner you seize that opportunity, accept the responsibility, and engage in the sustained effort to make positive changes, the more impact you will have. I hope you will do so in whatever ways best suit your talents and interests, and I wish you much success in your endeavors.

REFERENCES

Baum, N. (2007). Field supervisors' feelings and concerns at the termination of the supervisory relationship. *British Journal of Social Work, 37*, 1095–1112.

DeAngelis, T. (2005). Things I wish I'd learned in grad school. *Monitor on Psychology, 36*(1), 54–57.

Falender, C. A., & Shafranske, E. P. (2004). *Clinical supervision: A competency based approach.* Washington, DC: American Psychological Association.

Fouad, N. A., Grus, C. L., Hatcher, R. L., Kaslow, N. J., Hutchings, P. S., Madson, M.,…Crossman, R. E. (2009). Competency benchmarks: A developmental model for understanding and measuring comptence in professional psychology. *Training and Education in Professional Psychology, 3*(4, Suppl.), s5–s26.

Hoefer, R. (2005). Altering state policy: Interest group effectiveness among state-level advocacy groups. *Social Work, 50*(3), 219–227.

Kaslow, N. J., Grus, C. L., Campbell, L. F., Fouad, N. A., Hatcher, R. L., & Rodolfa, E. R. (2009). Comptency assessment toolkit for professional psychology. *Training and Education in Professional Psychology, 4*(4, Suppl.), s27–s45.

Lopez, S., & Prosser, E. (2000). Becoming an adaptive new professional: Going beyond Plante's principles. *Professional Psychology: Research and Practice, 31*(4), 461–462.

McCutcheon, S. R. (2009). Competency benchmarks: Implications for internship training. *Training and Education in Professional Psychology, 3*(4, Suppl.), s50–s53.

Plante, T. G. (1996). Ten principles of success for psychology trainees embarking on their careers. *Professional Psychology: Research and Practice, 27*, 304–307.

Safarjan, W. (2002). A primer for advancing psychology in the public sector. *American Psychologist, 57*, 945–955.

Staller, K. M. (2004). The structure of federal policy: Deciphering the United States Code. *Journal of Teaching in Social Work, 24*(3/4), 47–63.

Thomas, S. R. (2005). The school counselor alumni peer consultation group. *Counselor Education and Supervision, 45*(1), 16–29.

CHAPTER 12
FRUSTRATIONS, LESSONS, DISCOVERIES, AND JOY

At the conclusion of their internship, many interns feel a strong sense of accomplishment and satisfaction. They have enjoyed the opportunity to work with clients, have encountered professionals whom they respect and admire, and are pleased with their own work and what they have learned. This is the ideal. However, some interns also experience a sense of frustration and disillusionment as they end their internship.

Whatever your experience, this final chapter is designed to help put the internship into perspective. The following comments are based on impressions gathered from students, interns, supervisors, instructors, research and my own experience spanning more than 23 years of clinical and academic work. I begin by describing certain experiences and lessons that can dim one's enthusiasm for the profession. Then I conclude by offering some more positive thoughts that may help you maintain perspective and keep your spirits up through the hard times that inevitably come in any profession.

LEARNING FROM WHATEVER HAPPENS

Whatever happens at your internship, remember that it is just one experience. Do not make judgments about all settings, staff, clients, or yourself based on a limited sample. Even in the worst settings, with the most difficult clients, and with the most pathological staff members, there are valuable lessons to be learned.

To help you get a handle on what might frustrate or trouble you about your internship, I offer the following list of lessons that eventually occur to us all but are not always pleasant. The point is not to add to whatever woes you may already have discovered on your own but to validate what you may have encountered already or may experience in the future.

EXERCISE

Before reading my ideas, write your own impressions of the negative and positive lessons you have learned during your internship. Try to identify some of the things you have learned about people, systems, the function and outcome of treatment, life in general, and yourself as a person and as a helping professional.

LESSONS WE WISH WERE NOT TRUE

THE PEOPLE IN THE PROFESSION

1. Not everyone in the helping professions is equally able to help others. Some people are grossly incompetent. For some clients, tasks, or situations, we must include ourselves in the incompetent category.
2. Very few people who are, in fact, incompetent are willing to acknowledge that fact. Instead, most are terribly defensive about their skills and their work, and many believe themselves to be outstanding and gifted professionals in spite of objective evidence to the contrary.
3. Not everyone in the helping professions is really there to help others. Regardless of what they may profess outwardly, some are in the field primarily to satisfy their own needs. In some instances, this means they will act in ways that may be detrimental to clients, their agencies, and to you if they stand to benefit as a result.
4. For some people, honesty, openness, caring, and learning are not as important as power, status, appearance, and control. When working with these people, many of the things you believe are the right things to do may have exactly the opposite effect you intended. Do not let yourself become one of these people. If you are one of these people already, consider changing.
5. The people described in items 3 and 4 will probably not be interested in changing themselves. Either they do not think of themselves as just described, or they accept the description but do not find anything wrong with their view of the world. They may also think everyone else is just like them or worse.
6. Not everyone will like or respect you, no matter who you are or what you do. You should be open to feedback, but you do not have to be liked by everyone all the time.

THE SYSTEMS IN WHICH WE WORK

1. Ultimately, any system is only as good as the people who operate and use it. No system can succeed if it is run by incompetent or negatively motivated people.
2. Frequently, the people described in items 3, 4, and 5 of the preceding section are in charge of systems.

3. Even well-intentioned programs run by healthy, caring people sometimes do not work efficiently or well. Sometimes the very best efforts of the very best people are thwarted by bad systems or incompetent people running them.

4. Mental illness and a host of other social ills receive little attention and real support in our society. There is a lot of talk, and substantial sums of money are spent, but much of this is merely symbolic. In relation to where other monies and energy are allocated, what goes to these needs is minuscule. Changing this will require political involvement. Get involved!

5. Many of the problems we deal with as human service workers are rooted in the larger social and economic conditions of our society. Unless the root causes are addressed, systems implemented to deal with the effects are likely to have only limited success.

6. Prevention would work better than most treatments, but money for prevention is hard to come by, and most people do not want to take personal responsibility for prevention.

7. Coordination between different service systems can be nightmarishly complicated, inconsistent, and inefficient.

8. Sometimes rules and policies seem stupid, but they are based on sound reasons. Sometimes they are just stupid.

9. Much of your professional life, far too much, will be spent in meetings in which little gets accomplished. Learn how to conduct effective meetings yourself so that you do not waste other people's time or your own.

10. Much of your professional life will be spent on paperwork. Learn to deal with paperwork efficiently, but do not ignore it or neglect it.

THE CLIENTS WITH WHOM WE WORK

1. Many of your clients will be decent, deserving, and well-motivated people who, for a variety of reasons, you will be unable to help no matter how hard you try.

2. Some clients encounter such incredibly bad luck that it is hard to imagine how they survive. It is also hard to believe that life is in any way fair. Simply put, it isn't. Part of what we are about is trying to make the unfairness bearable.

3. Not all clients are motivated to get better.

4. Not all clients are decent and likable people.

5. Some clients are self-serving predators. They will steal from other people, will lie to you, and would probably hurt or even kill you if they thought it would help them. Do not pretend this is not true, or you will endanger yourself and others.

6. Some clients do not look, dress, act, talk, or even smell very nice.

7. Some clients are well motivated but simply lack the mental or emotional capacity to accomplish what they need to do to help themselves.

THE NATURE OF THE PROBLEMS

1. The kinds of people and problems we deal with are often overwhelmingly complex. They include psychological, biologic, social, economic, physical, spiritual, and genetic factors. This is one of the reasons treatment is so challenging.

2. You will have clients who are in desperate straits because of the social systems in which they live. Unemployment, lack of insurance, abusive families, sexism, racism, dangerous neighborhoods, and more all add to whatever other factors the client may present, and few, if any, of these factors can be dealt with directly by you.

3. Despite what we might wish to believe, everyone may be created equal in rights, but not everyone is created equal in abilities or temperament. Genetics, biology, and luck play far bigger roles than many of us realize in shaping who we are and in causing or contributing to certain illnesses. Some clients are apparently predisposed to alcoholism, schizophrenia, or bipolar disorder. Others will simply be less able mentally to prosper in this world or to comprehend certain therapy approaches. Still others will be quite well endowed intellectually, but their emotional responsiveness will be minimal.

4. Our understanding of biochemistry and behavior has increased immensely, but it still pales in comparison to what still remains to be discovered and what we need to know to help our clients. Many of the illnesses clients present have biological bases or will result in biochemical changes, and yet our ability to understand and correct these conditions is meager at best. However, many illnesses that are often treated biochemically have their roots in situational factors that, if changed, would largely "cure" the client's problems.

5. Chance, pure dumb luck, can make everything else irrelevant. A perfectly healthy individual gets in a car accident, and his or her life is changed forever. A woman is raped on her way home from work. A client who is unstable but coping loses his job and girlfriend on the same day, and it pushes him over the edge. A precious innocent child is killed in an accident or senseless act of violence. You can and should try to reduce some of these events by changing systems and people, but a degree of luck will always be present and can have an impact on us all in profound and sometimes terrible ways.

6. Many of the problems you deal with will be part of repeating cycles that are difficult to interrupt. A father who beats his children was himself beaten as a child. Children of alcoholic parents become alcoholics themselves. A child who lives in poverty and has a parent in jail winds up committing crimes himself.

7. Some of the problems we deal with are givens of existence. As such, we must not only help clients deal with those problems, we must deal with the same problems ourselves. Death, relationships, meaninglessness, responsibility, freedom, and uncertainty are all part of living, for client and clinician alike. We, too, are vulnerable.

THE LIMITS TO OUR KNOWLEDGE AND TOOLS

1. In the face of the lessons mentioned thus far, you will often feel you have no idea what the real problem is or how to treat it.

2. There will be times when you have a clear theoretical explanation about the nature of the real problem and its treatment, and you are sure you are right. Some of these times, you will be dead wrong.

3. In the face of the lessons mentioned thus far, you will often feel you know exactly what the real problem is, but it is part of the socioeconomic structure or some other system that you are powerless to influence or to change soon enough for a particular client.

4. Blaming the system rarely helps if that is all you do. You can change the system, but it takes work, commitment, and involvement.

5. Change takes time. In fact, it often takes a lot of time. You may never see in your lifetime the long-term effects, good or bad, of what you do for individuals or for society.

6. Often, no one, not the client, his or her family, his or her friends, you, or anyone else really knows what is going on with a client. Yet, somehow, you are expected to proceed anyway and do the best you can.

7. Many in the public, including perhaps your friends, family, and other professionals, will doubt the validity or value of what you do. This may be due to lack of knowledge, but it may also be due to good reasons. This can make it hard for you to believe in what you do yourself.

LESSONS ABOUT OURSELVES

1. You will not always live up to your own ideals as a professional or as a person.

2. You will not always be as competent as you would like to be.

3. There will be times when you do not work as hard as you believe you should. There will be times when you work too hard.

4. You will find yourself doing many of the negative things you believe clients should not do.

5. You will find yourself not doing the positive things you tell your clients to do.

6. There will be times when your own conduct could lead others to wonder about your motives and intentions.

7. There will be many times when you wonder if it is all worth it or if you should be doing something else.

LESSONS ABOUT THE LESSONS

The preceding lessons could easily lead one to abandon the field entirely or to stay with it but become cynical, jaded, and part of the problem instead of the solution. Do not let this happen to you.

The lessons I have described here are only part of the picture. You need to know that part because it is real and you will have to learn to deal with it. The good news is that you can learn to deal effectively with even the most difficult of these realities. Further, despite the negative aspects of clinical work, there are many positive rewards; on balance, these tend to outweigh the negatives. It is an honor and a privilege to get to do the kind of work we do. Even at the lowest points, it is worth remembering that and finding the joy. Human service is a calling, a science, and an art, and when practiced well, it can be deeply rewarding and life changing.

DISCOVERIES AND JOY

PEOPLE IN THE PROFESSION

1. There are many fine people in the profession. They are drawn to human services out of genuine concern and caring for others, and they have dedicated their lives and talents toward that end. In many cases, these people could make far more money doing something else, but they have chosen instead to pursue occupations that serve others.

2. People differ in skills and wisdom. By working closely with those more skilled than yourself and by continually being open to learning, your own skills can rapidly advance. By working patiently with others and sharing your own knowledge, you can help others learn and grow. We can all pass on to others what has been given to us.

3. Perhaps more than any other profession, the human services offer an expectation and opportunity for personal exploration and growth. This is not just about knowledge and technical skills; it is about who we are as people.

4. If you have certain natural abilities, do your best, work hard, listen, and learn, you will probably get along with most folks and will make some wonderful friends along the way. You may also do some excellent work for your clients, and their lives will be better as a result. Considering the choices, that is a pretty good way to spend your time and life.

THE SYSTEMS IN WHICH WE WORK

1. No system is perfect, but most can be improved by dedicated and competent effort.

2. Some systems really do help people. They may not be perfect, but without them the lives of many would be much worse.

3. It is possible to gradually change the root causes of problems. The process may involve personal change and political action alongside clinical work. The history of civilization is a history of painfully slow advances in how we care for and treat one another, but advances are indeed made, and each of us can contribute to them.

4. Change in systems begins with changes in ourselves.

THE CLIENTS WITH WHOM WE WORK

1. The task of personal understanding and growth is difficult and frightening. Although some clients will not be motivated to change, many will show great courage in the face of incredible obstacles.

2. Some of your clients will be extremely grateful for the help you provide as they struggle to improve their lives.

3. It is a privilege and responsibility to work with people who entrust a portion of their lives to our care. We must respect that responsibility and do our best to honor it.

4. Some of our clients will have lived lives and learned lessons that we have never dreamed of. We may learn more from working with clients than the clients benefit from their work with us.

THE NATURE OF THE PROBLEMS

1. The problems we deal with are extremely complex, but little by little we make strides in understanding them. This is how all knowledge progresses. We may not know everything we would like to know, but we do know some things and that can be very helpful. Our task is not to know everything already but to apply what we have learned, keep studying and learning, and keep moving forward.

2. Social change is slow, but change does happen thanks to the dedication and sacrifice of a few individuals working for the good of many. You can be part of the change process. To paraphrase Joe Hill, "Don't whine; organize!"

3. Differences in abilities and traits may be genetically influenced, but people are not ruled entirely by genes. Even those with severe limitations in many areas have certain abilities that bring them joy. Nurturing those abilities and strengthening others can make some extraordinarily challenging lives more pleasant. That can be a rewarding goal.

4. Life is uncertain, and bad things do happen to good people. For some, that is cause for despair; for others, it is the reason to make the most of every moment. The choice is ours. Watch out for simplistic answers.

THE LIMITS TO OUR KNOWLEDGE AND TOOLS

1. Although our tools are limited, research evidence shows that overall, the treatments we offer can and do make significant, positive differences in people's lives.

2. Differences in theories can be confusing and frustrating. Given the complexity of human existence, we should not expect it to be otherwise. Each theory adds to our understanding and can help us in our work. The trick is to use theories as tools and fit them to our clients rather than fitting clients to our theories.

3. No matter how frustrated you might become with the limits to knowledge or to your techniques, you are not alone. Every job or activity eventually has its limits. The challenge is to learn to deal with them constructively. That, indeed, is the challenge of life itself.

LESSONS ABOUT OURSELVES

1. You do not have to be absolutely perfect in order to help people. Some of your own most difficult struggles can help you find insights that will later serve your clinical work well.

2. You will make mistakes, but for the most part clients are resilient; if you do your best and recognize your limits, things will usually work out.

3. Each of us can make changes, but change takes time. As you work to improve yourself, you will come to understand the task your clients face.

4. There will be times when you wonder if it is all worth it, but there will also be times when it is crystal clear that something you have done has made a difference. Moments like that are rare enough in any work. When they happen in clinical work, they are especially valuable because people's lives change for the better.

5. You must find joy in your clinical work, but you must also find it elsewhere in your life. Because clinical work is so important, it will bring with it both highs and lows. Therefore, although you must be dedicated as a clinician, do not let that be the only thing that brings you satisfaction. Take care of yourself so you can care for others.

6. Completion of your internship is not an ending; it is a step along the way. Do not expect to ever be done with the process of learning and growth. That is what makes life and learning interesting. Make the most of it. You only get one chance, and it doesn't last that long.

CLOSING COMMENTS

Throughout the book, from the opening chapter to this sentence, I have encouraged interns to be open to new learning and to seek consultation frequently. Now it is my opportunity to put that advice into practice one more time myself. A book of this sort is never really finished. As soon as I write the final words for this page, I will begin to gather information from journals, colleagues, and students for the next edition. This is where I have the chance to learn from you, the reader. If you found this book helpful, if there are parts that were not useful, if I left things out that should have been included, if you have any suggestions for improvements, or if you care to share any personal anecdotes, I would welcome your input. You can write to me at this address:

Brian N. Baird, Ph D, 16628 76th Ave W., Edmonds, WA 98026

If you include your address, I will try to get in touch with you.

My goal in writing this book was to contribute to the quality of internship training and thereby enhance the quality of the helping professions. I hope I have met that goal, and I welcome your contributions to making the next edition still more useful.

Thank you for reading this book; I hope it has been helpful. I wish you success in your future studies and work.

APPENDIX A
INTERNSHIP SELECTION CHECKLIST

This checklist is designed to help interns and supervisors select placements that will best meet the intern's educational and training needs.

PREVIOUS FIELD EXPERIENCE

List any previous field experience you have had.

ACADEMIC CLASSES OR SKILLS TRAINING

List any course work or skills training that would be relevant to an internship (e.g., Human Development, Abnormal Psychology, Theories of Counseling, Assessment).

TIME

Carefully considering the requirements for your program and the various other commitments in your life, how much time can you realistically allocate to this placement each week? Please be specific about days and times you will or will not be available.

TREATMENT SETTING

What treatment settings would best match your abilities and interests at this time?

Indicate any prior course work or experience relating to such settings.

CLIENTS SERVED

What types of clients (e.g., ages, presenting concerns, ethnic or cultural backgrounds) are you most interested in working with at this point in your training?

Indicate any prior courses, training, or experience working with this group.

TREATMENT APPROACH

What theoretical orientation or treatment approach is most interesting to you at present?

Indicate any prior courses, training, or experience working with this approach.

LEARNING OPPORTUNITIES

What sorts of learning opportunities do you hope to have at your internship, and what level of involvement and responsibility would you like? For example, you might want to learn about intake interviews by first observing, then doing part of them with supervision, then doing a complete interview, and then doing a complete interview with a written report. List any opportunities you think would be interesting here. Also, note if you already have some experience in a particular area.

SPECIFIC COMPETENCIES

Identify specific competencies that you would like to improve during the internship. This might be basic skills such as writing intake assessments, conducting a mental status exam, improving therapeutic relationship skills, or improving SOAP note skills.

SUPERVISION STYLE AND PERSONALITY

What personal qualities of a supervisor do you think you would best work with?

What personal styles might challenge you but help you learn?

CAREER PLANS

What experiences will be most useful in helping your candidacy for a job or academic admission?

SAFETY AND RISKS

List any concerns you might have about the limits of your abilities or knowledge.

Identify any concerns or questions you have about your personal safety or risks relating to placements.

PEERS

Are there any other interns with whom you would particularly like to be assigned? If so, please indicate who and briefly describe your reasons.

Are there any other interns with whom you would particularly *not* like to be assigned? If so, please indicate who and briefly describe your reasons.

OTHER COMMENTS

Please identify or discuss any issues that you have not had an opportunity to address above.

APPENDIX B
PLACEMENT INFORMATION FORM

INSTRUCTIONS

This form is designed to provide information about agencies and programs interested in offering placements to interns. Copies of this form will be kept on file for students to review when seeking internships. Please answer all items, and feel free to include any additional information that you think important. Thank you for your time and interest in working with us.

Placement name: _____

Placement address: _____

_____

_____

_____

Phone: _____-_____-_____

Contact person: _____

Position title: _____

Phone: Work _____-_____-_____

             Mobile _____-_____-_____

Email _____

Web Address _____

Please provide a brief description of the services provided and the clients served by your program or institution:

_____

_____

_____

_____

Please indicate the qualifications you would like interns to have.

Degree level or year in school:

Freshman/Sophomore/Junior/Senior/B.A./B.S./M.A./M.S./Ph.D./Psy.D./Ed.D.

Majors acceptable: _____

Prior experience: _____

_____

_____

Other required qualifications: _____

Briefly describe the clients served, learning opportunities, responsibilities, and expectations for interns at your placement site:

_____

_____

_____

Please indicate what days and times are available for interns to be at your placement site. If you require that interns be present on certain days or times, please indicate those times:

_____

_____

_____

Briefly describe the supervision opportunities available to interns:

Supervisor name: _____

Supervisor degree and position: _____

Frequency of available supervision: _____

Supervisor's theoretical orientation: _____

Other information about supervision: _____

_____

Additional information about your program or the internship:

_____

_____

_____

APPENDIX C

INTERNSHIP LEARNING AGREEMENT RECORD FORM

Date: _____

Intern name: _____   Intern ID# _____

Intern address:

   Street: _____

   City: _____

   Zip: _____

Intern home phone: _____

Intern cell phone: _____

Intern email: _____

Internship site: _____

Internship address: _____

   Street: _____

   City: _____

   Zip: _____

Internship phone: _____

Supervisor name: _____

Supervisor degree and title: _____

Supervisor work phone: _____

Supervisor home phone: _____

Supervisor cell phone: _____

Supervisor pager #: _____

Supervisor email: _____

Description of internship setting:

_____

_____

Intern's schedule:

Day hours

Sun _____ Mon _____ Tue _____ Wed _____ Thu _____ Fri _____ Sat _____

Notes about intern schedule:

_____

_____

Supervision schedules:

Days _____   Times _____

Planned supervisory activities:

_____

_____

_____

Theory, techniques, and skills to be developed:

_____

_____

_____

INTERNSHIP GOALS AND LEARNING ACTIVITIES

In the space below, please list your learning and competency goals for the internship and the activities you and your supervisor agree upon to help you achieve those goals. Leave space under "Evaluation" to record an evaluation at the end of the internship.

Learning and competency goals	Learning activity	Evaluation
1.		
2.		
3.		
4.		
5.		

Intern signature: _____   Date: _____

Supervisor signature: _____   Date: _____

INTERN EVALUATION: SUPERVISOR FORM

Intern name: _____

Date of evaluation: _____/_____/_____

Supervisor: _____

Internship site: _____

INSTRUCTIONS

This form is designed to help supervisors provide feedback about the performance of interns. The form usually takes just five or ten minutes to complete, and your answers and comments will be much appreciated. This form will become part of the intern's record for this course and may be considered in assigning grades for the internship. Please answer each item using the scale provided. Space is provided following each category group for specific comments. Please also consider your evaluations in the context of the developmental stage of the intern's training. In other words, please indicate below at which level of training you see the intern (e.g., basic undergraduate, advanced graduate) and how he or she compares with others at that level. If you feel it would be helpful to put anything into context at the outset, please feel free to do so below. There is also additional space at the end of this form for general comments.

Intern's training and development level: _____

Initial comments: _____

_____

_____

_____

ANSWER CODE FOR EVALUATION ITEMS AND QUESTIONS

Please use the scale below to evaluate the intern's performance relative to others at comparable stages of education and training.
NA: Not applicable or not enough information to form a judgment

1. Far below expectations—needs much improvement, a concern
2. Below expectations—needs some improvement to meet standards
3. Acceptable—meets standards at average level for interns
4. Above expectations—performs above average level for interns
5. Far above expectations—a definite strength, performs well beyond average levels for interns

I. BASIC WORK REQUIREMENTS

_____ Arrives on time consistently
_____ Uses time effectively
_____ Informs supervisor and makes arrangements for absences
_____ Reliably completes requested or assigned tasks on time
_____ Completes required total number of hours or days on site
_____ Is responsive to norms about clothing, language, and so on, on site

Comments: _____

_____

_____

Suggested areas for further study: _____

_____

_____

II. ETHICAL AWARENESS AND CONDUCT

_____ Has knowledge of general ethical guidelines
_____ Has knowledge of ethical guidelines of internship placement site
_____ Demonstrates awareness and sensitivity to ethical issues
_____ Personal behavior is consistent with ethical guidelines
_____ Consults with others about ethical issues if necessary

Comments: _____

_____

_____

Suggested areas for further study: _____

_____

_____

III. KNOWLEDGE AND LEARNING

A. Knowledge of Client Population
_____ Knowledge level of client population at beginning of internship
_____ Knowledge level of client population at end of internship

B. Knowledge of Treatment Approach
_____ Knowledge of treatment approach at beginning of internship
_____ Knowledge of treatment approach at end of internship

C. Knowledge of Treatment Setting
_____ Knowledge of treatment setting at beginning of internship
_____ Knowledge of treatment setting at end of internship

D. Learning
_____ Is receptive to learning when new information is offered
_____ Actively seeks new information from staff or supervisor
_____ Has ability to learn and understand new information
_____ Has understanding of concepts, theories, and information
_____ Has ability to apply new information in clinical setting

Comments: _____

_____

_____

Suggested areas for further study: _____

_____

_____

IV. SKILL DEVELOPMENT

List specific skill and competency areas of focus for this intern during the placement (e.g., assessment, writing, interviewing, diagnosis, individual therapy, group therapy).

Performance   **Skill Area**

_____   _____

_____   _____

_____   _____

_____   _____

_____   _____

_____   _____

_____   _____

V. RESPONSE TO SUPERVISION

_____ Actively seeks supervision when necessary
_____ Is receptive to feedback and suggestions from supervisor
_____ Understands information communicated in supervision
_____ Successfully implements suggestions from supervisor
_____ Is aware of areas that need improvement
_____ Has willingness to explore personal strengths and weaknesses

Comments: _____

_____

_____

Suggested areas for further study: _____

_____

_____

VI. INTERACTIONS WITH CLIENTS

_____ Appears comfortable interacting with clients
_____ Initiates interactions with clients
_____ Communicates effectively with clients
_____ Builds rapport and respect with clients
_____ Is sensitive and responsive to clients' needs
_____ Is sensitive to cultural differences
_____ Is sensitive to issues of gender differences

Comments: _____

_____

_____

Suggested areas for further study: _____

_____

_____

VII. INTERACTIONS WITH COWORKERS

_____ Appears comfortable interacting with other staff members
_____ Initiates interactions with staff
_____ Communicates effectively with staff
_____ Effectively conveys information and expresses own opinions
_____ Effectively receives information and opinions from others

Comments: _____

_____

_____

Suggested areas for further study: _____

_____

_____

VIII. WORK PRODUCTS

_____ Reliably and accurately keeps records
_____ Written or verbal reports are accurate and factually correct
_____ Written or verbal reports are presented in professional manner
_____ Reports are clinically or administratively useful

Comments: _____

_____

_____

Suggested areas for further study: _____

_____

_____

Overall, what would you identify as this intern's strong points? _____

_____

_____

What would you identify as areas in which this intern should improve?

_____

_____

_____

_____

Would you recommend this intern for employment at his or her present level?

Please explain: _____

_____

_____

_____

_____

Would you recommend this intern for continued graduate studies?

Please explain: _____

_____

_____

_____

_____

Supervisor's signature: _____ Date: _____

Thank you for your time in supervising this intern and in completing this evaluation.

APPENDIX E

INTERN EVALUATION: INTERN FORM

Intern name: _____

Date of evaluation: _____/_____/_____

Supervisor: _____

Placement site: _____

INSTRUCTIONS

Your supervisor will be asked to complete an evaluation form designed to assess your performance during your internship. This form is provided to help you assess your own performance. It is essentially identical to the one given to your supervisor. The form usually takes just five or ten minutes to complete. It will become part of your record for this course and may be considered in assigning grades for the internship. Please answer each item using the scale provided. Space is provided following each category group for specific comments. Please consider your evaluations in the context of the developmental stage of your training. In other words, please indicate below what your current level of training is (e.g., basic undergraduate, advanced graduate) and how you compare to others at that level. If you feel it would be helpful to put anything into context from the outset, please feel free to do so below. There is also additional space at the end of this form for general comments

Intern's Training and Development Level _____

Initial comments: _____

_____

_____

_____

_____

ANSWER CODE FOR EVALUATION ITEMS

Please use the scale below to evaluate your performance relative to others at comparable stages of education and training.
NA: Not applicable or not enough information to form a judgment

1. Far below expectations—needs much improvement, a concern
2. Below expectations—needs some improvement to meet standards
3. Acceptable—meets standards at average level for interns
4. Above expectations—performs above average level for interns
5. Far above expectations—a definite strength, performs well beyond average levels for interns

I. BASIC WORK REQUIREMENTS

_____ Arrives on time consistently
_____ Uses time effectively
_____ Informs supervisor and makes arrangements for absences
_____ Reliably completes requested or assigned tasks on time
_____ Completes required total number of hours or days on site
_____ Is responsive to norms about clothing, language, and so on, on site

Comments: _____

_____

_____

Suggested areas for further study: _____

_____

_____

II. ETHICAL AWARENESS AND CONDUCT

_____ Knowledge of general ethical guidelines
_____ Knowledge of ethical guidelines of internship placement
_____ Demonstrates awareness and sensitivity to ethical issues
_____ Personal behavior is consistent with ethical guidelines
_____ Consults with others about ethical issues if necessary

Comments: _____

_____

_____

Suggested areas for further study: _____

_____

_____

III. KNOWLEDGE AND LEARNING

A. Knowledge of Client Population
_____ Knowledge level of client population at beginning of internship
_____ Knowledge level of client population at end of internship

B. Knowledge of Treatment Approach
_____ Knowledge of treatment approach at beginning of internship
_____ Knowledge of treatment approach at end of internship

C. Knowledge of Treatment Setting
_____ Knowledge of treatment setting at beginning of internship
_____ Knowledge of treatment setting at end of internship

D. Learning
_____ Receptive to learning when new information is offered
_____ Actively seeks new information from staff or supervisor
_____ Ability to learn and understand new information
_____ Understanding of concepts, theories, and information
_____ Ability to apply new information in clinical setting

Comments: _____

_____

_____

Suggested areas for further study: _____

_____

_____

IV. SKILL DEVELOPMENT

List specific skill and competency areas of focus for this intern during the placement (e.g., assessment, writing, interviewing, diagnosis, individual therapy, group therapy).

Performance	Skill Area
_____	_____
_____	_____
_____	_____
_____	_____
_____	_____
_____	_____
_____	_____
_____	_____

V. Response to Supervision

_____ Actively seeks supervision when necessary
_____ Receptive to feedback and suggestions from supervisor
_____ Understands information communicated in supervision
_____ Successfully implements suggestions from supervisor
_____ Aware of areas that need improvement
_____ Willingness to explore personal strengths and weaknesses

Comments: _____

_____

_____

Suggested areas for further study: _____

_____

_____

VI. Interactions with Clients

_____ Appears comfortable interacting with clients
_____ Initiates interactions with clients
_____ Communicates effectively with clients
_____ Builds rapport and respect with clients
_____ Is sensitive and responsive to clients' needs
_____ Is sensitive to cultural differences
_____ Is sensitive to issues of gender differences

Comments: _____

_____

_____

Suggested areas for further study: _____

_____

_____

VII. INTERACTIONS WITH COWORKERS

_____ Appears comfortable interacting with other staff members
_____ Initiates interactions with staff
_____ Communicates effectively with staff
_____ Effectively conveys information and expresses own opinions
_____ Effectively receives information and opinions from others

Comments: _____

_____

_____

Suggested areas for further study: _____

_____

_____

VIII. WORK PRODUCTS

_____ Reliably and accurately keeps records
_____ Written or verbal reports are accurate and factually correct
_____ Written or verbal reports are presented in professional manner
_____ Reports are clinically or administratively useful

Comments: _____

_____

_____

Suggested areas for further study: _____

_____

_____

Overall, what would you identify as your strong points? _____

_____

_____

What would you identify as areas in which you should improve?

_____

_____

_____

_____

Do you believe you are prepared for employment at your present level?

Please explain: _____

_____

_____

_____

_____

Do you believe you are ready for continued graduate studies?

Please explain: _____

_____

_____

_____

Intern's signature: _____   Date: _____

Appendix F

Emergency Contact and Procedures Information

Intern

Name: _____   Location in placement: _____

Primary work phone: _____-_____-_____ ext _____ Pager #

Secondary work phone: _____-_____-_____ ext _____ Pager #

Primary home phone: _____-_____-_____ ext _____ Pager #

Cell phone: _____-_____-_____ ext _____ Pager #

Email: _____

Placement Supervisor

Name: _____   Location in placement: _____

Primary work phone: _____-_____-_____ ext _____ Pager #

Secondary work phone: _____-_____-_____ ext _____ Pager #

Primary home phone: _____-_____-_____ ext _____ Pager #

Cell phone: _____-_____-_____ ext _____ Pager #

Email: _____

Alternative Contact Person at Placement

Name: _____   Location in placement: _____

Primary work phone: _____-_____-_____ ext _____ Pager #

Secondary work phone: _____-_____-_____ ext _____ Pager #

Primary home phone: _____-_____-_____ ext _____ Pager #

Cell phone: _____-_____-_____ ext _____ Pager #

Email: _____

Faculty Supervisor

Name: _____   Office location: _____

Primary work phone: _____-_____-_____ ext _____ Pager #

Secondary work phone: _____-_____-_____ ext _____ Pager #

Primary home phone: _____-_____-_____ ext _____ Pager #

Cell phone: _____-_____-_____ ext _____ Pager #

Email: _____

Alternative Faculty Contact

Name: _____   Office location: _____

Primary work phone: _____-_____-_____ ext _____ Pager #

Secondary work phone: _____-_____-_____ ext _____ Pager #

Primary home phone: _____-_____-_____ ext _____ Pager #

Cell phone: _____-_____-_____ ext _____ Pager #

Email: _____

OTHER RESOURCES

Crisis-line number: _____-_____-_____

Name: _____   Number: _____-_____-_____

Name: _____   Number: _____-_____-_____

EMERGENCY CONTACT AND PROCEDURES INFORMATION

On this page, list the step-by-step procedures to follow if you have reason to believe that a client is dangerous to self or to others. At the bottom of the page, complete the information for your local mental health agency that handles crises, the closest hospital that accepts mental health crisis referrals, law enforcement agencies, and an attorney you know who specializes in this area and can advise you. If you work in a setting where a crisis with a client might arise, speak with the individuals listed here to establish a relationship and know their needs and procedures. Complete this form and make the needed contacts at the start of your internship; then keep this form readily available at your work setting.

Step 1: _____

Contact person: _____   Phone number: _____

Step 2: _____

Contact person: _____   Phone number: _____

Step 3: _____

Contact person: _____   Phone number: _____

Step 4: _____

Contact person: _____   Phone number: _____

MENTAL HEALTH CRISIS UNIT

Contact name: _____   Phone number: _____

Contact name: _____   Phone number: _____

LAW ENFORCEMENT

Contact name: _____   Phone number: _____

Contact name: _____   Phone number: _____

HOSPITALS ACCEPTING CRISIS PATIENTS

Hospital name: _____   Unit phone number: _____

Address: _____

Hospital name: _____   Unit phone number: _____

Address: _____

ATTORNEY FOR CONSULTATION

Contact name: _____   Phone number: _____

APPENDIX G

ETHICAL GUIDELINES

Everyone taking part in an internship opportunity is expected to adhere to certain guidelines for ethical, responsible conduct and to adhere to federal and state laws and regulations. This is necessary for your own benefit and protection, as well as those of the clients, the placement agency, your instructor, your supervisor, and your academic institution. Certain basic guidelines are described in this appendix, but these are not exhaustive. As an intern you are also expected to learn and adhere to the broader ethical guidelines dictated by your relevant profession (APA, NASW, ASCA, ACA, etc.), as well as the guidelines specific to your placement agency. In addition, you must familiarize yourself with and follow federal and state laws and regulations (e.g., HIPAA, FERPA). If you ever have questions about ethics or responsible conduct, contact your instructor or the placement supervisor. At a minimum, interns agree to adhere to the following principles:

1. *Confidentiality.* The identity of clients or information that would reveal the identity of clients cannot be disclosed without the specific permission of the client and only according to the HIPAA and FERPA guidelines where they apply. The only exceptions are cases in which the client may be dangerous to himself or herself or others and in cases of abuse. In such situations, there may be a legal requirement to inform responsible agencies. There are also certain legal proceedings in which courts can order case notes and other records to be released. Interns must familiarize themselves with and adhere to confidentiality procedures of their placements and the laws of the state and federal governments. Personal notes pertaining to specific clients and any case material discussed in class must be prepared in such a way that confidentiality is maintained. Any records or communications involving electronic technologies (e.g., computers, email, PDA) must be protected with passwords, encryption, and any other means prescribed by the placement site, academic institution, HIPAA regulations, or other laws. Interns do not discuss cases in public settings outside of class or their internship, nor do they discuss their cases with persons who are not specifically authorized.

2. *Recognition of qualifications and limitations.* Interns must recognize the limitations to their training and abilities and must not exceed these in work with clients. It is incumbent on interns to recognize when clinical situations are beyond their knowledge or ability. When such situations arise, interns will seek assistance from their supervisors and instructors.

3. *Identification as interns.* Interns will explicitly identify themselves as interns to their clients, in reports, and in other professional activities. They will not misrepresent their training, qualifications, or status. Interns who will be at a placement site for a limited time will inform clients of that limitation at the outset of therapy and will consider it in their work with clients.

4. *Record keeping.* Interns will accurately and reliably maintain written and other records in a timely and accurate manner as required by their placement agency and by state and federal laws.

5. *Dual relationships.* Interns will strictly follow ethical guidelines regarding multiple relationships and will refrain from clinical work with persons with whom they are involved in other types of relationships. Such dual relationships may inhibit the effectiveness of the intern's clinical work and may jeopardize both clients and trainees. For example, it would not be ethical for a trainee to take as a client someone who was a fellow student in class. Similarly, coworkers, friends, and others should not be seen as clients.

6. *Prohibition regarding sexual conduct or harassment.* Under no circumstances shall interns become involved in sexual or romantic relationships of any sort with clients or their family members. Interns will also refrain from sexual harassment and will respect the sensitivity of others regarding sexual matters.

7. *Self-awareness and monitoring.* Interns will monitor their own emotional and physical status and should be aware of any conditions that might adversely impact their ability to serve their clients or placement agencies. If such conditions arise, interns should seek assistance and inform their placement supervisors and instructors.

8. *Ethics discussion with supervisor.* Each intern must discuss the ethical standards of his or her placement agency with the supervisor before performing any clinical work or client contact. Space is provided at the bottom of this form to indicate that such discussions have taken place and that the intern has been informed of ethical expectations, state and federal laws and regulations, and any other specific guidelines of the agency.

By signing below, the intern agrees to adhere to the guidelines listed above as well as those of the professional discipline, state and federal laws, and the specific placement agency.

Intern signature: _____   Date: _____

Site supervisor: _____   Date: _____

Instructor: _____   Date: _____

APPENDIX H

TREATMENT AGREEMENT AND INFORMED CONSENT

This form is designed solely for use as an example and template to help you develop a form suited to your own situation. Feel free to use parts of it to draft your own form. Be aware, however, that NO CLAIM IS MADE OF THE LEGAL STANDING OF THIS MODEL. You must craft your own information with an awareness of the legal and ethical requirements of your position, profession, setting, and state. Be advised that HIPAA guidelines require specific and separate notices, and it is advisable to give clients a consent notice specifying how medical records will be maintained and protected and who will or will not have access to them. Discuss any document of this kind with your instructor and supervisor before using it with clients.

LETTERHEAD FOR YOUR AGENCY

INTRODUCTION

As a way of introducing myself to clients, I have prepared this brief description of my background, approach, and other information that is important for you to know. Please read this carefully, and feel free to ask me any questions about what you have read or any other elements of your treatment. I know this may seem rather formal and that it covers a lot of information, but I believe it is important for clients to have as much information as possible so they can make informed decisions about their treatments. Again, if you have any questions or concerns at any time, please feel free to discuss them with me.

My name is _____ and I am a/an [intern, practicum student, etc.] presently studying at [institutional name] and working toward my [degree]. I have [previous academic qualifications and practical experience].

Throughout my work here, I will be under the supervision of [supervisor name]. His/her qualifications include [list qualifications]. The nature of our supervision will include [describe activities and frequency]. If you have any questions or concerns, please feel free to contact [supervisor name and agency phone number].

Crisis contacts: If for some reason you are unable to contact me or my supervisor, please contact [insert agency contact name and information].

Duration of my work here: My placement at this agency is scheduled to run from [start to stop dates]. On [end date] I will [move on, continue, or other plans]. At that time, clients I am working with will be [transfer or termination plans].

FEES

Fees for services are [describe fees]. All fees will be collected at the time services are provided. Billing procedures will be [describe billing procedures].

In addition to fees for time when I am meeting with you directly, it is also my practice to charge for time required for preparing assessment reports, telephone conversations lasting longer than _____ minutes, consultations, or meetings you have authorized as part of your treatment. I will be pleased to provide you with details of any such costs should they be necessary.

If it happens that you are involved in some way in a lawsuit that requires my participation, you will be responsible for fees associated with my professional time. Because of the demands of preparing for and participating in legal proceedings, my fees for this are _____.

Please be aware that in receiving my services you, not your insurance company, are responsible for full payment of fees. If you want your insurance company to pay for my services, please read your policy carefully to be certain about what your coverage provides. If you have any questions, call your insurance provider to be sure. I will be pleased to help in whatever way I can with this process. If conditions of your insurance policy limit the number of sessions your provider will pay for [explain your policy for managing this situation].

Please also be aware that your insurance company may request diagnostic information, a copy of your treatment plan, and case records in order to provide compensation. This information will then become part of its files. Insurance companies are generally quite responsible about keeping this material confidential, but that is something I cannot control or be responsible for. If you wish, I will provide you with copies of any material or correspondence I send to your insurer.

Finally, continuation of treatment depends on timely payment of fees. If you are unable for some reason to pay a bill as requested, please discuss this with me, and we will attempt to make arrangements as needed. However, I reserve the right to discontinue treatment based on nonpayment of fees.

CONFIDENTIALITY AND LIMITATIONS TO CONFIDENTIALITY

I place a high value on the confidentiality of information clients share with me, and I will make every effort to ensure that information about your case will be kept confidential. You should, however, be aware that legal and ethical requirements specify certain conditions in which it may be necessary for me to discuss information about your treatment with other professionals. If you have any questions about these limitations, please ask me about them before we begin treatment or at any time during our treatment. Such situations include [check your state laws before completing this]:

1. If I believe there is a danger that you may harm yourself or others or that you are incapable of caring for yourself.
2. If I become aware of your involvement in abuse of children, the elderly, or disabled persons.
3. If I am ordered by a court to release your records. This sometimes happens when clients are plaintiffs in lawsuits and psychological records are subpoenaed as part of that process.
4. If your insurance company requests records in order to verify the services received and determine compensation.
5. [In the case of minors, list any limitations and requirements requiring parental notification and the like.]
6. As part of the supervision process, I may discuss your case and share records and other materials [note if tapes will be used] with my supervisor [supervisor's name]. If you grant permission, I may also discuss your case as part of training group activities but your name and other identifying information will be kept confidential in these discussions.
7. [Depending on policy and law] I may also discuss information about your case with other personnel within the agency.
8. In the event that I die or become incapacitated, I have made arrangements for a colleague to review my records and ensure that clients I am working with receive continued care.

TREATMENT PHILOSOPHY AND FREQUENCY

Briefly, my approach to treatment is best described as [approach used]. In essence, this means [use layperson's terms to describe approach]. This approach to treatment is based on [briefly discuss any relevant research or theoretical literature]. I prefer this treatment approach, but there are other approaches available. If you are interested in learning more about these, I would be glad to discuss them with you.

The length of a typical session is [length]. The number and frequency of sessions depends on the client and the nature of his or her concerns. Typically, I see clients for [average number of sessions], but this can vary from as few as [ ] to as many as [ ]. By the [ordinal number of] session, we will discuss how treatment is going and how we expect it to proceed.

CLIENT RESPONSIBILITIES

In order for our work together to be successful, it is essential that clients attend sessions; make a sincere effort to work on the issues we are addressing; and follow through with elements of treatment, such as things to do between sessions, readings, and so on.

If for some reason you cannot attend a scheduled session, please call well in advance and at least 24 hours before your appointment. My schedule tends to be rather full, and if clients do not cancel appointments with sufficient time, others who could receive services are unable to.

Repeated failure to attend sessions or to provide adequate rescheduling notice may lead to termination of our work together.

MEDICAL ISSUES

If you have any medical concerns that I should know about, please be certain to inform me of them. I would also like to discuss how you would like communication and information exchanges, if any, between myself and your primary health care provider to be managed.

HANDLING CONCERNS

If any concerns arise at any point during therapy, I encourage you to raise them directly with me so we can work through them. If you feel you cannot deal directly with a concern or issue about your treatment, I will be glad to contact another professional who can help resolve any issues with you.

CONTACTING ME AND CRISIS PROCEDURES

Because of the nature of my work, there will be many times when I am with clients and am not immediately available by telephone. My normal office hours are _____ on _____. If I do not answer the phone, please leave a message and a number so I can return your call. If there is an emergency and I cannot be reached, please contact your physician, the emergency room at your local hospital, or the mental health center crisis line at _____.

CONCLUDING TREATMENT

I believe therapy should continue only until you have reached your goals or until it is no longer benefiting you. If I believe you have achieved your treatment goals or that you are no longer making progress or could benefit more in some other way, I will discuss this with you. If, at any time, you believe it would be best to discontinue treatment, you are free to do so, but please discuss this with me directly during a session together. Please also be aware that under unusual circumstances, including, but not limited to, failure to make timely payments for services, violation of other terms of this agreement, client threats or intimidation, I reserve the right to discontinue treatment at my discretion. Please also know that in the nature of internship training when my time at the internship has completed, I will leave this setting and, if you choose, you will be provided with assistance from another member of the staff.

ADDITIONAL ISSUES

I appreciate the time you have taken to read this. As I have said before, if you have any questions or concerns now or at any point during your treatment, please feel free to let me know. Please sign below to indicate that you have read this and have had a chance to ask any questions. When we meet, I will give you a copy of this to keep and refer to if you like.

I am looking forward to our work together.

Sincerely,

[Your name]

I have read this document, discussed it with [intern's or professional's name], understand the information contained, and agree to participate in treatment under the conditions described.

Client's name: _____   Date: _____

APPENDIX I
SUPERVISOR EVALUATION FORM

This form is designed to give interns the opportunity to provide feedback about the supervision they receive during their internship. This information will be useful in discussions with supervisors and will help your faculty instructor evaluate the learning opportunities at various internship sites.

Each item that follows asks you to indicate the frequency with which activities of supervision occurred, your satisfaction with the activities, or both frequency and satisfaction. Please rate frequency based on a percentage from 0 to 100, with 0 meaning that something never happened, and 100 indicating that the activity happened every time there was an opportunity as described in the item. Please rate satisfaction on a rating scale from 0 to 100, with 0 indicating that you were completely dissatisfied, and 100 signifying that you were completely satisfied. Frequency and satisfaction ratings need not be the same. For example, if you met for fewer than the agreed-upon times for supervision, you might rate the frequency at 75%. Your satisfaction might be anywhere from 0 to 100, depending on what you felt about this issue. Please try to evaluate each item separately from other items. Space is provided at the end for general comments.

PRELIMINARY REMARKS

If you think it will be useful to preface your responses with any introductory comments, please do so here. Additional space is available at the end of the form for general evaluative comments.

_____

_____

_____

_____

_____

_____

_____

_____

_____

_____

_____

_____

SCHEDULE AND AVAILABILITY

1. _____ Frequency
   _____ Satisfaction

   Overall during the internship, approximately how closely did the actual supervision contacts match the agreed-upon plan?

2. _____ Frequency
   _____ Satisfaction

   Apart from scheduled meetings, how available was your supervisor if you requested additional contact?

INTRODUCTION TO SETTING

3. _____ Yes _____ No
   _____ Satisfaction

   Did your supervisor give you a tour or arrange for a tour of the internship site?

4. _____ Yes _____ No
   _____ Satisfaction

   Did your supervisor introduce you to other staff when you began the internship?

5. _____ Yes _____ No
   _____ Satisfaction

   Did your supervisor discuss procedural matters, agency policy, and the like, when you began the internship?

6. _____ Yes _____ No
   _____ Satisfaction

   Did your supervisor discuss ethical and legal issues when you began the internship?

ACTIVITIES AT THE INTERNSHIP

Approximately what percentage of your time at the internship was spent in each of the following activities?

7. _____ Frequency
   _____ Satisfaction

   Observing the milieu of your setting or interacting informally with clients, but not directly observing or participating in treatment or other services

8. _____ Frequency
   _____ Satisfaction

   Interacting informally with staff members

9. _____ Frequency
   _____ Satisfaction

   Observing treatment, assessment, or other direct service with clients

10. _____ Frequency
    _____ Satisfaction

    Participating in or providing treatment, assessment, or other direct service with clients

11. _____ Frequency
    _____ Satisfaction

    Attending meetings other than supervision or informal conversation

12. _____ Frequency
    _____ Satisfaction

    Reading records, reports, and the like

13. _____ Frequency
    _____ Satisfaction

    Writing case notes, assessments, reports, correspondence, and the like

In the space below describe and evaluate any other activities you participated in during your internship.

14. _____ Frequency
    _____ Satisfaction

    _____

15. _____ Frequency
    _____ Satisfaction

    _____

16. _____ Frequency
    _____ Satisfaction

17. _____ Frequency   Overall, were you able to participate in the activities you had hoped to in the internship?
      _____ Satisfaction

18. What additional activities would have been useful to you during the internship?

_____

_____

_____

ACTIVITIES OF SUPERVISION

Approximately what portion of supervision time was spent in the following activities?

19. _____ Frequency   Using case notes or material to review your interactions with clients
      _____ Satisfaction

20. _____ Frequency   Observing the supervisor providing treatment, assessments, or other services to clients
      _____ Satisfaction

21. _____ Frequency   Providing services yourself under the direct observation of your supervisor
      _____ Satisfaction

22. _____ Frequency   Discussing institutional issues
      _____ Satisfaction

23. _____ Frequency   Didactic instruction in specific topics or skills
      _____ Satisfaction

24. _____ Frequency   Reviewing assessments or other reports you have written
      _____ Satisfaction

25. _____ Frequency   Reviewing case notes or other records you have written
      _____ Satisfaction

26. _____ Frequency   Reviewing assessments or other reports written by your instructor or other professionals
      _____ Satisfaction

27. _____ Frequency   Reviewing case notes or other records written by your instructor or other professionals
      _____ Satisfaction

28. _____ Frequency   Discussing your personal impressions, reactions, and adjustment to the internship
      _____ Satisfaction

29. _____ Frequency   Discussing your relationship with your supervisor
      _____ Satisfaction

In the space below, please describe and evaluate any other activities of supervision in which you participated.

30. _____ Frequency   _____
      _____ Satisfaction

31. _____ Frequency   _____
      _____ Satisfaction

32. What additional activities would have been useful to you in supervision?

_____

_____

_____

INTERPERSONAL ISSUES AND FEEDBACK FROM YOUR SUPERVISOR

The items below refer to how you were given feedback by your supervisor and to the quality of your relationship with each other. Please comment on your supervisor's performance in each of the following areas:

33. _____ Frequency   Recognizing areas in which your skills or knowledge are relatively strong
    _____ Satisfaction

34. _____ Frequency   Recognizing areas in which your skills or knowledge need improvement
    _____ Satisfaction

35. _____ Frequency   Recognizing and complimenting you for accomplishments or things you have done well at your
    _____ Satisfaction   internship

36. _____ Frequency   Letting you know when your performance has not been good in certain areas
    _____ Satisfaction

37. _____ Frequency   Providing emotional support
    _____ Satisfaction

38. _____ Frequency   Dealing with differences between you
    _____ Satisfaction

39. Based on your experience, briefly describe the ways in which you feel supervision was most helpful to you during your internship.

_____

_____

_____

40. If there was anything about supervision that was not helpful, please explain.

_____

_____

_____

41. In what ways do you think supervision could have been more beneficial to you?

_____

_____

_____

CLINICAL ACTIVITIES RECORD SHEET

Date	Total Hours On Site	Milieu Therapy-Observation	Group Therapy	Individual Therapy	Supervision	Testing/Assessment	Case Management	Staff Meeting	Education	Other

INSTRUCTIONS: For each day you are at your internship site, record the date in the left column, then the total hours for that date, followed by the approximate number of hours spent in each of the activities indicated in the columns to the right. This information will help you, your supervisor, and your instructor monitor the activities and learning opportunities you are involved in. It may also be useful in future applications (e.g., graduate studies, other internships, employment).

This form may be reproduced as needed by the purchaser of this textbook.

APPENDIX K
PLACEMENT EVALUATION FORM

INSTRUCTIONS

This form is designed to give interns a chance to evaluate the internship site at the conclusion of their internship. The evaluation will be useful to your instructor and to future interns who will be considering where to do an internship. Before answering any individual item, take just a second to review the entire form to see all of the items that will be addressed. Please answer all items, and feel free to include any additional information that you think is important.

Placement name: _____

Placement address: _____

Supervisor name: _____

SITE DESCRIPTION

Please describe, in your own words, the key services provided by this setting.

_____

_____

_____

_____

_____

Please describe the clients served by this setting. Include age ranges, presenting concerns, socioeconomic status, ethnicities, and so on.

_____

_____

_____

_____

_____

Please describe the treatment modalities provided, for example, group or individual therapy, family therapy, physical exercises, or occupational therapy.

_____

_____

_____

What are the professional backgrounds of the treatment staff on this site? Please list, to the best of your knowledge, the number of professionals by discipline and degree (e.g., 3 MSW social workers available at this site).

Numbers	Discipline	Degree Level

Please describe, objectively but in your own words, the physical qualities of the setting. Be sure to mention size, age of facilities, level of upkeep, aesthetic qualities, and so on.

_____

_____

_____

Please describe the setting of the institution (e.g., rural or urban, neighborhood).

_____

_____

_____

OPPORTUNITIES FOR LEARNING

Please list the various activities you participated in as part of your internship experience. For each activity, list the modality or instruments used (e.g., the activity might be therapy, the modality might be cognitive/behavioral or group-cognitive therapy; if assessment is the activity, identify the assessment tools used), the weekly frequency of the activity, the total frequency of the activity during the entire internship, the availability of supervision on a 1–5 scale, with 1 being no availability and 5 being maximally available, and the quality of supervision, with 1 being very poor and 5 being outstanding. Please provide any additional comments regarding the activity.

Activity _____   Modality or Instruments Used _____

Weekly Frequency _____   Total Frequency During Placement _____

Availability of Supervision _____   Quality of Supervision _____

Additional Comments _____

_____

Activity _____   Modality or Instruments Used _____

Weekly Frequency _____   Total Frequency During Placement _____

Availability of Supervision _____   Quality of Supervision _____

Additional Comments _____

_____

Activity _____   Modality or Instruments Used _____

Weekly Frequency _____   Total Frequency During Placement _____

Availability of Supervision _____   Quality of Supervision _____

Additional Comments _____

_____

Activity _____   Modality or Instruments Used _____

Weekly Frequency _____   Total Frequency During Placement _____

Availability of Supervision _____   Quality of Supervision _____

Additional Comments _____

_____

Activity _____

Modality or Instruments Used _____

Weekly Frequency _____

Total Frequency During Placement _____

Availability of Supervision _____

Quality of Supervision _____

Additional Comments _____

_____

Activity _____

Modality or Instruments Used _____

Weekly Frequency _____

Total Frequency During Placement _____

Availability of Supervision _____

Quality of Supervision _____

Additional Comments _____

_____

OVERALL IMPRESSIONS

Supervisor: Please give a brief description of your experiences with your supervisor. Be sure to mention strengths, areas of concern, and any suggestions for ways to improve the supervisory experience.

_____

_____

_____

Staff: Please describe the overall impressions of staff other than your supervisor. Include qualifications, professionalism, relationships with clients, and receptiveness to interns.

_____

_____

_____

Clients: Please describe your experience of the clients at this setting. Include overall client attitudes, motivations, receptivity to working with interns, as you observed them.

_____

_____

_____

Treatment or services provided: Please give your overall impressions about the nature and quality of the services provided at this setting. For example, do you think the services are provided well to the clients, and are they effective?

_____

_____

_____

Safety or other issues: Please comment about any issues (e.g., safety, hygiene) that you feel are either positive qualities about the placement or areas of concern.

_____

_____

_____

Ethical and professional standards: Please comment briefly about your observations concerning the ethical and professional standards set by the staff at this setting.

_____

_____

_____

FINAL SUMMARY IMPRESSIONS

Finally, please indicate the degree to which you would recommend this placement to other interns (from 1 to 5, with 1 being recommend against, and 5 highly recommend). Please briefly explain the reasons for this recommendation.

_____

_____

_____

_____

_____

_____

INDICES

AUTHOR INDEX

A

Abbas, A., 74
Abbott, A. A., 136, 137, 142, 143
Abramson, J. S., 68
Acuff, C., 48
Adkins, C., 95
Adler, A. B., 119
Adolph, J. L., 20
Agate, J., 69
Agency for Healthcare Research and Quality (AHRQ), 34
Ageson, A., 138
Aguirre, M. G., 15
Alter, C., 95
Alva, L. A., 48
Alvarez, A. R., 31
American Association for Marriage and Family Therapy
    (AAMFT), 34, 53, 55
American Counseling Association (ACA), 9, 33, 34, 150
American Psychiatric Association, 34, 53
American Psychological Association (APA), 33, 34, 53, 86, 119, 150
American School Counselors Association (ASCA), 9, 34, 150
Ancis, J. R., 79
Anderson, D., 36, 97
Anderson, J. R., 41, 153
Anderson, K. G., 69, 114
Anderson, S. A., 151, 155
Anderson, S. K., 53
Anderson, W., 125
Annis, L. V., 141
Antle, B., 41, 45
Arches, J., 121
Arcinue, F., 59, 115
Armenian, H., 21
Aronson, E., 120, 121
Arredondo, P., 34, 86
Arum, R., 95
Asamen, J. K., 137
Ashkanazi, G., 36
Aten, J. D., 2, 6, 118
Atkinson, D. R., 88
Auerbach, C., 6, 38

B

Baerger, D. R., 45, 46
Bahrick, A., 80
Baird, B., 97, 104, 131, 169

Baird, K. A., 48
Baker, C. A., 57, 141
Baker, E. K., 113, 116
Baker, S. B., 57, 74
Ball, V., 21
Baltimore, M., 57
Banich, M., 49
Barker, R. L., 101
Barlow, D. H., 21
Barnes, P., 32
Barnett, J. E., 37, 38, 40, 49, 50, 53, 57, 70, 113, 114, 122, 148, 150
Barret, B., 41
Bartell, P. A., 54
Bashe, A., 36
Baum, N., 151, 161
Becker, B. R., 118
Becker-Blease, K. A., 57
Beebe, R. S., 33
Behnke, S., 33, 42, 49, 59, 60, 81, 150
Beier, E. G., 71
Benefield, H., 36, 41
Benjamin, G. A. H., 44
Bennett, B. E., 35, 39, 46, 55, 103, 108
Berberoglu, L. S., 110
Berger, M., 20, 47, 132
Berger, S. E., 47
Bergeron, R. L, 36
Berliner, S., 120
Berman, A. L., 35, 46
Bernal, M. E., 86
Bernard, J. M., 57
Bernstein, B. E., 35, 41, 44
Bernstein, J. H., 59, 69, 114
Betz, R. L., 27
Beutler, L. E., 21
Biegel, G. M., 129
Bike, D. H., 116, 131
Binder, R. L., 141
Bingham, R. P., 150
Blashfield, R. K., 114
Bliese, P. D, 119
Bludworth, J., 76
Bodenhorn, N., 41, 49
Bogo, M., 2, 12, 13, 54, 68, 69, 70, 71, 74, 75, 81
Boisvert, C. B., 21
Bongar, B., 46
Bonner, M., 20

SUBJECT INDEX